HAND-BELL RINGING
The living tradition
RINGING FOR GOLD

The annals and development of hand-bell tune ringing from its birth in the mid 1500s

By Peter Fawcett

Edited by Philip Bedford

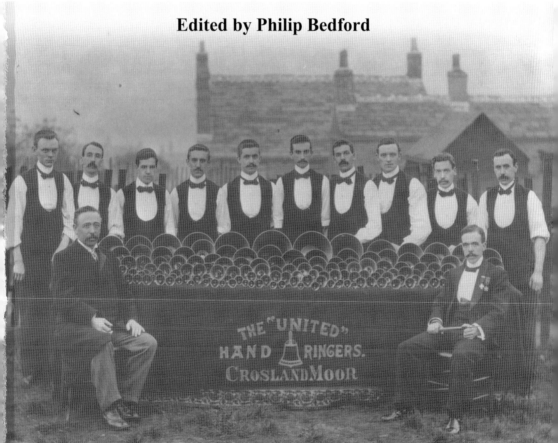

Published by Donald A. & Philip Bedford

First edition published 2012 by Donald A. and Philip Bedford,
Handbell Music Publishers,
44 Nunnery Fields, Canterbury, Kent, CT1 3JT, U.K.
Email: akaneandphilip@yahoo.com.au.
Tel & Fax: +44 (0)1227 454662

Edited by Philip Bedford.

Distributed in the USA and Canada by 'From the Top Music', 2700 Vista Grande NW, #105, Albuquerque, NM 87120, 702.489.6594, 505.228.5276, Toll Free: 1.866.951.0053, Fax: 505.839.4554, <www.fromthetop.com>

British Library Cataloguing-in-Publication Data
A catalogue record of this book is available from the British Library

Library of Congress Cataloguing-in-Publication Data applied for

ISBN 978 0 9538290 6 4

Design, Illustrations and Layout by Bruce Michael Baillie

Printed in Great Britain by
The Amadeus Press, Ezra House, West 26 Business Park, Cleckheaton, BD19 4TQ,
Tel: 01274 863210, Fax: 01274 863211

To the Memory of Jean Sanderson
First Archivist of the Handbell Ringers of Great Britain
Mentor and Friend

Contents

N.B. Throughout this book Peter has used the traditional spelling 'hand-bell', except where it appears without a hyphen as part of a name.

Sponsors

Anne Doggett, Wendouree, Victoria, Australia.

Paul Marshall, Brighouse.

Gwyn and Roger Gillard, Belmont, Victoria, Australia.

Mr. and Mrs. Michael Rhodes, Liversedge.

Ian Hayes and Christine, Okehampton.

Colin Armitage, Breedon-on-the-Hill.

Richard Offen, Mount Claremont, W. Australia.

J. Fraser Clift, Kemsing.

Christopher E. Carter, Bradfield.

Hazel Bradey, Ecclesfield.

Richard J. Hartnell, Darlaston.

Jane and John Willis, Okehampton.

David Kirkcaldy, Steyning.

Raymond Clayton, Hoghton.

Philip R. Wild, Gedling.

Central Council of Church Bell Ringers Library.

Keith W. Scudamore, Mangotsfield.

St. Mary's, Tenby, Handbell Ringers.

The Rev'd. Norman J. Smith, Hayling Island.

Margaret Farnie, Cocklake.

Len and Mary Porter, Oxford.

Margaret Anne Wells, Winnersh.

Julie (Peter's niece), Brighouse.

David A.C. Matthews, Tytherington.

Vivienne Davies, Raglan.

Vic Cox, Dronfield.

Estuary Bells of Teignmouth.

Oxford Diocesan Guild of Church Bellringers.

Patricia A. Foster, Shelley.

Anthony Hayes, Loughborough.

Alan and Margaret Hartley, Totley Rise.

Handbell Ringers of Great Britain.

Elizabeth Wright, Sale.

Frank Beech, Stone.

Roger and Christine Lazenby, Leeds.

Ecclesfield Handbell Ringers.

Janie Grabham, in memory of Edna Grabham née Bedford, Hyde.

Lindsey Trevarthen, Swinscoe.

Brian Buttery, Grantham.

Malcolm Fairbairn, Oxford.

Frank and Meg Wood, Bowness -on-Windermere.

Heather I McLean, Murthly, Perth.

Susie Fawcett, South Africa.

John P. Partington, Rochdale.

Roger Thomas, Knighton.

Sheila Warburton, Burnham.

John Atkinson, Beverley.

West Midland Region, HRGB.

Patrick J. Brennan, Pontefract.

Kathryn Harrison, West Yorkshire.

Sue Allen, Launton.

Allan G Keen, Bilton.

A. Ryan Price, Emersons Green.

Maureen Dewhurst, Chapeltown.

Clifton Hand-bell Ringers.

Rachel Giles, Gower.

Andrew, Claire and Kimberley Ford, Beverley.

Bingley Handbell Ringers.

Toos Koster, Beverley,

Stan and Jennie Nuttall, Sheffield,

Michael Wright, Teignmouth.

Hugh O'Malley, Leeds.

Jackie and Mary Dwyer, Leeds.

Jo Flannery, Leeds.

Alex and Val Freeman, Berrow.

Dick & Ruth Fawcett, Cleckheaton

Henry Balmforth, Gomersal.

Yorkshire Hand-Bell Ringers Association

EST 1903

Editors Foreword

It is irrelevant whether or not this book is a financial success. It is a book that had to be published.

Peter Fawcett is a craftsman gardener. He is not a professional researcher, a professional writer or a professional musician. But he is a man with an unusual vocation (some might call it an obsession) – to preserve in detail the memory and traditions of past hand-bell tune ringers, and to give advice and guidance to current ringers to help them avoid the pitfalls of the past - and it has taken him 35 years of detailed research to do so. Had Peter produced this work under the supervision of a university supervisor there is no doubt that it would have earned him a PhD. However unlike academic research historians, whose main method of gleaning information is to trawl through other academic texts, Peter adopted a more basic research approach. As an example it went something like this: He would go to the Manchester Archives and read all the microfiched copies of the "Eccles Gazette" for 1862. In the copy for 12th July he would find a reference to the Eccles Temperance Hand-bell Band who had performed at the Working Men's Club the previous Tuesday and that their leader was one Mr. Jas. B. Barker. He had not previously heard of the band or their leader. The band had never competed at Belle Vue and it appeared in no other records. He would then phone all the 'Barkers' in the telephone directories covering Eccles and the surrounding areas asking if they knew of any hand-bell ringing ancestors. Ninety-nine per cent of the time the answer was negative, sometimes quite rudely so. Just occasionally someone would reply "Oh yes, I think my Auntie Glad knows something about that. In fact I think there are still some hand-bells under her bed. I remember finding them when I was little. She's ninety two now you know." Using this approach over 35 years has produced some amazingly original material – from a complete collection of original music from Hyde dating from before 1855 showing their progression from number music to staff notation, to the original Mears Challenge Trophy from the Belle Vue Competitions, and a wealth of material between.

Peter's style of writing is original, often humorous, and in places quite exciting (for example his description of the rivalry between Crosland Moor United and Crosland Moor Public at the turn of the century, and between Glossop and Shelley thirty years earlier).

When Peter asked me if I would edit his work and include within it an analysis of the music rung by ringers over the past couple of hundred years or so, I felt honoured, but also daunted. Should I attempt a massive re-write to turn the book into a stodgy but politically and academically acceptable learned treatise? When my brother Don and I first read Peter's draft four years ago the answer became obvious. Here was the writing of a man with a passion, a passion which shows through on every page. It needed no re-write - a little bit of correction and a little bit of addition maybe – but it is eminently readable and stands tall on its own unique merit. Don and I believe that it will stand the test of time and become the foundation work, the basic source material for future hand-bell researchers and historians. That is why I said at the beginning that it is irrelevant whether or not this book is a financial success. It is a book that had to be published.

Philip Bedford
Past President,
Handbell Society of Australasia,
International Handbell Committee Member

January 2012

Introduction

While I have done my best to research and record the development of hand bell ringing through the ages, I regard my work as a guide to further research rather than a fully complete document. It is not definitive and nor could it be as there is much still to be found, for example information about hand-bell ringing in the years before 1855 when the Belle Vue contest began. It was a very old art then as was stated in the report of the very first British Open. Perhaps research by a University is what is required. Indeed if any of you have other hand-bell related items from the past – newspaper cuttings, photos, music, hand-bells, anecdotal stories about eccentric hand-bell ringing Great-Great-Uncle Egbert which have been passed down through the family etc., please would you let me know. My email address is <ringingforgold@gmail.com>.

I was inspired by the work of Cecil Sharp who went around England in the early 1900s to find traditional singers and dances and record them. In modern times, the great folk motivator Ashley Hutchings impressed me. Also in the 1970's folk singer Peter Bellamy discovered an unknown traditional singer Walter Pardon. However the art of musical hand-bell ringing has largely been passed over by the media with a lack of information being one contributing factor. I hope therefore that this work will generate their interest.

I began my researches with an open mind. I have always been interested in all aspects of tradition, no matter where or what. In my time I have been involved with Folk music, Morris dancing, Choirs, Brass bands, Irish music and of course Hand-bell bands. This freethinking gave me the distinct advantage of looking at the hand bell movement from a multi traditional standpoint. I hope to lay to rest once and for all, modern myths and untruths, which have hindered the modern movement since 1967. My involvement with hand-bell ringing began with my love of Irish music in the early 1970's. I happily frequented an Irish pub in Leeds called the Regent where Irish traditional music was played. I was extremely impressed by their commitment and love of their music, and the way they passed their traditions on to the young. I was enthusing about this to a musician at the Regent called Johnny Gillard, who suggested that I might find some Yorkshire traditions in my own area. I took up the challenge and began looking for Morris dance traditions. One winter's day in Haworth I bought a book by H.N. & M. Pobjoy, called Hartshead cum Clifton, which was a history of the area near where I grew up. In one of its pages was a reference to the Clifton Hand-bell Ringers, stating "A newspaper article in 1958 said the bells were still in store in the village of Clifton - is this still so?" Well here was the local tradition that I had hoped to find. After making enquiries at Kirklees Hall Estate where I had worked when leaving school, I was told to go to the Armytage Arms public house where I would find Stanley Hudson, and he might know where the bells were. It was on Boxing Day 1974 when Mr Hudson told me the bells were in Lister's wire mill at the bottom of Clifton Common. I then sat on the idea until November 1975 when I decided to take a look. I mentioned this to Audrey Round of the Brighouse Echo, who then beat me to it. She phoned me excitedly saying that there were hundreds of bells. I had expected to find a dozen. I went to look for my self and instantly realised I had discovered a really big tradition. In side one of the boxes of bells was a Belle Vue list of bands that had won prizes.

After re-forming a band of ringers in the village of Clifton my mind began to wonder if I could find out anything about the other bands on the Belle Vue list and here are the results.

One aspect of my research which cannot now be repeated is the oral interviews (some of which I audio recorded) with people who were actually members of the bands contained in this book (or could remember them) as they have now all passed on - the last being in 2010. But this is their story – a story that has never been told, until now.

Peter Fawcett   **November 2011**

Chapter 1 - Origins

In looking for the origins of the art of musical Hand-bell ringing, it would be quite a simple matter to say that tune ringing appeared to owe its beginnings to church towerbell ringers in England, who perhaps practised change ringing on cold winter nights in the comfort of the local public house, but evidence suggests that it was not quite so simple, nor so recent.

Whilst 'hand-bell set' is the name given to the musical instrument which was developed in England in the Middle Ages, it developed from the earlier organica tintinnabula (Organisation of little bells of different tonal pitches) and the cymbala (9 to 16 small bells of different tonal pitches suspended on a cross bar). Both the

**Fig. 1: Chinese Pien Chung
from about 12th Century BC**

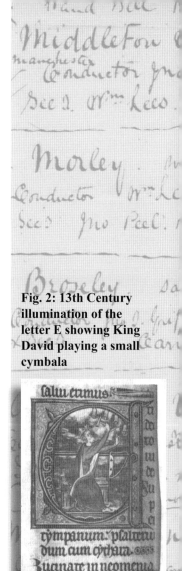

Fig. 2: 13th Century illumination of the letter E showing King David playing a small cymbala

Fig. 3: An Organica Tintinnabula from the 11th Century

tintinnabula and the cymbala had previously been popularly used in religious worship throughout Europe from well before the time of the Norman Conquest of England in 1066 AD, until the 15th century. Indeed the cymbala can trace its history back with little developmental change to the pien-chung of China 2500 years before.

After large bells had moved outside the Church in the Italian province of Campania in Paulinus' time, hand-bells continued their development within the Church. A cappella chanting (voices only) was replaced in popularity by more elaborate modes of liturgical accompaniment, which included bells, stringed and wind instruments and small organs. Many mistranslations of the Latin "cymbala", used both for cymbals and bells in early times, exist in psalms today, e.g. "Praise him upon the loud cymbals (big bells), praise him upon the well tuned cymbals (tuned hand-bells)." Early illuminations show small chimes of hand-bells hung from rods and tapped with small wooden hammers, and in the early middle ages instructions for sung masses included the use of bells to double up on the tenor line. (Perhaps church choirs have always been short of tenors - singers not church bells! In those days the tenor line carried the melody.)

1

In a scene from the Bayeux Tapestry, embroidered shortly after the Norman Conquest, two accolytes are shown walking beside the coffin of Edward the Confessor on its way to interment in Westminster Abbey. They are ringing hand-bells to keep evil spirits from entering his body before it reaches its final resting place in the protection of the holy building.

Readers who would like to know more about the early development of bells should read Percival Price's excellent book "Bells and Man" published by the Oxford University Press.

On the recording, "The Mediæval Sound" made by the late and sadly missed expert on early music, David Munroe, in the 1970s,

Fig. 4: Bellringing Accolytes on Bayeux Tapestry

these mediæval bells were played in a duet with a tenor flute. The bells play a plainsong melody, and the flute plays the second part, to produce a very pleasant sound. The recording also includes a duet of mediæval bells and treble recorder. The bells used in the recording, made by the Whitechapel Bell Foundry in the 1970s, were copies of the mediæval originals.

So the advent of making music on small bells was nothing new by the time change ringing on tower bells and hand-bells had begun in England in the early years of the seventeenth century.

Therefore change ringing on hand-bells and the subsequent ringing of tunes only perpetuated an idea that already existed - that of playing tunes on small bells.

There is evidence that Henry VIII made thousands of pounds by selling off bells and other treasures in the first half of the 16th Century from the Monasteries he had destroyed during the Reformation. But Henry did like music, and music, singing and dancing carried on as before.

It was during the reign of Henry VIII's successor Edward VI (1547-1553) that I found my earliest reference to hand-bells. Whilst looking through the parish records of St Leonard's Church, Middleton, Lancashire, I found the following inventory of 1552 (original spelling):

One sensec of brasse ij Crosses of Brasse and Lead payr of organs, A payre of rigalles ij chaleces of sylur p'cell gilt - wt patens, It'm in the steple, V, Bells And on Litll bell (i.e. Sanctus Bell), ij hand belles.

So from this record we know that there were hand-bells in church steeples in 1552 thus predating change ringing proper. However it is interesting that this date is about the time that change ringing became possible on tower bells. Although the art as we know it today probably did not develop until about 1660, it was about 1550 that two technical advances made change ringing possible on tower bells: the full circle wheel which enabled a bell to be balanced mouth upward for a short time at the end of each stroke, and a bell founding technique which enabled the tenor of a ring of eight tower bells to be only about 3 times as heavy as the treble, enabling the light bells to be heard when they rang between the heavy bells. Prior to this the tenor bell would have been far heavier in relation to the treble such that the treble (and other light bells) would not have been heard clearly when all the bells were rung in quick succession.

These early hand-bells could possibly have been used to practise swing chime ringing that was known to have taken place before the development of change ringing although this is unlikely as we know that swing chime ringing went quite quickly out of fashion once the full circle wheel had been introduced. So, if anything, the hand-bells found in the steeple would have been used for the elementary or proto-change ringing which had already started to develop, though even this was not very likely as the clapper fitting was still very crude. Therefore the 'hand belles' to which

3

the Middleton inventory refers most likely were those that at this stage were still being used to produce music as part of the church service – not in the styles we have today but with mallets.

In 1625 Charles I became king and from 1629 to 1640 he ruled without reference to Parliament, raising money illegally and he became unpopular. In 1642 Civil War broke out between the Royalist forces of Charles I and those of Parliament led by Oliver Cromwell.

The Royalists were defeated and the war ended in 1649. Charles I was beheaded and England was proclaimed a Republic. In 1653 Cromwell dismissed Parliament and made himself Lord Protector.

There followed one of the darkest periods in English history. The Puritans, the extreme Protestant clergy who now came to power, held views of strictness in morals and religion to the exclusion of almost everything the people enjoyed. There was to be no music, dancing or singing. Church organs were taken out and destroyed along with many other musical instruments: harps, fiddles etc.

Although bells were no longer allowed to be used for religious purposes, and many were taken from the steeples and sold for their metal content along with other church property, records do show that, in many areas there was a "fully compensating increase in ringing for secular occasions".

It was generally not a good time to be a church bell ringer because of the risk of being declared Papist. But bellringers have always been a stubborn lot and it is quite possible that during these hard times both change and tune ringing were practised secretly using hand-bells, perhaps with soft leather tied round the clappers, so that Cromwell's forces, the "Roundheads" could not hear them outside the house. We know for example that Oliver Palmer wrote his change ringing compositions in Hebrew to avoid suspicion of Popery, although the use of hand-bells for in-hand tune ringing at this time was unlikely because of the crude clapper assemblies.

In 1660 the Stuarts were restored to the Throne when Charles II was crowned King. All the old traditions of dancing, singing and music making were celebrated once more. At Castleton in Derbyshire there has been a celebration of the Restoration every year since 1660. The celebration is known as the Castleton Garland, where a huge bell made of flowers is worn by a man who rides a horse around the village, accompanied by his lady. The man then casts off the bell and it is hoisted up the tower to represent the return of bell ringing. The man under the bell represents the exiled king in hiding, and the casting off of the bell represents his restoration to the Throne. Until the mid-19th Century the ceremony was organised by the Castleton church bellringers who themselves danced a morris behind the King and his Lady during their procession. The Restoration and repair of the churches was a lengthy process, but hand-bells, being readily available, would have been used by towerbell ringers while the restoration work was carried out. In many cases bells had to be re-hung and new bells cast.

During this period itinerant bell founders played an important role. These were men who worked from a base, but would travel around the country with a wagon and horse team, stopping and setting up their stalls at country fairs. These founders would carry a small amount of bell metal with them, probably bought en route, enough to make a few bells and would advertise their presence and encourage people to bring in old bells to be recast. By this time, itinerant bell founders had been plying their trade for at least 500 years, and even during the Puritan Republic their work was still needed. There are many references to bells being repaired and installed during this period e.g. from the parish records of Wallasey St Mary:

…until 1658 when the churchwardens accounts are first regularly entered in the Registers. The entries concerning the bells become very frequent, being chiefly for new ropes, repairs to the bells and frames, 'oyle' and 'liquour' to grease the bells, 'skins' to hang the clappers, a 'planke for wheile spokes and a pese to mend ye frams', and in 1676 'extended at Letting the great bell downe, on the workemen and some others of the p'sh 1s 6d'. In 1672-3 the churchwardens received £1 3s 3d for '31 pounds of bell mettle' cut out of the great bell, and in the same year 6s 6d was paid to one Lanckshaw, an itinerant bell founder, 'that undertooke to cast the little bell and faild.

There are also tales of itinerant founders, when desperately short of metal, going into public houses and buying up pewter beer mugs from which people were still drinking! This would explain the mixed composition of metal used in the casting of some of the early bells. These itinerant founders would often go off on a tour of several counties, for two, three or even four years and then return to their home base for a time before embarking on another lengthy journey. Some founders would simply knock at the door of a vicarage and ask for work and if a tower bell was required, would cast it on nearby common land, or in the churchyard or even inside the church itself in some cases.

But it is the casting of hand-bells at country fairs which is the most interesting aspect of the work of the itinerant founders to our story. This very act helped spread the art of musical hand-bell ringing and its importance cannot be underestimated. The itinerant founders had prospered after the disruption caused by Henry VIII's Reformation. They usually offered to recast bells on the spot as there would then be no carriage charges, usually very high as the roads were so bad and travelling difficult and expensive, particularly for large tower bells.

As with the tower bells, from the mid 16th century onward there had been a minor revolution both in handball design and use. Sets of bells of up to 1½ diatonic octaves were being produced independent of a frame, with leather looped handles on each bell.

It is not my intention here to give an account of all the bell founders in England, as bell founding is a specialist subject in itself and is beyond the scope of this book. Rather, I shall give a brief outline of how the making of hand-bells developed, giving the best examples of founders who cast hand-bells and the changes that were made to them throughout the 17th and 18th Centuries. I will describe 19th and 20th Century bell founders later in our story. For those of you who would like to know more detail about the history of hand-bell founding in the UK I suggest you read William Butler's excellent book: "Musical Hand-bells – a Comprehensive History of the Bells and Their Founders"

The itinerant founders built furnaces on the spot from clay or fire bricks and these were only used once. The bell metal was put straight onto the bricks and a plug was left in the bottom for the metal to run out into the moulds. Charcoal was used to fire the furnaces. Low Moor, near Bradford, has a history of metal making dating from the 17th Century and the remains of many of these early furnaces can still be seen there today.

Some of the itinerant bell founders were monks displaced by the Reformation, who had learnt bell founding in the monasteries and had used their experience and knowledge in maintaining a livelihood.

However just how important the itinerants were to the development and spread of musical hand-bell ringing we do not know, and just who they were is difficult to ascertain, especially in the case of the North of England. The Belle Vue contests helped strip the North of old hand-bells that had been cast by the early founders because, in order to win Belle Vue a band had to have the very best bells available. So, as bells wore out with the constant use they received through constant rehearsals and contests, they were traded in and a new set of bells bought. Thus there are very few, if any, ancient bells left in the North.

In the South of England fortunately some ancient hand-bells have survived to the present day possibly partly due to the absence of contest ringing. The surviving bells, however, provide a record of the way in which ancient hand-bells were made and worked, greatly adding to our knowledge and understanding of early tune ringing and of the bell founders who cast them.

Aldbourne in Wiltshire was the base of the Aldbourne foundry which was the business of the Cor family. The first of this family was Robert Cor (1694-1724) who was joined by his brother William Cor (1696-1722). Robert and William were succeeded by Oliver Cor (1725-1727) and the last of the Cors, John Cor (1728-1750). The Cor family cast their initials and their maker's mark - a dabchick - inside their bells. William Cor was the first bell founder to cast bells in a sand mould and to attempt rough tuning with a file.

The oldest set of musical hand-bells I have found in carrying out research for this book, were cast by the Cors.

I was told by a fellow hand-bell ringer that he had seen a set of 12 musical hand-bells whilst visiting the former home of William Shakespeare's mother's family in the village of Wilmcote, 3 miles from Stratford-upon-Avon in Warwickshire. He told me they were displayed in a glass case making it impossible to inspect the inner part of the bells, but he did notice they had solid strikers. I hastily wrote a letter to the archivist of the Shakespeare Birth Place Trust enquiring about the bells and of the possibility of my being allowed to inspect them. The reply was in the affirmative, with the archivist adding that the bells were not believed to be of a great age. At hearing this I felt a little disappointed but remembering that my friend had said the bells had solid metal strikers I decided to go and see them for myself. I received permission to see them on the Wednesday and I was in Stratford-upon-Avon the following Saturday.

On my arrival at the Tudor farmhouse, which is preserved as a museum of farming and rural life, I was taken to the barn where the bells were kept. I had a basic knowledge of ancient bells and so, as soon as I looked at the 12 bells in the glass case I immediately realised that the bells were indeed old ones, very old I thought, as they had not been turned on a lathe but had been filed on the outside in an attempt to tune them. The case was then opened and I carried out an inspection.

The bells were made of bronze and had originally been cast as a set of twelve as they were numbered from 1 to 12 in Roman numerals, roughly stamped on the large copper rivets that fixed the very long leather handles to the bells. Bells No's 1,2,3,11 and 12 had not been filed at all, but the others had all been filed on the outsides and

7

bell No. 5 had been filed a little on the inside. This, of course is consistent with hand-bell founders' practice before the advent of the tuning lathe. They cast many bells of each note and picked out the best to form the basis of the set, then some of the bells would be filed to bring them roughly in tune with the others to form a ringable set

The bells had the maker's dabchick mark. Four of the bells had the initials W. R. COR on the inside, the dabchick being placed over the letter R which formed the feet of the bird. The letters were the initials used when William and Robert Cor worked together from 1694 to 1722. Two of the bells had no initials at all, and six bells had the initials O. R. COR which were the initials used by Oliver Cor, between 1725 to 1727. So the bells were probably cast by Oliver Cor using some of the same moulds originally used by William and Robert Cor.

Thus these bells must have been cast in or before 1727 which could make them the oldest complete set of musical English hand-bells in the world. The staple assemblies were even more interesting to me than the bells themselves. The clappers were made of iron and had a solid metal ball striker which was simply bent around a "horseshoe" of iron fixed into the bell. At the base of the striker, around the horseshoe were two collars of thick leather. I then realised that these collars were not washers, but were placed there to stop the striker hitting the bell twice and acted as an early form of the brass springs that were later used. These leather collars must have been somewhat inefficient but would have probably sufficed for the simple "in hand" ringing that was practised at the time.

Fig. 5: The bells cast by Oliver Cor 1725 - 1727, now at Stratford-upon-Avon

It is remarkable that this set of bells has survived to our time and even more remarkable that none are missing and all the fittings and handles are as they were when Oliver Cor made them, only one striker is missing and two bells are cracked.

As Bill Butler pointed out at a 1988 Handbell Symposium Workshop, it would have been on such a set that the Rambling Ringers Club rang their changes and their tunes sometime prior to 1734. The account of this ringing society is recorded in the oldest contemporary record of hand-bell ringing – William Laughton's notebook of 1734 (lodged in the Guildhall Library, London – see handwritten extract at Appendix 9). As well as recording theirs and other's changing ringing endeavours (e.g. of the College Youths' country trip to Kent and France "One course of Cinques

8

on the Hand Bells on Friday ye 2d of June 1732 at Calais in France & another when they were half seas over.") the notebook sets down the words of two songs then follows them with some lines of music written in numbers for ten bells:

35670787	07677539
65434356	96567678
66566427	63572461
78638790	321235467

This is the earliest known surviving hand-bell music, written in an "aide memoir" number notation, which mimics the way change ringers still write out their methods. It appears to be for the bottom 10 bells of a set of 12 bells with the bell shown as number 4 in the 'music' being 4b (1½ diatonic octaves - in modern bell number music: 1-12 plus 6b), a useful set for both tune ringing and change ringing. This is because having a 6b enables changes for eight bell ringing methods to be rung on the light eight (2-8), as well as the eight heavy bells of the 12 (5-12). It also means that the set can be used for all those melodies which flow both above and below the tonic – like the one above. Similar hand-bell sets, with a 6b, in a variety of keys, are still found in church belfries throughout Britain e.g. Thorpe Bay in Essex.

Here is a transcription of the music into staff notation using Philip Bedford's best guesses at the rhythm and note durations, given the words of song – though the last line does not scan very well. We do not recognise the tune. Perhaps if someone experiments with different rhythms and note values they may produce a more recognisable melody!

Bill Butler went on to say that "some people instantly recognised that hand-bells could be used as a source of entertainment and that they could make money with them. Roger Smith, who performed at St. Bartholomew's Fair, London in 1760, rang eight bells on his own. The Norwich Mercury for 1760 records that the celebrated Frankling was ringing there, performing in a similar manner.

Ringers often appeared as part of music hall acts. George Histon and W.H. Johnson were two such who who rang ten bells each, four in each hand and one on each foot!! Another performer like this was William Farthing, who died just a hundred years ago. He used to ring ten bells on his own, but had two in each hand, one on each elbow, one on each arm and one on each foot. He rang tunes on his own in this way, and also rang touches of Bob Royal. With the aid of another ringer he used to ring Bob Maximus!"

But I digress. After the era of the Cors had passed it is noted that a founder named Edward Read was at Aldbourne from 1751 to 1753, after which the Aldbourne foundry was taken up by Robert Wells. There were two people with the name Robert Wells, so here I shall term them 1 and 2.

Some of Robert Well 1's, bells are still in use today. There are one or two Wells bells in the set of bells that were used by the Warnham Hand-bell Consort (Sussex) in the 1980s and 1990s before they disbanded.

The time from approximately 1740 to 1830 which straddled what is known as the "Age of Enlightenment". It was a period of rapidly increasing commercial and industrial prosperity, largely resulting from a series of inventions which greatly stimulated the textile trade. This Industrial Revolution completely changed the social and economic life of the nation. Therefore it is no surprise that during this time came changes in the way hand-bells were designed, made and rung. Indeed the popularity of hand-bell ringing increased rapidly. When Handel immigrated to England in 1740 he heard hand-bells being rung in several of the homes into which he was invited. This, together with the ringing of so many church bells caused him to name Britain "The Ringing Isle".

It would seem that Robert Wells 1 (1760-1780) was one of the first founders to bring about major changes to the design and the manufacture of hand-bells, his bells being tuned more accurately than those of the Cors, and Wells also made great and important changes to the staple assembly of his bells. The simple horseshoe of iron cast into the bell on which to hang the clapper, as used in the Cor bells, was replaced by a clapper mounting which was fixed through a hole drilled into the top of the bell and secured by a pin through the argent. The clapper was constructed of bell metal instead of iron; the clapper ball was drilled in both striking faces and leather striker pegs inserted into the holes. The horseshoe shaped iron staple was replaced by a bronze "staple" in the form of a clevis into which the staple end of the clapper was attached with a staple pin made of leather or wood. In the meantime another founder, Henry Symondson had replaced the leather collars, with brass springs which were riveted onto the clapper mounting to prevent the bell giving a double ring. The clapper now moved in one arc only back and forth. This arrangement was much more effective and efficient than anything used before. The resulting bells had a longer life and a much more musical sound, not now

10

being metal to metal. Because of the improved staple assembly, the ringers had more control over the ringing of the bell which enabled expression to be used when playing tunes. A similar type of staple/clapper assembly is still used by the Whitechapel and John Taylor Foundries.

After Robert Wells 1 came Robert Wells 2 (1781-1799) and also his son James Wells (1781-1825).

Robert Wells 1 was one of the first founders to put a casting number on the dome of each of his hand-bells. Of his bells that exist today the largest bell known of is 22C. There is also an 8C, so the number of bells of different sizes and notes cast by him must have been at least a diatonic three octaves, twenty-two in number from 1C to 22C, although he most likely cast at least the most used accidentals when required, which is an indication of what range of hand-bells tune ringers used during the 18th century.

The Wells family used the same patterns as had been used by the Cors, but after James Wells, the Aldbourne Foundry and their patterns, like many others, were bought up, by Mears of Whitechapel.

Probably the most well known of the travelling founders was James Bridgeman who initially worked for the Wells family and then at Whitechapel. He later moved back to Aldbourne to set up his own foundry from about 1830-1858. James Bridgeman visited fairs and markets and made a good sale to farmers of his latten bells, which were used on draft horses to warn oncoming traffic of their approach. His latten bells were similar to his hand-bells but had iron clappers hung from a staple and were hung usually four to a 'belfry' to ring a distinctive chord as the horses moved. It is thought that he cast all his bells with the iron crown staple and then snapped them out of bells for tune ringing before drilling a hole for the clapper assembly.

While the Wells family was producing bells in Wiltshire, a Hertford bell founder named John Bryant 1782-1825 instructed his tuner and second in command Henry Symondson 1782-1845 to develop patterns for the production of hand-bells.

At the end of the 18th century the vertical lathe was first used in the tuning of English tower bells. This machine was first installed at the Whitechapel Bell Foundry, London, where it was driven by donkey power. The Whitechapel Foundry believe a tuning lathe may have been installed as early as 1738. This lathe replaced the earlier system of hand chipping and filing of bells and also led to increased output, but it was only used to tune bells on the outside.

Very soon the lathe principle of tuning was applied to hand-bells by Symondson at Hertford and by Mears at Whitechapel. Prior to this, founders had simply cast a number of bells, picked out the best and filed them to pitch as the Cors did, but overtones were still completely neglected.

But it is thought that it was Symondson who first started tuning the inside of hand-bells as well as the outside - probably in the late 18th or early 19th century, this practice was taken up by Whitechapel although a set of Thomas Mears' hand-bells of 1812 vintage, which were returned to Whitechapel for a refit 50 years ago, were not turned on the inside.

John Bryant was highly regarded, both as a founder and a man of integrity, who cast some excellent hand-bells of a high quality, some of which are still in use today. This is an indication of how the hand-bell standards had risen from the days of the Cors. In 1825 Bryant died penniless and was buried in a pauper's grave - a sad end for a man of such enterprise.

Henry Symondson is important to the story of the development of hand-bell ringing, in that he cast many bells - mostly hand-bells, which he initialled. This is evidence of the growth and popularity of musical hand-bell ringing that took place after the introduction of bells with better tuning and the improved Wells type of staple assembly. Later, Symondson's Foundry at Hertford and Tottenham Court Road, London was bought up by Mears of Whitechapel who had a growing dominance of bell founding during the 19th century. Symondson then joined John Taylor, who had moved his foundry to Loughborough in 1839. Taylors cast a set of bells for Heptonstall hand-bell ringers around 1900. These bells are now used by Hope (Baptist) Hand-bell Ringers, a stone's throw from Heptonstall. The bells were refurbished at the Loughborough Foundry in the mid 1980s. The Hope Hand-bell Ringers were formed in the early 1960s when the Rev D Irvine got together a small band. After two years he left and Mr George Bungay took over as conductor. After a period of activity the bells fell into disuse until 1979, shortly after which the band's present conductor Julie Ming took over. In 1984 Hope were the first winners of the three and a half octave class in a new competition for hand-bells in connection with the Mrs Sunderland Music Festival.

But I digress again. By 1900 the most popular hand-bells were cast by the Whitechapel Bell Foundry. Whitechapel hand-bells were made popular by bands such as Almondbury, Liversedge and Crosland Moor United. Established in Aldgate, London in 1420 the Foundry moved to Whitechapel, less than a mile away, in 1583, across the road from its present site at 32 and 34 Whitechapel Road, to which it moved in 1738. The hand-bells produced by the Whitechapel Foundry today are of the same basic design as developed by Robert Wells (1) 1760-1780.

Whitechapel hand-bells are known for their mellow tone and for their beautiful leather handles. The Foundry still uses traditional craft-based techniques in the production of their hand-bells, the patterns for which, have been continually extended and improved. In 1986 the Foundry cast a monster "Low 32G", the largest hand-bell the Foundry produces. The traditional tuning skills have been handed down for generations, from father to son. These skills are now augmented by the use of electronic equipment, capable of registering pitch to within one hundredth of a semitone.

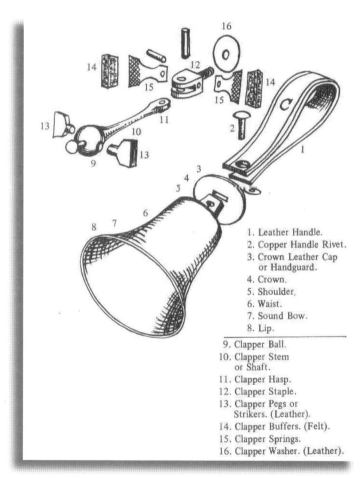

Fig. 6: Parts of an English Hand-bell

1. Leather Handle.
2. Copper Handle Rivet.
3. Crown Leather Cap or Handguard.
4. Crown.
5. Shoulder.
6. Waist.
7. Sound Bow.
8. Lip.

9. Clapper Ball.
10. Clapper Stem or Shaft.
11. Clapper Hasp.
12. Clapper Staple.
13. Clapper Pegs or Strikers. (Leather).
14. Clapper Buffers. (Felt).
15. Clapper Springs.
16. Clapper Washer. (Leather).

Reproduced with the kind permission
of C.T. Richards Esq.

One of the families with a long association with the Whitechapel Foundry are the Olivers. The line began in 1860 with George Oliver and ended with the retirement of Ernest Oliver in 1986.

13

Ernest worked at the Foundry for 56 years, the same number of years that his father, Bert had worked there when he retired in 1929. Ernest's grandfather, George, served at the Foundry for 68 years. His cousin, George Oliver, also worked at the Foundry, a remarkable line of service, in a British company that exports bells of all kinds around the world.

From 1865 to 1968 the Foundry traded as Mears and Stainbank and in 1968 took on the present name of Whitechapel Bell Foundry Ltd, although many people still continue to use the former name.

Fig. 7: L. to R. Ethelbert Oliver (1898 - 1929), George Oliver (1860 - 1918), George Oliver (Ethelbert's nephew) (courtesy David & Dianne Pickett)

Fig. 8: On the right is Ernest Oliver in 1981 with bells from Clifton, Brighouse which he was tuning (photo: John Atkinson)

Musical Hand Bells.

THE ABOVE ILLUSTRATES A CHROMATIC OCTAVE.

MEARS & STAINBANK,

Church Bell Foundry

(Established 1570)

32 & 34, WHITECHAPEL ROAD, LONDON, E.

(Near St. Mary's Station).

Musical Hand Bells.

Their sizes are distinguished by numbers. No. 1 of about 2½ inches diameter, being tuned to Note C. Lower C's (removed an octave apart) are numbered 8, 15, 22 & 29, and measure respectively 3½, 4½, 7 & 10½ inches.

The principal enquiry for Hand Bells is to further the practice of change-ringing in connection with Church Bells. Small sets for this purpose usually consist of 8, 12, or 15 Bells in the

DIATONIC SCALE.

Tenor No.	22 C	21 D	20 E	19 F	18 G	17 A	16 B	15 C
	£ s.	£ s.	£ s.	£ s.	£ s.	£ s.	£ s.	£ s.
Peal of 8 Bells	5 10	5 2	4 15	4 8	4 0	3 16	3 12	3 10
„ 12 „	7 7	7 6	6 16	6 6	6 0	5 18	5 13	5 10
„ 15 „	8 8	7 15	7 7	6 16	6 6	5 15	5 15	5 10

Any set can always be increased—the cost of additions being seen from the following Table of Single Bells.

SINGLE BELLS.

NOTES	No.	Price.	No.	Price.	No.	Price.	No.	Price.	
C or C ♯	19	55/-	22	19/-	15	11/-	8	11/8	No. 1 and
D „ D ♯	28	45/-	21	17/-	14	10/-	7	7/-	smaller
E	17	38/-	20	16/-	13	9/6	6	6/9	Bells
F „ F ♯	16	30/-	19	15/-	12	9/-	5	6/6	
G „ G ♯	15	26/-	18	14/-	11	8/6	4	6/3	5/6 each.
A „ A ♯	24	23/-	17	13/-	10	8/-	3	6/-	
B	23	21/-	16	12/-	9	7/6	2	5/9	

(The usual Ringing Fittings are included in the above prices).

Tune playing upon Hand Bells has become a popular form of entertainment, and there is now a considerable demand for long sets of Bells, some of which consist of as many as 170 in number, being five-and-a-half octaves in the Chromatic Scale, with many of the notes in duplicate and triplicate, and costing over £80. The following Table shows the cost of

PEALS IN THE CHROMATIC SCALE.

TENOR.	2 Octaves (25 Bells)	3 Octaves (37 Bells)	4 Octaves (49 Bells)	5 Octaves (61 Bells)
	£ s. d.	£ s. d.	£ s. d.	£ s. d.
29 C - -	30 0 0	35 10 0	39 0 0	42 0 0
28 D - -	25 0 0	30 15 0	34 5 0	
27 E - -	22 0 0	27 0 0	29 10 0	
26 F - -	20 10 0	25 0 0	27 15 0	
25 G - -	18 10 0	23 0 0	25 0 0	
24 A - -	16 15 0	21 0 0	23 0 0	
23 B - -	15 0 0	19 10 0	21 10 0	
22 C - -	14 10 0	18 0 0	20 10 0	
21 D - -	13 5 0	17 0 0		
20 E - -	12 5 0	16 0 0		
19 F - -	11 5 0	15 10 0		
18 G - -	10 10 0	15 0 0		
17 A - -	10 0 0			
16 B - -	9 5 0	13 5 0		
15 C - -	9 0 0	12 10 0		

CHURCH BELL ROPES of best Russian hemp, coloured wool sallies and soft flax ends. 11/6 per rope up to sixty feet in length, 6d. per rope extra for every additional ten feet.

Fig. 10: Whitechapel Bell Foundry - Master Founders since 1420

Master founders since 1420

1420	Robert Chamberlain of Aldgate
1426	William Chamberlain
1456	John Daniel
1470	John Daniel's Successor
1487	I. W.
1500–1515	Thomas Bullisdon
1506–1522	William Culverden
1523	Thomas Lawrence
1538	John Owen
1553	Thomas Kempe
1574	Robert Mot
1606	Joseph Carter
1610	William Carter
1616	Thomas Bartlet
1632	John Clifton
1640	Antony Bartlet
1675	James Bartlet
1700	Richard Phelps
1735	Phelps and Lester
1738	Thomas Lester
1752	Lester and Pack
1769	Lester, Pack and Chapman
1776	Pack and Chapman
1781	Chapman and Mears
1784	William Mears
1787	William and Thomas Mears
1791	Thomas Mears I
1805	Thomas Mears and Son
1810	Thomas Mears II
1844	Charles and George Mears
1861	George Mears and Co.
1865	Mears and Stainbank
1873	Robert Stainbank
1884	Alfred Lawson
1904	Arthur Hughes
1916	Albert A. Hughes
1945	Albert A. and William A. Hughes
1950	Albert A., William A. and Douglas Hughes
1964	William A. and Douglas Hughes
1972	William A., Douglas and Alan Hughes

Hand-bells from the Whitechapel and Taylor Foundries have been found in all parts of the country, but there is no evidence of bells from the other aforementioned founders being found in the North of England. This is not particularly surprising because the North had a number of foundries of its own, but even so no examples of 18th century hand-bells have been found in the Northern counties so far. One factor which could explain the absence of ancient bells, is, as already mentioned, the contesting aspect of bell ringing in the North, which resulted in a great turnover of hand-bells. Also a great many northern bells have been displaced as a result of the countrywide revival which began in the mid 60s. Therefore evidence of 17th and 18th century hand-bells used in the North is limited and more research is needed in this area.

There are, however, records of 16th, 17th and 18th century bell foundries in the North, although I have not seen any hand-bells cast by them. Most bell founders who cast tower bells could also cast hand-bells, so the following foundries may have done so.

There was a foundry at Wigan, Lancashire, the only one known in that county. This was operated by John Scott (1658-1664), William Scott (1673-1701), Ralph Ashton (1703-1720) and Luke Ashton (1724-1750).

At Wath-on-Dearne (Yorkshire) was another northern foundry, carried on by T Hilton (1774-1808). There was also the Rotherham (Yorkshire) foundry of Joseph Ludlam and A Walker (1733-1760).

There was also the great York foundry which existed for about a hundred and fifty years. First in this line was Rowland Oldfield (1586-1615), who was followed by William Oldfield (1601-1642) whose tower bells are fairly common in Yorkshire. He was succeeded by William Cuerdon (1650-1678). After Cuerdon migrated to Doncaster, the York foundry then passed to Samuel Smith, who carried on founding until 1709. When he died, his son Samuel (1709-1731) took over.

Edward Seller whose bells were similar to the original York founders's started a rival foundry in York in 1710. Edward Seller died in 1724 and a second Edward took his place, until he died in 1764. The last in this line of founders was George Dalton (1752-1789) and G and R Dalton (1783 – 1807).

The development from ringing country tunes on 12 Cor type hand-bells to the ringing of full orchestral pieces of music, using upward of 70 bells, took about a hundred years and its development was accelerated by the introduction of "four-in-hand" ringing, probably introduced following Robert Wells' (1) invention of the new staple assembly. "Four-in-hand" ringing, requiring the use of two bells in each hand, set at right angles to each other so that they may be struck independently with a flick of the wrist, impossible using bells with the old lap-over Cor type of staple assembly.

After "four-in-hand" there came "off the table" and subsequently the "Yorkshire Method" of ringing hand-bells. How this development took place we shall see later in the story although all four styles (2 in hand, 4 in hand, Off the Table and Yorkshire Method) can still be found in use by different bands throughout the world where English style hand-bell ringing has been adopted.

It has been said that the development did not extend to the South of England where tune ringing on any scale was non-existent until after 1967. However this is not true. Teams using large hand-bell sets ringing both 4 in hand and off table developed concurrently both in the north and the south of England – and indeed in the colonies. S. Mary's Prittlewell in Essex had a semi chromatic set of two and a half octaves of Stockham hand-bells down to 22C presented to them in 1869 by Octavius Wigram and there was an extensive volume of secular music with the bells when they were brought out of mothballs in 1966. The Royal Poland Street Ringers were in London with a long set of 163 bells in the 1880s. They undertook 4 major tours in Europe in the late 1800s at the request of the European monarchies. (After the last tour, they sold their bells to a Swedish group called Norrländska Time Players, probably from Söderhamn, [who were later taken over by Fredsklockorna in Nässjö], and taught them to ring in the original mouths down off table style). The Temperance Ringers in London had 82 bells in the 1880s and rang off table, mouths down on their tenor and bass bells and 4 in hand on their treble bells.

Fig. 11: Hand-bell Ringers at the Temperance Fete – from the Graphic, 3rd August 1872

Dr. Barnardos Boys HBRs in London in 1909 used a similar number and the same style (Their bells went to the Websters at Weldon nr Corby [via a church in Peterborough] to be used by the Weldon ringers), Brookhampton in W. Australia rang in the same style but on 3 octaves in 1904 (and still do in 2011), and so did the Maryborough band

in Queensland, Australia at about the same time.

In South Australia the Mount Torrens Primary School's first (incomplete) set of 4½ octaves were lent to them in perpetuity by an elderly local, who in turn had had them given to him in his youth by a similarly elderly local who had been left them by a Vaudeville performing relative. That set contained at least three Henry Symondson bells which therefore would probably date them from somewhere between 1782 and 1845. The Barrett Brothers, from Burra South Australia, ringers of musical glasses and hand-bells at the turn of the 19th/20th centuries used their bells in their evangelising work throughout South Australia, Victoria and New South Wales. The Handbell Society of Australasia's Handbell Herald for January 1990 records that the Barrett Bros' three octaves of bells turned up again in Adelaide, in the possession of one of the grandchildren (now well past retirement age!). Apart from the bass bell, which was being used as a doorstop, none of the bells had been used for a long time and were about to be put on the market.

Figure 12 to 16 show more examples of the 4 styles of ringing.

Fig 12: The Bellringers. A painting by Thomas R. Lamont (1826-1898). Although not the usual style of 2-in-hand ringing, the Offenham Ringers rang in this style (ringing on the up-stroke) at HRGB's 3rd Annual Rally at Worcester in 1969

Fig. 13: The Bedford Family Carol Ringing in 1973. (L to R Sylvia, Don, Philip, & Mai)

Maybe the belief that hand-bell development had not spread to the south came from the fact that the North was separated from the rest of the country by distance and the poor state of the roads and this made travel hazardous, expensive and slow. Also Pennine Hills further isolated the towns and villages within them. It is recorded that Northern people were notoriously rough, and many visitors were shocked by the fierce inhabitants, who were suspicious of strangers and resistant to any kind of change.

John Wesley wrote on 9th June 1757.

"I rode over the mountains to Huddersfield. A wilder people I never saw in England. The men, women and children filled the streets And seemed just ready to devour us"

In April two years later he wrote.
"Preached near Huddersfield to the wildest Congregation I have seen in Yorkshire"

But why had sets of hand-bells become so large by the late 18th century, when there is evidence of sets of up to 50 bells being used? During research for this book, I have spoken to old veteran hand-bell ringers who were told in their younger days,

Fig 14: The Norbury Hand-bell Ringers were the first band registered with HRGB. Bill Hartley, HRGB inaugural chairman is on the far left

Fig 15: The Mt Torrens Ringers, South Australia & the Okabe Kindergarten Koto band representing the Handbell Society of Australasia at the International Handbell Symposium in Japan in 1998 using a version of the "off table bass bells, 4-in-hand trebles"style to play 'Sakura' & 'Moon over the Ruined Castle'.

Fig 16: Ecclesfield in the late 1950s ringing in the Yorkshire Off-table Style on a long set of bells (Granville Mitchell is in the far row on the left hand side) (Photo: Conrad Gregory)

when they began ringing, that hand-bell bands had been formed as a result of tower cum hand-bell ringers meeting "Folk musicians" in public houses. One man who told me this is Mr Arnold Calvert, a former Almondbury ringer from Huddersfield. He was told this by his former conductor at Almondbury, the late Harold Godward, a hand-bell ringer of great experience, who died in 1979. Who the "Folk Musicians" in the pubs were is impossible to say. It is possible, though unlikely, that they were Waits whose positions

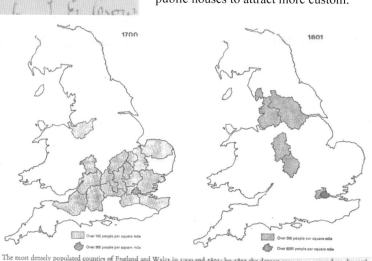

Fig 17: England Population Densities 1700 and 1801

1700

1801

Over 100 people per square mile
Over 500 people per square mile

Over 200 people per square mile
Over 5000 people per square mile

The most densely populated counties of England and Wales in 1700 and 1801: by 1801 the denser areas were centred on the coal and iron fields. These maps are based on average density. In fact some parts of each county were much more thickly populated than others; north Lancashire, for example, had very few people.

had been abolished by the Municipal Reform Act of 1835, or they could have been morris dance musicians, or more likely a local fiddler and concertina player who were always welcomed in public houses to attract more custom.

I believe the answer lies in the Industrial Revolution, the rationale behind the rapid expansion of the hand-bell movement at that time, and the way in which that important historical event influenced the lives and in turn the music of the people. The Industrial Revolution in Britain took place approximately between 1730-1830. This revolution went hand in hand with the Agricultural Revolution which started before it but was accelerated by the Enclosure Acts of the 18th and early 19th centuries. Whilst as a result of these Acts small farmers received compensation for their land, it was very little, and the loss of rights of the rural population led to an increased dependency on the Poor Law. Only a few found work in the increasingly mechanised, enclosed farms. Many relocated to the towns, or cities (or colonies) to try to find work in the emerging factories of the Industrial Revolution. Those men that stayed on the farms usually had to serve a seven year apprenticeship, and sign an agreement that they would not marry until their time was finished. Even then they would then need to work for a few years before they could support a wife. No wonder many young men did not take on this kind of agreement and went to look for work in the towns. The areas most affected by the enclosures at this time were areas with waste lands, which were the West Country and the Northern Counties.

Although there was hardship and poverty, it did not affect everyone and those who were willing and able to change and migrate to the large industrial towns that were springing up in the Midlands and the North, eventually prospered to varying degrees. My own ancestors migrated from Wensleydale in the rural North Riding of Yorkshire to the industrial West Riding during this time.

Mills were now the work places of the people. Forests of tall

20

chimneys blackened the sky with their smoke. Many people hated the changes which brought about the end of their rural lifestyle. But many of the small rural villages were close to the industrial areas, enabling some people to travel to the towns to work. People of those days thought nothing of walking 5 miles or even further to work and back. (If this were suggested today, people would be aghast!) Mills were often built in the rural villages which in some cases merged with, or grew into towns, with the influx of large numbers of people.

The changes and conditions that prevailed during these times are very well put together in a dialect poem by Professor F W Moorman - "A Dalesman's Litany" - composed sometime before 1919. The poem is unique in that Moorman was not a Yorkshireman, but was born at Ashburton in Devon and came to the North as Professor of English Language at Leeds University, where he made a special study of Yorkshire dialects.

A Dalesman's Litany

It's hard when fowks can't find their wark Wheer they've bin bred an' born;
When I were young I awlus thowt I'd bide 'mong t'roots an' corn.
But I've bin forced to work i' towns, So here's my litany:
Frae Hull, an' Halifax, an' Hell, Gooid Lord, deliver me!

When I were courtin' Mary Ann, T'owd squire he says one day:
"I've got no bield for wedded fowks; Choose wilt ta wed or stay?"
I couldn't gie up t'lass I loved, To t'town we had to flee:
Frae Hull, an' Halifax, an' Hell, Gooid Lord, deliver me!

I've wrowt i' Leeds an' Hudthersfel', An' addled honest brass;
I' Bradforth, Keighley, Rotherham, I've kept my bairns an' lass.
I've travelled all t'three Ridin's round, And once I went to sea:
Frae forges, mills, an' coalin' boats, Gooid Lord, deliver me!

I've walked at neet through Sheffield loins, 'T were t'same as bein' i' Hell;
Furnaces thrast out tongues o' fire, An' roared like t'wind on t'fell.
I've sammed up coals i' t'Barnsley pits, Wi' muck up to my knee:
Frae Sheffield, Barnsley, Rotherham, Gooid Lord, deliver me!

I've seen grey fog creep ower Leeds Brig As thick as bastile soup;
I've lived where fowks were stowed away Like rabbits in a coop.
I've watched snow float down t'Bradforth Beck As black as ebony:
Frae Hunslet, Holbeck, Wibsy Slack, Gooid Lord, deliver me!

But now, when all wer childer's fligged, To t'coontry we're coom back.
There's fowerty mile o' heathery moor Twix' us an' t'coal-pit slack.
An' when I sit ower t'fire at neet, I laugh an' shout wi' glee:
Frae Bradforth, Leeds, an' Huthersfel', Frae Hull, an' Halifax, an' Hell,
T'gooid Lord's delivered me!

Bield - shelter; wrowt - worked; addled – earned; bairns – children; loins – lanes; sammed up – picked up; bastile soup – workhouse soup; childer – children; fligged – flown away; slack – powdery coal-dust.

The Litany was set to music by the late David Keddie and made famous by Tim Hart and Maddy Prior, so here it is:

Dalesman's Litany

The enclosures coincided with the rise in population. Such large numbers of people concentrated in these areas now made it possible for hand-bell ringers to form subscription bands, which enabled them to buy larger sets of bells. The people took great pride in their hand-bell ringers, who in many cases provided the village with its only source of music, as there were no brass bands. (They didn't come until after 1815 when the valve was invented), and there were few other musical instruments available, these being still rare and expensive and made mainly on the continent, apart from home-made instruments like the pipe. The hand-bell bands were the first public subscription bands of the working class masses. The Napoleonic wars, which ran from 1793 to 1815, brought hardship to those engaged in agriculture, but indirectly benefited the lot of the industrial worker. As many as one in ten men of military age were serving in the armed forces, this reduced unemployment and workers in the iron and textile industries were able to demand good wages. The effect on industry and agriculture of the wars was to stimulate production. Uniforms and blankets were needed and this stimulated the textile industry. Ironworks were busy making chains, anchors, guns and nails.

The hand-bell ringers of this time who lived and worked in the new industrial areas, with higher earnings found themselves able to afford larger sets of bells, but still through subscription rather than individually.

In the 1835 House of Commons Report on the hand-loom weavers' petitions, it was stated that the hand-loom weavers of 1795 were "a frugal and industrious people supporting many friendly societies"

I don't think it unreasonable to assume that men who had to co-ordinate both mind and body in the operation of hand-looms, would also make excellent hand-bell ringers, where the same co-ordination is required.

Changes in industry brought changes in the way goods were manufactured. There came the invention of new machines with names like the "Spinning-Jenny" and the "Spinning Mule". The "Jenny" was invented in 1764 and did the work of eight hand spinners. The "Spinning Mule" was invented in 1779 and proved to be an improvement on the "Jenny". The introduction of these machines brought about a short period of prosperity for the hand-loom weavers and the croppers (The finishers of woven cloth) and there were hardly enough hand-loom weavers to keep up with the supply of yarn coming from the new spinning machines. In 1812 hand-loom weavers could earn between 17 to 19 shillings (85p to 95p) per week, which was a lot of money in those days. The croppers could earn about 25 shillings (£1.25) per week. They were often paid 5% of the value of the finished cloth. No wonder they went about in fine clothes in the evening. But changes were on the way.

The entry of America into the war in 1812, combined with several bad harvests meant the price of food soared as no grain could be imported. Virtually all the ports were closed. These factors, plus high unemployment caused a great deal of distress and starvation. America's entry into the war made matters worse, cutting off a third of the textile exports and thus increasing the level of unemployment.

The advancement in spinning technology created a need for the mechanisation of weaving, and in 1785 the first power loom was invented by Edmund Cartwright, but its introduction was slow, due to design faults. The power loom was first used in the Lancashire cotton industry. Following a series of improvements, Richard Roberts, a Welsh millwright working in Manchester, developed in 1822, a power loom with a cast iron frame capable of mass production.

In 1787 another machine, called a shearing or cropping frame was invented. Around 1812 two blacksmiths called Enoch and James Taylor of Marsden, near Huddersfield, worked themselves up into machine makers and began to make shearing frames, which could do the work of 10 skilled hand-croppers. To be out of work in those days often meant starvation, so it is not surprising, that as the use of these machines became more widespread, the well paid and skilled hand-loom weavers and croppers, became fearful for their livelihoods and the loss of the independence of working at home, and put up strong opposition to these new machines.

In 1806 there was a House of Commons "Report on the State

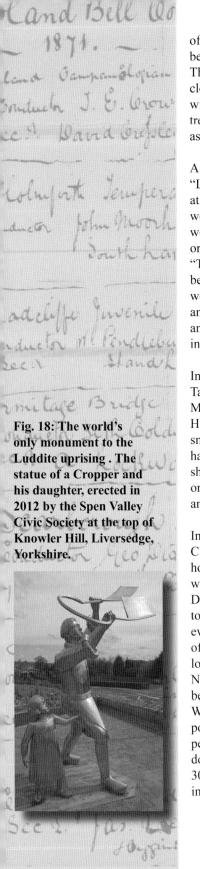

of Woollen Manufacture in England" which had been necessary because of the opposition to the growth of factories and machines. The croppers combined with clothiers (The men who made and sold clothes) and raised over £10,000 for legal expenses and sending witnesses to give evidence, but all in vain. Their delegates were treated with scant regard and all appeals were rejected, and it was assumed that opposition to the new machines would soon die out.

A body of rebels grew in the North of England, calling themselves "Luddites", from Ned Ludd, who had smashed a machine in anger at Nottingham. There was unrest and tension. The first Luddites were the croppers, and, later, the hand-loom weavers. The croppers were in a good position to create trouble. It was said of their strong organisation, known as the "Institution" or Croppers' Union, that "The despotic power they really possess and exercise is beyond belief". The croppers were the elite of the Woollen industry and were highly skilled workers. Their hand shears were 4 feet long and weighed up to 50lb and they had a reputation for being riotous and heavy drinkers, and very difficult for their employers to keep in control.

In February 1812, shearing frames, made by Enoch and James Taylor, were smashed, after being dragged from carts on Hartshead Moor. The Taylors also made large hammers, known as "Enoch Hammers". These same hammers were used by the croppers to smash the shearing machines, which gave rise to the call "Enoch hath made thee and Enoch shall break thee". The breaking of shearing frames became widespread. The Luddites were very well organised - not a wild rabble, but a well disciplined band, masked and drawn up in military style ranks.

In April 1812 there was a Luddite attack on Rawfolds Mill, near Cleckheaton, Yorkshire (only a few hundred yards from my home) when the Luddites were routed by the military. There were deaths of both mill owners and Luddites during these times. Discontent smouldered on and in 1820 there was an ambitious plot to capture Huddersfield in Yorkshire, by an all out attack, but this eventually came to nothing. In 1834 came the threat to the jobs of hand-loom workers, when George Hattersley and Sons made a loom specifically for the worsted industry, but it was smashed at Nabwood, near Shipley, Yorkshire. There had been power looms before. In 1826 one example was at the power loom factory of Walters and Lund, at Macclesfield in Cheshire, where there were power loom riots. One report stated that a mob of 3,000 to 4,000 persons threw stones at the factory windows and broke down the doors. Another report of the same riot said that there were 200 to 300 persons! The growth in the use of textile machinery became immense and, as the Luddites feared, earnings fell.

Fig. 18: The world's only monument to the Luddite uprising . The statue of a Cropper and his daughter, erected in 2012 by the Spen Valley Civic Society at the top of Knowler Hill, Liversedge, Yorkshire.

The 1835 "Report on the Hand-Loom Weavers' Petition to the House of Commons" gave mixed views on rates of pay, but it was clear that earnings were lower. A top earner in weaving could earn 15 shillings per week (75p) if he were lucky, but most workers seemed to be earning 6 to 8 shillings per week (30 - 40p). In the Huddersfield district, where hand-bell ringing was popular, a great number of weavers, it was stated, did not earn more than 4 to 5 shillings (20 - 25p) per week when trade was good. In Bolton, Lancashire, earnings were lower still with weavers on around twopence three farthings per day (just over 1p).

By 1850 wages had improved. Huddersfield power loom and hand loom men could earn 14 to 15 shillings (70 - 75p) per week, but the average earnings were around 11 shillings (55p) per week.

In other areas where hand-bell ringers existed, around 1850 wages were of a similar rate. Dewsbury in Yorkshire became the centre of the shoddy industry, which began in nearby Batley about 1813. The shoddy trade made cheap cloth by reworking ground up rags. Shoddy workers could earn 18 to 22 shillings (90p to £1.10p), more than the power loom workers in Huddersfield. Manchester spinners could earn 9 to 11 shillings (45 -55p) per week. At Macclesfield in Cheshire, silk weavers' earnings were 10 to 12 shillings (50 - 60p) per week.

The above are good examples because hand-bell ringers from all these areas were amongst the first competitors in the early days of the British Open Hand-bell Ringing Contest, which was first held at Belle Vue, Manchester in 1855, by which time conditions for the working man had somewhat improved.

The French Revolution of 1789 had given people ideas about the rights of man and his lot in the world, and the British Government became fearful of a popular movements in Britain, and were petitioned by the mill owners, disturbed by the strength of fighting against them. The result was the Combination Acts of 1799/1800, which made combinations (unions) of workmen illegal. The Acts failed to prevent the formation of combinations and some trade unions continued openly, whilst others operated underground.

The Acts were rigorously used against the factory workers of Yorkshire and Lancashire and workers were imprisoned. The Acts prevented working classes from being able to better their wages and conditions of employment. Workers could be fined for having factory windows open, for washing themselves, lateness, absenteeism; and even whistling was finable. The chief deterrent was dismissal. Some employers used methods of "Shame". Robert Ward of Bradford in Yorkshire made children hold up a card in which the offence was written for all to see.

Cand Bell Co
_1871. —_

...and Campanologian
Conductor J. E. Crow...
...David Cuf...ter

Colnforth Temper...(?)
...ductor John Moorh...
South ha...

...adcliffe Juvenile
...ductor W. Pendlebu...
...ec... St and L

...mitage Bridge
...onductor Seth Gold...
...c. A. Lockw...

...carborough
...onductor Geo D...a
...y E. B. Newton. 16 m...

Hyde
...nductor S. Brier...
...Organi...(?)
...e... S... Wes. Hy...

Oldham.
...onductor David
Sec... Jas. L...
...ippin...

The Combination Acts were repealed in 1824. A Meeting reported in the Stockport Advertiser of "a meeting of the working classes" held at the Star Inn, Stockport, Cheshire in January 27th, 1825 shows how much the workers hated the Combination Acts. The meeting passed a resolution stating:

"That we the working classes of Stockport, were long oppressed by and discontented with these oppressive statutes, demminated (sic) Combination Laws; and now express our gratitude to the Parliament for repealing those Laws, which reduced honest industry to pauperism, to misery, to general suspicion and discontent and deprived them of time and means of instruction. We can feel more than grateful for the repeal of the Combination Laws. We've heard that application is to be made for legislature for the repeal of those oppressive laws"

The report went on to condemn those who violated the law, but that the Acts should not be brought back.

The workers had come to look upon their employers as tyrants. Some employers felt that there was a need to improve relations between themselves and their employees and make their workers happy with improved conditions in their factories. Thereafter the use of the stick and the strap on workers was forbidden, the working day reduced to twelve or even ten hours per day. Some employers built chapels and schools and workers outings were arranged. Employers found that production did not fall and indeed large profits were made.

It would seem that such moves benefited hand-bell ringing in that some bands received grants of money to purchase bells. The local gentry encouraged people to take up agreeable leisure activities and were known to have given financial support to hand-bell ringers. We shall see examples of this later.

One point to consider is that hand-bell bands, unlike other forms of bands, such as brass, could not be used for political demonstrations or marches – "a good thing too" thought employers and the gentry. It was also felt generally that such leisure time organisations would keep people away from the evils of drink, and this was also in line with the early Victorian belief that music was "a force for the moral elevation of the working people".

Fortunately, there were some good and fair employers. Josiah Wedgwood of the potteries was one example. Arthur Taylor, in his History of Brass Bands mentions a Preston (Lancashire) factory owner who, in 1844 paid for 650 of his employees and 70 friends to go on a pleasure trip to Fleetwood. Such 'Works-trips' continued well into our own time, but with the advent of the working man's car, such trips became obsolete and most ended in the 1960s - rather regrettable I think! Now everyone goes to Fleetwood in their antisocial 4 seater cars, instead of all pals together in a "Shara" (from charabanc), a single decker, often uncomfortable, motor coach used for Works day outings to the seaside after the Second World War until the early 60s.

The efforts of the mill owners and local gentry seemed to have an effect, as there was less unrest and fewer strikes in areas where such measures were taken.

Eventually an Act of Parliament was passed in 1847 (Fielden's Act) which limited the working hours of women and young persons in textile mills to ten hours per day. This was extended to workers in other industries in the 1860s.

The lowering of working hours would have benefited the hand-bell movement as there would have been more leisure time for band rehearsals. The decrease of working hours of the 1860s coincides with the increase in the popularity of hand-bell ringing.

"Church Bands" were another influence on the development of musical hand-bell ringing. These bands played for the church service after the Puritans decreed in 1644 that all organs should be removed from the church. The tradition of these church bands lasted about 200 years and were widespread throughout England and were most common between 1780 and 1830. Some of the instruments used were the viol (fiddle), bass viol ('cello), serpent, clarinet, ophicleide and the bassoon. The bands often played in galleries erected for them at the west end of the church, these being imitations of galleries in the great Tudor houses where minstrels entertained. The tune "Cranbrook", a carol rarely used today, is almost the only survivor of a very large repertoire of church music. The tune is however used by "Yorkshire Folk" today, when they sing "Ilkey Moor Bah T'at". The church choir would occupy seats in the west gallery alongside the church band.

The novelist Thomas Hardy was a great church band enthusiast. He mentions them in one of his best-loved novels "Under the Greenwood Tree", which portrays vividly the lives of the Mellstock choir members and its old established west gallery musicians.

The church bands played many hymn tunes and short verse anthems or hymns for the choir. They would often "Double up" as village bands for dancing.

By the second half of the 19th century all but the smallest churches had acquired either a small organ or harmonium. The old village musicians were turned out and replaced by an organist. These changes happened because of church reform from the Oxford Movement. Changes in doctrine led to changes in the services, in church furniture and allied to a change in musical taste, to a demand for a different kind of music. The displaced village musicians resented the change. "A chist o'whistles" was the contemptuous name given to the intruding organ. The instruments in many cases belonged to the church, so the village musicians were often left with nowhere to play and no instruments.

This situation would seem to have had a bearing on the development of hand-bell ringing in the second half of the 18th century, as the demise of the church bands coincides with the increase in popularity of hand-bell ringing, and it is probable that many church band and choir members became hand-bell ringers. It is recorded that many of the early hand-bell ringers were also members of the choir or glee singing parties or village choirs. Also hand-bell ringing was most popular where there was a strong choral tradition, for instance in Yorkshire and Lancashire.

Both church bands and choirs used staff notated music and taught music to their members, using the system of Tonic Sol-fa, which was also a method used by the hand-bell ringers of the 19th century.

Indeed, C. W. Fletcher of the Royal Criterion Hand-bell Ringers and Glee Singers published an instructional book on hand-bell ringing in 1888 ("Hand-bell Ringing", pub. J. Curwen & Sons) which recommended the adoption of Tonic Sol-fa notation as "the best that could possibly be devised for hand-bell ringing". In justification Fetcher said "...it is believed the method of the Royal Criterion Hand-bell Ringers [will] compare favourably with that of other ringers who adhere to an older style. This is indeed proved by the criticisms of the Press, from the Times downwards, and by the numerous applications for their services being received from various parts of the world. The members believe that they have secured the best existing system, one by which the most complicated harmony can be perfectly played. There is no doubt, however, that this is largely due to the Tonic Sol-fa method, which they adopt." The system obviously worked for Fletcher's 5 strong hand-bell band, as they rang on a long set of 109 bells (5 octaves with duplicate top 4 octaves), using the mouths down off table method, ringing up to 15 bells each.

The use of Tonic Sol-fa by hand-bell bands gives further credence to the idea that church bands and choir members joined hand-bell bands, after the introduction of an organ in a particular parish church. Looking for evidence that would corroborate this I checked the record of the dates when organs were installed in churches where hand-bell ringers were known to have existed before 1855.

At Leigh Parish Church, Lancashire, the organ was erected in 1777. At Ripponden Parish Church, Yorkshire, the second church of three built in 1729, had a gallery in the west end of the church and the first organ was introduced into the church in 1828, and they then disbanded the old church band. The instruments belonged to the church. At Middleton in Lancashire the organ was erected in 1825, and in Eccles in 1811.

Perhaps, the organ installed at Leigh Parish Church is the best example. The point being that church band musicians, replaced by an organ, against their will in 1777, would have not hung around for brass and reed bands to develop, but would have joined, or set up the Leigh Hand-bell Band.

In the 18th century the connection between ringing and religion had become more and more tenuous. The standards of behaviour in most country and village belfries became appalling with cursing, swearing and smoking being normal, and in many towers a barrel of beer, or even gin and brandy was always "on tap" in the ringing chamber. Spirits too in those days were cheap but taxation of spirits in later years was to change this. Such habits were normal for the times.

The Temperance Movement originated to encourage people to drink beer rather than gin. My local Methodist Church at Hartshead Moor held fundraising events to set up a working men's club, which still operates to this day. Unfortunately the church closed about thirty years ago! (A few examples of the amount of ale and spirits drunk by people connected with the church will be given later). In the light of this situation it is not surprising that before long a deep rift developed between the towerbell ringers and the clergy. Incumbents were locked out of the tower by the ringers. The ringers reserved the right when and when not to ring.

Changes came as a result of the Oxford Movement which brought church reforms. In 1839 the Cambridge Camden Society was formed and from then until 1868 it influenced virtually every aspect of the Anglican Church throughout the country.

The towerbell ringers found themselves and their bells under close scrutiny and this often resulted in the clergy regaining control of the bell tower, though for the following thirty years some ringers fought for the restoration of the privileges and rights that they had enjoyed before.

One of the more drastic means of achieving control of the tower and ringers was to lengthen the bell ropes, so that they came down to the bottom of the tower and to abolish the ringing chamber and take out the chamber floor. The result of this was that the ringers were in full view of the congregation and so would have to improve their behaviour. Also the clergy had the keys to the church and tower, thus they had overall control of the ringing. The antagonism between the towerbell ringers and the clergy became acute and to make matters worse the clergy forbade ringers to engage in prize ringing contests which took place between towers. Eventually the custom of change ringing for prizes died out in about 1850.

The result of all this friction between the clergy and the tower bell ringers would then seem to have a bearing on the formation of bands of hand-bell ringers. Tower bell ringing normally could now only be carried on in connection with church services. Hand-bells however, could be rung in rooms outside the jurisdiction of churches, for example in a room at the local public house, and, unlike swinging tower bells, which can not be used to ring tunes, hand-bells do not have that restriction, as the more musical of the tower bell ringers would have already realised. Thus, because (as stated before) hand-bells could be purchased quite easily and were freely available, and the fact that the ringers also had their own accommodation where they could drink and do as they wished without any interference from incumbents or church wardens. We know that many tower bell ringers took this option and also became hand-bell tune ringers (e.g. the Lancashire Ringers who, from 1846 toured the world on two occasions as tune ringers as

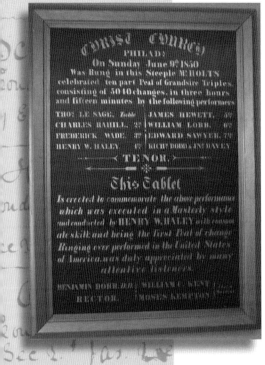

Fig 19: Peal Board commemorating the first Peal in the USA (courtesy Dianne Cermak)

I detail later, also taught change ringing on tower bells in the British colonies. Another band, again taken to the USA by P.T. Barnum (confusingly still called the Lancashire Ringers) even rang the first true peal outside Britain when, ringing Grandsire Triples, they rang a peal of 5040 changes at Christchurch, Philadelphia on 9th June 1850.) This could explain why many bands of hand-bell ringers had no connection with the church as early as 1855, even though some of their members may have been church tower bell ringers, but I will give more examples of such bands later on in my story.

There was one event which took place every year, to which all of the aforementioned groups visited and enjoyed. This was the "Wakes". The word "Wake" comes from the custom of "Waking" or watching the church on the eve of the dedication of the church. Every rural parish had its "Wake" every year and most of them had two, one on the day of dedication and another on the birthday

30

of the saint to whom the church was dedication. The festival of the dedication was then discontinued, leaving the "Saints" day festival. Up to the year 1536 the Wakes were held inside the church and arranged by churchwardens, who made house to house collections to finance the festivities.

Because churches were dedicated to different saints, their saints day festivals were held on different days throughout the year. It is interesting that many of the usual saints to whom parish churches are dedicated have their feast days in the summer months: St Barnabas on 11th June, St John on 24th June, St Philip and St Paul on 29th June, St Thomas on 3rd July, St Christopher on 25th July, St Mary on 15th August and St Bartholomew on 24th August. However there were complaints that the number of holidays had been excessively increased to the detriment of civil government and secular affairs. The "Wakes" had become popular, not only with the inhabitants of the particular parish, but to others who flocked from neighbouring towns and hamlets. Peddlers and hawkers attended to sell their wares. Ale was brewed by churchwardens in the church, which led to them sometimes being called "Ale-Wardens". Rioting and bad manners and drunkenness had crept into the festivals, so in 1536 an Act of Convention was passed by King Henry VIII which ordered that all "Wakes" should be held on the same day, the first Sunday in October. The Act caused much dissatisfaction and in most places tradition and habit were too strong for the authorities and the original dates were still adhered to. The Act did remove the "Wakes" from the church into the churchyard, where booths were erected.

By now the Wakes had spread out into the whole village or town near the church, bear-baiting, bull baiting and cock fighting were part of the proceedings.

In 1579 a group of ecclesiastical commissioners consisting of Henry, Earl of Derby, Henry, Earl of Huntingdon and William, Bishop of Chester held a meeting at Manchester and issued a mandate against pipers and minstrels making and frequenting bear-baiting and bull-baiting on the Sabbath days, or on any other days and also against superstitious ringing of bells, wakes and common feasts, drunkenness, gaming and other vicious and unprofitable pursuits. (So at least we know there was some bell ringing going on at this time, even though it was superstitious!)

Such orders to suppress the Wakes were made all over the country to little effect. Eventually the cruel and barbarous practice of bull-baiting was abolished in 1835. But what importance were these Wakes to the development of hand-bell ringing?
Well the Wakes, as stated, became very popular and people would save money all year to spend during the Wakes which were usually

held at the end of the summer, in August and September. There was much singing and drinking and reed bands would play in the public houses throughout the duration of the Wakes. The tower bell ringers always rang on all festive occasions and celebrations of any kind, the winning of a battle, for example, and often had access to a set of hand-bells and as stated before could and did ring tunes on their hand-bells as well as changes.

I have already described how church bands, choirs and tower bell ringers took to ringing hand-bells as a form of making music and that hand-bells, unlike other musical instruments, were readily available to buy and that the suppliers in the early days were bell founders, who travelled round the country seeling their wares. The Wakes therefore were an ideal market place for bell founders like the Cors and Wells founders, who were very happy to sell hand-bells to anyone who requested them. Therefore there was no need to order bells from a foundry miles away and travel over poor roads to collect them, or pay carriage fees.

Hand-bell ringing became very popular in areas where wakes were held and as mentioned earlier, throughout the duration of the Wakes, hand-bell ringers would ring in the public houses of the district. The Wakes attracted many people from the surrounding areas, who would travel in an assortment of carts, crammed with as many passengers as it was possible to hold. It is therefore only natural that hand-bell tune ringers from one village would visit the Wakes of another nearby village or town to ring tunes in the pubs and enjoy the merriments. This probably resulted in the exchange of thought and ideas between different sets of hand-bell ringers. It was at this stage, I feel, somewhere between approximately 1760 and 1790 that hand-bell ringing in the North of England started to develop into "larger Bands" of tune ringers, using 30 to 40 bells, rather than being tower bell ringers, ringing tunes on the small sets of bells used to practise change ringing and carols. It was not only hand-bell ringing which was developing and changing during these times, but all forms of music. New ideas were developing. The violin, was replacing the viol. Orchestras were growing larger, although at this time they were also known as "Bands". Change was the order of the day, not only in music, but in lifestyles, and it is worth remembering that at this time, as already stated, the church bands were being disbanded and replaced by the organ, and there was also the friction between the clergy and the tower bell ringers to bear in mind.

The Industrial Revolution caused a shift in population from the South to the North. At this time the Northern hand-bell ringers were developing new techniques of ringing hand-bells.
The Wakes were responsible for the introduction of the most important event in the development of musical hand-bell ringing:

"The Contest". A feature of the Wakes were competitions for just about everything from Archery to pancake racing.

The Stockport Advertiser of the 25th of July 1825 contains the following paragraph,

"Didsbury Wakes (Manchester) will be celebrated on the 8th, 9th and 10th of August. A long bill of fare of the diversions to be enjoyed at this most delightful village has been published. The enjoyments consist of ass races, for purses of gold; prison-bar playing and grinning through collars, for ale; bag-racing, for hats; foot-racing, for sums of money; maiden plates, for ladies under twenty years of age, for gown-pieces, shawls etc., treacled loaf-eating, for various rewards; smoking matches, apple dumpling eating, wheelbarrow-racing, the best heats; bell-racing and balls each evening. The humours of Didsbury festival are always well-regulated, the display of youths of both sexes vying with each other in dress and fashion, as well as cheerful and blooming faces, is not exceeded by any similar event and gaieties of each day are succeeded by the evening parties, fantastically tripping through the innocent relaxation of country dances, reels, etc., to favourite tunes, at the 'Cock' and the 'Ring of Bells' Inns."

Because of the hand-bell ringing that took place in public houses during the time of the Wakes, some of the pubs could have been named the "Ring of Bells" as a result, so it does not always necessarily follow, that pubs were always named "Ring of Bells" as a result of tower bell ringing that took place near by. For example, at Hyde in Cheshire, a traditional home of hand-bell ringing, there is a pub called the "Ring O' Bells" with no church tower near it. The nearby Saint Thomas' Church has no tower. So could that have been where the Hyde Hand-bell Ringers practised or played during Wakes time?

The word "Bell-racing" in the report is, I feel, a mistake by the printer and should have read "Bell-ringing", therefore indicating that part of the proceedings was a bell-ringing contest. Both tower bell and hand-bell bands are known to have competed on such occasions andat these Wakes contests there would have been perhaps only two or three bands at the most taking part, and the drinking of ale and gin would have been as important as the contest itself, perhaps more so.

My friend, the late John Terry, always maintained that the earliest contests for hand-bell ringing were held in public houses, long before the advent of the Belle Vue contests in 1855. At the Eccles Wake (Lancashire) in 1830, a handbill stated that there would be Bull-baiting plus other events and that the Wake would conclude with a fiddling-match by all the fiddlers who attended, for a piece of silver.

So contests were not something invented by the Brass Band

SADDLEWORTH RUSHBEARING.

Fig 20: Saddleworth Rushbearing from an oil painting (between 1747 & 1789). Rushbearings and Wakes were popular with hand-bell ringers who played in public houses during the feasts.

Fig 21: Saddleworth - the Oil Painting

movement as many people have mistakenly suggested. The Wakes, with their long history, would have had competitions long before these examples and this could be another reason why sets of hand-bells had grown so large by the 1790s in the North of England. Wakes in Yorkshire were often called "Feasts" and in other places like Halifax they were known as "Wakes", as they were in Lancashire, in some parts, such as Elland in Yorkshire, the Wakes were called the "Tide". People would clear out their homes and put up new curtains for the coming feast, which is where some suggest that we get the word "Tidy" from "Getting ready for the tide".

In other areas the Wakes took the form of a "Rushbearings". This came from the practice of gathering rushes from the moor and spreading them over the stone or earthen floor. Each year the old rushes would be taken out and the fresh ones strewn over the floor of the church. By the 18th century, Rushbearings were held only every few years as an added attraction to the annual Wakes. Rushbearings were strongly encouraged by some church wardens, and this is where our bell ringers come into the rushbearing picture. The rushes were gathered from the moor, cut and tied into neat bundles and placed on a "Rushcart" which was sometimes hired from the local undertaker. The bundles of rushes were stacked on the cart to form a pyramid, a branch of oak being inserted at the top to make the pile firm. The Rushcart was finally decorated with ornaments, flowers, ribbons and usually a piece of silver. To the cart were attached pulling ropes, which were from twenty to thirty yards long, across which chains were secured or wooden poles. The cart was pulled around the district by Morris Men, or sometimes horses pulled the cart, visiting public houses and the homes of the "well-to-do" people where the Morris Men performed their dances. The procession would eventually arrive at the church, but at what time!

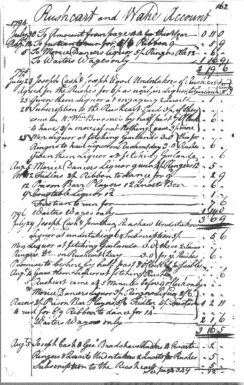

Fig. 22: Didsbury Rushart and Wakes Accounts – check Saddleworth or Didsbury or both from the original
Part of the 1805 accounts reads: "Aug 5 Ringers 6 Quarts for Rushcart 4/-"
And in 1808 it reads "July 17th Garland Carriers, Ale 3/-, for ringers 3/-, for Rushes Dancers Musicians Ale 5/-, Fiddler 7/-"

Whilst researching at the City of Manchester Cultural Studies Centre, I came across the Didsbury Rushcart and Wake's accounts, which were included in the Churchwardens' accounts. The accounts are an extensive record of payments to people who helped with the Rushcart. One thing these accounts show is the amount of ale and gin drank in order for them to carry out the task!

The interesting aspect of these, especially the 1794-6 accounts is the way in which the churchwardens group together the fees of the "Morice Dancers" and those of the "Ringers", could it be that these ringers were both tower bell ringers and hand-bell ringers and that they rang tunes for the Morris Dancers to dance to? Or did they simply ring tunes in the pubs where the Rushcart and the Morris dancers visited? Certainly the latter applied at some Rushbearings, but in the case of the ringing of tunes for the Morris dancers in this case I think not, as the accounts also mention "Dancers musicians".

I decided to check on whether hand-bell ringers in other parishes could have rung for Morris Dancers. The village of Ripponden near Halifax in Yorkshire has a long history of Rushbearings and had hand-bell tune ringers as early as 1855. Holmfirth (Yorkshire) also had Rushbearings. Hand-bell ringers existed in 1855. Middleton in Lancashire had hand-bell ringers in 1855 and the village had Rushbearings. (Indeed as I have already shown they had hand-bells as far back as 1552!) So there could be a connection between Morris Dancers and hand-bell ringing, but more research is needed in this area, if evidence is to be found.

At Manchester Cultural Studies Centre in the archives department I came across a poem: "A pituresqe Description of Furton Fair and it's pernicious consequences" by W. M. Sheldrake written in 1789. It is a very long poem by any standards. From page 18 it reads (original spelling. Where an 'f' comes within a word this is read as an 's'):

Fig. 23: The oldest known photograph of Hand-Bell Ringers, Middleton Parish Church Bell Ringers - 1853 The oldest known photograph of a Brass Band is from 1855.

MIDDLETON PARISH CHURCH
BELL RINGERS 1853.

THOMAS   THOMAS   THOMAS   JAMES   SAMUEL JOHN
ARROWSMITH. FALLOWS. BUCKLEY. BUCKLEY. SAXON. HEYWOOD.

"But' Mongft th alarming and atrocious crimes,
Which are attendants on thefe dregs of times,
And dregs of men, none, 'tis prefum'd is worfe,
Or close subject them to a dire a curfe
As brutal fights, for which they are renown'd
In all the diftricts of the country round
So that 'tis doubters bad beyond compairing,
Unlefs to follith HOLCOME'S curft rufh-bearing;
But as 'twas fatiz'd by an abler pen,
I'll fay but little on that theme again,

Yet, if reports are true, as prudence tells,

'The laft's urival'd and bears of the bells,
Becaufe their interludes and tragic play
Are chiefly acted on the Sabbath-day,
Poor fools, how eagerly they ply their lore,
And to their tawdry garlands add one number more;
Which proves, alas! As oftimes is the case,
That pure religions banish'd from the place"

The reference to "Holcome's curst Rush-bearing" followed by "the last unrivalled and bears off the bells" possibly, though unlikely indicates that hand-bell ringers rang the music for the Morris dancing at Rushbearings. As the type of Morris dancing traditionally performed in the North of England, was danced in clogs, the reference "bears of the bells", could have been a reference to hand-bells although it may to refer to the crotals (Noddy bells) that were attached to the Morris men's legs - not that they were traditional in the North West of England. It makes food for thought, but again more research will be needed before anything can be proven.

(Although the Bedford Family Ringers often include Morris Dance tunes in their repertoire, and two of the Bedfords were, for many years Morris and Country Dancers, they have only accompanied Morris Dancers once - "Ring O' Bells" from the Litchfield Tradition. It was not a success, being in the open in a town square in South Australia. Although it looked good, the bells were too quiet and the dancers, with bells around their calves, and the public were too noisy. So Peter is right. It is unlikely that hand-bell ringers ever regularly accompanied Morris Dancing, though they may have accompanied country dancing, especially if they were lead by a flute or violin as we know some teams were in the early 1800s. Ed.)

The Wakes were a very enjoyable time for the majority of people who had never have travelled further than the nearest market town. People would dress up in their best and gaudiest clothes. The inns were crowded with drunken people which is not surprising looking at the Didsbury Wakes accounts! Also in the pubs was the singing of folk songs, according to contemporary reports the singing of chorus songs went on all day long! Seldom in those days did a woman enter a pub, which may well be another reason why hand-bell ringers were all men, as that was the place where a lot of the ringing was practised and performed.

While the Wakes were popular, hand-bell ringing was popular, but when the railways came and the Wakes began to wane, there also followed a decline in hand-bell ringing. One of the first passenger lines was opened in 1830 carrying people from Liverpool to Manchester. After this the building of railways boomed and within forty years England was covered with a network of railways. This enabled both people and goods to move about the country at a pace thought impossible only fifty years before. The railways now made it possible for bells to be transported quickly and efficiently from the foundry to the customer, although better roads and canals had already improved travel and transport. With the coming of the railways, excursions to the coastal and spa towns became popular and as a result the Wakes declined and in many places only the name and the date of the holiday remained. However, some festivals did keep going as before, and in those places at least, hand-bell ringing also kept going.

Some villages today still have excellent Wakes. Two examples are the Saddleworth and the Sowerby Bridge Rushbearings in West Yorkshire. So when church bands were dying out and the population was growing in the North, hand-bell ringing was very popular and the number of bells used increased for a number of yearsuntil the railways came (1832/35) and the Wakes began to fade. Then hand-bell ringing also went into decline as was reported in an unnamed newspaper cutting I discovered at the Manchester Cultural Studies Centre (see page 46 below). Was the decline of the Wakes and coming of the railways the only reason that hand-bell tune ringing went into decline?

I think there was another and more significant reason for this decline in hand-bell tune ringing, during this period. The growth of Brass Bands coincided with the decline of hand-bell bands. In fact the railways actually helped the growth of Brass Bands as many were engaged to play at the seaside towns for the excursionists in purpose-built bandstands. They were also hired for elections and other outdoor events. Another advantage of playing in a brass band was that the player could practise at home and even play a tune on the instrument on his own, which was something the hand-bell ringer could not do. He could only play tunes when all the other ringers were present. Also many hand-bell ringers would be able to read music, which would have made them ideal recruits for brass bands. Therefore the opportunities for brass band musicians were very attractive to the hand-bell ringer and it would seem that, with the decline of the Wakes, many hand-bell ringers took to the playing of brass instruments and joined brass bands during this time up to 1855. However, despite this decline, some hand-bell bands continued through this period. Indeed the first hand-bell competition at Belle Vue, Manchester in 1855 was held only two years after the first brass band competition.

Brass band historians usually cite three strands of eighteenth and early nineteenth century music making, which are said to have merged to form first the wind band and then the brass band. These strands were the Waits bands, the church band and the military

38

band. However Waits historians have strongly deny to me that Waits had any involvement. I believe that there were still three strands which merged eventually to form brass bands, but instead of one of the strands being the Waits, that strand was actually the hand-bell ringers whom we know had been playing music on hand-bells for at least a hundred years before any form of brass band was known. Therefore I read things differently from my brass friends. I would say that often tower bell ringers and the church bands merged to form hand-bell bands, and then some of the hand-bell, military and wind bands came together to form brass bands.

Enderby Jackson, a key figure in the 19th century band development, of whom we shall hear more later, said in his writings of the 1890s in an article entitled

"ORIGIN AND PROMOTION OF BRASS BAND CONTEST":

"Certain classes of mill-, foundry- and factory-bands were able to purchase full sets of instruments of one maker and these rapidly became favourites with the public for their tunes and equality. Most of the members of this class of band were then - as they are now - drawn from the weekly wages earning classes, many working as colliers, iron founders, leather workers, mill hands, wool and cotton, shoddy not excepted, weavers etc. Those born and bred amidst the rugged hills and lovely dales of West Yorkshire and North East Lancashire were especially charmed with the richness and resonance of the new music. From their childhood these people invariably show a deep love for the music of nature, as well as for that acquired by them as art". He then goes on to say *"Their hands, horned and often malformed by their daily toil, were well served in these new instruments by the short easy manipulation, three fingers sufficing to work the mechanism of the three equidistant pistons".* His last statement has stuck ever since it was published in the 1890s and has been used as a reason why hand-bell ringers played music on bells. Rough, horned hands they might have had, but this was not the reason they took to the ringing of hand-bells. It was for the reasons already mentioned. Jackson goes on *"Being at that time a young Yorkshire solo flautist and trumpeter and travelling with a theatrical company, 'My professional' with the amateur brass bands then rapidly forming and my services were frequently requisitioned both in the towns and villages to arrange music for the new musicians. The beautiful and romantic country around Leeds, Bradford, Dewsbury, Batley, Bramley, Huddersfield, Holmfirth, Accrington, Ossett, Blackburn, Stalybridge, etc with the many hamlets nestling in and around the wild mountainous ridges of the rugged and stony backbone of England, separating Yorkshire from Lancashire, began to swarm with rival formations, which were frequently subsidised by public subscriptions and formed an important element in the village recreations.*

In a few years almost every village and group of mills in these districts possessed its own band. It mattered not to them how the bands were constituted or what classification of instruments was in use."

Jackson's last statement shows that in those days a band was a band, which included a number of different types of instruments, including hand-bells. He goes on "Each man made his own choice, and the teacher found music suitably arranged for their proficiency. If these things were cleverly managed, music was the result and music was the love and pride of these people and their ever abiding pastime". Jackson now enters into the subject of hand-bell ringers. "Excellent bands of hand-bell ringers had long abounded in these districts and they certainly surpassed in brilliant and astonishing play, any similar formation of the present day". His last statement, I feel, was not correct as by 1890, standards had risen above those of the days before 1860. Perhaps his memories were such happy ones that he looked upon the hand-bell ringers of his youth in a much better light, but not to take anything away from the early ringers, they must have been very good indeed. To the old man in the evening of his life, looking back, even the sun seemed to shine brighter, when he writes about the repertoire of these early hand-bell bands - grand and sacred choruses, airs with variations, waltzes, quadrilles, country dances and even florid operatic selections, formed their repertoires. "The close practice of these pieces solaced their long winter evenings and in the bright golden summer time enlivened the village green. Wives, daughters and sons enjoyed the music, which formed a really excellent accompaniment to the healthy open air dancing of the lads and lasses"

This confirms my thoughts that hand-bell ringers did play for dancing, but ringing 4 in hand with perhaps violin accompaniment I feel. Later in his article he writes "North country bell ringers have long maintained their reputation of being good readers of music, the members of the bands usually forming the village and church choirs of the places of worship in their districts, clubs of glee singers abounded amongst them, with madrigal societies scattered here and there, and the practices of these clubs, in addition to glees, extended to the works of Handel, Bach's cantatas, with Haydn's and Mozart's Masses".

Later in his article he says, "These industrious, hard working, bell ringing, glee singing, passionate lovers of music formed the 'Golden ore' from which our noted, world-known, amateur brass bands were formed and from which, as the best men left the country, they were recruited". The last sentence probably refers to the men who went to fight in the Crimea which tends to confirm later research by brass band historians showing Enderby Jackson's memory to be a bit faulty and fanciful in his later years. Brass bands actually developed concurrently with the other 'poor man's music' of the time between the 1830s and 1850s rather than after it, and it is most likely that the 'golden ore' supplied recruits for all the poor man's bands of the period – brass, concertina and hand-bells. However this article is still important in that it gives clues as to what type of lives the people had and their activities - which gave rise to this 'golden ore' hand-bell. Enderby Jackson comes into our story again as we now come to the most significant and important one single event in the whole story of the development of musical hand-bell ringing - the Belle Vue Hand-bell Ringing Contest. The run up to the contest is interesting and important, and had its effect on the success of the contest.

Chapter 2
- Belle Vue – The First Revival

The Belle Vue Zoological Gardens were opened to the public by John Jennison in 1837, who created them from a 36 acre waste plot of land at Gorton, Manchester, taking the name from a public house near the site called "Belle Vue House". Jennison then set to work and made "Belle Vue" the grandest and most popular pleasure gardens in the North. There was a lake and gardens, all types of entertainers were engaged, including jugglers, conjurers and the very popular clog dancing, in fact all the things that had been popular at the Wakes. There was also the new attraction of the Zoo. Not that many people had even heard of an elephant, let alone seen one in 1850, when the first one in Lancashire came to the Zoo. There was also dancing to the Belle Vue's own mixed band, playing for dancing all the popular tunes of the day, which in fact were similar to the tunes played by the hand-bell ringers, but more of this later.

Fig. 24: The Crystal Palace C. 1861

In 1847 Jennison had the first greyhound track in the world built at Belle Vue. Belle Vue was self sufficient in that it carried out all functions entirely independently e.g. baking, and providing actors for the spectaculars. It even had a print shop to print its own programmes and tickets. But the story of this musical contest starts in London, not in Manchester, at the Great Exhibition held at the Crystal Palace in 1851, which was the brain child of Prince Albert. The Palace was a massive glass built auditorium. The working classes were encouraged to visit the exhibition, using the excursion trains which were laid on for the event. The exhibition signalled a new era of some stability in the country. The Chartists were dying out, with the gradual reforms ending in 1848 with the failure of their last petition to Parliament, although Chartist conventions were held up to 1858.

At the exhibition was a musician born at Hull in the East Riding of Yorkshire, named Enderby Jackson who I have already mentioned - remember him as he comes into our story again. In the late 1830s the young Enderby Jackson joined a new band formed in his native Hull in 1836, in which he played in the trumpet section. In 1845 there was a contest held at Burton Constable Hall, in which both brass and wind bands took part. This was the time when wind, brass and reed bands were changing over to brass only. (Perhaps this change to all brass was brought about by the influence of hand-bell ringers who had been used to playing on one instrument with a clear pure, and distinctive tone – the hand-bell set, and they found that the brass band produced a similar pure and distinctive tone?) Back to the Burton Constable Contest. This event must have made its impression upon the young 9 year old Jackson, who was playing flute at the event with a Quadrille band for the dancing. For a number of years he worked as a musician in a travelling theatre, around the North of England and played at the fairs that visited the various wakes during that time. It was during these travels that Jackson came into contact with hand-bell ringing bands who were often also at such fairs and wakes.

Some of the Wakes still existed. At Oldham in 1859 the Wakes were reported to be very well attended "On Sunday many came from the country in carts and other vehicles, capacity was of the conveyance, not the strength of the horse, as usual fixing the number in each conveyance. Extra trains were put on, the fair ground thronged and had a theatre, two circuses, a conjuring booth. An exhibition of arts where the music consisted of bagpipes and a song, several rush-carts were drawn through the town, one 'The Bardsley Brow Cart' was accompanied by a set of thirty Morris dancers".

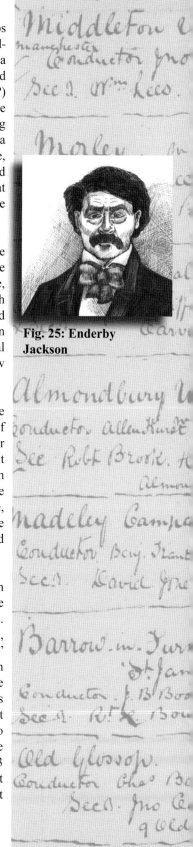

Fig. 25: Enderby Jackson

No doubt Jackson would have witnessed such events, and by the time of the Great Exhibition of 1851 he was an ambitious musician of great enthusiasm. At the Exhibition at which brass bands and other musicians took part, I wonder if hand-bell ringers also took part. It was at the Exhibition of 1851 that Jackson met two brass band men who were equally enthusiastic - James A Melling of Stalybridge (Lancashire) and Tallis Trimnell of Chesterfield in Derbyshire, "Both young musicians full of ardent zeal in spreading the love of music broadly among the teeming population of operatives and miners surrounding their central districts" he wrote later.

Jackson discussed the growth and progress of brass bands in Yorkshire and of contests at fetes, fairs and other events (e.g the Wakes), and on the system of giving prize gifts at these events. Later in his life, in the 1890s, Jackson wrote a number of articles, already mentioned, in periodicals such as the "Musical Opinion" and the "British Bandsman", which are a useful record of 19th century music making, but are written in a romantic vein, which one has to bear in mind when reading through them. In these articles he indicated that he had provided the idea of musical contests at Belle Vue, but there is some doubt amongst band historians as to whether this was correct. Jackson said in another article in the 1850s, that the idea of a contest did not occur to him until 1853 when he visited Doncaster races and saw horses win prizes. It seems that he could have discussed the idea of holding contests at

Belle Vue with Melling and Trimnell at the 1851 Great Exhibition, but that it was Melling who took the initiative - and that counts for a lot. Talk is one thing, action another. Jackson said later that his lack of direct participation at Belle Vue was because he had to help with arrangements for a Royal Visit to Hull at the time and he also claimed that the manager and owner of Belle Vue stole his idea. "Mr Jennison, of 'Belle Vue Gardens', Manchester, listened to some of his band and seized my plan, I now knew the anguish of the inventor who sees his scheme falling into the hands of others…..".

Fig. 26: Front Cover of a Belle Vue Advertising Brochure

It must be said that Jennison was also at the Great Exhibition as he afterwards hired professional musicians he had seen there to play at Belle Vue. It is thought that John Jennison and James Melling probably deserve more of the credit than they have been given for the starting of the Belle Vue Contest.

Both men died at a young age, Jennison on the 20th September 1869 and Melling on the 10th November 1870, and when Jackson made his claims it was 20 years after their deaths and nobody challenged Jackson on the matter. Basically the idea of a Contest was nothing new, and the inspiration may well have come indirectly from the Wakes as all three men would have been to such events. The facts are that in 1852 Jennison, encouraged by Melling, held an experimental contest at Belle Vue for drum and fife bands. The event was a successful one and Jennison announced that it would be repeated the following year and not only that, but "He would further organise an advanced tested system of educating higher

44

Fig. 27: John Jennison, the Creator of Belle Vue Zoological Gardens

Fig. 28: Aerial View of Belle Vue Zoological Gardens

Fig. 29: The Ballroom, Belle Vue, where the British Open was held from 1855 to 1926, pictured here in the 1880s. It was destroyed by fire on 17th January 1958 (Photo courtesy Manchester Cultural Studies Centre)

culture in the loftier spheres of musical art among the working classes of Lancashire and Yorkshire….through the medium of carefully organised competitions for brass bands".

In September 1853 the first brass band contest, took place at Belle Vue with far more people attending than anyone had thought possible. The local press estimated the crowd at 16,000. But the event did not go smoothly. Trains were late, delaying the start of the contest, and the food ran out. Another important aspect of the

46

contest was the special excursion trains, which had been arranged for the contest with careful negotiations, by which the railway companies were persuaded to allow cheap fares and lay on extra trains for special events at Belle Vue. The idea of cheap excursions had been adopted by Thomas Cook in 1841.

Jennison, pleased by the success of the contest, began to plan further musical competitions. In June 1854 there was a reed band contest at Belle Vue and this was another highly successful contest. By now Jennison was elated by the response to his contest and he now turned his attention to others to see which would be his next new musical contest at the gardens, and in the summer of 1855 announced that there would be a hand-bell ringing contest at Belle Vue with "the view of leading to the adoption of a higher class of music than hitherto in bell ringing".

So, as can be seen, the idea of a hand-bell ringing contest was part of a gradual progression of contests at Belle Vue. The story of the first hand-bell ringing contest at the Gardens is told in an unnamed newspaper cutting I discovered at the Manchester Cultural Studies Centre. The report is a valuable account of the state of hand-bell ringing in the years up to the contest, which was held on Monday, September 24th 1855. I have added the number of bells used by each band taking part in the contest from a contemporary report from another newspaper. The report is a valuable record of the type of music played by hand-bell ringers and the number of bells used up to 1855 and also gives the aims of the contest.

"PRIZE HAND-BELL RINGING BELLE VUE GARDENS

Yesterday afternoon, twelve sets of hand-bell ringers, comprising 113 ringers, contended for six different prizes, at the Belle Vue Gardens, in the presence of a very large company, difficult to estimate as regards number, because never brought together, but probably some 15,000 or 16,000. The ringing took place in the large new saloon, in which there is said to be standing room for 10,000 persons and which was as full as it well could be, whilst there seemed to be almost as many persons outside as within, parading the gardens and occasionally joining the auditors of the contest.

Hand-bell ringing is old rather than novel in many parts of Lancashire, having been more general than at present in rural places, before the time when Wakes began to wane. Although there are sets of ringers here and there, it is considered that in later years there has been a falling off in this branch of musical art. Public exhibitions of its performance have been rarities and have seldom been witnessed except in public-houses, during Wakes, in neighbourhoods where a set of ringers had been kept together. Hence a contest of hand-bell ringers was a novelty and as such

47

had special attractions.

The competitions for the prizes occupied the orchestra in the saloon, a corner of which was reserved for the judges, who were Mr Elijah Roberts, Eccles; and Mr Seed and Mr William Waddington, Manchester. Thirteen sets of ringers had been entered to compete for the prizes; but one, from Uttoxeter (Staffordshire), was unable to do so, owing to the absence of one of its leading members. Therefore the number of sets was reduced to 12. Each had selected its own music, in accordance with conditions made known some weeks ago, when it was stated that, as the prizes were offered with the view of leading to the adoption of a higher class of music than hitherto in bell ringing, the judges would be guided in their decisions by the most exact and scientific performance of difficult, complicated and classical music, rather than by the effective performance of simpler and popular airs, requiring less musical skill and practice. We subjoin a programme of the pieces performed as the selection of the different sets shows to some extent the musical ability of members of each.

The sets are given in the order in which they rang, which was decided by lot; and each set played two pieces and then retired until its second turn came around:

Shortly after the programme was finished the decision of the judges was announced as follows:

Name of Band & Pieces Rung	Number of Performers	Number of Bells
1. **Ripponden**, Nr Halifax – Auld Lang Syne & Keel Row; Katty O'Lynch & Elfin Waltz, first figure (Labitzky)	9	44
2. **Salford Harmonius Youths** (Lancashire) – Medley Waltz (Henry Johnson) & Sturm March Galop; Weber's Last Waltz & Rondo from the overture Guillaume Tell (Rossini)	7	53
3. **Hurst Brook** (Ashton-under-Lyne) Lancashire – Ap Shenkin & Hungarian Schottische; Caller Herrin' & Albion Polka	12	51
4. **Oldham Senior** (Lancashire) – Bell Waltz with introduction and coda (Johnson) & Grand Introduction and Polonnaise (H. Johnson); Selection from Elfin Waltzes (Labitzky) and English Hornpipe	8	32
5. **Oldham Junior** – Caller Herrin' & Jenny Jones; Copenhagen Waltz & Cheer, Boys, Cheer	9	32
6. **Holmfirth** (Yorkshire) – Lord Hardwicke's March & Song: Mariner's Grave with Introduction; Rouse, Brothers, Rouse (Arr H. Pogson) & Grand March	11	53
7. **Glossop (eight brothers)** Derbyshire – Deonady's Waltz & Bonny Oldham; Jenny Jones & Keel Row	8	43
8. **Stoke-upon-Trent** (Staffordshire) – Jenny Lind Polka & Introduction and Waltz; Blue Bells of Scotland & Introduction and Galop	9	43
9. **Leigh** (Lancashire) – Waltz No. 1 (Mozart) & Lesson 24 (Hook); Water Piece (Handel) & Grand Promenade March (Holt)	12	51
10. **Sheffield (Crookesmoor)** Yorkshire – Bell Waltz (Johnson) & Bell Polonaise with Introduction (Johnson); Chimes Polka (Johnson) & Bluebells of Scotland with Variations (Johnson)	8	50
11. **Hyde** (Cheshire) – Charming May Polka & Abbotsford Polka; Opera Schottische & Anglo French Alliance Polka	10	46
12. **Middleton** (Lancashire) – Hornpipe Waltz (Mozart), Cheer, Boys, Cheer; & the Huntsman's Chorus (Kalkbrenner)	10	42
Uttoxetter (Staffordshire) – did not play	7	46

No 9 (Leigh) First prize £10
No 4 (Oldham, Senior) Second prize £5
No 2 (Salford) Third prize £3
No 12 (Middleton) Fourth prize £2
No 10 (Sheffield) Fifth prize £1
No 11 (Hyde) Sixth prize 10s

*The decision gave general satisfaction; but some persons were
rather disappointed that first prizes had not been awarded to
the musical pieces which had elicited most applause from the
company. To such, however, the rule laid down for the guidance
of the judges and of which all competitors were equally aware,
will be sufficient explanation. With one or two slight exceptions,
the programme was adhered to; and in the opinion of the Judges
the ringing of the successful sets was excellent, whilst non critical
listeners set it down as very good and pleasing music. An unusually
effective display of the siege of Sebastopol, for which the night
was remarkably favourable, concluded the entertainments for the
majority of visitors, most of whom were from neighbouring and
distant towns".*

This report is very important to our story as it shows that the
number of bells used by hand-bell ringers had not increased since
the 1790s "Dalton" set of 50 bells which Crosland Moor United's
Secretary mentioned earlier, and as can be seen by looking at the
list of music played at the contest. A larger number of bells would
have been unnecessary for such music _- the waltzes, polkas and
country-dances then played by the bands.

Fig. 30: Crosland
Moor Public are
pictured in the
Ballroom, Belle Vue
at the 1913 British
Open

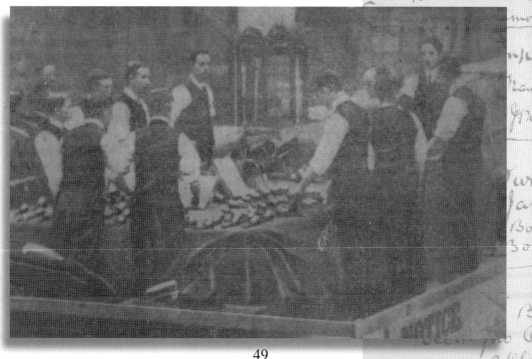

Fig. 31: The Lancashire Ringers at the Adelphi Theatre, London

Three of the bands taking part in this contest, Oldham, Salford and Sheffield (Crookesmoor) had music arranged for them by Henry Johnson (1822-1892), who was the leader/conductor of the Oldham ringers. Henry Johnson must have been a well known figure and arranger of music for hand-bells, as twelve years earlier, in May 1843, he appears on an engraving published in the "Illustrated London News" entitled "The Lancashire Hand-bell Ringers" at the Adelphi Theatre, London. This band was almost certainly Oldham, as records show that they did a tour of England appearing with a Professor Anderson, the great "Wizard of the North".

Anderson seems to have been a promoter, as it was stated in "Church Bell", (records of Oldham Parish) in December 1871 that they had been "Taken in hand" by him.

In the Illustrated London News engraving of 1843 Mr Johnson is seen "Counting the ringers in" with his fiddle bow. In Mr Johnson's hand is a fiddle with which he would have led the music.

It is this combination of fiddle and hand-bells which would have been ideal for playing for country dancing, and perhaps this was the combination used if hand-bell ringers played for a village dance, but this is where more research is required.

The Lancashire (Oldham) hand-bell ringers, said the London News article, used a chromatic three octaves and a perfect fourth of 42 bells, with which they performed "The most difficult overtures, waltzes and quadrilles". Interestingly this band is reputed to have won one of the ringing competitions which were run at Belle Vue during the five years immediately prior to the start of the famous National Hand-bell Competitions in 1855.

HISTORICAL NOTES

We can only pay our debt to the past by putting the future in debt to ourselves—Lord Tweedsmuir.

The Lancashire Bell-Ringers, at the Adelphi Theatre

The tintinnabulatory feats of these "Seven sons of Camponology" have excited considerable interest at the Adelphi theatre, on the same evenings with the performances of the great Wizard of the North. The ringers are stated to be natives of Lancashire, a county celebrated in the annals of Campanology. The precision with which each performer takes up the required note, and his management of the bells so as to give effect to the most delicate and piano passages, or to others as loud and martial as a military brass band, are truly surprising, as well as their general improvement, by incessant practice, since their last performance in the metropolis. Their bells, forty-two in number, form the chromatic scale in the compass of three octaves and a fourth, thus enabling them to perform the most difficult overtures, waltzes, quadrilles, &c. It would be injustice not to mention with praise the conductor of the Campanologian band Mr. H. Johnson, whose skill has mainly contributed to the perfection of their performances.

Ringing, by the way, is a practice which is said to be peculiar to England, which, for that reason, and the dexterity of its inhabitants in composing and ringing musical peals, wherein the sounds interchange in regular order, is called the Ringing Island. Formerly, too, men of rank practised bell-ringing as a pastime. The treatise on this subject at present in highest repute, is "Campanologia Improved," 1733, where the reader will find all the terms explained of single, plain bob, grandsire bob, single bob minor, grandsire treble, bob major, caters, ten-in, bob royal, cinque, and twelve-in or bob maximus, with all their regular permutations.

Taken from The Illustrated London News for the week ending 13th May 1843.

50

The engraving of the Lancashire Ringers published in the Illustrated London News shows the bells on the table standing upright with each ringer with a bell in each hand giving the idea that they rang one bell in each hand. The pose was probably the idea of the

Fig. 32: Lancashire (Royal Cumberland Youths) Ringers, (from an engraving found by R.L.Meyer)

engraver, so he could make his sketch and do the engraving later (and even today most modern photographers ask ringers to hold a bell in each hand - an awful practice I feel). Another engraving of the Lancashire Ringers on tour in the USA which came to light in the 1960s, found in a second-hand shop in London by Raymond L. Meyer of the Beacon Hill Ringers in the U.S.A. (It was reproduced in the book "The Art of Handbell Ringing" by Nancy Poore Tufts), handbellshows 5 ringers ringing "4 in Hand". However, we know that this band was not the same one that performed at the Adelphi, and were probably not even from Lancashire, and they had less ringers and no separate conductor.

More information is found in the autobiography of the American impresario P T Barnum (Pub 1855), in which he says, of the original band, that while he was in London in 1844, he heard of the Lancashire ringers performing in Ireland, so he arranged to meet them in Liverpool and engaged them for a 12 month American tour. (Interestingly the Saunders News Letter of 31st May 1842, which can be found in the tower of St. Patrick's Cathedral Dublin says "The seven Lancashire bell ringers on sets of 27 and 42 hand bells are to perform at the Portobello Zoo Gardens on the 3rd of June 1842." They had earlier performed in the Theatre Royal, Abbey

Street, Dublin in March 1842. Whether this was the tour during which Barnum signed them up for his American tour, and the date in his autobiography was in error, or it was an earlier Irish tour I do not know)

Once in the USA he often billed the Lancashire Ringers as "The Swiss Bell Ringers", made them grow long moustaches, wear Swiss mountain clothes, and forbade them to speak English during performances. At other times he billed them as the Lancashire Ringers.

In 1850 Barnum wanted to repeat his success, but this time, although he still called the touring group the Lancashire Ringers, he had signed up to a 12 month's contract, four members of the London based towerbell change ringing society the Society of Royal Cumberland Youths, (Barnum having had them commended to him by the Mears Foundry). The fifth ringer signed was an accomplished hand-bell ringer, not a towerbell ringer (and therefore probably not a Cumberland Youth), and he was not, as far as we know, a member of the then existing Lancashire (Oldham) Ringers.

In 1863 all the cotton crops in the USA were destroyed during the American Civil War. "......This caused a great amount of distress in the cotton spinning districts of Lancashire, so George Coppin, a well known impresario of the time, brought the Lancashire Hand-bell Ringers (to Australia) as a speculation........", and there they toured on and off for another eight years until they returned, still ringing, via Honolulu and the USA to England. This time we do know that the band were once again from Oldham.

Whilst in Australia, not only did the Lancashire Hand-bell Ringers tour through all states giving "a performance (which) is most extraordinary", including making a side tour off to India in 1865, but they also helped local tower bellringers ring their full circle swinging big bells, including, as the Melbourne "Age" at the time reported, ringing on the St James, Melbourne "church bells, several peals in the Grandsire method in the art of change ringing, being the greatest achievement ever accomplished in any of the Australian Colonies". Nor was their towerbell ringing restricted to change ringing. As the Adelaide Observer reported in 1866 they "visited the Town Hall .....for the purpose of practising upon the Albert Bells Several chimes....were performed upon six to eight bell, and ....'Home, Sweet Home' was also played, the chiming being in general very correct, and of a superior character throughout. It was performed by means of the ropes, two bells being allotted to one ringer."

Years later, the Oldham Chronicle reported from a letter sent by the band from Honolulu (dated 27th August 1871). The four signatories to the letter were, Samuel Naylor, formerly of Jackson Street, Oldham; John Whittaker, Lower West Street, Peter Mills, Barker Street and S Harrison, North Moor. The writers said they left Auckland, New Zealand on the 10th August 1871 on an American steamship for Honolulu. They went on to say they would sail to San Francisco next and then towards home. Even in Honolulu the Oldham men remembered the "Wakes" stating that they would not be without a Wakes dinner.

The Oldham Chronicle article gave the names of the other members of the band, saying that four of its members who returned to Oldham were; John Wrigley, Isaac Ogden, Samuel Mills and Henry Hunt Patterson; it also listed William Stott and J Isherwood who died in Australia and William Cooper who died in America. There is no mention of what became of the other members.

You have to sit back and wonder at the achievements and enterprise of these men, taking on two world tours, one of one year duration and the second one lasting eight years.. Today people would gasp at the suggestion of even a eight week tour.

But back to the 1855 Belle Vue Contest, "The Keel Row", "Jenny Jones", "The Bluebells of Scotland" and "Ap Shenkin" were all tunes used for Northern Morris dancing, but these were also popular tunes of the day. It can also be seen from the list of music played, that the first influences of classical music came from Mozart, Rossini and Handel, who were all influential composers of church music. George Fredrick Handel (1685-1759) wrote operas, but after 1737, he concentrated on the writing of oratorios and through this medium Handel captured the hearts of the Northern people. He even described hand-bells as the English national instrument and included hand-bells in his oratorio 'Saul'. The county of Yorkshire and in particular the West Riding, was the area where his music was rapturously received by everyone, including hand-bell ringers. The most beloved (though not, perhaps the finest of Handel's oratorios), was the "Messiah" which today still is performed widely in Yorkshire, and in fact towards Christmas there are still many productions of the Messiah in chapels and concert halls.

Another important aspect of the first Belle Vue hand-bell contest were the aims of the contest: "That as the prizes were offered with the view of leading to the adoption of a higher class of music than hitherto in bell ringing" and that "The judges would be guided in their decisions by the most exact and scientific performance of difficult, complicated and classical music, rather than by the effective performance of more simple and popular airs, requiring less musical skill and practice". However, with the exception of the the Salford Youths and Leigh Hand-bell Ringers most of the music played at the Contest, did not come into this category with most of the pieces played being simple country dance tunes. This was the music of the wakes ringers, traditional country music, which was probably the only kind of music known to many of them, who largely came from isolated country villages such as Glossop. The Leigh Hand-bell Ringers' music however did come within the aims of the contest, so it is no surprise that they won first prize. The style of classical music which became popular at the competitions had developed between 1740 and 1780, through the works of Joseph Haydn (1732-1809), Wolfgang Amadeus Mozart (1736-1791) and their contemporaries.

So even at the time of the first contest in 1855, classical music was beginning to filter through to the working classes through church music. Note also that in the report of the competition, the writer states that hand-bell ringing was old rather than novel, and in another report of the contest, hand-bell ringing was said to be "very old" which is further evidence of the tune ringing bands that existed in the 1700s.

The attendance at this first contest was a full house. The ballroom, which had only just been built, was 74 yards long and 35 yards wide and held 10,000 standing. There was also almost as many people outside parading the Gardens. The ballroom, it would seem from reports, was not altogether ideal for the listener. The correspondent of the Huddersfield Examiner in 1907 complained that, even beneath the performers' platform some of the softer passages could not be heard. The effect, he said, "At the best, was singularly pleasant but one had always the impression of listening to music at a distance……From the farther end of the ballroom one could hear nothing but a faint, far-away pealing, so small is the carrying power of the muffled bells".

Of course it was only necessary that the adjudicators should be able to hear from their hessian box near the orchestra, but the fact that it was hard to hear the music didn't affect the attendance at all. The room was full for almost every contest; although of course people not only came for the contest but to see Belle Vue's other attractions as well.

The contest was an instant success and the reasons for this success are simple. The idea of all the Belle Vue contests, which had began in 1852 with the drum and fife bands contest, was that they were to be part of the Belle Vue Wakes week. The organisers of Belle Vue would have certainly known how popular the Wakes had been in villages all over the North up to some 20 years earlier and they also knew how popular any form of competition was for the spectators, (Even today just consider the size of the spectator following of World Cup Football, or alternatively, and surprisingly, competition ballroom dancing. I read the other day that 'Strictly Come Dancing', a television weekly knockout competition had a UK following of six million. It does not appear to be gambling that attracts such a huge following but the excitement of a competition itself). So their idea was to create a kind of Super Wakes at Belle Vue which would attract the people of the towns and villages where Wakes had been, or still were, popular. For the occasion even a Rushcart was hired "At a great expense" to complete the scene and parade the gardens.

The display of the "Siege of Sebastopol" was given in front of a long lake. Such displays of sieges, battles and other great British victories were a regular feature of Belle Vue, throughout its life. The actual "Siege of Sebastopol" was the fall of the Russian stronghold in the Crimea, which fell on Monday 10th September, 1855 and on that day the parish bells of every tower in the land were rung, some continuing to ring until between two and three o'clock on the following Tuesday morning. The tower bell ringers no doubt seized a chance to have a good ring on this occasion, but imagine the outcry if that were to happen today!

The writer of the unnamed newspaper report of the Belle Vue Contest also said that hand-bell ringing up to then had been rare and seldom seen except in public houses, during Wakes, and in neighbourhoods where a set of ringers had been kept together. In order to check on this, I had a look at records of the places where Wakes existed and found that all the home towns of 19th century hand-bell bands had evidence of Wakes or were near to other places where Wakes existed.

Cheap excursion trains were put on for the contest, as they had been for all the other contests. Not only that, but the ringers taking part in the competition were carried free of charge, which in the days of low wages was a great incentive for the bands to take part. It was also a day out, to be looked forward to by everybody, to the wonderland of Belle Vue. Another important aspect of this contest, is that it seems from all the reports I have read, that there is no indication at all, that any of the 13 bands that entered were connected with the church other than the fact that some of their members were also church tower bell change ringers. So it appears that the bands were all independent of the church, probably being subscription, patronage, military volunteer, or mill or other works bands. It was a feature of these contests throughout their life that most of the bands were not connected to a church. Later we will meet hand-bell ringers who were connected with a church, but is must be stressed that hand-bell ringing was not at this time particularly a church activity, and many bands never had any connection with a church at any time at all.

55

Looking at the size of the sets of bells that the ringers of the first Belle Vue Contest were using, it would seem that the method of ringing used by many of the bands taking part in the contest, was to ring the treble bells 4 in hand, with the others being rung off the table with the bells in an upright position, (with the bell mouth facing downwards on the table). However ringing either the tenor and bass bells mouth downwards, or with a well-damped 4-in-hand technique, would enable a good band to play anything, including classical music in full harmony. In fact some of the earlier music put out by the prolific 19th century hand-bell music publisher William Gordon was clearly written for 4-in-hand ringing for the treble bells and cannot be played as allocated 'off table'. These methods of playing were those commonly used by the Wakes hand-bell ringers, and many bands still used these methods in the 1870s - though these were bands who did not enter the Belle Vue Contest, therefore perhaps feeling no need to change their style. (Indeed the mouth down off table bass and 4-in-hand treble style is still used, as mentioned later, by the Brookhampton Ringers in Western Australia, the style having been taken to Western Australia during the 'gold rush' period in the 1890s, and by Fredsklockorna in Sweden.)

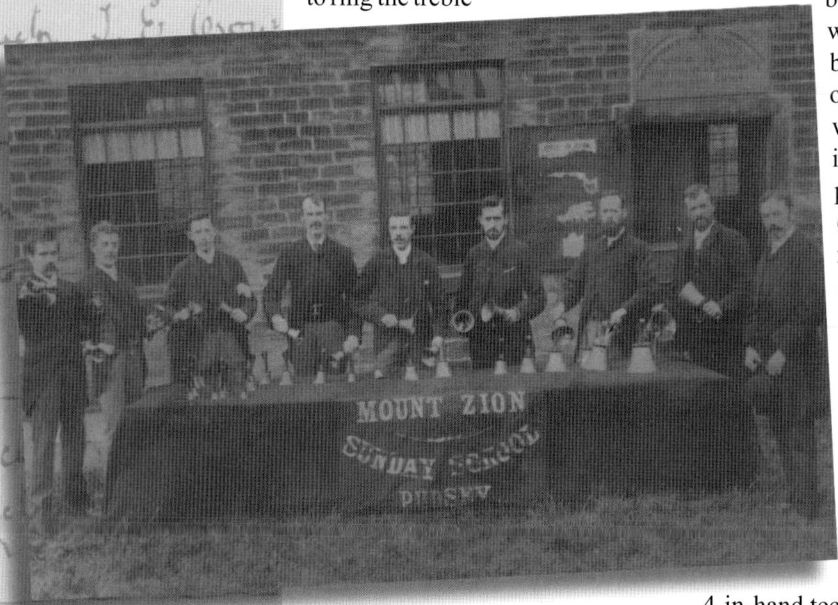

Fig. 33 Pudsey Hand-bell Ringers taken in the 1870s - note the treble ringers holding their bells 4-in-hand with the others ringing in the mouths down off-table style

An example of such a band of hand-bell ringers was Pudsey, near Leeds, who do not appear to have ever entered any contests.

How did the ringers at the first Belle Vue Contest in 1855 arrange their music? A difficult question, but there are some clues as to how this was undertaken.

During my research I found, almost by chance the original music of the Hyde Hand-bell Ringers some of which dates back to before 1855. Much of it is written in a hybrid form of numerical notation, including such complicated pieces as "The Caliph of Bagdad" by Boieldieu and Rossini's "Tancredi" Overture with individual

56

scores for the trebles, tenors and bass parts. Their later music is taken directly from piano scores with each part having a copy of the complete piece but with copious handwritten notes on which notes to play! Unfortunately I cannot ascertain when Hyde switched from number music to staff notation.

Mr William Butler sent me a small book entitled "The Hand-bell Ringers Tune Book", by Daniel Scholefield published about 1852. Daniel Scholefield was a Yorkshireman who lived in Trinity Street,

Huddersfield, a printer by trade, he worked for J Bairstow, of Cross Church Street. Utilising the services of his employer, he printed from time to time, leaflets containing ringing information and he produced pamphlets on various subjects such as "Scholefields Concertina Tutor".

As can be seen "The Hand Bell Ringers 'Tune Book'" is for only 15 bells and is in letter notation. But one aspect of interest is that the music has many gaps where ringers are not ringing, so it would appear that each ringer rang only his own bells. Could this be a clue to how the music was arranged by the Belle Vue hand-bell ringers? Mr Scholefield advertised tunes for sale as played by the Huddersfield Campanologian Band, (as he called it) amongst these, were - "Hallelujah Chorus" and the "Occasional Overture". Mr Scholefield also offered to arrange music for hand-bells at "The most reasonable terms" but unfortunately none of these arrangements have come to light for historical analysis. Mr Scholefield's further publications were, "The Bell Ringers Companion" and "A Supplement to the Clavis". The latter suggests that he was a towerbell change ringer as well as a hand-bell tune ringer because the Clavis Campanalogia was still one of the main change ringing instructional manuals of

THE

HAND BELL RINGERS TUNE BOOK,

PART FIRST,

BY D. SCHOLEFIELD, HUDDERSFIELD.

BEING A COLLECTION OF TUNES ARANGED IN AN EASY MANNER FOR THE USE OF THOSE PERSONS NOT UNDERSTANDING MUSIC.

HUDDERSFIELD:

PRINTED BY J. BAIRSTOW, BOOKSELLER, 34, CROSS CHURCH STREET.

Fig. 35: The Hand-bell Ringers Tune Book - D. Scholefield 1852

EXPLANATION.

Lay out a Peal of FOLLOWING Bells, in any key, and always call the Tenor Bell A.; the next above B.; the next C.; and so on in the regular course of the Alphabet; (omitting the Letter j) beginning at the Tenor and ending at the smallest Bell.

The top row of Letters is the Air, those below the Bass, for Example in the Tune O'DEAR WHAT CAN THE MATTER BE, the three first Notes in the Air, are m m m, or three blows with the Twelfth Bell, reckoning from the Tenor. The Bass Notes, a, c, e, or the Tenor, the third from the Tenor, and the fifth from the Tenor.

An Accidental Sharp marked thus, ... *
A Single Bar, do. do. .... |
A Double Bar, do. do. .... ||
A Repeat, do. do. .... :||

N.B. The following Tunes as Played by the Huddersfield Campanologian Band, may be had

ARANCED TO MUSIC, BY D. SCHOLEFIELD, 79, KING STREET.

Hallelujah Chorus, 3s., Overture Occasional, 3s., Anthem Sound the Loud Timbrel, 9d., Rise Bells, with variations, 9d., Lord Hardwick's March, 9d., Napoleon's March, 9d., Aurora Waltz, 6d., each, English Waltz, 6d., each, Polkas, 6d., each, &c., &c.

ANY TUNE ARANGED TO MUSIC, FOR THE HAND BELLS ON THE MOST REASONABLE TERMS.

the time, and had had a major influence on the future course of change ringing when it was first published in 1788.

The Huddersfield Hand-bell Band, which he conducted, had two members of his own family amongst its twenty-two

LIVERPOOL HORNPIPE. 12 BELLS.

e d, c a c e, h k m k, l i k h h g f e, d f a f c e c e, b a b c d c b a, c d e e h k m l,
l i k h h g f e, m k h k l i g i, h h h :||: e, h k h k g i g i, f e f g h g f e, d f d f e
e g e e e
c e c c c
a b a a a

e c e, b a b c d c b a, c a c e h k m k, l i k h h g f e, m k h k l i g i, h h h :||
e g e e e
c e c c c
a b a a a

GLEE. POOR MARY ANN. 12 Bells.

h h g f h, i i h g e, f f f g g g h k h :|| l k l m, n m l k, l k i h, k i h g, h h g f h,
e c c d f g g e e b d d d e e c f e i h i k l k i h i h g f e d c b e e e d f
c c b d e c c b a a a b b b d c c c b d
a a b b a a

i i h g e, f f f g g g, h k h :||
g g e e d d d e e e f e
e e c b b b b b d e

members, but I feel that this number of ringers would not have been one band, but two; a senior and a junior band as was the normal practice at the time. I feel that they would have rung the trebles 4 in hand and the tenor and bass would be rung off the table, as with the example given of Pudsey Hand-bell Ringers, using five chromatic octaves. The Huddersfield Band was, according to Scholefield, the first to use staff notation rather than a number or letter system, but to which year was Mr Scholefield referring when he made this claim? If in fact the history of the Huddersfield Band dated from the 1700s then I feel this claim could be true, but I would doubt the claim if it referred to 1852. More research may provide the answer.

So at the present our knowledge of how the first Belle Vue ringers arranged their music is very limited. The only other comment on the subject that could be made is that, if any of the bands were connected with a church tower bell band, then they probably used a number or letter system of notation. The ringers who previously had broken with the church and had then formed bands using military volunteer band, and church band musicians, and choir members, would possibly have used staff notation.

The wording for the guidance of the adjudicators at Belle Vue was that "The judges would be guided in their decisions by the most exact and scientific performance of difficult, complicated and classical music, rather than by the effective performance of simpler and popular airs requiring less musical skill and practice". So this first historic contest now set a target for the hand-bell ringers. They could now win something of far more importance than any local wakes contest - the British Open Championship of Great Britain. The challenge was now on.

One other important factor in the holding of the contest at Belle Vue was the introduction of the penny post in 1840. Before this, it would have been very difficult to publicise the contest and make contact with bands on a national basis to invite entries.

In 1856, the year following the first contest, no winners are recorded, only a list of entrants. Was there a contest, or was it called off at the last moment? An advertisement appeared in the columns of the Manchester Guardian on Saturday, September 20th, saying that the contest would take place the following Monday, September 22nd, commencing at 3pm, the Belle Vue Band would play for dancing after the judges' decision was made known. The Assault of the Malakoff would be given by Bruce and his assistants with "A gorgeous display of fireworks" at 8.15pm. Another advertisement in the Manchester Courier gave the names of the entrants, which were, Oldham Senior (Lancashire), Holmfirth (Yorkshire), Saint George's Bolton (Lancashire), Saint Thomas

59

HAND-BELL RINGING CONTESTS

AT BELLE VUE, SINCE 1861.

1855	1856	1857	1858	1859	1860	1861
[Bands Entered.] Leigh	[Bands Entered.] Dalton	[Bands Entered.] Harmaley	[Bands Entered.] Harmaley	[Bands Entered.] Harmaley		1 Wigan
Middleton	Holmfirth	Holmfirth	Dewsbury	Dewsbury		2 Shelley
Oldham Senr.	Leigh	Leigh	Holmfirth	Holmfirth	No Account of	3 Leigh
Salford	Macclesfield	Pendleton	Leigh	Liverpool	Contest.	4 Uttoxeter
Sheffield	Oldham Senr.		Pendleton	Pendleton		
	Pendleton		Wigan	Salford		Extra Prize—
	Prestwich			Wigan		Wigan.

1862	1863	1864	1865	1866	1867	1868
1 Shelley	1 Uttoxeter	1 Wigan	1 Uttoxeter	1 Uttoxeter	1 Uttoxeter	1 Shelley
2 Uttoxeter	2 Meltham	2 Oldham	2 Dewsbury	2 Dewsbury	2 Shelley Junr.	2 Batley
3 Wigan	3 Wigan	3 Whitworth	3 Wigan	3 Shelley	3 Dewsbury	3 Broseley
4 Dewsbury	4 Oldham	4 Dewsbury	4 Shelley		4 Meltham	4 Wigan
Extra Prize—Wigan.						

1869	1870	1871	1872	1873	1874	1875
1 Shelley	1 Shelley	1 Glossop	1 Old Glossop	1 Old Glossop	1 Holmfirth Tem.	1 Holmfirth
2 Scarboro'	2 Hyde	2 Holmfirth	2 Holmfirth	2 Holmfirth	2 Holmfirth	2 Shelley
3 Leeds United	3 Elland	3 Elland	3 Batley Carr	3 Huddersfield	3 Armitage Bdg.	3 Dalton Victoria
4 Broseley	4 Leeds	4 Armitage Bdg.	4 Hyde	4 Glossop	4 Disley	4 Huddersfield

1876	1877	1878	1879	1880	1881	1882
1 Shelley	1 Shelley	1 Shelley	1 Old Silkstone	1 Old Glossop Jr.	1 St. Thos. Hyde	1 Honley Tem.
2 Dalton Victoria	2 Dalton Victoria	2 Dalton Victoria	2 Old Glossop Jr.	2 Barnsley	2 Old Glossop	2 Birch Vale
3 Huddersfield	3 Huddersfield	3 Huddersfield	3 Dalton Victoria	3 Hinchcliffe Mill	3 Hinchcliffe	3 Leesfield
Holmfirth Tem.	4 Meltham	4 Old Silkstone	4 Elland	4 Dalton Victoria	4 Elland	4 Old Glossop Jr.

1883.	1884	1885	1886	1887	1888	1889.
1 Dewsbury	1 Liversedge	1 Almondbury.	1 Almondbury	1 Liversedge	1 Dewsbury	1 Liversedge
2 Hyde	2 Dewsbury	2 Liversedge	2 Liversedge	2 Almondbury	2 Mirfield	2 Mirfield
3 Elland	3 Almondbury	3 Dewsbury	3 Mirfield	3 Whitefield	3 Almondbury	3 Tintwistle
4 Cheddleton	4 Dalton Victoria	4 Birstall	4 Holmfirth	4 Mirfield	4 Whitefield	4 Dewsbury
5 Dalton Victoria	5 Howard Bros.	5 Lepton	5 Birstall	5 Holmfirth	5 Liversedge	5 Birstall, St. Saviour's

Fig. 36: Belle Vue Prize Winners List 1855 – 1889

Pendleton (Lancashire), Macclesfield Original (Cheshire), Leigh (Lancashire) the previous year's winners, and Saint Bartholomew's Prestwich (Lancashire). Of these Holmfirth, Oldham and Leigh had entered the first contest the year before. There were three bands of ringers who were attached to churches and one other band that seems to have been independent - Macclesfield Original - seven bands, a drop of five entries from the previous year's contest. The list of prizewinners, published by Belle Vue themselves, had always had an entry for the year 1856, simple saying "Bands entered" and giving a list of the bands. All the copies of the list I have seen say the same.

So the contest was advertised in two newspapers on the Saturday before the Monday when the contest was supposed to take place, so was it cancelled at very short notice? . There wasn't a mention of the contest in the Manchester Guardian or Courier subsequently. Could there have been a flood or a violent storm that stopped the event? I think not, as nothing unusual happened weatherwise, reading the newspapers. I believe that the reason the results of 1856 are not recorded - only the bands entered - is simply that when the first list of winners was printed in 1889 nobody had kept (surprisingly) proper records. As can be seen from the list from 1889 (Which I found in the Shelley Archives) no winners were shown for 1855-56 57 58 59 and 1860. The following year the list was more complete, due to the intervention of Shelley's Fred Taylor. Some of the EXTRA Prizes from the early contests however were still missing from the final list published in 1926 because no one could remember them. However I have done what they could not do as easily. I visited several Libraries, Manchester, Huddersfield, Stockport, Stafford etc and found the missing details in contemporary newspapers of the day. The only ones I have not found were the 1856 results. I have looked and looked. But I do not think it was cancelled. Because of the lack of detail on the earlier published lists I believe the contest did take place. So it was not swept away in a flood, just lost through bad memory.

The next ten years of the contests were ones of fluctuating numbers of entrants, although the attendance remained high. The following year, there were again seven entries with 68 performers - Hurst Brook (Ashton-under-Lyne), Barnsley, Dewsbury, Leigh, Holmfirth, Whitefield and Pendleton. Four of these were from Lancashire and three from Yorkshire. Each band performed four pieces. Two were fixed by the judges and two were of their own selection. Whitefield did not take part. Leigh and Holmfirth were asked by the judges to play again to see who would receive the first prize of £15. The result of this was that Holmfirth was awarded the first prize. For some reason, only the first four names were put on the list of prizewinners. A reason for this could have been that a list of prizewinners could only be sold if there were enough contests to put on it and by the time there was, people had forgotten who the other bands were!

At the 1858 contest there were six entries, most of which had entered before, apart from Wigan Parish Church who were competing at their first Belle Vue Contest.

In the same week Charles Dickens appeared before an audience at the Free Trade Hall in Manchester to read from his own writings. I wonder if he was there in the audience at Belle Vue, to see the Holmfirth Hand-bell Ringers win the first prize for the second year running?

The year also saw the last 4-in-hand horse coaches to leave Manchester in October. The rivalry of rail and steam had run all other coaches off the road, but the old "Derby Dilly" still held its own. It was thought that

Fig. 37: Belle Vue Hand-bell Competition Flyer 1862

Fig. 38: Belle Vue Hand-bell Rules and Contestants 1862

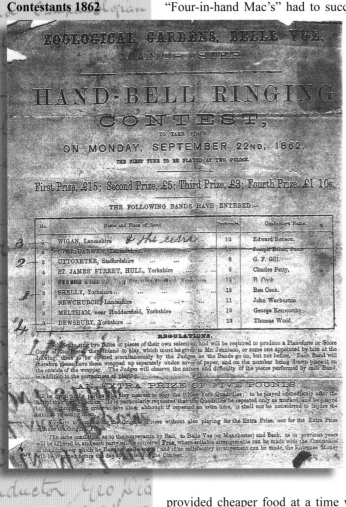

the railways would not find their way through the Peak District of Derbyshire, but the Midland line did so and the last of the old "Four-in-hand Mac's" had to succumb to the might of the iron horse, although horse drawn coaches, buses and trams were still used in towns and cities.

A note in the local paper said that the public should not encourage begging. By this time the second generation of factory workers was more accustomed to the discipline of industrial work and life in towns and was more able to adjust to the capitalist system. The first co-operative store had been opened in Rochdale, in Lancashire in 1844, founded by 28 workmen amongst whom were seven flannel-weavers. The aim was to cut out the middleman, by the establishment of a retail shop. They sold goods at the normal price and members were given a "Dividend" after the profit was known. The Co-op movement had an obvious appeal to the poorer classes and by 1875 there were over a thousand Co-operative Societies in the country, which provided cheaper food at a time when the poor, whom Charles Dickens so often wrote about, found it hard to make ends meet.

1859 was a historic year in the development of hand-bell ringing in England. It was also the year of "What might have been" for hand-bell ringing. It is also the year when Enderby Jackson, who organised his first musical contest at Hull in 1854, re-enters our story, and as usual Jackson didn't do anything by halves. Jackson's first love was for brass bands and one of his ambitions was to introduce brass band contests to London. The Crystal Palace had now been moved from its original site in Hyde Park, to a new site at Sydenham. The manager of the Palace at Sydenham, Mr R K Bowley, who was described by Jackson in his writings of the 1890s as a "Self made man", was selected from some six hundred applicants for the job. Bowley was interested in Jackson's idea of holding a brass band contest at the Palace, but wanted some proof that the working man could be persuaded to come to London to watch it. To provide proof that the workingman would come to London for such contests, Jackson took the historic decision to bring a hand-bell ringing contest to the Crystal Palace. Jackson brought twelve bands of ringers and their supporters to Sydenham. Jackson always put in a great deal of preliminary organisation for his contests. Six months before the event he would set out on a public relations exercise to visit the towns in the North where bands existed, meeting band officials, encouraging the setting up of new bands and supporters club to accompany them to the contest. He arranged with the railway companies that competing bands would travel to the contest free of charge; and their families could travel for example, between Leeds and London for about 4s.6d. (approx 22p) in the special excursion trains to the contest. Jackson was able to do this as he had already proved to the railway companies the value of musical contests on previous occasions, and the railway companies advertised the contest on their posters. The hand-bell bands who took part came from; Dewsbury, Barnsley, Holmfirth, Huddersfield, Lythe (near Whitby) - all from Yorkshire, and from Lancashire came Salford, Pendleton, Wigan, Oldham, Liverpool, Accrington, and Stalybridge from Cheshire, each band containing twelve players.

Of the twelve bands, who Jackson described as "Twelve picked bands, of our best hand-bell ringers", three - Lythe, Accrington and Stalybridge had never entered any of the Belle Vue hand-bell ringing contests held up to that time, which seems strange as the last two bands named, were on the doorstep of Belle Vue. So why hadn't they attended the previous competitions? Perhaps the thought of playing at the Crystal Palace, London, was so spectacular and wonderful to them, they just could not resist it. Jackson didn't say who won, but the contest must have been successful as the Crystal Palace management was satisfied that Jackson had the necessary organising ability and had proved his point that the working man would come to London to watch musical contests. They then gave their permission for a brass band contest to be held the following year.

That was the one and only contest for hand-bell ringing to be held at Crystal Palace. It was probably held in July. One can only wonder about the effect and direction hand-bell tune ringing would have taken if there had been further contests for hand-bell ringing at the Crystal Palace. I think it could have led to the establishment of a stronger hand-bell ringing movement in the South, which would have strengthened the whole of hand-bell ringing in Britain, and could have resulted in a much stronger movement, much more able to resist the decline of later years up to our own time. Why did Jackson hold a contest for hand-bell ringing instead of one for brass bands? Why did the Crystal Palace management agree to an experimental hand-bell contest first, instead of holding a brass band contest as an experiment? Probably because hand-bell bands were already well established and well known, where as brass bands were only in their infancy.

At least hand-bell ringers can claim it was they who paved the way to London for the brass band movement to stage contests there, a tradition which is still carried on today. The hand-bell contest was also the first musical contest held at Sydenham. Enderby Jackson held four brass band contests at Sydenham, but became disenchanted with the management there and extended his activities as an impresario, arranging tours abroad for people. In 1871 Enderby Jackson went to Australia for three years, taking with him a man who was a member of a pierrot company (forerunners of clowns). Perhaps he was a former friend whom he had met during his travelling days. Enderby's last days were spent painting and writing at his home in Scarborough where he died in 1903 aged 77.

John Jackson, Enderby Jackson's Grandson found amongst his grandfather's papers the following reference to the Crystal Palace Hand-bell Competition:

At the 1859 contest for hand-bell ringing at Belle Vue, the Holmfirth hand-bell ringers were making their first bid for the championship. The rule was that if a band won the first prize three times in succession, then that band was declared "The Champions of Great Britain". The local press estimated the crowd at 20,000, although of course The Ballroom where the contest was held, could only hold 10,000 people standing, which is what it seems they did.

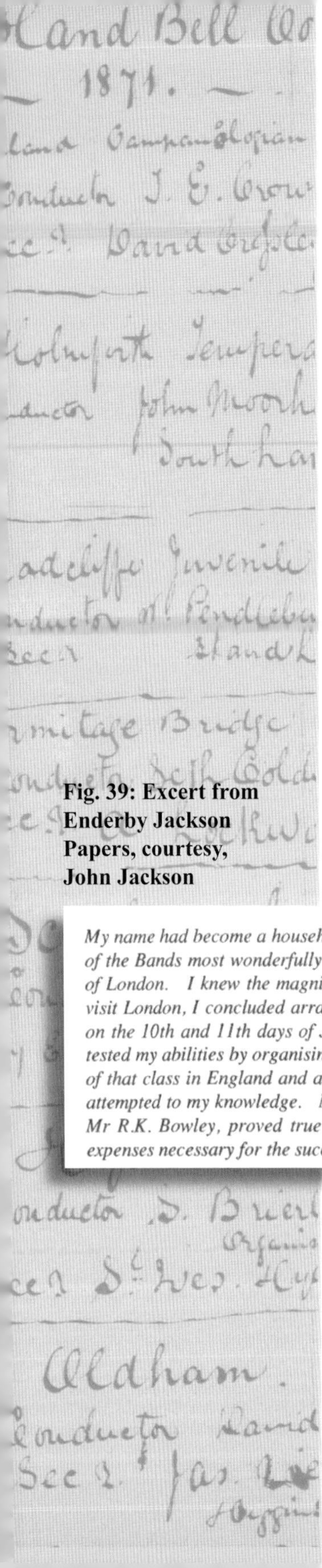

Fig. 39: Excert from Enderby Jackson Papers, courtesy, John Jackson

My name had become a household word in the homes of the British working man and, as I found the Quality of the Bands most wonderfully improved, I determined upon displaying their proficiency before the critics of London. I knew the magnitude of the venture so, backed by the zeal of my best Bands who wished to visit London, I concluded arrangements with the Crystal Palace, Sydenham, to hold my first contest there on the 10th and 11th days of July 1860. I may mention the same Company had the previous year 1859, tested my abilities by organising for them a Hand-Bell Ringing Contest when I took twelve of the best bands of that class in England and achieved a success, wonderful in its way, which has not since that time been attempted to my knowledge. Mr Price, a large dealer in Woollens, one of the Directors, and the Manager Mr R.K. Bowley, proved true and fast friends who were not deterred by the seeming magnitude of the expenses necessary for the successful carrying out of a "Jacksonian Brass Band Contest".

Again only six bands entered, five of whom had entered in previous years and one new name in the line up, that of Liverpool (Bell Methodists) who were perhaps fired into enthusiasm by their adventure to the Crystal Palace earlier in the year, and were probably the first Methodist ringers to take part. The numbers of ringers varied between eight and twelve in each band, and played from an elevated platform, the contest lasting nearly five hours. Each band performed four pieces of its own selection. The Dewsbury and Holmfirth bands had to compete again to decide the second prize, the reporter of the contest saying that the Holmfirth ringers were very expert at reading music. Pendleton however were the winners of the first prize thus denying Holmfirth the championship.

Another development at the contest was the addition of an extra prize for the band that played "nearest to copy" the fifth figure of Julien's "Martha Quadrilles", this prize being won by Wigan. To commemorate this success the tower bells of Wigan Parish Church were rung at one o'clock in the morning to the astonishment of the people who lived in that part of town, many of whom seemingly believed that either the town was enveloped in flames or that the French had landed!

The addition of an extra prize would seem to be a first attempt at getting the bands used to a set test piece. "The contest was conducted in good spirit and friends of the performers gave hearty cheers".

1860 saw two more new names on the list of entries, those of Shelley who were conducted by Ben Cooke, who also rang first treble, and also the name of Heckmondwike, conductor Mr T Roberts. Both were from Yorkshire. Also taking part were Wigan, conductor William Mason, Barnsley (Samuel Wilkinson); Holmfirth (Henry Pogson); Dewsbury (H Metcalf); and Pendleton (James Green), who were the winners for the second year running. Pendleton's address was given as the May Pole Inn. There was also another extra prize and again the winner of this was the Wigan band.

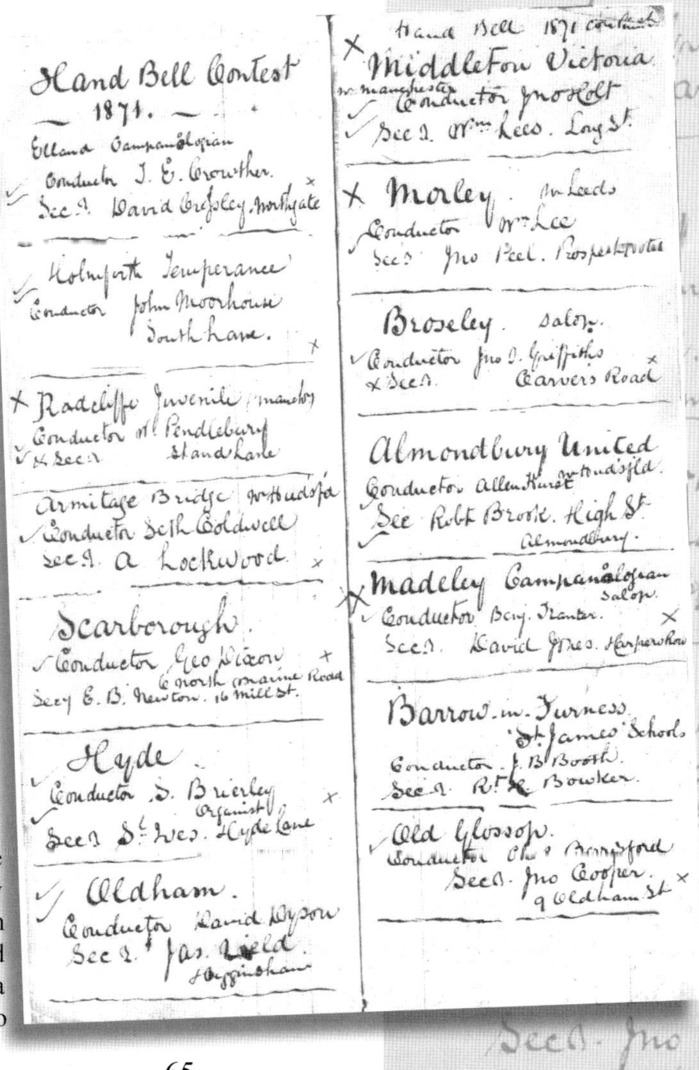

In the following year, 1861, Wigan won first prize, playing Jupiter Quadrilles and the Farmers Rifle Galop. Shelley who played selections from "Martha" closely contested them, Wigan also won the extra prize for playing nearest to

Fig. 40: Two pages showing the 1871 Contest from the Book in which James Jennison (the Proprietor of Belle Vue) kept a record of all the Entries for the Hand-bell Contests, reproduced courtesy of Cheathams Library, Manchester

ZOOLOGICAL GARDENS, BELLE VUE, MANCHESTER.

HAND-BELL RINGING CONTEST,

TO TAKE PLACE

ON MONDAY, SEPTEMBER 21st, 1863.

THE FIRST TUNE TO BE PLAYED AT TWO O'CLOCK.

First Prize, £15; Second Prize, £5; Third Prize, £2 10s; Fourth Prize, £1.

THE FOLLOWING BANDS HAVE ENTERED:—

No.	Name and Place of Band.	Performers.	Conductor's Name.
1	SWAN MEADOW MILLS, Wigan.	12	William Mason.
2	WIGAN.	11	Edward Benson.
3	MELTHAM, near Huddersfield.	12	G. Kenworthy.
4	SHELLY, near Huddersfield.		G. Stephenson.
5	HECKMONDWIKE Campanologian, near Leeds.	12	Thomas Roberts
6	OLDHAM.	11	David Dyson.
7	UTTOXETER.	9	G. F. Gill.

REGULATIONS.

Each Set to ring two tunes or pieces of their own selection. The Judges will observe the nature and difficulty of the pieces performed by each Band, in addition to the correctness of playing. N.B.—Any new system of judging proposed, will be considered, and if thought by the majority of the Bands entered to be superior to the one formerly adopted, will be used on the occasion.

AN EXTRA PRIZE OF FIVE POUNDS

will be given for a piece to be played by each Set, a Pianoforte Copy of which will be sent two months before the Contest to each Band entered for the Original Prizes; to be played immediately after the last of their own selection. The Set who play the nearest to copy to be the winners. No extra entrance money to be paid.

N.B.—No Band to play the same pieces they have played at any previous Contest.

All the Bands to furnish Pianoforte copies of the pieces they intend to play at the time of drawing.

No party to compete for the Original Prizes without also playing for the Extra Prize, nor for the Extra Prize without the Original Prizes.

The same conditions as to the conveyance by Rail, to Belle Vue (or Manchester) and Back, as in previous years will be adhered to, and each party will be conveyed Free, where suitable arrangements can be made with the Companies of the lines over which the Bands wish to travel; and if no satisfactory arrangement can be made, the Entrance Money will be returned.

copy, the overture to the "Home Flowers Waltzes". The weather wasn't good but still at least 10,000 people turned up. Two more names were present, those of York (W H Howard), Meltham and Stocksbridge, both of which were conducted by Henry Pogson who had conducted Holmfirth from the beginning of the contest in 1855. Uttoxeter (G Richardson) also came to compete again for the first time since they withdrew from the contest. Interestingly Henry Pogson seems to have been an important and successful conductor/arranger who was employed by a number of bands in their attempt to succeed at the various competitions between 1855 and 1874. (see Appendix 2).

FIRST

BY FIFE AND DRUM BANDS,

ON WHIT-TUESDAY, JUNE 6th, 1865.

TWENTY-FIVE POUNDS will be given, which, with the Entrance Money, 20s. each Band, will be divided into Prizes, the particulars of which will be given after the entries are complete. N.B.—A Side Drum will be given to the best Band as in former years, in addition to the first prize.

REGULATIONS.

No Band to exceed Twenty-five Performers, Conductor included.

Each Band to perform two tunes or pieces, one of their own selection, and one sent to them five weeks before the Contest.

No Professional Musician will be allowed to play in any Band.

CONDUCTORS.—Any Professional Man may act as Conductor for what Bands he may be engaged (without limit to number), but will not be allowed to play in any.

Entries to close on Tuesday, April 25th, 1865.

SECOND,

BY BRASS BANDS,

ON MONDAY, SEPTEMBER 4th, 1865.

FIFTY POUNDS will be given, which, with the Entrance Money, will be divided into four or five Prizes.

REGULATIONS.

Amatuer Bands only allowed to play. A Professional Musician may act as Conductor, and may also perform on any instrument, he may also act for as many Bands as he thinks proper, but not to play as a member in one Band, and Conductor in another. The members of each Band must have played together once a week for six weeks before the day of the Contest. A person being a member of another Band, will not be disqualified, but no one to play in more than one Band at the Contest. Entrance Money, 20s. each Band, to be sent on or before Tuesday, July 25th, 1865. Two pieces to be performed, one of which will be sent six weeks before the Contest, arranged for the Cornets to be played in B flat; Sopranos in E flat or D flat, at the players' option; and a piece chosen by each Band, which must also be played with Cornets in B flat.

The number of competing Bands not to be less than five, and no Band to exceed 20 in number, Conductor included.

N.B.—No Band to play the same pieces they have played at any previous Contest at Belle Vue.

THIRD,

HAND-BELL RINGING,

ON MONDAY, SEPTEMBER 25th, 1865.

By Sets of not more than twelve performers, First Prize, £15.; Second Prize, £5. Entrance Money, 10s. the Set to form the Third and Fourth prizes.

REGULATIONS.

Each Set to ring two tunes or pieces of their own selection. The Judges will observe the nature and difficulty of the pieces performed by each Band, in addition to the correctness of playing. The two pieces to be plaid in succession.

N.B.—No Band to play the same pieces they have played at any previous Contest at Belle Vue, except they should be required to play off, when they may play one of their old pieces.

All the Bands to furnish Pianoforte copies of the pieces they intend to play at the time of drawing.

Entries to close on Tuesday, August 15th, 1865.

GENERAL REGULATIONS.

The same conditions as to the conveyance by Rail, to Belle Vue (or Manchester) and Back, as in previous years will be adhered to, and each party will be conveyed Free, where suitable arrangements can be made with the Companies of the lines over which the Bands wish to travel; and if no satisfactory arrangement can be made, the Entrance Money will be returned.

All disputes respecting parties being Professional to be submitted to JOHN JENNISON, JUNR., with known particulars, and his decision to be final; also in all other cases before the playing takes place, afterwards the decision of the Judges to be binding. Gentlemen of the highest professional standing and respectability will be selected for the office, and will (where practicable) be brought from distances widely apart.

Post Office Orders to be made payable to JOHN JENNISON, Belle Vue, Manchester.

By the 1862 contest it seemed that the word had really got round that hand-bell ringing was on its way back to popularity as there were now nine entries! - three of them, Over Darwen, Hull Saint James Street, and Newchurch who had not entered before.

What was now happening is comparable with our own time, the word getting around and bands were being formed or re-formed in towns and villages where they had existed before the decline of the Wakes, and a look at a list of where Wakes had existed confirmed this to be true.

Shelley were winners of the 1862 contest, and the extra prize for playing "New York Quadrilles" went again to Wigan. In the next year 1863 the Wigan Ringers were the cause of the contest's first rough house. The problem was that some bands learnt to play a good contest piece which they repeated year after year. The extra prize would seem to be an attempt to encourage bands not to repeat themselves, but some bands, including Wigan, persisted in doing so. Not only that, but they also had the effrontery to learn and to win the extra prize every year! Following this experience a rule appeared for the 1863 contest stating that "Each band should give two tunes of its own selection and should not repeat any tune they had given at a former contest".

Did Wigan take any heed of this new rule? No they did not. There was grumbling when the Wigan Ringers took the platform and played a piece which they had given at a former contest and then they were asked to perform a second piece, which they did - but this was also a tune they had played on a previous occasion. This, in the words of a reporter of the day, "Caused both difficulty and delay; which must have been just too much for the audience. The result was a rough house, and the Wigan band, in the words of one of the ringers, Charles Jowett 'received a fusillade of sods and stones; and something bordering on a free fight was indulged in'. Thereafter "Charlie" was rather fond of pointing out a facial wound he received in the scrap as he did when recalling his memories of the occasion to the Wigan Observer in 1913! It must be remembered that the other bands of ringers taking part in the contest were seated in the orchestra at the rear of the platform, and it was the audience that was in uproar. Also, sodding (throwing sods of earth) was normal practice in the North at that time when people got angry. In the end all was calm when it was decided that "The Wigan and the Meltham band, which was next in the order of merit, should each play another tune". When this was done the second prize went to Meltham and third to Wigan, with Oldham coming fourth. Then came the contest for the extra prize, each band played the last figure in Coote's "Oure Lancers" and just to rub the salt in with the audience, Wigan again took the first prize! Wigan had now won the extra prize for five years running for which they were awarded a silver medal each. It would seem that they were "Medalled off" as the extra prize was dropped after this - hardly surprising.

Wigan returned again the next year, in 1864 to win the first prize in the open contest and continued to appear in contests until 1869 after which they must have retired from the contest field altogether although the band continued operating at least until 1870.

The results of the interview by the Wigan Observer with Mr Jowett give an insight into the world of hand-bell ringing in the 1860s. By 1913 when the interview took place, Mr Jowett was the only ringer left alive, and gave the names of the other members as: Edward Benson (conductor), Daniel Dix, W Richards, Jas Dix, Peter Mather, Thomas Richardson, Peter Buckley, William Buckley, John Brears, Edward Smith, Peter Finch and Thomas Wilkinson.

Mr Jowett who was by now 76 years of age was full of stories about the early contests at Belle Vue. The Wigan band, he said, was in great demand and played in various parts of the country and numerous visits were made to halls of the landed gentry; where they were always well received.

On one occasion, the ringers visited Duxbury Hall, the residence of Squire Standish, who was so pleased with the rendering of "All Good Lasses" and other popular tunes, that he gave them a generous donation. Before they left they gave a rendition of "Old Fowler" and bade the Squire a hearty "Good day". Then they proceeded homewards, but had scarcely gone fifty yards when the sound of gun fire stopped them in their tracks and on looking round the old Squire was seen, gun in hand, pointing in their direction. The volley was intended as a parting salute, but the ringers were glad to beat a hasty retreat.

On another occasion, the bands received from Haigh Hall, what to them was a mysterious message in crabbed handwriting, but were unable to decipher it. Neither "Owd Rector Gunning" nor the church clerk could tell what it said, and it was finally decided that Mr Jowett should go to the Hall the next day and make enquiries. At the Hall he was welcomed by a "fine lady" who answered his call, whereupon he asked if the "Colonel" (Sir James Lindsay) was at home. "The Colonel is not at home", replied the lady smiling, "but the General is". News had just arrived at Haigh that the higher distinction had been conferred upon the "Colonel".

It was then said that the indecipherable message was an invitation to the ringers to give entertainment at the Hall, where they appeared a few days later. Mr Jowett said *"The company at Haigh were ta'en up with our playing, and t'owd earl danced a reel in red knee breeches to the ringers' accompaniment"*. His last statement adds more weight to the surmise that handbells were used to provide the music for dancers, as Mr Jowett expressed no surprise at the Earl's dancing a reel.

The practices of the band were first held at the home of the mother of one of the band members, but as the band grew, this became inconvenient, so the bells were removed to the Parish Church belfry. Several of the band were also towerbell ringers at the church, but they soon had to find fresh headquarters, and eventually the bells were housed in a room at the rear of the commercial hall where practices were held for a "considerable time". The bells used by

Wigan, a set of seventy nine, were made by Charles D'Albert of London, but it was stated that four or five of the largest bells were added by a local maker, stated to be possibly Mr Roger Bolton.

When Wigan disbanded, the bells came into the possession of one of the ringers and it was always understood that it was his intention to hand them over to some responsible authority for future care, but this intention was never fulfilled and the bells were forgotten, and in 1913 found their way to a local brass foundry as scrap. Fortunately Mr Gilbert C Hall, a tower ringer at the Parish Church, on hearing a rumour that the historic bells were at the scrap yard he went to see Mr W H Barker, the head of the firm and related the history and romance attached to the bells, and made an appeal for their rescue from the melting pot, which was successful. The bells were handed over to Mr Hall with the understanding that there must be no further sale of the bells, which were said to be of magnificent tone – and the bells still exist today. It just needs someone to start using them again.

In the same year of Wigan's first prize win in the Open at Belle Vue 1864, another band from the town entered for the first time, called Wigan Swan Meadow Mills who had 11 ringers in their number. This band was placed third in 1865 and fourth in 1868, but on the Belle Vue list of prize winners were simply listed as "Wigan" for those years, which has confused the two bands' records on the Belle Vue list of winners until now. The Band was provided with sponsorship by James Eckersley owner of the Swan Meadow Mills factory in Wigan. He was also Mayor of Wigan and MP for the town 1866-1883. Also taking part at Belle Vue in 1864 were the Batley Prince of Wales Hand-bell Ringers, named in honour of the Prince. The band was based in a public house, the George Hotel in Wellington Street, Batley in Yorkshire.

The band had 12 ringers, which is an indication of how popular hand-bell ringing was becoming in the industrial mill towns of the North of England. Batley were to enter on quite a few occasions during the next ten years at Belle Vue, and in 1868, a second band was entered - "Batley Junior".

In the years 1865-66-67 the Belle Vue Contest was won each time by Uttoxeter Hand-bell Ringers from Staffordshire, who, by winning the first prize for the third year in succession were declared the "Champions of Great Britain", the first champion band since the beginning of the competition. The conductor of this band was a Mr G F Gill and had only eight members, which shows the high quality of the ringing, winning with eight members, when the average number of ringers in the other bands was ten, and they used 49 bells.

In November 1983 I decided to travel to Uttoxeter to see if I could discover more about the town's famous ringers. After making local enquiries, I was directed to the William Salt Library in Stafford. I soon found reports about the band in newspapers of the day, which stated that Mr George Richardson had founded the band in 1839. Mr Richardson, it said, had been the band's leader since its formation, and the band became champions on Mr Richardson's 58th birthday. When the band returned from the Belle Vue Contest "the church bells sent forth many peals in honour of their chief ringers". The Uttoxeter ringers were presented with the Belle Vue gold medal for winning first prize, and because they had won the Contest three times in succession each ringer gained a special silver medal subscribed for locally. These were presented at a special ceremony by the founder of Belle Vue Gardens, John Jennison "Amidst scenes of the greatest enthusiasm" in Uttoxeter Town Hall. The Uttoxeter Hand-bell Ringers were also tower bell ringers and while I was in Uttoxeter I noticed the Church had a very large bell tower and I think it is possible the band could have also held their hand-bell rehearsals in the tower ringing chamber.

The rule at the time (1867) was that any band who became champions by winning three times in succession would be barred from competing for the following three years. The newspaper report said that "The band now stood in the position of champion, on which laurels they may now well 'Rest and be thankful'", which is what they must have done, as they never entered the British Open again, as Wigan had done before them. Uttoxeter's last official concert was in Uttoxeter Town Hall in October 1880, but they gave several concerts in the district after that date.

Later, a new band of ringers was formed in Uttoxeter. An article in the Bell News and Ringers Record of April 1912, said there had been a revival of the art of hand-bell ringing in the town, and the new band of young ringers included young men whose fathers had been in the original band. They also used the same bells, which brings us back to the fact that a tradition can lie dormant for years and then spring into life, as long as the bells are kept in the district so the tradition can live again. The Bell News article also said that there were, at the time (1912), only two members of the old band were still alive.

The Staffordshire Advertiser for September 1868 said that the Wakes were being held in Uttoxeter, but not in the usual gay manner they usually were, owing to there being no races there.

The existence of Wakes in Uttoxeter and the formation of the hand-bell band in 1839, well before the start of the Belle Vue Contests, is further evidence that hand-bell ringing was popular where Wakes existed, and the fact that at least four bands of hand-bell ringers operating in this area of Staffordshire (Stafford, Cheddleton, Stoke on Trent and Uttoxeter) is an indication that there were probably local contests held at these Wakes for hand-bell ringing. Uttoxeter's success at Belle Vue in 1866 brought a significant development in the actual ringing of hand-bells, but this development did not originate from Uttoxeter in Staffordshire, but from the ringers of Shelley in the West Riding of Yorkshire. Shelley, who had won first prize in 1862 were strong rivals of Uttoxeter at Belle Vue. In the contest of 1866 Shelley became the first band to develop the use of duplicate bells, when they used 2 bells of the same size and note. In 1867 Shelley took things a stage further and used triplicate bells of the same size and note. Such sets of bells containing duplicate or triplicate bells of the same notes became known as 'long sets', and sets with no duplicates or triplicates became known as 'straight sets'.

Prior to the introduction of duplicate bells it was necessary at the start of each piece, for bells being rung off table to be allocated to a ringer such that no more than two bells would ever have to be rung quickly in succession. This usually meant that the bells would need to be reallocated for the next piece thus wasting time between each piece. This was not a problem for 4-in-hand ringers, nor for ringers with duplicate and triplicate bells. Some say that the introduction of duplicate bells allowed more difficult and complicated music to be played. However the use of duplicate bells did not particularly enable a band to play more difficult music. It just overcame the need to re-assign hand-bells between pieces for those teams ringing off table. A good and properly allocated off table band, or a well-damped 4-in-hand band can play music which is just as difficult as that played by a band using a long set. For example, the music played at Belle Vue by Uttoxeter in 1865, the first year of their three successive wins was, the "Overture to Italiana in Algeria" (Rossini). At the same contest Uttoxeter also played "March of the Men of Harlech". The bells would have been rung four-in-hand plus off the table for the bass bells. The difficulty of the pieces offered for the competition obviously got harder as the years went by because, in the Belle Vue Contest of 1869, Shelley played Haydn's "Surprise Symphony" and in the words of two of the Shelley band, "(It) was a great achievement at this Contest".

At this contest in 1869 Shelley were clearly head and shoulders above all the other bands, though the Glossop band from Derbyshire played the "Merry Bells Polka" eight times over from memory, which is clear evidence that some bands played without any music.

The Wigan bells are pictured below.

The use of duplicate bells also meant that larger sets of bells were now used. At the first contest in 1855, the greatest number of bells in use was 53, but when the Wigan band disbanded in about 1870 they owned a set of 79 bells.

Chapter 3 – Evolutionary Development

But how had hand-bell tune ringing on a large scale developed? And how did the ringing of 12 bells in hand grow into the ringing of 70 bells plus all from a table?

This development consisted of a series of identifiable stages, which can still be seen in their various parts of development today.

Initially, with the Cor hand-bells, the clapper was prevented from leaning on the lip of the bell by up to three leather collars, which also provided the slot to encourage the clapper to swing in one arc only. Thus 4 in hand ringing was possible and did take place (Bill Butler's book on bell founders, and the Oxford Book of Music show an etching of one Roger Smith at Saint Bartholomew Fair, London, ringing 4 in hand [and 2 on head, and 2 on feet] in about 1760!). However 4 in hand was made much easier and more accurate with the invention of the "Wells type" staple assembly. As previously stated Robert Wells (1) master founder between 1760-1780 invented an improved staple assembly which consisted of two brass springs affixed to a clevis of bronze, in which the clapper was retained. Through the clapper and the clevis, a hole was drilled through which a wood dowel was inserted, on which the clapper pivoted. The brass springs prevented the clapper resting on the bell, thus enabling the bell to continue to sound after being struck. Also the clapper could now only move in one plane, back and forth within the confines of the clevis. This gave the ringer much more control over the way in which four bells could be handled.

The above type of staple assembly was used in all English hand-bells made until the early 1970s and is still used by the English and Dutch Founders today. However, in the USA, Jake Malta, through Schulmerich Carillons Inc. and then Malmark Inc. introduced design innovations which improved the clapper assembly, making them more adjustable and providing a ringer with greater dynamic control.

From four-in-hand developed the ringing of bells from a mattress covered table and subsequently the Yorkshire method of ringing hand-bells.

The above explanation of the development was taken further during my association with the late John Terry, a former veteran hand-bell ringer and a member of the Low Moor Hand-bell

Ringers and also a tower bell ringer in Low Moor, Bradford, Yorkshire.

John Terry has been a great influence on the direction and content of this book. I met John in 1978 and for the next four years he proved to be a great help to me in my research of the development of musical hand-bell ringing. John Terry died in November 1982 age 75.

In the early 1920s John Terry had joined the Low Moor tower bell ringers and soon became a member of the Low Moor hand-bell ringers. He would often arrive for rehearsals early, and being young and keen and full of zest for his hobby, as he was throughout his life, he would converse on the subject of hand-bell ringing with the oldest member at the time, James William Emmott, a big man of 21 stones, known locally as Bill "O" Tom's (meaning son of Tom). J W Emmott was a ringer of 60 years experience in those days which would take his earliest recollections of ringing back to the 1860s. John Terry himself took part in his first British Open at Bell Vue in Manchester at the age of 14.

The following is an account of the development of hand-bell ringing after the introduction of four-in-hand ringing, worked out by John Terry and the writer and is put forward as a basis for further discussion and investigation.

The technique of four-in-hand came in useful during tune ringing activities as it was then possible for tunes to be rung with very few ringers. It has been said that at this stage of the development no attempt was made at damping. However I do not think that this would have been the case. Certainly many 4-in-hand bands would not have damped their bells, or at least not adequately at that time, in the same way that many 4-in-hand teams today still do not damp their bells adequately. But in fact it is very easy to damp four-in-hand bells against the body and it would have been so then. Remember, Handel included hand-bells in one of his oratorios. He would not have been happy for the individual bells to sound longer than the note durations written in the music, and so ruin his harmonies! (My brother Don and I still feel the same way for all the compositions and arrangements that we have put together over the years for four-in-hand ringing. Ed.)

The music used, if the ringers were tower cum hand-bell ringers, would have been based on the same numbers that they used for change ringing on tower bells.

If the ringers were former members of church bands or choirs, then staff notation, or tonic sol fa in the case of choir members, probably would have been used.

The development of four-in-hand arose out of a two-fold desire of tune ringers – to enable fewer ringers to ring more bells, and to extend ringers who were becoming bored with ringing tunes with only one bell in each hand. In change ringing however, ringing one bell in each hand was already a big mental challenge, and there was rarely a need for more than five or six ringers to ring together, and most often a change ringing band at this time would only have three or four ringers. Ringing four-in-hand to changes would have been quite a mental feat (although it has been done. In the early 1960s I remember seeing the son of Alf Bowell, a former bell founder in Ipswich, ringing Grandsire Triples and Plain Bob Major four-in-hand after Sunday Evensong service ringing in the ringing chamber of St Mary-le-Tower. Indeed George Symonds and Charlie Sedgeley, who used to ring with him, told me that they could remember father and son Bowell ringing plain courses of Double Norwich Court Bob Major 4-in-hand. Ed.)

These ringers had come to enjoy ringing hand-bells four-in-hand, so later, in order to improve the sound and range of the music played, the ringers added more bells both through the tenors and into the bass, and above the trebles.

When the larger bells were added to the bottom tenors the ringers found that these bells were too big and cumbersome to ring four-in-hand, so the ringers then had the idea of placing the large bells on a table, on which they had first laid their overcoats. In this way, the bells were ready for ringing and the lower tenor and bass ringers were still able to ring four bells each like the rest of the ringers. The bells were placed on end with the mouth facing downwards on the table.

The ringers rang more or less the bells they held in hand when they started ringing the tune, the musical arrangements used by the ringers at this time would have been relatively simple with the bells being rung at a pace which allowed time to put a bell down and pick up another from the table when required.

Therefore, the trebles were now rung four-in-hand and the lower tenors and bass were rung from a table, and this was the birth of the first form of "Off the table" ringing.

As more complex music was tackled, extra bells were added to the set, therefore a larger table was required and the ringers overcoats were replaced by an enveloping, purpose-made cloth cushioned by an underlay of blankets.

With the use of a table, the ringers required more space, those still practising in the belfry, (unless it was a large ringing chamber) taking alternative accommodation. Many, it would seem, moved into public houses, although remember some bands were formed in public houses and never had any connection with the church. Shelley Hand-bell Ringers are an example, as the band was formed before Shelley Church was built (although it is not known where they rehearsed).

What is now known as the "Off table" or "Yorkshire" ringing style where bells lie on their sides on a table with their handles toward the ringers, was developed by the Shelley Hand-bell Ringers of Huddersfield, and, as previously stated, first used in public at the 1866 British Open Hand-bell Competition at Belle Vue in Manchester. As also explained, prior to this, (from about 1780 onwards), the ringing styles had always been either two or four-in-hand on sets of up to 50 bells, with later, just the bass bells being placed mouth down on tables and rung in a proto-off table style (described more fully later in this section). Thus the Lancashire Ringers, when they were first signed up by P.T. Barnam to go to the USA in 1844 (They first started touring in England in 1841) were probably such a four-in-hand/mouth down off-table bass band, and were again when they went to Australia in 1863. Although the five ringers, (who were essentially London based and effectively a different band) who undertook the second Barnum USA tour in 1850 were 4-in-hand only.

As previously stated Shelley HBR were also the first to use duplicate and triplicate hand-bells to avoid the need for re-allocation between pieces.

The competitions, of which there were many local ones, as well as the British Open at Belle Vue, were the main means of disseminating hand-bell information at that time, and thus following the 1866 competition, other teams gradually changed their style, so that by the 1880s the majority of large northern bands were fully "off table" using "long sets" of bells i.e. sets containing duplicate and even triplicate bells. It is interesting that before the 1878 the Belle Vue competition pieces tended to be traditional and Music Hall hits of the day, but after that there was a swing toward more classical music although many bands were reluctant to change.

Crosland Moor, Saddleworth, and Elland were the best "off table" teams at the beginning of the 20th Century.

The style reached its apex in the first part of the 20th century but then, partly as a result of the decimation of the Great War and the effects of the Spanish Flu, apart from a handful of bands, faded away. The last competition at Belle Vue was held in 1926 and the last organised by the Yorkshire Association in 1932.

Most bands at this time were public subscription bands so that when they declined and then disbanded, the bells were often put into the church for safekeeping - and then often later sold when the church needed money for repairs. This was the case with the two sets of over 100 bells each (practice set and concert set!) of the Saddleworth Ringers, which were sold in the early 1970s and the 70 Horbury bells, which were sold from a church stall individually in 1958 and realised about £60.

Fig. 42: The "Fredsklockorna" (Peace Bells), Sweden Photo: Michael Wright

(Comment by Editor: In hindsight I regret to say that I was a party to this practice. When my late wife Sylvia and I went to live in Nuneaton, Warwickshire in 1970 we set up the Windscape Ringers using an ex vaudeville long set which we bought from an elderly ex chorus girl in Sheffield. Although many of them were cracked, there was a middle three octaves that were useable. We then bought a 4 and half octave set new from Petit and Fritsen in Holland as the Vaudeville set were not very good. When we decided to go to Australia in 1975, as Peter explains later in the book, we bought the Todmorden long set from Todmorden Unitarian Church. Ed)

The tradition was kept going by a few bands in Britain, including the Ecclesfield Hand-bell Ringers, Norbury and the Thurlstone Bell Orchestra, and one band in Sweden and two in Australia, Brookhampton and Maryborough Queensland. It was fully revived in the late 1960s with the resurgence of hand-bell ringing in the U.K. and the setting up of the Handbell Ringers of Great Britain.

In Australia, the Brookhampton Ringers from the deep south of Western Australia still ring in the "4-in-hand trebles, mouth down off-table bass" method of the early nineteenth century. The Royal Poland Street Ringers of London, towards the end of the nineteenth century, also used the mouths down off table style, but for all their bells (after previously using the four-in-hand method plus later the mouth down bass). In this off-table style the bells are placed mouths downwards upon the tables, and are picked up with the hands turned inwards and rung on the up stroke as the hands are rotated back to their normal position. Royal Poland Street used to tour extensively throughout Europe, especially performing at the command of the European Royal Families, and sold their bells at the end of one such tour to what is now one of the few Swedish groups, the "Fredsklockorna", which still rings in the same 19th century mouth down off table style as did the Royal Poland Street Ringers.

But I move ahead too fast! I will explain this in more detail later in the book.

So some bands in England were still ringing in the "4-in-hand trebles, mouth down off-table bass" method of the early nineteenth century in the 1870s, as the photograph of Mount Zion, Pudsey Hand-bell Ringers (near Leeds, Yorkshire) shows, as were, as already stated, the Royal Poland Street Hand-bell Ringers (1872) and even much later still, Todmorden were still using the method as shown in an engraving of 1901; and also as stated Brookhampton and Fredsklockorna still do. However this method would have been considered at least thirty years out of date by most bands at the beginning of the 20th century, let alone the 21st Century, but even today, leaving aside Brookhampton and Fredsklockorna, some bands still use a combination of four-in-hand and off the table - but with one difference; the bells on the table are laid on their sides, which is another part of the development to which we shall now return.

As stated the method of ringing the treble bells four-in-hand with the lower tenor and bass off the table, is probably the method used by the hand-bell ringers taking part in the British Open Hand-bell Tune Ringing Contests at Belle Vue, from the first contest in 1855 up to 1866, when for the first time in history, duplicate bells were used. At the 1866 contest the Shelley Hand-bell Ringers used 2 bells of the same pitch for some notes, which was described as "Double Bells" and at the following year's contest of 1867 used "Treble (Triple) Bells" which was the use of 3 bells of the same pitch.

The above particulars of the introduction of duplicate bells were printed on a leaflet published in 1911, by two former members of

...and Bell Co
1871.

...and Campanologian
...conductor J. E. Crow...
...d David Crossle...

...Colnforth Temper...
...ductor John Moorh...
...South ha...

...adcliffe Juvenile
...ductor M. Pendleb...
...ec.:.   Standl...

...mitage Bridge
...nductor Seth Cold...
...ec.: A Lockw...

...carborough
...onductor Geo Di...
...E. B. Newton...

Hyde
...ductor D. Brie...
...Organis...
...ec.: St Ives Hy...

Oldham.
...onductor David
...Sec.: Jas L...

the Shelley Band, Fred Shaw and Artha Cook. (Note the unusual spelling of Mr Cook's Christian name). The details were taken from the band's minutes book by them.

Until 1866 the bells were still rung with the trebles four-in-hand and the others off the table with the bells standing on end in an upright position on the table. After its introduction in 1866, more and more teams laid their off table bells on their sides, and more and more of them enlarged their sets with duplicates and triplicates, especially of the trebles. Thus, rather than ringing their bells in the linked four-in-hand style which had previously prevailed, the treble ringers were able to ring many more than four bells each off table, in some cases up to two octaves of bells each.

These changes brought about a difference in the sound produced by bells which were automatically stopped "ringing on" by being replaced on the padded table after being rung, rather than in-hand ringers being required consciously to damp their bells when required. Indeed, like some four-in-hand teams today, it was likely that many bands did not consciously damp their bells at all. It all depended on the musicality of their leader, and the type of music being played. In these bands the bells were rung in much the same way as a piano is played when the sustaining pedal is pressed down - more like a carillon.

Shelley, being the first band to ring hand-bells as described, would explain why this system of ringing became known as the "Yorkshire Method". The method was invented by the Yorkshire men of Shelley, near Huddersfield.

But why had Shelly found it necessary to make changes in their ringing methods and to use duplicate bells? The reasons are simple enough, the development of using duplicate bells was the result of gradual changes that had been evolving since before the British Open Hand-bell Contest began, from the time when Robert Wells (1) introduced improvements to the design of hand-bells, between 1760 and 1780, but this evolution had been accelerated by the desire to win prizes, first at Wakes contests and then at Bell Vue.

The very fact that in order to win the first prize at this contest, the winning band had to give the best rendition of the most "difficult, complicated and classical music" meant, not only playing more complicated music, but the improvement in technique was also a major consideration and a deciding factor in the adjudication.

It became necessary for the hand-bell bands to experiment, and possibly gain by the results, when competing against other bands. In turn each of the other bands at the contest would keep a keen eye on all the other competitors for any new methods they themselves could use, everyone benefiting from the exercise.

These developments can be summed in the adage: NECESSITY IS THE MOTHER OF INVENTION.

So if it had not been for the British Open Contest at Belle Vue providing the impetus, I feel that hand-bell ringing may not have developed past the four-in-hand stage, although to be fair, some teams were already ringing their bass bells in the mouth down off table style, and there was pressure from the foundries to sell more and larger sets of bells too .

The use of duplicate bells made tune ringing much easier for both ringers and arrangers, as when one ringer could not ring a particular note and neither of his neighbouring ringers could reach the bell required, because they were ringing other bells, then if another bell of the same note was available, it could be played by one of the other ringers around the table who was not ringing a bell at the time.

This new system meant that even more complicated music could be performed, than when using the old four-in-hand method plus off the table system at the bass, as the top flight bands had reached the upper limit of that system. It is interesting to note that earlier music published by William Gordon of Stockport, Cheshire was arranged for the bass ringers to ring off table and the treble ringers to ring four-in-hand, whilst music he published later was arranged for off-table playing throughout.

The use of duplicate bells seemed to go unnoticed by the press, as contemporary reports make no mention of it. Duplicate bells were first used at the 1866 British Open, which for a number of reasons wasn't all that successful, only 4 bands entered, one of which was unable to take part due to "the indisposition of its leader" and to make matters worse, it rained all day, as a result the attendance was a poor one, but things looked up the following year in 1867 when there were 9 entries and in 1868 there were 10.

One interesting piece of information in the contemporary report of the 1866 contest at Belle Vue was the details of the judges, which stated that one of the judges was a "Mr Thistlewood, professional hand-bell ringer, Liverpool". In 1865 one of the judges was a "Mr Thistlewood of Manchester" - the same man who had moved? I wonder. From this report we know that there were professional hand-bell ringers at the time, although there had been others. As I have already stated, early as the 1840s, the Lancashire Hand-bell Ringers (Oldham) had toured England and the USA

The Hand-bell Movement was now becoming well established,

81

with bands starting up in a number of places. The entry list for the Belle Vue Contest of 1869 was the biggest so far with 18 bands in the line up, all of which competed. The 1869 contest had the greatest number of bands competing in the whole of its 65 year history, although there would be a larger entry list in other contests later. The bands in the line up for this 1869 contest came from as far afield as Shropshire and Warwickshire, counties with centres of large populations and industry such as Iron, coal, and the production of hardware for the ever-growing population, and also for the Army and Navy. The list of entrants for the 1869 contest shows how widespread hand-bell ringing had now become. The eighteen bands were: Society of Ringers, Rawmarsh, Rotherham, Yorkshire; Swan Meadow Mills, Wigan, Lancashire; Scarborough, Yorkshire; Armitage Bridge, Yorkshire; Batley Junior, Yorkshire; Glossop, Derbyshire; Holmfirth, Yorkshire; West Bromwich, Warwickshire; Clayton West Junior, Yorkshire; Leeds United, Yorkshire; Hyde, Cheshire; Old Glossop, Derbyshire; Royal Albert, Birmingham; Thurlstone, Yorkshire; Broseley, Shropshire; Shelley, Yorkshire; Burnley, Lancashire; and All Saints Society, West Bromwich, Warwickshire. Astonishingly that year saw the one and only contest for change ringing on hand-bells held at Belle Vue on the same day. The bands who took part in this were: St Peters, Sheffield, Yorkshire; St Marie's, Sheffield, Yorkshire; Ashton, Lancashire; Saddleworth, Yorkshire; Halifax, Yorkshire; Wakefield, Yorkshire and Hyde, Cheshire.

It was at this contest that the Shelley ringers started a sensational run of success, which must have amazed their rivals, when they played Haydn's "Surprise Symphony".

In the leaflet published in 1911 by Shelley's secretary Fred Shaw, and Artha Cook (both treble ringers in the band), they claimed that this was the first introduction of "high class" music at the Belle Vue Contest, which, in effect was suggesting that when music with "high class" titles had been played before 1869 at Belle Vue, the bands had only played the tuneful easier parts of the music. However an analysis of the Hyde number music from 1855 shows that complicated hand-bell arrangements of classical music were already being played by bands before Shelley's performance of the "Surprise Symphony".

The inclusion of West Bromwich, Royal Albert Birmingham and All Saints Warwickshire in the entry list will no doubt be surprising to most people today up to now, it was thought that the influence of the Belle Vue Contests was restricted to the Northern Counties of Yorkshire, Lancashire, Cheshire, Derbyshire and Staffordshire, which for the most part was true, but they were not the only counties to be represented at the contests for in future years. there were to be bands from further a field, such as Loughborough

(Leicestershire) who competed from 1865 onwards, Barrow-in-Furness St James (Cumberland) 1871 to 1873, Lincoln 1872 and 1876, Workington (Cumberland) 1873 and Wolverhampton St Peters Collegiate (Staffordshire) 1876, Madeley (Shropshire) 1870 and 1871, but the entries from these places seems to have faded away by the late 1870s.

Therefore we do know that by 1869 news and fame of the Belle Vue British Open Championship of Great Britain Hand-bell Ringing Contest had spread at least throughout the north and the midlands of the country.

The following year, 1870, the Shelley ringers won the first prize for the third year in succession, therefore becoming "Champions of Great Britain". They played Symphony No. 1 in E Flat by Haydn (the eighth in the set he wrote for Solomon).

This meant that there had been two champion bands in succession, first Uttoxeter 1865, 1866 and 1867, who had retired from the contest field, and now Shelley 1868, 1869 and 1870. So out of the last six contests there had been only two winners, and up to this time there had been no rule which barred a band from competing if it won the contests three times in a row.

John Jennison had died in September 1869, and the organisation of Belle Vue was now in the hands of his son George, who was head of Belle Vue until 1878. George was "The mind that developed Belle Vue" and he enforced the rules regarding championship winners that "Any band winning three times in succession was to be barred the following three years", which meant that Shelley were now out of the running for the next three years. This must have seemed very harsh indeed to the Shelley ringers.

Things came to a head when, during the years when the Shelley band were debarred from competing, 1871, 1872 and 1873, the Old Glossop Band (Derbyshire) took first prize in each of these years and so became the new champion band.

Hand-bell ringers from Glossop, first entered the contest in 1869, when two bands from Glossop entered under the names "Glossop" and "Old Glossop". Both bands had the same conductor, Robert Wild, but had different secretaries. In 1871 the first win of Old Glossop's triple success, the band entered under the name "Old Glossop" but only the name "Glossop" was printed on the list of prizewinners. The conductor of Glossop from 1871 onwards was Charles Berrisford. Apart from the 1869 contest, only one band from Glossop entered for further contests.

In 1872 the band entered under the name "Old Glossop" and 1873

they entered as merely "Glossop" but on the list of prizewinners was printed the words "Old Glossop". Further confusion is created by the fact that in 1874 a Glossop band entered as "Glossop Howard Brothers" and only the words "Howard Brothers" was printed on the list of winners. In 1879 and 1880 Old Glossop Junior won prizes in the contest. In 1881 they were listed as "Old Glossop" again, and in 1882 they were listed as "Old Glossop Junior"! If this isn't enough confusion in 1884 they were listed again, taking fourth prize as "Howard Brothers".

All of this leads me to think that Glossop, Old Glossop, Old Glossop Junior, Howard Brothers and Glossop were synonymous.

Fig. 43: Rivals of the 1870s – (Top) Glossop who were uniquely made up of eight brothers plus their secretary and their conductor, Charles Berrisford of New Mills, (Below 1878) Shelley with Ben Cooke centre holding the baton. He was one of the greatest figures in the history of hand-bell ringing

The Glossop band is unique in the annals of hand-bell ringing as it was remarkably made up of eight brothers called Howard.

After Glossop's triple wins of 1871, 1872 and 1873, the band claimed the "Championship of Great Britain", "This", in the words of Fred Shaw and Artha Cook, two of the Shelley ringers, "the Shelley band could not allow, as the three contests were not open ones".

The result was a special challenge contest between the Glossop band and the Shelley band at Belle Vue, Manchester, on December 28th, 1874 for the great prize of £50.00 and the championship. Shelley played "Symphony No 1 in the Solomon Set" by Haydn, "Symphony No 11 in B flat by Haydn, and "Overture to Zanetta" by Auber.
Glossop played "Symphony No 1 in the Solomon Set"…Haydn, "Half hours with the best composers,Mendelssohn etc" by W.H.Callcott, "Gloria" (chorus) from the 12th Mass…Mozart.

Fred Shaw and Artha Cook were right. Shelley won the championship.

While I was researching for this book, I was told there was information and a photograph of the Shelley hand-bell ringers in

Shelley Parish Church (which was built in 1866, the heyday of the Shelley Hand-bell Ringers).

One dark and stormy November night I travelled to the hill-top village and stopped to ask a man if he could direct me to the vicarage. "Yes", he said and described where it was. "It's down the road on the left, up a dark drive, mind you it's a spooky looking place, a big Victorian building, it looks the type of place that when you knock, the door will fly open and a vampire will fly out at you". I took one look at the place and decided to call back during the hours of daylight!

I called back at Shelley vicarage a few weeks later (during daylight) and as a result found information and a photograph of the band. I also confirmed that the formation of the Shelley hand-bell ringers predated the building of the church.

The years of Glossop's triple win are of interest to our story, as reports of the Belle Vue Contest of these years show how standards of performance had risen since Shelley played the "Surprise Symphony" in 1869. For example, in the contest of 1873 there were 18 bands comprising upwards of 180 performers, and not one band played any simple country tune as they had done before 1869 and a little afterwards, as can be seen from the entry list and music performed:

Hyde (Cheshire) - selection from "La Traviata"
Meanwood, near Leeds, Yorkshire - overture "Tancredi"
Barrow-in-Furness (Cumberland) - "Kyrie" and "Gloria" from Mozart's Mass
Workington (Cumberland) - selection "Der Freischutz"
Scarborough (Yorkshire) - overture "Tancredi"
Broseley (Shropshire) - movement in "Hearts of Oak"
Elland (Yorkshire) - "Kyrie" and "Gloria"
Batley Carr (Yorkshire) - "Kyrie" and "Gloria"
Brighouse (Yorkshire) - overture "Tancredi"
Thurlstone (Yorkshire) - overture "Caliph of Bagdad"
Bingley (Yorkshire) - selection from "Martha"
Disley (Cheshire) - music "Warriors Joy"
Queensbury (Yorkshire) - Handel's "Hallelujah Chorus"
Loughborough (Leicestershire) - Napoleon's "Grand March"
Huddersfield (Yorkshire) - overture "Caliph of Bagdad"
Glossop (Derbyshire) - "Kyrie" and "Gloria"
Holmfirth (Yorkshire) – Rossini's overture "Cenerentola"
Old Glossop (Derbyshire) - "Half hours with the best composers Mendelssohn etc" by William Hutchins Callcott

It is also likely that all of these bands were now using the Shelley system of duplicate bells rung from the table, with all of the bells

Fig. 44: Belle Vue Tune Ringing Contest Programme 1899

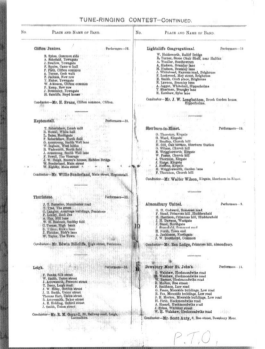

laid side-on, instead of ringing the trebles four-in-hand and the tenor and bass mouth down from the table. Four-in-hand ringing was probably never seen at Belle Vue again. The "Yorkshire Method" of Shelley had become the norm, although bands like Pudsey, near Leeds, who did not enter the competitions, were not influenced by these "new methods" used at contests and felt no need to change. They thus continued to ring their trebles four-in-hand and their bass mouth down from the table – and, as I have already explained, some hand-bell bands in Britain continued to do so for years afterwards, in some places to within the living memory of some of the former ringers with whom I talked; and of course, again, as I have already mentioned, at least two teams in the world have continued using the system from when they were set up in the 19th century to the present day (Brookhampton, Western Australia and "Fredsklockorna", Sweden).

But there was still further room for the development and improvement of music and ringing methods used, as the Manchester Courier's reporter put it, in his report of the 1874 contest at Belle Vue. "Although there was a general weakness in the bass parts, the ringing on the whole was fully up to the average merit" The significance of this report is that although there had been great improvements in the type of music played, there was still a weakness in the bass section.

In 1867 a rule was put in the book by the Belle Vue management, that from then on each competing band had to send the name and address of each of its ringing members. These were published in the programme a month before the contest for all to scrutinise. This was to prevent bands from borrowing players from another band. This hadn't been a problem in the Hand-bell Contest, but it had been going on in the Brass Band Competition and came to a head after Clay Cross Brass Band won the 1867 brass band contest, when it was claimed that in fact Clay Cross were an amalgam of the best players from three bands.

This rule has provided excellent material for research, as the list of names and addresses of players and conductors showed how many ringers were in each band and also showed the movement of conductors and ringers between bands. Unfortunately the earliest programme my research has produced is for 1860.

Although there was movement between bands, this was mainly conductors, rather than hand-bell ringers where there was only a small amount of transference from one band to another, and usually even then, only when a band disbanded. However the conductors would conduct any band that would pay them!

One conductor who conducted several bands was George Boys, who conducted both Huddersfield Albert and Honley Temperance in the 1876 British Open at Belle Vue. The year after, in the same contest, he conducted again Huddersfield Albert and also Woodroyd.

In other country areas of England during this period, hand-bell ringing rarely developed past the 12 bell plus a couple of semitones stage, with tower ringers playing carols at Christmas, being the main activity, as at Halesworth on the Norfolk coast.

However some bands in the South of England in the 1880s had developed much further than the 12 bell stage and even took part in contests, as can be seen from a contest that took place at Cold Ash in Berkshire on June 30th 1885.

The contest took place in the grounds of the Revd J M Bacon, who organised the event. Mr Bacon, according to the "Bell News and Ringers Record", organised his first contest in 1882. This proved to be very successful. The contest seemed a leisurely affair in that it took place on a Tuesday afternoon. "The fine sunny weather added to the relaxed atmosphere and was enjoyed by the large

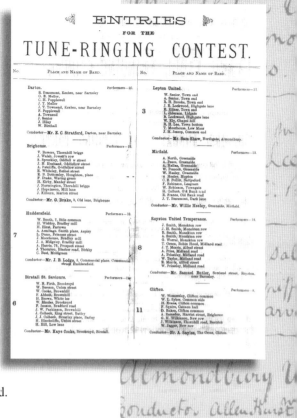

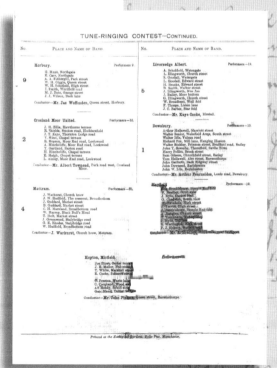

crowd. The fine weather also kept a larger number busy in the hay fields", said the correspondent.

The bands competing were: **Cold Ash Hand-bell Ringers, whose members were; Rev J M Bacon, R Law, E Shepherd, E Mathews, W Mathews, T Stroud and J Prescott.**

Reading Temperance Hand-bell Ringers - C H Taylor (secretary), W Allen (conductor), G Noyes, G Taylor, G Tombs and A Taylor.

Abingdon Hand-bell Ringers - E Young, H Sheard, J Viner, A Carter, E Webb and H Bright.

Highclere Hand-bell Ringers - C Knapp (captain), E Smith, J Head, A Knapp, F Lawrence and E Hopkins.

Hampstead Norris Hand-bell Ringers - T Barlow, J Pummle, J Quelch and T Warman.

Lambourn Hand-bell Ringers - J Hillier (captain), T Fowler, E Hewitt, J Pottinger and J Dudley.

The adjudicator was a Mr W Newell

The competition was divided into three classes, (1) for tune playing on sets of more than 20 bells; (2) for tune playing or "call changes" on smaller sets; (3) for change ringing.

In Class 1 Reading Temperance were a long way ahead of the other two competitors, Abingdon and Cold Ash. Reading also had a larger set of bells, a photograph of the band, taken in 1889 was published in "Reverberations" (the journal of the Handbell Ringers of Great Britain) and shows Reading used a set of 51 bells at the time. At the end of concerts, Reading's leader would deliver a powerful temperance address - unlike the Northern bands, who made for the nearest bar.

The report says Abingdon used 23 bells, the number of bells of Cold Ash used is not stated.

The 1889 photograph of Reading shows the band using the pre 1867, old method of ringing with all the bells standing upright on their ends, with the treble ringers playing their bells in the four-in-hand style, and the tenor and bass bells being rung from the table.

In Class 2, Lambourn, Highclere and Hampstead Norris used "a different style of ringing including simple airs and various peals".

In the change ringing class Abingdon came first, ringing 120 Grandsire Doubles. In second place were Cold Ash, the only other entrant. Not a bad line up of entertainment for a sunny Tuesday afternoon in the country.

Although hand-bell ringing south of Birmingham in any organised form was rare until relatively recent times there certainly was plenty of hand-bell ringing in the South at that time though probably not using the Yorkshire method but, as I have already mentioned, still in either the old mixed style, like the Royal Poland Street Ringers (using a 6 octave long set) and the Barnardo's Boys in London also using a long set, or fully 2 or 4 in hand like St Mary's, Prittlewell in Essex on 2½ octaves (ringing from number music, whose bells date from 1869 cast by George Stockham of Lincoln's Inn, London), Ealing Hand-bell Ringers on 3½ octaves, and a band thought to have been based in Ilford, in Essex, whose Warner's bells went down at least to 26F# and also date from the 19th century (The rest of their bells were melted down as part of the "War Effort").

Reading through Jennison's ledgers, I discovered an exercise book in which all the entering bands, their conductors and the addresses of the bands were written, and sometimes the number of bells owned by the band. The addresses show the extent of the influence of the pub. The listings are from 1856 - 1874. (see Appendix 4)

In 1856 St Thomas' Pendleton's address was given as the May

Fig. 45: A whiskery band of gentlemen pose with their 12 bells - Halesworth Company of Ringers, Norfolk 1876
The importance of the British Public House in the development of the art of hand-bell ringing cannot be underestimated. I would say the public house played as much importance in this development as its neighbour the church.

89

Pole Inn. 1857 Hurst Brook H.B.R. (Ashton-under-Lyne) address, The Ring O'Bells. 1857,Whitefield H.B.R. - The Black Horse. Salford Original H.B.R. - The Saddle Inn. 1861, Heckmondwike H.B.R - The Queens Hotel, in 1863 Heckmondwike had moved a 100 yards down the road to the Lower George Inn. Also in 1863 Oldham H.B.R. - Coach and Horses Hotel. 1864, Batley - Prince of Wales H.B.R - George Hotel. 1865, Heywood H.B.R. - Kings Arms. 1869, Royal Albert H.B.R. Birmingham - Coach and Horses.

The above were the bands whose addresses were given as pubs. The others bands entering were listed under the band's secretaries' names and addresses, and some of these may well still have used the local pub as their practice venue.

These are just a few examples of bands who practised in public houses. It is worth remembering that, at this time there was no instant music in pubs like we have today, no putting 10p in a slot to get three minutes of music from a jukebox. All music heard had to be made by the people themselves, and anybody who could make music and enliven other people's lives under the light of the gas mantle or oil lamp was popular and welcome. A Landlord and his customers would be pleased to have a band practise in his pub, which, in those days had separate rooms for each purpose, smoke room, games room and the music room.

With bands using between 36 and 53 bells it would have been no problem to pack up the bells and put them away in a cupboard between rehearsals. This task would have become much more difficult towards the end of the century when sets of up to 200 bells were being used. Putting these away and setting them out on the table at rehearsal would have been tiresome, and in any case the bands with such large sets of bells, found it much better to leave the bells set out on the table permanently so they could just walk into the room and begin rehearsals immediately, without having to set out and pack up afterwards. It could have been for this reason that there seemed to be a movement away from holding rehearsals in pubs towards the end of the 19th century, as publicans don't like their rooms to be in continuous use by anyone. Bands then made increasing use of clubs, mills, rooms next to or above shops, cricket clubs, school basements, specially built rehearsal rooms, in fact anywhere they could leave the bells set out on the table. The pub bands had fulfilled a social function and would have had a ready supply of recruits, because a hand-bell band already had a complete instrument, so there was no need for a new recruit to buy his own, Another benefit was travel. Band members would perform at concerts in interesting places and go and compete in the hand-bell ringing contest at the famous Belle Vue Gardens, Manchester. This would have been thought of as a wonderful treat and an exciting experience to those people who for the most part led dreary, dull, overworked lives in isolated villages or smoky northern towns, when a trip to the nearest market in a neighbouring town or village was a long way and was the highlight of the week.

Therefore to go to Belle Vue on a Wakes holiday in September was something really to look forward to, and when they arrived - well the crowds for a start, where else could they see 20,000 people all in one place - and the city of Manchester, wasn't it big? Wasn't it grand? The people, the shops, all of it, people would find fascinating - even in the 1920s when my friend the late John Terry went with Low Moor H.B.R. As he said "We were amazed at the scale and size of everything, that was one of the things about Belle Vue".

One band that carries on the tradition of the pub bands is Beverley Town Hand-bell Ringers, who were formed in 1981 and used to practise in the East Yorkshire market town's Cross Keys Hotel. The band presently use a set of 109 bells made at the Whitechapel Bell Foundry, London in 1981. The band's conductor is John Atkinson, who until 1980 was conductor of Beverley St Mary's Church Handbell Ringers. Mr Atkinson is one of a new generation of hand-bell conductors who have learnt the skills and acquired the knowledge of the art of Yorkshire hand-bell ringing by listening to what experienced Yorkshire hand-bell ringers had to say, and acting on the advice they had had to offer–. As a result, the Beverley Town Handbell Ringers have attained a high standard and were the first band to win the hand-bell contest, held in connection with the Hull Competitive Music Festival in April 1988. Our old friend and early hand-bell impresario, Enderby Jackson would have smiled!

Jackson, who, as already mentioned, organised the one and only hand-bell contest at the Crystal Palace in 1859, was born in Hull where there was a band called St James' Steet Hull Hand-bell Ringers. They entered the British Open in 1862 when the small band of only 6 ringers was conducted by Mr Charles Petty of 6 St James Street, Hull. Another band in the region was St Andrews, Kirkella, Hull, where a set of 25 Shaw bells was purchased for the towerbell ringers in the 1880s. The present band at Kirkella was formed in 1975 using these 25 Shaw bells, but in 1981 the bells were sold and replaced by a new set of 49 Whitechapel bells. In 1985 the band won third place in the hand bell contest at the Harrogate Competitive Music Festival gaining 87 marks out of a possible 100.

The winners of the 1985 Harrogate Contest (the first time a hand-

Fig. 46: A Staffordshire Triumph. Stonnall after their historic victory in the first ever hand-bell class at Harrogate Competitive Music Festival in 1985. The band used the Crosland Moor chippy choppy style of ringing (photo: Peter Fawcett)

Left to right: A. Thornton, V. Gall, D. Middleton, Betty Amphlett, R. Duckers, Harry Amphlett, Colin Gall (Conductor), P. Duckers, E. Claverley, B. Bacon, F. Middleton.

bell class was included in the competition) were Stonnall Hand-bell Ringers from Staffordshire who gained 89 marks. Their conductor was Mr Colin Gall. In winning the contest Stonnall may well have been the first Staffordshire band to win a hand-bell competition since our old friends Uttoxeter won first prize at Belle Vue in 1867. It was also the first time a Staffordshire band had won a contest on Yorkshire soil. The Stonnall Ringers were formed on New Year's Eve 1972 in the village pub, the Old Swan. The band used 4 octaves of bells.

Also in the East Yorkshire region are the Cottingham Hand-bell Ringers who began in 1963 using a set of 20 bells under the direction of Mr Ian Booth, more bells having since been added to make up the present set of 51 bells spanning 4.5 octaves.

St Mary's Beverley Hand-bell Ringers began in 1968 with 10 borrowed bells, ten years later the band purchased 60 Whitechapel bells.

A few miles away from Cottingham is Hessle where there is another hand-bell band.

As a result of the activity of these bands the tradition in East Yorkshire is now stronger than ever before.

During the 1860s, 70s and 80s, there operated a rather interesting band, which I have already mentioned in passing. It was not based in the North of England, or even the Midlands, but in Poland Street, London, their address being given as 17 Kennington Terrace. S.E. They were known as the Royal Poland Street Hand-bell Ringers and what makes this band even more interesting is that they travelled extensively, were quite well known, were non-competitive and were a band of only 5 ringers.

The history of the band is at present rather hazy, but they adopted the name "Royal" after they had been invited by Queen Victoria to Osborne House on the Isle of Wight, on August 14th, 1870 on the birthday of Princess Beatrice.

The Poland Street Hand-bell Ringers seemed to make a habit of performing for royalty, for included amongst their invitations were invitations from the King of Belgium, the Crown Prince of Denmark, Archduke Charles Louis of Austria, the King and Queen of Greece on their visit to London, and the Prince and Princess of Wales (December 26th, 1872 and January 1st, 1873) at Sandringham.

In 1874 the band were at Inverary Castle, Scotland playing for the Duke and Duchess of Argyll. In 1877 they again entertained Queen Victoria at Windsor Castle. Queen Victoria's patronage must have had an effect on the popularity of the Poland Street Ringers, whose travels also extended to Brighton (Sussex), Aylesbury (Buckinghamshire) and even more surprising they appeared at Rochdale (Lancashire) for three days in 1886, and Bury (Lancashire) in 1887 in the North of England, the home of long-set hand-bell ringing. The above mentioned are just the concerts about which we have evidence, but there must have been others and it is known that in the early 1880s they even toured the USA. As already mentioned at the end of one of their European concert tours they sold their then current set of bells to Fredsklockorna in Sweden who still ring in the mouths down off table style.

All reports speak in glowing terms of the powers and skill of these ringers and that the 5 men used a set of 131 bells cast by Whitechapel. Among the tunes they played were "The Village Bells - introducing chimes, psalms, chants and hymn tunes", "The Harmonious Blacksmith", "Rory O'Moore", "The College Hornpipe", "Scots Wha' Hae", "The Bluebells of Scotland" and "Home Sweet Home with variations". William Gordon of Stockport sold arrangements of all these pieces at the time and it is likely that his arrangements were those used by the Poland Street Ringers. They also included in their repertoire a hand-bell march from "Norma", and "Morceaux" from Mozart's 6th sonata in which 82 bells were used, so the standard of the band and the level of skill of the individual 5 ringers must have been very high.

By the kind courtesy of the Editor of the *British Workman*, I am enabled to gratify my readers with a representation of performers with hand-bells, which will illustrate how these are to be handled for tunes or changes. Mr. Duncan Miller, formerly of Poland Street, London, and his four musical friends have justly merited the epithet of "Royal," by which they are well known. The skill of these musical amateurs is most wonderful. They are all temperance men, engaged in business during the day; but by a wise employment of their leisure evening hours, they have acquired such remarkable musical skill as justly entitles them to the epithet by which they are now known since the 14th of August, 1870, the birthday of the Princess Beatrice, when Her Majesty honoured these diligent and persevering gentlemen by inviting them to perform at Osborne House.

Fig. 47: The Royal Polan Street Hand-bell Ringers - From Bells of the Church: a supplement to the Church Bells of Devon - The Revd H.T. Ellacombe 1872

Interestingly the history of Birstall St Saviour's Hand-bell Ringers (Yorkshire) says that Birstall purchased the bells of the former Royal Poland Street Hand-bell Ringers in 1901. Migration of hand-bell ringing industrial workers and miners in the late 1800s was responsible, I feel, for the introduction of hand-bell ringing to the industrial areas in the central belt of Scotland, where there were the same industries as in the North of England, those of coal, spinning and weaving. (In the same way that an English miner had taken hand-bell ringing in the 4 in hand/mouth down off table style to Kalgoorlie in Western Australia when he migrated there in search of gold, taking his hand-bells with him, and from there to Brookhampton in Western Australia where they are still used.)

Another Band I have mentioned several times in passing needs another mention here and that was Dr Barnardo's Famous Musical Boys, otherwise known as Dr Barnardo's Hand-bell Ringers who rang from sometime before 1887 to at least until 1943 when their bells were sold to a church in Peterborough. Dr Barnardo had founded his first orphage in Stepney, East London in 1870 after having been taken to a hiding place of hundreds of boys on a rooftop in Whitechapel. They were avoiding the orphan's then current alternative of "The Workhouse". Musical education was given a prominent and integral place in the Barnardo curriculum. As Dr Barnardo said in an article about his orphanage, Leopold House:

"Considerable attention is always paid to musical training at Leopold House. All my little Hand-bell Ringers, whose music is universally appreciated, are from this Home. Five or six of these little fellows, with their table of bells, have attended public meetings in connection with the Homes for several years past. To these were added in 1887 a party of half a dozen little Scotch Bagpipers. The latter, gay in their tartans, and tuneful in their lilts, have become at once the most attractive of all my wee musicians".

As time went on more instruments were added and the 'Musical Boys' increasingly accompanied the Deputation Secretaries (the fund-raisers of their day) on their tours throughout the country, a policy that was extended worldwide as their reputation for excellent musicianship grew. This included a trip to Australia and New Zealand in 1891/92. They even had a piece of music, "the Granville Waltz", especially written for them by their instructor and accompanist, Henry Aaron. Whilst digging around on the Internet I found the following write-up about one of their fund raising performances:

Fig. 48: Dr Barnardo's Musical Boys (courtesy Barnardos)

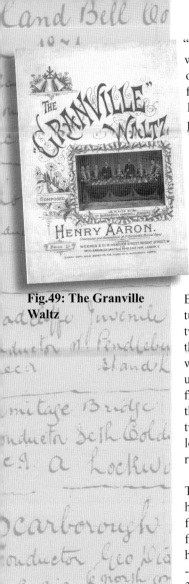

Fig.49: The Granville Waltz

"In 1912, a grand two day bazaar and exhibition in connection with Dr. Barnardo's Homes for boys was held in the grounds of Glasclune House, North Berwick, Scotland, kindly granted for the occasion by Dowager Lady Kinross. Within the house Dr. Barnardo's Musical Boys gave an excellent and varied performance with hand-bell, mandolin, ocarina, dulcimer fairy bell and other selections, including a musical march by the pipers in Highland dress. Later three flying machines from an Aerial Circus performed over the house and town." (Interestingly in 1944 Barnardo's purchased Glasclune firstly to be used as a girls home and then a home for both boys and girls in 1953. It remained as such until 1975 when it became a specialised home for emotionally difficult children. The house was burnt down in April 1979 the children all being safely rescued).

I have watched archived footage of "the Famous Barnardo's Boys" ringing on hand-bells, an Indonesian bamboo Angklung, tubular bells, straps of sleighbells, and a zylophone accompanied by two pianos. Three of the five hand-bell ringers clearly demonstrate the mouth down off table method of ringing, picking the bells up with the backs of their hands facing inwards then swinging them up and over to ring them on the downward sweep of the arc in one fluid movement. They make no attempt to damp their bells other than when they replace them on the table to pick up another. The two treble ringers ring their bells four in hand with the handles looped through each other in the traditional English style though ringing the upper bells inwards.

The Barnardo's Musical Boys were not the only 'waifs and strays' hand-bell band existing at the turn of the 19th/20th century. I have found reference to at least one other - the Refuge Handbell Ringers from the Strangeways Children's Shelter, Manchester, UK, and have seen a photograph of them (from the Manchester Archives - <http:www.flickr.com/photos/manchesterarchiveplus/6765645331/>) dating from 1904.

Several bands operated in Scotland during that time, including; Paisley, Dundee, Arisaig and at St Mary's Cathedral, Edinburgh. The band at Edinburgh used a set of 77 bells in the range 001C – 29C made by George Welch of London who was a successor to George Stockham. These bells were bought in 1884, although there was a set of hand-bells at St Mary's prior to this. Evidence of outside influences at St Mary's is documented in their minutes books which I read, for it appears that in 1879 a Mr Samuel Bennet came to St Mary's as the first tower bell instructor. Mr Bennet in fact came from Hyde, a Cheshire town where hand-bell ringing was very strong at the time. Mr Bennet may have started some tune ringing on the old bells before the 1884 bells were purchased. He returned to Hyde in 1883. In 1884 St Mary's tower minutes books record that a Mr John S B Archer of Cromwell Road, South Kensington was engaged as a member of the society in recognition of his abilities in "the practice of hand-bell music and otherwise". Mr Archer may have been a former member of the Royal Poland Street Hand-bell Ringers who were based in the area from which he came - South Kensington.

It would seem from all the information and records I have looked at, that none of the hand-bell bands of the central belt area of Scotland ever entered any contest at Belle Vue.

During the years 1871-72-73 when Shelley were debarred from competing at Belle Vue, the band were not idle, and performed in 63 concerts during these years.

The band also published a booklet containing a full list of engagements from the formation of the band in 1864 to Christmas 1873 with opinions of the press on the band, all of which must have raised the status of the band in the eyes of the public. The band's engagements included not only many local concerts, but also more prestigious engagements such as:

1871 - the Goole Regatta on July 10th and 11th; Grand Concert, the College, Ilkey, Yorkshire on November 21st
1872 - Pullan's New Music Hall, Bradford, Yorkshire on March 15th; Music Hall, Great Horton, Bradford on March 16th; Bazaar, St George's Hall, Bradford on April 17th;
1873 - Concert, Drill Hall, Macclesfield, Cheshire on January 31st and February 1st; Morgan's Popular Concerts, Mechanics' Hall, Bradford on March 1st and 3rd. On March 4th they performed at Morgan's Popular Concerts again - this time in the Merchanics' Institute, Leeds, Yorkshire. On August 9th they were again in Bradford for two performances at an art treasures exhibition. On August 16th again they were in Bradford for the Grand Fete at Lister Park. The Art Treasures Exhibition organisers must have been very impressed with the band as they engaged them for four more performances, on August 29th and September 20th.

Looking at Shelley's list of engagements one can see that at this time hand-bell ringing was regarded as popular entertainment. This is borne out by the type of music Shelley and probably all the other bands played at their concerts. As their 1873 booklet says: "Their programme consists of "Overtures, Selections, Choruses, Glees, Waltzes & Co and all the most popular music of the day"; so in fact Shelley were almost a "pop group".

Although Shelley were debarred from competing at Belle Vue at this time, there were other contests which Shelley entered.

In 1872 they won first prize at a contest at Elland, near Halifax. On the 2nd of August 1873 they took 3rd prize at another contest held at Blackley, near Halifax and on September 1st of the same year they gained 1st prize at a contest at Barrow-in-Furness, Cumberland.

Two months later there was an interesting contest at Heckmondwike (Yorkshire) Co-operative Hall. All the walls in the town and surrounding towns were thoroughly posted with placards announcing in a flaming and attractive type, that "The Hand-bell Contest was to take place on November 8th, 1873 at 5.30p.m." The poster also stated that "Each band was to ring a selection marching from the railway station to the Hall", about a quarter of a mile, the report of the event went on; "At this the public seemed somewhat excited and a feeling of interest was aroused with people who appeared taken by storm at the announcement of such an uncommon entertainment."

The ploy of arousing the public's interest by marching to a contest, was first used by our friend Enderby Jackson with brass bands, and had it not been for the fact that Jackson was in Australia at this time, I would have said that he was the organiser of the contest. The reporter actually does not say who the organiser was so the mystery remains.

This is the only example of marching hand-bell ringers during the 19th century I have so far encountered, although I know that there have been marching and processional hand-bell ringers during the 20th century, both in England and overseas. (The Mount Torrens Ringers from South Australia used to march annually in a veteran car parade through Birdwood in the Adelaide Hills during the 1980s, each ringer's music being pinned to the ringer in front. Ed.) When the time came for the hand-bell ringers to march, Shelley were the only band to do so! The other seven entrants did not bother. Some were busy elsewhere in the town. The Holmfirth Temperance Ringers held their final rehearsals at the Railway Hotel, (So much for temperance!). They then went to the Market Place where they played several tunes before going on to the Hall followed by a large concourse of people. Eventually the Hall was "Full to it's utmost capacity", so the organiser would, no doubt be well pleased despite there being only one marching band.

The bands who took part were - Almondbury, Batley Carr, Queensbury, Elland, Huddersfield, Brighouse, Holmfirth Temperance and Shelley, who took the first prize of £10. Each band were asked to play two selections. Shelley played "Grand Symphony in D" and the Overture "Zanetta" with 8 ringers. The second prize of £5 was taken by Holmfirth with 10 ringers who played the Overtures "Cenerentola" and Rossini's "Il Turco in

Italia", with Almondbury taking the £2.10s third prize with "Caliph of Bagdad" and "Martha". The fourth prize was £1 - Mozart's 12th Mass "Kyrie and Gloria" rendered by the Batley Carr Ringers. The event finished at about 10pm. It was suggested that a contest be held annually, but this never came to fruition.

Another of Shelley's achievements during the years they were debarred at Belle Vue was a concert with an orchestra at Manchester's Free Trade Hall, which was later to be burned down and replaced by the present Hall. The concert was held on the 10th January 1874. The event was Mr De Jong's Popular Concert. Mr De Jong, in fact gave numerous "Popular Concerts" at various centres of entertainment throughout the north of England, and did summer seasons at Blackpool, one of the newly emerging seaside resorts.

For Mr De Jong's concert, the Shelley Band did something which, as far as I know, has still not been attempted by any band of hand-bell ringers since. They played the Overture "Caliph of Bagdad" in conjunction with Mr De Jong's orchestral band of 75 players. Reports of the performance said that the effect of orchestra and ringers was "extraordinarily fine"

The Free Trade Hall, which was built on the site of the "Peterloo Massacre", held over 7,000 people, but it was sadly destroyed in an air raid during the 1939-45 war and was replaced by the present hall.

Shelley it would seem, did not enter the actual 1874 Belle Vue Contest held in September, preferring to challenge Glossop at Belle Vue in late December and therefore deciding the issue of who were the real champions. Shelley's other rivals, Holmfirth Temperance were making their own challenge for Shelley's crown, as they won first prize at Belle Vue in 1874 and again in 1875, when Shelley came second. At the 1875 contest there was another of the "Extra Prize" contests for the playing of Quadrilles from Alfred Cellier's "The Sultan of Mocha" but who won this extra prize is not mentioned in reports. Holmfirth, only about 3 miles from Shelley, were now in the position of only needing to win again in 1876 and they would be the "Champion Band" themselves.

In 1876 the day of the contest arrived. It always fell on the local holiday in September known as "Honley Feast Monday" to Huddersfield folk, but Holmfirth ringers got off to a bad start, when they lost their bells on the way to Belle Vue. Apparently a porter took the boxes of bells out of the van at a station on the way and left them on the platform. However the bells were recovered in time for Holmfirth to perform last.

99

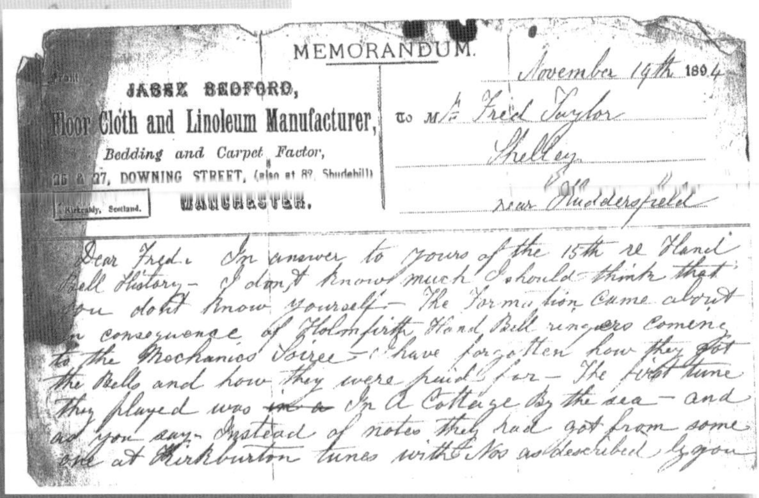

Fig. 50: (Above and below) Jabez Bedford's memo on the formation of Shelley

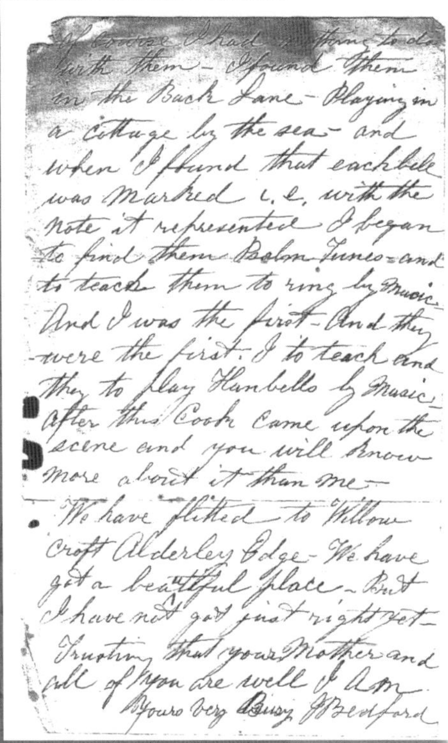

This cannot have helped their championship attempt as they could only manage fourth place, with rivals Shelley collecting the first prize of £15. Fourteen bands entered, but only eleven competed. It seems that it was usual for some of the bands to withdraw on the day of the contest. The Holmfirth Band apparently had had a direct bearing on the formation of the Shelley Ringers. Jabez Bedford of Shelley said, in a letter of 1894, that "The formation of a band of ringers in Shelley came about as a consequence of the Holmfirth Hand-bell Ringers giving a concert to the Mechanic's Soiree in Shelley, after which a band was formed in Shelley."

Shelley, with 10 ringers, rendered Beethoven's Symphony No 1 for which they must have put in hours of practice to ensure that this time there would be no "slip ups". The band's performance was considered by the adjudicators to be worthy of the highest commendation and "perhaps the most marvellous achievement in hand-bell ringing ever known". On the same day as the 1876 British Open, there was a "Supplementary Contest" wherein seven bands played the "War March of the Priests" from Felix Mendelssohn's "Athalie".

The result was 1st (£4.00) Park Lane, Keighley, (Conductor - Thomas Broadbent); 2nd (£3.00) Holmfirth Temperance, (James Charlesworth); 3rd (£2.00) Shelley, Ben Cooke; 4th (£1.00) Underbank United, Holmfirth, (James Moorhouse).

There were to be other successes for Shelley, as in 1877 they were again in first place at Belle Vue "British Open" and there was yet another "Extra Prize" contest in which all the bands performed an arrangement of the Overture to the "Marriage of Figaro" - Mozart, the piece being sent out to each band only 14 days before the contest. Shelley also won this prize. I wonder what the reaction

100

would be from today's bands on being given the piece to learn and perform in 14 days time!

The Shelley Band were now on target for a second "hat trick", which was something no band had previously achieved.

George Jennison, described as "the mind that developed Belle Vue" died in 1878, having been one of seven sons of the founder of Belle Vue, "Honest" John Jennison. George was succeeded as head of Belle Vue by his brother James, a post he held until 1917.

Until 1877, the bands competing at Belle Vue had always chosen their own test piece (apart from the extra prize contest), but eventually it became very difficult for bands to choose different, more difficult pieces and therefore a joint request on the part of the ringers for a suitable test piece to be used, was made to Jennison, and the following year a test piece was sent out by Jennison to each band on entering, about two months before the contest and the "own choice" was dropped.

The piece chosen in 1877 was Mozart's "Sonata No 5".

The set test made the contest easier for the adjudicators to judge, and it was also easier for the conductors who had to write out the music in individual parts for their ringers.

The entries came from Leesfield (lees); Park Lane, Keighley; Huddersfield Albert; Honley Temperance; Broseley, Shropshire; Dalton Victoria, Kirkheaton; Meltham Temperance; Penistone; Old Silkstone; Barnsley; Holmfirth Band of Hope; and Shelley. All of these competed with the exception of Holmfirth, who withdrew. There was a very large attendance of spectators for the contest. The winners were Shelley, achieving their second "hat trick". The judges considered the playing of the bands superior to that of previous years, saying the expression and execution of the first 3 prize winners was excellent. Also they said that the expression of the fourth placed band, Old Silkstone, was better than that of the bands placed above them.

Apparently Silkstones's execution had let them down, but they must have taken heed of the judges advice, as one year later they returned to win first prize in the contest. Also in 1877 there was another innovation by Jennison, a second contest for bands who had not taken a prize in the championship contest, and the winners of this second

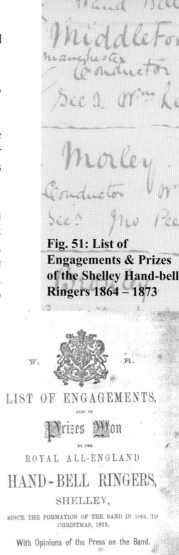

Fig. 51: List of Engagements & Prizes of the Shelley Hand-bell Ringers 1864 – 1873

contest were New Mills, Derbyshire with Honley Temperance 2nd and Park Lane, Keighley 3rd. This second contest was not repeated in later years, for which there seems no reason.

After Shelley's second hat trick, they were again debarred from competing - this time for two years instead of three as before, but about this time the amount of available work in Shelley declined considerably, and several of the members had to move away from Shelley to find employment, one of these men being the conductor Ben Cooke. Shelley's original band was partly broken up and sadly they were never to compete at Belle Vue again. The band had performed at over 400 concerts and they considered that their greatest reception had been at Mr De Jong's Concert at the Free Trade Hall, Manchester in 1874. Shelley's band appeared at 22 contests and won 15.5 first prizes.

The original ringers were- Fred Shaw, Artha Cook, Jesse Cook, Alfred Haigh, Elliot Kilner, Christopher Alderson (who had one of the bells placed inside his coffin), William Shaw and Ben Cooke, conductor. There were six others who joined the band who did good service, Charles Berry, George Haigh, Andrew Barden, George Henry Taylor, Henry Roberts and William Mosley.

The Mechanics' Institute Soiree, December 27th 1880 was the last time the old band played together, and the concert room was packed for the occasion with 500 people. During this evening there were speeches, poetry and songs. The Shelley Ringers played their rendition of "Kyrie and Gloria" by W.A. Mozart, their very first piece, "In My Cottage" with variations, the song "Matty's Sweetheart" by Arthur Sullivan, which was a popular song of the day, "Bluebells of Scotland" with variations. The last pieces to be played were Handel's "Hallelujah Chorus" and "God Save the Queen". The band was formed on August 24th, 1864 and dissolved on April 18th 1883, bringing to a close an era in which Shelley had played a leading role in the development of hand-bell ringing as we know it today. Shelley were the great innovators of their time bringing new methods, new music and changes in the way hand-bells were held and played, the effects of which can still be seen today in many parts of the world over 130 years later.

Among the Shelley papers I found the following poem which was written early in their history:

A History of the Shelley Hand-bell Ringers

Gentlemen and Ladies before I begin,
You mun grant me one favour, that's to make less din,
You shall have a short history of this jolly party,
Of Shelly Bell Ringers, and I think they're all hearty.

You shall have it very plain, the real old sort,
And when I've done my best, I expect you'll find fort;
So if you'll all for a while pay attention,
Their names to you I'll just try to mention.

There's Ben Cooke, Joe Addy, and Bill Shaw,
That's tidy ringers, but you must know;
That there is others in the lot,
Whose names you'll find I've not forgot.

Ben Booth, George Stevenson, and Jack Hoyle,
You'll not find better on British soil;
Barden Taylor, and Harry Berry,
You'll not find bad, no, not so very.

Joe Green, Joe Addy and Jess Cook,
Rather younger than the others look;
These three lads, though they are juniors,
You'll not find much behind their seniors.

So now that you've got every name,
We'll drink their health and wish them fame;
I hope they always will be jolly,
Love music, yet still keep from folly.

Not very long since they were no bells in Shelly,
But they got two a piece did Jack, Bill, and Berry;
Barden had same, and Kike, and Ben,
It just made a dozen, and then they were men.

These didn't do long, they wanted some more,
So they was two or three entered to raise their store;
They wor Cook and Stevenson and Taylor, his sen
And Jabe Bedford did a bit, and it made just ten,

They sent up to Lunnan, to get some new ones,
And Holmfirthers tried them to see if they were true ones
When they'd gotten all these they still could'nt do,
They wanted another ringer or two.

George Addy entered, Jess Cook, and Joe Green,
Joe Tunnacliffe did a bit but now's seldom seen;

They went on a while till they thought they were able,
To get some new books, besides a new table.

When they'd get'n these they thought they'd some store,
But like all ats doing weel, they wanted some more;
Not very long since, a month or two,
Instruments were all the talk, and nowt else would do.

I believe its impossible to be satisfied,
For these are all getten, they want some at beside;
I think they wor never such a set made,
Taking all things together for msuie and trade.

There is Weavers and farmers, beside all the ringing,
And bass players and fiddlers, and Barden, he spining,
There's Fluters and Singers they are ready for tramping,
There is Harry, Berry, -- he slubbin,-and Stevenson he stamping.

There is two or three more, I'm put all in reight,
There is Blacksmith, and Clogger to keep all straight;
If you'd been in Shelly this last six weeks,
You'd a seen such scenes as one cannot speak.

Some trying Candlesticks to see if they'd fit,
Some marching with opheclide he what a seet;
I'll bet some tried a tunnel to see if it would saand,
It caused such an allahballo taan raand.

But if yo wor in Shelley nah, at Sundays at morns,
You'd be reight fair tain we trams and saxhorns;
There is Berry with Tram, and Stevenson plays bass,
And Cook with D Flat with a Magenta face.

There is three cornopeans, Barden Kike, and Jess Cook,
And Booth wiring in with double bass at Woodnook;
There is Bill Shaw playing sax, and George Addy same,
Jack Hoyle and Joe Green will make players if they frame.

First day they were getten, thy were a regular shine,
Cook playing sax and Bill Shaw wor trying;
And then at neet thy changed the seen,
Taylor with fiddle, Berry playing and Green.

They took em to school on Tuesday at neet,
To have em tried raand to see if they wor reet,
They wor six or seven at they thought would pass;
And they wor three or four more wor'nt worth brass.

They've got em exchanged you must bear in mind,
And in a few week's more a new band you'll find;
I'll just give you now a programe of this lot,
I think they would nearly furnish a cot.

They've table and seats, and flocks for a bed,
Young women will be saying thy want to be wed;
They've two stands, a lamp, now I leave you to guess,
A new can, besides books and bags, what a mess.

They've pens, ink and paper that's been made by steam,
And a box to put books in to keep 'em all clean;
They've a tub 'at's on sale at will make a meal kist,
There is two at main things yet up a my list.

There is band and bells, now just pay attention,
And other small things too numerous to mention;
Folk may think and talk but they'll all be aght'
That says they've been getten with talking abaght.

For I think I may say and be within bands,
Taking all things together they've cost sixty paands;
So now my friends, I will conclude with this,
That music in its place is nout amiss.

Any band of today which uses duplicate bells and plays all the bells from a padded table can thank Shelley and the Belle Vue Contest which helped in the evolution of such developments. Some of Shelley's musical arrangements can still be heard today, as some of these were passed onto the bands of hand-bell ringers in the Huddersfield area, many of which were arranged by one of Shelley's treble ringers - Fred Shaw, born in Shelley in 1847. He was a miner by trade, and also a competent musician, "a clarinet player whose services were in great demand". He was a ringer with Shelley from the band's beginnings in 1864, and was the band's conductor for the last 3 years of its existence. Fred Shaw also arranged quite a number of popular airs and supplied Crosland Moor in the early 1900s with twenty-one arrangements, one of these, "Auld Lang Syne" with variations, being still in Crosland Moor's collection of music, and other bands' in the Huddersfield area today.

Fig. 52: Two Pages from Promotional Flyer for the Royal All- England Hand-bell Ringers, Shelley

ROYAL ALL-ENGLAND
HAND-BELL RINGERS,
SHELLEY.

The above Ringers refer with pride that they have been highly appreciated in all their previous Engagements in city and towns where they have appeared, and have won golden opinions from the press. They are now open for engagements to Concerts, Entertainments, Demonstrations, Festivals, Galas, Agricultural, Horticultural and Floral Shows, Exhibitions, Evening Parties, &c.

These unrivalled performers are nine in number, and have a Peal of 111 Handbells, having won Six Prizes at the Annual Contests, Belle Vue, Manchester. This feat never having been accomplished by any other Band of Ringers.

The First time they competed, in 1865, they won the Fourth Prize by the Overtures "Caliph of Bagdad" and "Tancredi."

In 1866, they won the Third Prize by the Overture to "Guillaume Tell," and a selection from "Faust."

In 1867, they won the Second Prize by the Overture to the "Occasional Oratorio," and a selection from the Opera of "Martha."

In 1868, they won the First Prize by the Overtures to the "Occasional Oratorio" and "L'Italiana in Algeria,"—Ten Bands competing.

In 1869, they won the First Prize by a selection from Haydn's "Surprise Sinfonia,"—Eighteen Bands competing.

In 1870, they won the First Prize by a selection from Haydn's "No. Grand Sinfonia,"—Fourteen Bands competing.

In a Handbell Ringing Contest at the Huddersfield Horticultural and Floral Society's Annual Exhibition, in 1869, they won the First Prize by the Overture to "Henry IV." and "L'Italiana in Algeria."

Their Programme consists of Overtures, Selections, Choruses, Glees, Waltzes, &c., and all the most popular music of the day. For terms. &c. apply to the Hon. Sec.

F. SHAW Shelley, near Huddersfield

10

Saturday and Monday Evenings' Entertainments.—"These have been marked by characteristics which, if not wholly new and novel, have not before been carried out on so extensive a scale in the Mechanics' Institution, or elsewhere in this town. We mean the appearance of the All-England Handbell Ringers. The company of ten, with a peal of 111 bells, did marvellous execution, and with the most difficult music; and the fact that they cannot have music stands, proves that they have arrived at great proficiency in their art. They commenced with the overture 'Caliph of Bagdad,' all the intricacies of which they dexterously mastered, and the sounds throughout the whole gamut showed that their singular instruments were sweet and full toned. In the waltz 'Queen of Beauty,' and the selection from Haydn's 'Grand Symphony,' they showed to equal advantage, although it was obvious that in these the bells could not produce any such effect as a band of wind and stringed instruments. In 'The Hallelujah Chorus,' which is so much better known, the effect was greater, and the repeated strokes more distinct and clear. In the Songs, including 'In My Cottage, &c.,' and 'The Star-spangled Banner,' they gave every satisfaction."—Leeds Times, Saturday, March 8th, 1873.

Harrogate Horticultural and Floral Fete, Chalybeate Spa Grounds.—"The principal novelty of the day was the performance of the Shelley Handbell Ringers, which formed a most pleasing variety to the music of the splendid Leeds Model Band, which again played in the grounds. The concert in the evening was very much better attended, and every thing passed off most spiritedly. Miss Blanche Cole was encored in her first song, 'Bid me discourse,' But perhaps the most popular, as well as most novel feature of the concert was the performance of the Shelley Handbell Ringers, who played Handel's 'Hallelujah Chorus,' the American 'Star-spangled Banner,' and Haydn's 'Grand Symphony.' The way in which these eight performers manipulate 111 bells, is really extraordinary, and the rich flow of sweet sounds, in perfect time and harmony is really marvellous."—Harrogate Advertiser, Saturday, August 30th, 1873.

Entertainment at Dewsbury.—"One of the most successful amateur entertainments it has been our pleasure to witness took place on Saturday night, in the Primitive Methodist school-room, Dewsbury, under the auspices of the Ravensthorpe British Workman, and the committee of this admirable institution will have no cause to regret having got up an entertainment out of their own district, for there was a very large attendance to hear the performance. When we say that the Royal All-England Handbell Ringers were present, and performed selections of music, our readers—at least those of our readers who have heard these clever handbell ringers—will at once come to the conclusion that the audience had a rich treat, and their conjectures will be correct. The overture, 'Occasional Oratorio' (Handel), by the ringers, was warmly received, and the next the band gave was 'The humming bird,' an imitation of a musical box,' which obtained the encomiums of the assembly. The next selection was from the opera of 'Martha,' and its execution was a splendid performance, every note being brought out with distinctness, and some of the passages with a softness that was pleasing to the ear, and the bell ringers, when they left the stage, were loudly applauded. The overture in the second part of the entertainment, entitled, 'Zanetta,' created much enthusiasm, as also did 'Constancel's' waltz, by Masson. 'Hark, the Curfew's Solemn Sound' (Attwood) followed, and the bell ringers finished their part in the entertainment by rendering the 'Hallelujah Chorus' in a manner as only the Shelley Handbell Ringers can perform it. At the conclusion the musicians were loudly cheered.—Dewsbury Reporter, Saturday, November 8th, 1873.

In 1913 Fred Shaw was interviewed by the Huddersfield Examiner in the village of Blackburn, near Sheffield, where he was living at the time. Unfortunately Mr Shaw was lying in a critical condition, as a result of an accident at Rainforth Colliery near Rotherham, where he was manager. It seems that while inspecting the workings he was struck by some falling timber which broke his back.

Whilst reading the report of the interview it occurred to me that the band spirit and camaraderie needed for the work of the miners is also reflected in Hand-bell ringing - both activities requiring the same qualities. It is also interesting to note how many hand-bell bands were established in mining areas. For instance hand-bell ringers from Annesley and Newstead Byron (Nottinghamshire) competed at Belle Vue in 1910. Annesley is about 20 miles from Sheffield, the nearest other recognised centre for hand-bell ringing, but there was a colliery at Annesley, which could explain why hand-bell ringing was in the village - it travelled with the miners and when they moved they took their traditions with them. Another miner's band was formed in the 1890s at Lepton, near Huddersfield.

A report of 1907 in the Huddersfield Examiner said "Nearly all the players came from Yorkshire mining towns and villages,'All collier lads' as an admirer from Barnsley put it".

In 1907, Shelley's Fred Shaw was the adjudicator of a hand-bell ringing contest held at Linthwaite near Huddersfield, and his remarks made at the contest give us a clue as to the way in which Shelley arranged their music. In his remarks he advised bands "Not to take piano pieces, but write from the orchestral parts, first and second violins" and "Not attempt runs on the big bass bells such as G size 25, or G in the bottom line in F clef". Mr Shaw went on "This bell is about eight inches in diameter, weigh 6lb, length about 15 ins. Compute how far this has to travel to get a stroke. This octave is too heavy in tone for quick passages. From G11 to G18 is the best part to put in some good harmony and runs. Bands should only show score copies of what they intend to play" signed FRED SHAW, adjudicator. By this time - 1907 - there had been more changes, some of which of course, Mr Shaw disapproved, but more of these later.

A further indication of Shelley's method of arranging the music came from my friend late John Terry. Mr Terry was taught hand-bell ringing in the late 1920s by Kaye Cooke, who was the son of Ben Cooke, the conductor of Shelley. Mr Terry said the method of writing out the music taught to him by Kaye Cooke was as follows; (but from a piano arrangement): "The notes in the treble clef are written in the treble book and the notes up to about top F in the bass clef are written in the bass book. All the notes from bass F to say G on the second line in the treble clef are written in the tenor book".

It was not only the ringing methods and music that had changed and advanced as a result of the contests, changes to the bells themselves had taken place. Bands were aiming at a higher standard of music required a higher standard of bell with improved handling capabilities and a better tone.

The stiffened handles must have been introduced when bells started to be flicked from a table in the new Yorkshire style of ringing, which came in with Shelley. This new technique was carried out much more skilfully and easily with stiffened handles, especially when playing more advanced music that had been made possible by the new ringing style.

The clapper mountings were now made with a screw thread which was tapped through the top of the bell into the argent onto which the handle was riveted, thus making it much easier to remove the clapper by simply unscrewing it whereas before this improvement, the handle had to be removed before the clapper and mounting could be taken out. More care was taken about the choice of felt with which to cover the strikers on the tenor and bass bells, which produced a better and more controlled sound.

There was also a gradual improvement in the tone of the bells themselves and tone was all important to the bands that competed at the Belle Vue Contest, as 10 marks out of 100 were given for tone.

Bell founders like James Shaw and Son of Bradford, Yorkshire were quick to perceive the fact that points were awarded for tone in competitions, and used this in their efforts to persuade bands to buy their bells and further pointed out that bands using their bells had won prizes.

In their catalogue of 1887 Shaw's were proclaimed to be "The largest manufacturers of musical bells in the world" and then added more importantly "PRIZE MEDALS AWARDED SPECIAL MENTION BY JURORS FOR GREAT PURITY OF TONE". An advertisement for Shaw's bells in 1908 said "GOLD AND SILVER MEDALS AWARDED".

Mears and Stainbank, now the Whitechapel Bell Foundry, London were also attempting to catch the buyer's eye when they advertised in the Yorkshire Hand-bell Ringers Association's Contest Programme of 1912, "At the annual contest held at Belle Vue, Manchester, the FIRST PRIZE for the last fourteen years in succession has been awarded to bands using our bells and on twelve of these occasions the SECOND PRIZE also"

Bands were keen to keep their bells in prime condition as any bell out of tune, used in playing the Belle Vue Competition piece, was treated as a wrong note by the adjudicator and a point was deducted each time that bell was rung.

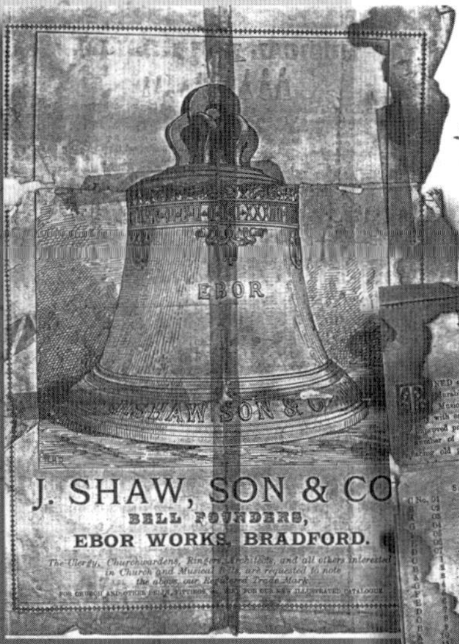

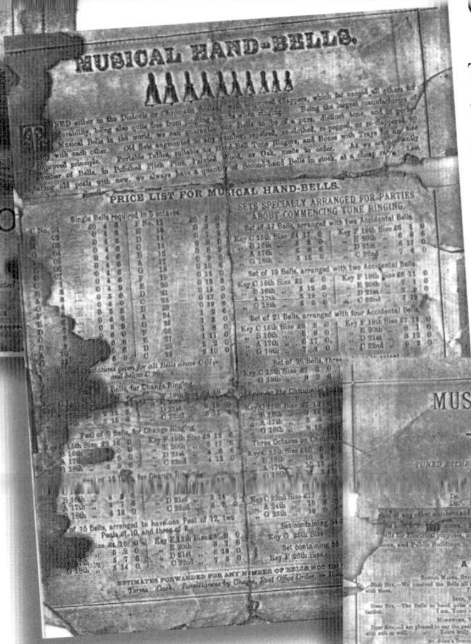

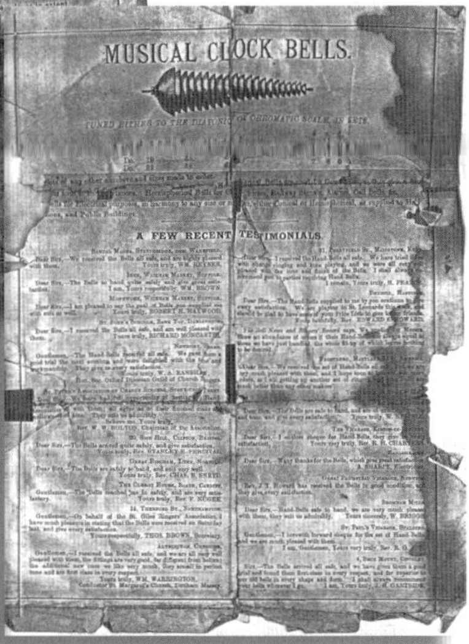

Fig. 53: J. Shaw - Hand-bell Price List – C.1887
Mr Shaw had long practical experience and genuine enthusiasm for bell ringing, and set himself to work out the many delicate and difficult problems connected with the production of a perfect set of bells.

The fact that bands wanted to have the best set of bells possible for contests had a knock-on effect which was beneficial to people in areas wishing to start a new band of hand-bell ringers, in that when it was felt that a set of bells could no longer be kept up to contest standard, it was sold off or traded in and a new set bought. This resulted in a healthy second-hand trade in hand-bells.

This thriving second hand market enabled new bands to start up with a limited amount of capital expenditure. Prices were low as there were plenty of second-hand bells about. Shaw's Bell Foundry of Bradford would take old bells in part exchange from bands purchasing new sets and declared in their 1887 catalogue - "As we are constantly replacing old peals with new, we always have a quantity of second-hand bells in stock, at a cheap rate". Imagine present foundries making such a claim in their catalogues today!

J Shaw, Son and Company was established in 1848 by James Shaw, who set up his bell foundry at the Ebor Works, Lyndhurst Street, off Leeds Road, Bradford in Yorkshire.

All types of bells, bell machinery, fittings and accessories including tables, boxes and bell mattresses, were all manufactured at the Ebor Works, as was every process in bell making, from the casting of the bell metal to the finished product. Shaws made bells for churches, schools, factories, ships, fire stations, clocks, cattle, and of course they made musical hand-bells. The highest award of a gold medal at the Royal Yorkshire Jubilee Exhibition in 1887 was won by Shaws for their bells.

So there was a gradual improvement in the quality of bells, which was to continue into the twentieth century.

The fact that Shaw's Bell Foundry existed in the centre of the area in which hand bell ringing was a fast growing developing art form, was an influential factor which aided the popularity of the movement, as the foundry was, with the coming of the railways, within easy reach of towns in the North of England.

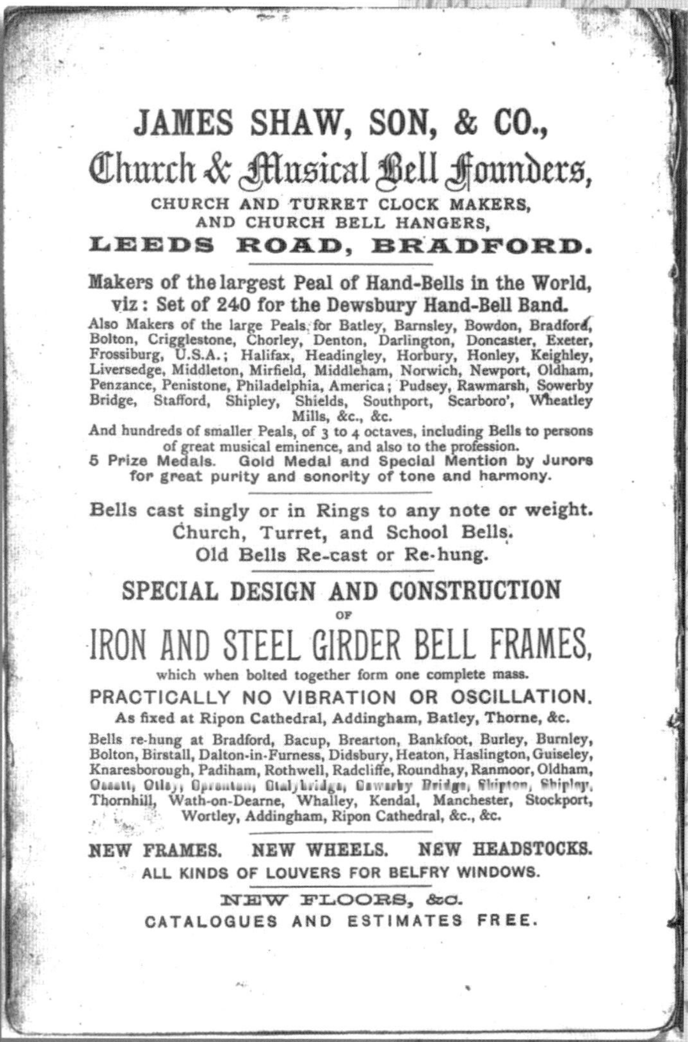

JAMES SHAW, SON, & CO.,

Church & Musical Bell Founders,

CHURCH AND TURRET CLOCK MAKERS,
AND CHURCH BELL HANGERS,

LEEDS ROAD, BRADFORD.

Makers of the largest Peal of Hand-Bells in the World, viz: Set of 240 for the Dewsbury Hand-Bell Band.

Also Makers of the large Peals for Batley, Barnsley, Bowdon, Bradford, Bolton, Crigglestone, Chorley, Denton, Darlington, Doncaster, Exeter, Frossiburg, U.S.A.; Halifax, Headingley, Horbury, Honley, Keighley, Liversedge, Middleton, Mirfield, Middleham, Norwich, Newport, Oldham, Penzance, Penistone, Philadelphia, America; Pudsey, Rawmarsh, Sowerby Bridge, Stafford, Shipley, Shields, Southport, Scarboro', Wheatley Mills, &c., &c.

And hundreds of smaller Peals, of 3 to 4 octaves, including Bells to persons of great musical eminence, and also to the profession.

5 Prize Medals. Gold Medal and Special Mention by Jurors for great purity and sonority of tone and harmony.

Bells cast singly or in Rings to any note or weight.
Church, Turret, and School Bells.
Old Bells Re-cast or Re-hung.

SPECIAL DESIGN AND CONSTRUCTION
OF
IRON AND STEEL GIRDER BELL FRAMES,
which when bolted together form one complete mass.

PRACTICALLY NO VIBRATION OR OSCILLATION.
As fixed at Ripon Cathedral, Addingham, Batley, Thorne, &c.

Bells re-hung at Bradford, Bacup, Brearton, Bankfoot, Burley, Burnley, Bolton, Birstall, Dalton-in-Furness, Didsbury, Heaton, Haslington, Guiseley, Knaresborough, Padiham, Rothwell, Radcliffe, Roundhay, Ranmoor, Oldham, Ossett, Otley, [illegible], Stalybridge, Sowerby Bridge, Skipton, Shipley, Thornhill, Wath-on-Dearne, Whalley, Kendal, Manchester, Stockport, Wortley, Addingham, Ripon Cathedral, &c., &c.

NEW FRAMES. NEW WHEELS. NEW HEADSTOCKS.
ALL KINDS OF LOUVERS FOR BELFRY WINDOWS.

NEW FLOORS, &c.
CATALOGUES AND ESTIMATES FREE.

Fig. 54: J. Shaw Advertisment of 1890

By 1870 the railways facilitated transport to and from Shaw's Foundry allowing bells of all kinds to be sent to almost any part of the country by rail. Shaw's bells became very popular everywhere, especially in the North of England where the large bands of contest ringers were developing. A few smaller sets of up to 50 bells were even exported to America, where they are still in use today.

There were a number of other founders who supplied hand-bells to the Northern contest ringers, although they had a smaller share of the market than Shaws or Mears of Whitechapel.

George Stockham had his foundry in London and supplied Almondbury with a set in 1873 and also Honley Temperance won the British Open at Belle Vue in 1882 using a 5 chromatic octave

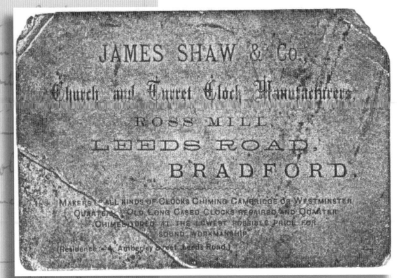

**Fig. 55: J. Shaw
Business card**

set of 90 Stockham, which were cast in 1876 and ranged from 01C to 28D. The set included 31 duplicates. Keighley Parish Church Hand-bell Ringers also used Stockham bells about this time, as did Oldham, Lancashire, who purchased a set in 1875 and Horbury, Yorkshire, who bought a set of 111 in 1876.

Stockham also sold many bells in the South of England, so it would seem his bells were popular in the 1870s and 80s. Stockham used the pattern of a previous founder William Dunn of Bloomsbury, London, who cast a set of bells down to 26F for St Peter's Collegiate Church, Wolverhampton, amongst others. After Stockham retired, his patterns went to George Welch, who cast a large set of bells for Hayfield in Cheshire with which the band entered the British Open at Belle Vue in 1890.

Referring back to the question of when the Shaw bell foundry closed, this matter has been subject to much speculation amongst bell historians. The company advertised in a contest programme in 1912, which gives no hint of any decline.

I have even made contact with descendants of the Shaw family who can throw no light on the matter.

One theory is that the foundry was bombed during one of the German Zeppelin raids during the first world war. Another theory I have heard is that the foundry caught fire and their patterns, which were made of white metal, were destroyed. Either of these theories could be correct or was it a combination of the two? As there was no reason as far as I can see that the company should have ceased trading otherwise.

Shaw bells seemed to be the most popular hand-bells in use during the mid 1800s until the 1890s when Mears and Stainbank of the Whitechapel Bell Foundry started to become more popular. The use of Shaw bells was made popular by prize winning bands such as Dewsbury and Liversedge Albert and Horbury, all bands of the West Riding of Yorkshire.

Dewsbury had figured in the Belle Vue entry list as early as 1857 when they competed with 12 ringers who used a set of 52 bells. This band was in and out of the prizes (mostly in) for the following ten years. Dewsbury's conductor in 1862 was Thomas Wood whose address was shown in Jennison's ledgers as the Three Measures Arms, which was probably their headquarters at the time.

In 1866 the town of Dewsbury almost had a double celebration, when the town's brass band won first prize in the British Open Brass Band Contest, and the hand-bell ringers just missing out by coming second in the hand-bell contest, both contests being held at Belle Vue. Although the Dewsbury Hand-bell Ringers had several conductors during these years, they put in a final appearance at Belle Vue in 1870, but were not amongst the prize winners, after which this particular band went into recess. Dewsbury were to rise again, successfully winning first prize at Belle Vue in 1883. Their rise to fame began in 1877 when Mr William Senior, landlord of the Wakefield Arms in Back Wilton Street (a pub no longer in existence) purchased a second-hand set of 56 bells from the Batley Hand-bell Ringers, probably from a fellow landlord at the George Hotel where the band was last based and did reasonably well up to about 1870. With these bells Mr Senior formed a band, the original members being John Garforth, Sam Wolstenholme, Tom Hellawell, Walter Idle, Walter Senior (the landlord's 13 year old son), Scott Auty (who was later to conduct Dewsbury Moor St Johns at Belle Vue in 1899), John Blackburn, Danny Firth, Mr Haley, Ned Wormald and John Henry Dixon. 5 of these were also tower bell ringers.

The first few years in the life of the band were uneventful, but the ringers laid a good foundation for the future by assiduous practising under the conductorship of a Mr Birch.

The landlord's son Walter Senior, a member of the Dewsbury Band, was interviewed by the "Dewsbury District News" years later in the 1930s when some of his remarks are revealing.

"We had some good times together. When we first started with only 56 bells we found some pieces a bit difficult to play, and when we were fast anywhere for a note we had to throw the bells from one to the other to keep the melody going. It was hard work

SHAW, SON & Co.,
BELL FOUNDERS,
Lyndhurst Street, Bradford.
MUSICAL HAND-BELLS A SPECIALITY.
Prize Medals Awarded. Special Mention by Jurors for great purity of tone.

TUBULAR BELLS.
In any Key, Diatonic or Chromatic Scale. For all purposes.

TAPPING BELLS.
Arranged for Change Ringing, or for Tune Playing in any Key Suitable Stands made in oak, &c., or polished brass.

MUSICAL CLOCK BELLS.
Tuned either to the Diatonic or Chromatic Scale, in sets. Sets of any numbers or sizes made to order.
Hemispherical Bells of all sizes and weight. Large Hemispherical Bells are used for Cemeteries, as they give a deep sonorous tone at short distances. Hemispherical Bells for Clock Chimes, Railway Signals, Alarms, Call Bells, &c.
Bells for Electrical purposes, in harmony to any size or number, either Conical or Hemispherical, as supplied to halls, mansions, and public buildings.

SHAW, SON & Co.,
Leeds-rd., BRADFORD, Yorks.

This advertisement was included in the programme for the Yorkshire Handbell Ringers' Association's seventh annual Tune Ringing Contest at Sunny Vale Gardens, Hipperholme, on Saturday, May 7, 1910. Admission was 6d.; seats were 3d. extra.

Fig. 56: Shaw & Son Advertisment - 1910

Fig. 57: Dewsbury Hand-bell Ringers about 1897. The conductor with his baton in the centre is Arthur Fearnsides (Image Courtesy of the Kirklees Image Archive: www. kirkleesimages.org.uk)

when we had to change bells like that".

The technique of throwing bells to one another seemed to be employed by all the bands with small sets of bells without duplicates, and must have been quite spectacular, and would have been used by most bands until Shelley developed the use of duplicates in 1866.

Following Mr Birch, William Lee took over the conductorship of the Dewsbury Ringers. Mr Lee had conducted the Batley Ringers to 2nd place at Belle Vue in 1868 and Batley Carr to 3rd place in 1872. In 1883 the Dewsbury Ringers shot to fame by winning the first prize at Belle Vue after years of being unplaced in the contest.

The test pieces for the 1883 contest, music from Auber's "Mansaniello" and Verdi's "La Traviata" were arranged by Henry Parker, who was one of a long family line of managers at Belle Vue, which started in 1862 with William Etherington Parker. The Parkers always did the spadework at Belle Vue and the family was to continue to do so right into the 1920s. Henry Parker also arranged music from Donizetti's "Lucrezia Borgia" and "Rondo in C" by Hugo Wolf, in 1882.

Dewsbury were now to go on to become one of the three most influential bands that were to shape the further development of hand-bell ringing over the next seventeen years and into the twentieth century, the others being Liversedge Albert, and Almondbury United, all Yorkshire bands.

Dewsbury won first prize at Belle Vue in 1883 with their conductor William Lee, and again in 1888 and 1890 with their new conductor Arthur Fearnsides, (William Lee had by this time been appointed conductor of Mirfield) after which the band had a lean spell with three years out of the prizes, however winning again at Belle Vue in 1894 and 1897. (A tragic event concerning Mr Lee was recorded in an Dewsbury Reporter article in 1939. "Mr. William Lee, conductor of Dewsbury and Mirfield Ringers was also solo trombone player in Dewsbury Old (Brass) band. He had been out with the band in the afternoon of Boxing Bay, and when he came home for his dinner the meat was just cooked. He cut off a piece of meat with a knife and put it in his mouth. The meat got fast in his throat and in a few minutes he was choked to death." A concert was subsequently organised of all the Dewsbury Bands (hand-bell and brass) for the benefit of his widow.)

Before the 1888 contest, bands throughout the country put in every moment they could spare at practice and in the Dewsbury and Liversedge camps excitement was at fever pitch.

One day the Dewsbury band went to listen to Liversedge practising the test pieces, the overture to Auber's "Crown Diamonds" and the "Cuckoo Polka", - dispelling the present day myth that the old contesting bands would not allow visiting by other competing bands!

The opening of Crown Diamonds was a slow movement and Dewsbury's conductor Arthur Fearnsides had his band practising it according to this tempo. But the Dewsbury Ringers were alarmed on listening to Liversedge to find them playing the same movement at a much more rapid tempo. The Dewsbury Ringers thought their new conductor must have made a mistake and appealed to Mr Fearnsides to have the piece played faster. He would not, even though all the band were against him, and told the ringers flatly: "If you go to Belle Vue with me you will have to do as I want to do" - this ultimatum was accepted with some bitterness. The day of the contest came and hearing all the bands playing "Crown Diamonds" at the fast tempo adopted by Liversedge, one of the Dewsbury Ringers remarked significantly "We're either a long way off or we've won it".

"We've won it" shouted Mr Fearnsides, who no doubt looked all his band in the eye with a wry smile.

After this success, the band bought, in 1889, a new set of 186 bells "Such as rejoiced the hearts of hand-bell ringers of the old

Fig. 58: One of the Silver Medalions awarded to Members of the Dewsbury band (this one to R. Hodgson) when they won the Yorkshire Challenge Cup in 1911 (courtesy Colin Armitage)

school" wrote the band's chronicler. The bells were purchased from James Shaw of Bradford, and while other bands were now turning to Mears bells from Whitechapel, Dewsbury stayed with Shaws and continued to do so throughout their history. Perhaps they preferred the tone of Shaw bells rather than the more mellow Whitechapel bells - bells of the "Old school" perhaps.

The Dewsbury Band, flushed with their British Open success and new bells, were on their mettle, and in 1890 were so confident of winning first prize at Belle Vue again they were openly boasting that it was as good as won long before the contest day. The test piece was the overture from Suppé's "Poet and Peasant" opera and a melody from "Songs without words" by Mendelssohn. The Dewsbury band won first prize. However they were not to win first prize again after their previous brilliant achievements and the band began to lose ground. The reason given was the dropping out of older members and their replacement by younger men who took time to mature. Despite this they still managed creditable results in the British Open at Belle Vue, taking 3rd prize in 1908, 4th in 1909 and 1910, and 5th in 1911. They also had success in local contests, winning the Yorkshire Shield in Section Two of the Yorkshire Hand-bell Ringers Association Championship in 1909. Section Two was limited to bands using no more than 49 bells and no duplicates.

After this success, Dewsbury were promoted to Section One in 1910 and won the title of Yorkshire Champions in 1911, winning the Yorkshire Challenge Cup gaining 125 marks, four points clear of the second placed band Crosland Moor Public. The test piece was the overture from Mozart's "Don Giovanni".

This was a very good win for Dewsbury's young players as the competition of the early twentieth century was keen and was of a higher standard than the 1890s, and the style of playing had changed, so bands had to adapt to these changes. The Dewsbury band comprised: A Heeley, A Young, M Senior, A North, M Willoughby, C Broadley, R Hodgson, W Hellawell, W Young and A Woodhouse, the conductor was Arthur Fearnsides who had been with the band since 1888.

During research for this book I received information that a former member of the Dewsbury Band, Arthur Young lived at a house in Bradford Road, Batley Carr and had a photo. I went to the address, knocked on the door and a woman (who turned out to be Mr Young's granddaughter) answered. I asked if Mr Young lived there, "Well he did do" was the reply, "why, did you want him?" she asked. When I told her of my research she said "Oh, I think you'd better come in, he died in 1939". However I did get a photo of her grandfather standing by himself, at the side of the

Yorkshire Challenge Shield in 1911. The amazing thing about my visit was that the family had occupied the house since the 1890s and was moving to another district some 10 miles away on the day of my visit, so had I been one day later I would have missed them, probably forever.

The Dewsbury Hand-bell Ringers were a pub band and held rehearsals in various pubs in the town, the main one being the now demolished Foresters Arms in Wakefield Road. The Dewsbury bells still exist and are protected by a trust deed, but they narrowly escaped extinction in 1918. The Dewsbury Ringers had been so depleted when members were "Called up" for military service in 1916 that the organisation folded up, and the bells were sold to a local scrap merchant Harry Darnborough. However Mr Darnborough thought it a shame that such good bells should be wasted and to his eternal credit, he offered them to a number of hand-bell ringing enthusiasts at Earlsheaton (a village on the edge of Dewsbury), who formed themselves into a band after the war in 1919. One of the band, Willie Hellawell had been a member of the pre-war band, the others members were: James Crowther, Arthur Senior, Hubert Talbert, Joe Hewitt, Hemingway Dransfield, Aden Terry and Lawrence Terry. As Mr Hellawell had been with the Dewsbury band before (as had his father before him) and therefore would have been familiar with the procedure, he was appointed conductor and secretary of the new band who made their headquarters at the Park Hotel. Again it can be seen that it was an experienced ringer who ensured the continuity of the tradition, a thought well worth remembering by younger ringers in today's bands, as the day may come when the continuity of their bands' tradition rests with them alone.

The Earlsheaton Band gave concerts all around the district but did not enter any contest of which I am aware. This band carried on until the early 1930s, after which an effort was made by Earlsheaton Parochial Council to build a band among boys of the Sunday School, but nothing much came of it. With the bells still residing in Dewsbury there is always a chance of a revival of the town's great hand-bell tradition if someone took an interest.

Dewsbury's great rival was Almondbury United. Almondbury is a village near Huddersfield and has a long and glorious tradition of hand-bell ringing, embracing seven first prize wins and a championship in the British Open and two tours of the USA. The band must be considered one of the great ringing bands of all time.

The ancient village of Almondbury had a tradition of change ringing from the early 1800s, but not until 1873 were the first band of tune ringers formed, amongst whom were several change ringers

115

and men who had a slight knowledge of music. The success of Shelley, Dalton and Holmfirth ringers (all nearby villages) in competition must have been an influence on these men in deciding to take up tune ringing.

It was in the early part of 1873 when the band at Almondbury was formed with a set of 81 bells purchased by public subscription from G Stockham. Rehearsals were held in a room over a local butcher's shop. The first conductor was Chas Broadbent and by September 1873 the band were ready to enter the British Open Championship at Belle Vue, in which they gained third prize, although on the list of prize winners the name of Huddersfield appears. This was because the band entered as "Almondbury, near Huddersfield" and lack of space would not allow such a long title, so the words "Almondbury near" were dropped from the printed list of prize winners.

At one period a Mr A Hirst was said to be "tutor", Henry Pogson who had arranged some of Holmfirth's music for the first Belle Vue competition back in 1855, and most probably conducted them at the contest, took the baton at Almondbury's final rehearsals. Mr Pogson also conducted a number of other bands at Belle Vue in the 1860s including Stocksbridge (1861) near Sheffield, and Meltham also in 1861, Armitage Bridge (1869), but was mostly associated with Holmfirth Temperance and was possibly their resident conductor. Mr Pogson was a well known figure in the world of music making in the Huddersfield area at the time.

One of the delights of researching a subject that has strong connections with one's home area is that information can appear from the most unexpected sources. In 1986 I was reading the Huddersfield Examiner and who should be featured but none other than Henry Pogson, along with his photograph, up to then I had no idea of what he looked like or any details other than his hand-bell

Huddersfield Daily Examiner, Monday, December 1, 1986

Singing his praises

AFTER over 130 years, due credit can at last be given to the unsung hero of Pratty Flowers, otherwise known as The Holmfirth Anthem.

Ever since it was first published in the 1850s the name on the sheet music has attributed the arrangement solely to Joe Perkin, then the conductor of Holmfirth Choral Society.

But, as Miscellany revealed last week, the arrangement was a dual effort between Perkin and another choir member, Henry Pogson.

When Perkin asked Pogson to put his name to the music as well the bashful Pogson is said to have replied: "You can have all the glory, I am content to be of service."

But this photograph puts the record straight.

It is provided by Mrs Audrey Jones, of Douglas Avenue, Dalton, who is a great grand daughter of Henry Pogson.

The picture shows the three men behind Pratty Flowers soon after the composition had been completed.

On the left is Mr C S Floyd, then president of the Holmfirth Choral Society, who commissioned the tune and to whom the music was dedicated. In the middle is Joe Perkin, the choir's conductor, and on the right, holding the original copy of Pratty Flowers, is Henry Pogson.

Said Mrs Jones: "The part he played in arranging Pratty Flowers has always been known in the family, but he was a quiet person who got pushed into the background."

Monday Miscellany — Compiled by Andrew Flynn

activities. In fact he was the co-writer of the popular local song "Pratty Flowers", otherwise known as the Holmfirth Anthem, which ever since its publication in the 1850s has been attributed to Joe Perkin, then the conductor of Holmfirth Choral Society (an organisation which still flourishes). The story being that when Perkin asked Pogson to put his name to the music as well, the bashful Pogson is said to have replied: "You can have all the glory, I am content to be of service".

But back to Almondbury, reports say that in the 1870s the band became "disorganised", but in the early part of 1883 a concert was given in Almondbury by the relatively famous Dalton Victoria hand-bell ringers after which a desire spread amongst the young lads of the village to form a band of ringers.

A start was made using the old Stockham bells, which reports again say "the disorganised band had left in trust", leaving bells bought by public subscription in trust for future use is a common practice in the North of England, no more so than Yorkshire and Cheshire, where I have found bells still kept in trust, after over sixty years of inactivity. Fortunately many of these sets of bells are now being brought back into use again.

A ringer from the old band, Fred Littlewood was appointed their conductor. Several rooms were used for rehearsals, but the room which was in the main their headquarters, was Long Croft, which they were to use for many years.

By 1884 the old Stockham bells had become worn and only fit for practice. The Shelley band had been dissolved a few years earlier and negotiations were held with the former secretary of Shelley, Fred Shaw, who had possession of Shelley's 145 bells, and Almondbury purchased them from him on Good Friday 1884. After a winter's practice, the band thought they had become real exponents of hand-bell music, and after being formed for less than twelve months they made their first appearance on a contest platform. This was at a contest held at Kew Gardens, Southport on July 5th 1884, one of the few contests to be held outside Belle Vue. This contest attracted some of the best talent of the day. The Almondbury ringers were confident they would win a prize, as they had done a large amount of practice.

Each band had to play its own selection for one contest, but for a special contest each band had to perform a piece especially arranged by Fred Shaw "In my Cottage" with five variations, for a prize of £5, a large amount in those far off days. This prize was won by Almondbury and they came second in the other contest, playing Haydn's Symphony No. 1.

117

Fig. 60: A Fine Body of Men - Almondbury United 1900, taken after their championship win. L to R back: H. Stead, J.W. Bothroyd, Ben Lodge (conductor), J. Stansfield, J. Stead. L to R front: J.H. Godward, F. Stead, H. Harrison, J.W. Dawson, A. Jenkinson, J.A. North. It was said that J.W. Bothroyd rang the bass 29C (C3) as if it were a treble. He was a stone mason!

Encouraged by this achievement they entered for the British Open Contest at Belle Vue in the following September. With their early success they gained many followers who travelled from the village with them to Belle Vue to hear and see how they would fare against the famous bands of the day, Liversedge, Dewsbury, Huddersfield, Dalton and the other well established organisations with considerable experience of the contesting world. Almondbury were awarded third prize and to crown their first year's work they appeared at a contest in Derbyshire at Glossop Drill Hall in the following month and took fourth prize with the overture to Boldieu's "Caliph of Bagdad", and Haydn's Symphony No. 1.

This was then the beginning of what would become, after years of hard and determined effort, the first "Champion Band" since the days of Shelley.

Early in 1885 their conductor Fred Littlewood, under whom they had made such a splendid entry in the contesting arena, retired. His place was taken by Ben Lodge, also known as a "Brass Band Man" as they are called in Yorkshire, and it was he that was to guide them to the top.

Ben was successful right from the start and took them to the British Open at Belle Vue, at which they won first prize and a gold medal.

118

They went on to win first prize again in 1886, which meant that in 1887 they would now be competing for the Championship for the three wins in a row.

In April of 1887 the Almondbury hand-bell ringers received an invitation to play before the Prince and Princess of Wales, but turned down the offer, the reason given that they had to wear evening dress and this they did not have.

In September 1887, interest in Almondbury village was at fever pitch for the British Open. Surely Almondbury had done enough to win? Even one of the Liversedge Ringers thought so! But it was not to be. Undaunted, Liversedge went on to win, with Almondbury coming second. During the next ten years Liversedge remained one of Almondbury's greatest rivals, with successes for both bands, but in 1900 the Almondbury United Hand-bell Ringers secured their third win in a row at the Belle Vue British Open to become the Champions of Great Britain, the first band to do so since Shelley, and the first band to do so since the sending of set test pieces to each band began in 1878. For this achievement they received a gold medal and silver championship medals for each member of the band. The test piece was from Lortzing's opera "Czar and Zimmerman".

During all this time many concert engagements were undertaken in Huddersfield and surrounding Pennine villages and towns and further afield including Manchester Botanical Gardens and Free Trade Hall, Birmingham Town Hall twice, Newcastle Exhibition for five days, Sheffield, Nantwich, Leamington, Ashton-under-Lyne, Stockport, Mexborough, Rochdale (three times), Leeds, Stalybridge, South Kirby, Saddleworth. The list was endless.

In becoming Champion Band the men from Almondbury were now barred from competing at Belle Vue for one year (the Jennison's were not to repeat the mistake of the 1870s when they barred Shelley for three years).

Almondbury were then given something to do for a year or so, when just after the British Open in late September they received an offer proposing that the Band or part of it should tour North America.

After negotiations with a London agent, an agreement for a band of six players to travel was reached with the promoters in the USA, the Redpath Lyceum Bureau of Boston, which promoted the education of the working classes (See Appendix 7 for a copy of the contract). It had been hoped that the full band would be able to go, but the Bureau said their concert parties did not exceed twelve people, which had to include other entertainers. Before the

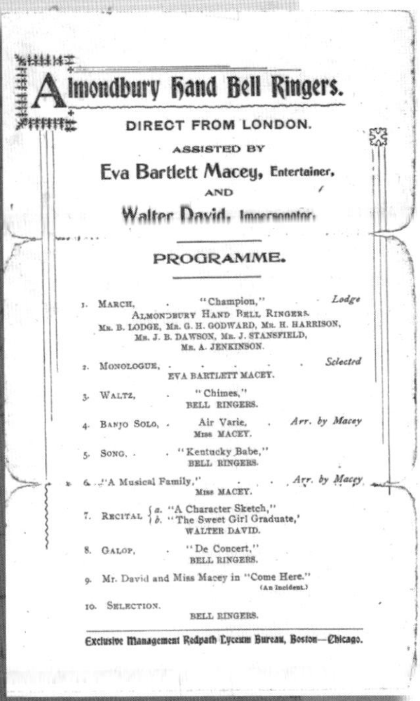

Almondbury Hand Bell Ringers.

DIRECT FROM LONDON.

ASSISTED BY

Eva Bartlett Macey, Entertainer,

AND

Walter David, Impersonator.

PROGRAMME.

1. MARCH, . . "Champion," . Lodge
   ALMONDBURY HAND BELL RINGERS.
   MR. B. LODGE, MR. G. H. GODWARD, MR. H. HARRISON,
   MR. J. B. DAWSON, MR. J. STANSFIELD,
   MR. A. JENKINSON.

2. MONOLOGUE, ... Selected
   EVA BARTLETT MACEY.

3. WALTZ, . . "Chimes,"
   BELL RINGERS.

4. BANJO SOLO, . Air Varie, . Arr. by Macey
   MISS MACEY.

5. SONG, . . "Kentucky Babe,"
   BELL RINGERS.

6. "A Musical Family," . . Arr. by Macey
   MISS MACEY.

7. RECITAL { a. "A Character Sketch,"
             { b. "The Sweet Girl Graduate,"
   WALTER DAVID.

8. GALOP, . . "De Concert,"
   BELL RINGERS.

9. Mr. David and Miss Macey in "Come Here."
   (An Incident.)

10. SELECTION. . . .
    BELL RINGERS.

Exclusive Management Redpath Lyceum Bureau, Boston—Chicago.

Fig. 61: Example Programme for the Almondbury Hand-bell Ringers 1901 USA Tour

departure of the band, a complimentary dinner was held for the band in the Woolpack Inn. Speeches were made by two local doctors, a local councillor, the chairman, and the vicar who admitted he hadn't even heard the ringers! Speakers almost ran out of superlatives to describe the band, and one of the doctors gave advice on how not to be seasick!

The band of six took all 163 bells with them. The tour was all expenses paid and they left Huddersfield Station on Thursday, September 26th, 1901 for Liverpool where they sailed in the steamship "New England" for Boston. On the Wednesday they gave a concert at sea. (See Appendix 7 for a copy of the programme)

The band gave 200 concerts, travelling 17,000 miles by railway and visited 26 States, for which the band was paid £36.00 per week, quite a sizable sum in 1901, and at some venues a collection was also taken.

The six who went on the first tour of the USA and their occupations were: George Henry Godward, a beamer; Harry Harrison, a tenterer; Joshua Haigh Dawson, a Mason; Joe Stansfield, a Healder; Albert Jenkinson, a Tinner and Ben Lodge whose occupation was not mentioned. Ben Lodge was the band's conductor, but went as a ringer, as one of the six.

One of the six, George Henry Godward, who along with F Stead had previously been a member of the Dalton Hand-bell Ringers who were based at Kirkheaton, wrote a diary of the trip, which is an interesting first hand account of the tour with its glories and hardships. The diary is far too long for it to be included here in its entirety, but interesting excerpts included an account of the first of their concerts in Boston, of which he writes; "We are giving our first concert in Boston tonight before all the critics, we are introduced to the Shipp Brothers Hand-bell Ringers mandolinists and banjoists. The lady that is travelling with us has travelled with them, we get encored for every piece and they want more" writes Mr Godward. In fact the Shipp Brothers went under the name of the Imperial Bell Ringers (not to be confused with a later band of Yorkshire ringers of the same name). The U.S.A. Imperial Ringers were formed by William Shipp of Dorchester, Massachusetts and were five men who also played harp, guitars, banjos and piano. They must have been amazed at Almondbury's high standard of ringing.

From letters of commendation of Almondbury (Set out in Appendix 7) sent to the organisers of the tour, The Redpath Lyceum Bureau, we can get an idea of the difference in the standard between

American and English hand-bell ringers of 1901. A letter from Edgar T Farrill of Lebanon N. H, "The bell ringers are a success from the word go. We have listened to the Swiss and Spaulding bell ringers, but the Almondbury company is the finest thus far". Another letter from John W Lee of Plymouth, Mass. said "Nothing like their work has been heard here and unless they return, will not be for many a season". The above was printed by the Bureau in an advertising pamphlet entitled "What they say about the Almondbury Hand-bell Ringers". The Swiss Ringers may have been the Lancashire Ringers from Oldham, England, although equally could have been any number of American teams like the Spaulding Ringers - four men and three women who were formed in 1866 by a John Spaulding as the "Spaulding Brothers' Swiss Bell Ringers". They were also vocalists, violinists, harpists and comedians and performed all of the above as well as hand-bells! The Spaulding Brothers' Swiss Bell Ringers toured the United States and Canada extensively, and at a fourth of July concert in the city of Boston in 1867 they performed to more than 9,000 persons in the music hall. But it would seem their standard of performance was not up to that of Almondbury's.

From engravings I have seen of American bands of the nineteenth century it would appear that all the bands played the bells in the Yorkshire method of pre-1866, with all the bells standing on end on the table to be simply picked up and rung openly when required, which by English standards, at least for competition ringing, was 40 years out of date.

When in Greensboro, North Carolina, the Almondbury Ringers encountered racial discrimination for the first time, something unheard of in their native England. In fact black people would have been very rare in England at this time. However Mr Godward writes, "here we see for the first time two separate waiting rooms, one for white and one for colored people". The Almondbury men were taken to the local tobacco sales by the young men of the Y.M.C.A. - Mr Godward writes; "It was a sight we may never see again, there are 200 heaps of tobacco leaves and the auctioneer walks up and down the rows and sounds like as if he were singing a song when he is asking for bids".

In Charlotte, North Carolina, the Almondbury men walked out to the cotton fields, speaking with some of the black people, who were picking cotton. The workers told them they received very poor wages, which kept them on the poverty line.

The Almondbury Ringers gave a concert in the Y.M.C.A. to a full house.

After arriving at Fredericksburg, Virginia, at 1p.m. the Almondbury men went to dinner and then to the Opera House, where they would be performing in the evening, to check that the bells had arrived, when there was a cry of "Fire!" – A steamer by the wharf, which was just about to start for Baltimore had caught fire. Mr Godward takes up the story; "One of the deckhands after lighting his pipe, throws the match down and it ignites something on the low deck and they cannot put it out, it burns the vessel to the water edge". Mr Godward adds with a touch of Yorkshire humour; "It was a fine sight and would have been had it been dark". The name of the vessel was the Richmond, which was on the paddle box, which was the final part of the boat to fall into the river. Next day, the Almondbury party started out for Frederick, 114 miles away, stopping off in Washington to see the White House.

A few days later they were performing in Avondale, Pennsylvania on November 20th, 1901. The hall where they performed was packed with people standing in the aisles and with seats on the platform. The band was given a good reception, having to respond twice to one selection and encored for all the others. Mr Godward writes with all the confidence of a Yorkshire man when he added; "There are another party of Swiss hand-bell ringers advertised for the 23rd, but we think it will go hard with them where we have been".

The "Swiss Hand-bell Ringers" could have been one of any number of American bands, who used the name "Swiss" as a norm after Barnum had brought over the Lancashire hand-bell ringers from Oldham to the U.S.A. in 1844 and called them "Swiss" as Barnum thought it sounded better. Although the Swiss Hand-bell Ringers mentioned by Mr Godward could have been the Todmorden Hand-bell Ringers, also from Yorkshire, who toured the U.S.A. in 1889 and 1901. As I have already said, Todmorden were not a competition band and I have found no reference to them ever competing. It would seem from an engraving, which came to light recently that the band used the pre 1867 system of "Four-in-hand" for the trebles and the rest of the bells standing on end on the table, which in 1901 in the North of England would have been very old fashioned. However this may have been an old engraving because amongst their music were well used William Gordon arrangements which could only have been played using the Shelley off table style for all bells.. Their bells and music were revived by Philip and Sylvia Bedford when they bought the Todmorden bells in 1975. The Todmorden church needed a new roof and Sylvia and Philip Bedford, who were about to emigrate to Australia, needed another set of bells. They were leaving their new 4 ½ octaves of Petit and Fritsen hand-bells with the UK Midlands hand-bell band they had founded five years earlier, "The Windscape Ringers" (who still ring today - 2011 as "Hartshill Windscape"). The Todmorden bells comprised a set of 6 chromatic octaves from 29C

[C3], plus a duplicate further two chromatic octaves (from 18G[G4]) totalling 98 bells which the Bedfords sold to the Australian band, "the John Donne Ringers" (whom they had taught to ring in the Shelley off table style during their first three years of residence in Adelaide, South Australia before returning to England for a year, for their "$1000 cure"). Sadly the John Donne Ringers have been in recess for many years now, but perhaps will restart one day using the original Todmorden bells and music

But let us return to our Almondbury friends. In Vineland, Philadelphia, the band felt really welcome, as Mr Godward's brother lived four miles outside the town, where they had "Yorkshire pudding made in America" as Mr Godward put it. His brother introduced them to lots of Yorkshire people who had settled in the area. Mr Godward writes "in the afternoon we go to the club and hear a few Old Country glees sung by Yorkshire people - it sounds like being at home again".

The 12th December saw the band arrive in New York, where they were to stay until the New Year at the Meyer's Hotel at Hoboken. On their first day in New York they gave a concert six miles away, "In a distant part of the town" at Hasbrook Hall College. The concert was a good one, after which the band had their first holiday since the start of their tour, after a total of 54 concerts in almost as many days, which is an exhausting schedule by any standards, but in those days men were men and used to hard work. The holiday was far from most people's idea of a holiday, for a start the Meyer's, where they were staying, was a German hotel and the band were not satisfied with the food "the menu is like pig's meat" wrote Mr Godward.

After giving two small concerts on the 14th of December, the band had no bookings and seemed to spend most of their time repairing boxes and tables with a few rehearsals in between and walking around New York. Boxes and tables seemed to be constantly being broken, "They have no mercy on baggage here" wrote Mr Godward in a reference to the treatment handed out to the luggage by the railways.

When Todmorden's Handbell Ringers ruled the world!

IN 1889, the Todmorden Handbell Ringers were hailed as "the best organisation of their kind in the British Empire" by an American newspaper.

The Boston Daily Globe printed this statement during the Handbell Ringers' tour of the United States and Canada.

An old poster advertising this tour was featured recently in the 'Todmorden News'.

Providing answers

It had been bought several years ago by the owner of Fagin's antique shop, Mrs Linda McCormick, who was interested to know more about the performers.

Mrs Nellie Crabtree, aged 92, of Todmorden has duly provided some answers.

Mr John Mitton, who appears second from the left on the poster, although she was not born when the Ringers left for their American tour, she can recall many stories about the group.

Four of the five members were Mr Mitton, Mr Holt Chadwick, Mr H. F. Postlethwaite and Mr Fred Dennett, the great uncle of Coun Eric Dennett.

Despite the adulation of the critics, the Ringers' tour of America was ill-fated. They were let down by an inefficient agent who only found venues and potential audiences where the Ringers had arranged to visit Todmorden due to lack of money.

Hopes dashed

A venture which began with high hopes of fame and fortune ended in bitter disappointment, although this did not put an end to the musical ambitions of the Ringers.

Dennett, Postlethwaite and Chadwick formed the nucleus of the Ringers. Fred Dennett played village bells, fairy bells and musical glasses and after the American tour he added the autoharp to his instrumental repertoire.

H. F. Postlethwaite performed solos on the musical glasses and also played duets with Holt Chadwick on the handbells.

Holt Chadwick, who was John Mitton's brother-in-law, at one time kept the New Inn before becoming the landlord of the Fountain Inn.

Besides being a handbell ringer, he was an accomplished vocalist and sang both humorous songs and ballads.

Mr John Mitton was a weaver at Waterside Mill when he became involved with the Handbell Ringers.

Church connections

This connection with the Fielden brothers links the Ringers with the Unitarian Church. There is some suggestion that the handbells belonged to the Fieldens and it was in the Church and Sunday School that the Ringers practised.

Mr Joseph Haigh Crossley, the manager of Todmorden Industrial Co-operative Society, appeared with the Ringers at Tadcaster Town Hall in March 1889. The programme simply says he performed solo on the piano.

Whether this was just a one-off performance or whether Mr Crossley is the fifth man in the poster is not certain.

The Ringers' repertoire was quite varied. Opening with a march, the programme would include a number of airs — English, Irish or Scottish — interspersed with songs from Holt Chadwick and solos, duets and trios on particular sets of bells. A great favourite was a selection from Verdi's 'Il Travatore' and the programme would usually conclude with "Auld Lang Syne." A noticeable addition after the American tour was "Home Sweet Home".

Encores!

Programmes indicate that the Ringers performed with great success at the Crystal Palace, Liverpool, Manchester, Leeds and York.

The Boston Globe says: "The Todmorden Bellringers have made a great hit, and nightly are encored on almost every selection they play. There are five of them and they come from Todmorden, in the north country, England. They are Handbell ringers and they swing liquid melody throughout the upper register.

"By the deft manipulation of numerous Bells, varying in weight from eight and a half pounds to two and a half ounces, they produce not only the solemn peals of grand Cathedral notes, but the tintinabu-lations of fancied fairy chimes. Church bells, sleigh bells, fire bells wedding bells, funeral bells, door bells, dinner bells, breakfast bells, supper bells, horse-car bells.

Like a farmer!

"They play "Il Travatore" with ease, and popular tunes well from their mystic metal as melifiously as syrup drips from a maple tree. On a table covered with green baize, and draped with velvet, are placed the necessary bells to supply the proper notes. At a preconcerted signal, the Todmordians grasp the leather straps and big bells, smaller bells and tiny bells are uplifted, sawyed in the air, and the big melody is sent travelling on its long journey through the exhibition building.

"We might say wrung out of them, for as the bells stand on the cloth they are verily dumb bells and the manner in which the music is evoked is not unlike the manner in which a farmer wrings the neck of a chicken."

Best in the world: Todmorden's Handbell Ringers

123

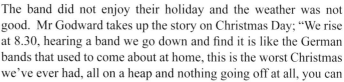

Fig. 63: Almondbury United in 1935, Harold Godward is sitting front centre.

The band did not enjoy their holiday and the weather was not good. Mr Godward takes up the story on Christmas Day; "We rise at 8.30, hearing a band we go down and find it is like the German bands that used to come about at home, this is the worst Christmas we've ever had, all on a heap and nothing going off at all, you can imagine what it is like being amongst foreigners and cannot tell a word that is spoken and people coming in and no one that you know to speak to, only yourselves".

The New Year saw the band on the move again, on the second part of their tour, travelling 371 miles from New York to Rochester near Lake Ontario on the night sleeper train on January 4th, after giving a concert at the local music hall. The band were disappointed not to be able to visit Niagara Falls the next day, their rest day, as another concert had been added on that day.

On the 13th of January they performed at the Y.M.C.A. auditorium, Grand Rapids, Michigan, where they had their largest audience so far, with the hall full of between 3 to 4,000 people, "It looks like a sea of faces" remarked Mr Godward.

When at Keobuk, Iowa, the band walked down to the Mississippi River, which was frozen, the ice being 11 inches thick, Mr Godward said, "There are men cutting it with ploughs and horses into squares and storing it" which to men from Huddersfield must have seemed a strange sight.

In St Joseph, Missouri, a local band of hand-bell ringers, the Dunbar Troupe, a male quartet as well as singers, went to Almondbury's concert at the Opera House where the Americans examined Almondbury's bells. The Dunbar Troupe's own bells were from Taylors, "but not so good as Almondbury's" they said.
February 22nd: the band was playing at Fredonia, Kansas to an audience "like rowdies". "They stamp, shout and whistle like lunatics", exclaimed Mr Godward who went on to say "The hotel here is nice and very clean, kept by a giantess over 6 feet high and built in proportion".

Two days later they played in Eldorado Springs, Missouri, where the performance was at the Court House. Straight after the concert the band had to set out in 2 buggies to drive to Walker to make a

train connection, a distance of 14 miles across the Prairies at night!
"The roads being like ploughed fields. Some time we are one foot
deep in mire, the next the same in snow. It takes us from 10.10pm
until 2.20am to reach Walker". The band's connecting train was
due in at 6am!

On the 1st of March they performed in a mining city with the warm
sounding name of Cheer. Out of its 4,000 inhabitants 1,000 were
English.
Four days later and the band were at Cedar Rapids, Iowa, where
a matinee was given for the inmates of the local jail. At the jail
they were told the story of one of the prisoners who was caught
through his love of music. He had murdered a man, then escaped
to the wilds of the Klondyke, a favourite retreat for criminals
in those days, where he continued with his love for playing the
violin. Detectives sent word to see if there were a newcomer to
the Klondyke who played the violin. The reply was "yes" and
that was how he was found and caught and was now leader of the
prisoner band.

In Cincinnati, Ohio, March 18th, the band performed in the Music
Hall to 4,500 people. "The hall," said Mr Godward, "was 192 feet
long, 122 feet wide and 62 feet high", which must have made the
Almondbury men think Huddersfield Town Hall was like a village
hut.

Early April and the men were back in New York for their last few
concerts before boarding the ship for home on May 7th.

On their return to Huddersfield on May 15th, members of the band
must have felt glad to be back in good old-fashioned England,
but even in Huddersfield the world was changing. When the
men returned they found that the tramways in the town had been
electrified during their absence.

The band was given a grand reception on their arrival. The Lindley
Brass Band played, and with the same friends who had given them
a send off 9 months earlier, sang "Home Sweet Home" and "Auld
Lang Syne", thus providing a suitable ending to the tour, which, for
the men from Almondbury, must have seemed like visiting another
planet. The diarist Mr Godward died at the age of 42 in 1904.

The following October Almondbury made a second tour of the
U.S.A. and Canada, but this was a shorter trip with two different
ringers in the line up. Returning to Huddersfield in February 1903
gave the band ample time to return to the contest stage of Belle
Vue.

It is often taken for granted that a successful band has a group of ringers who have remained together for a long time and have welded themselves into a musical unit, but analysis of the Almondbury Bands that went to the United States and Canada reveals the fact that, of the twelve young lads who commenced in 1883, only six were still with the band at the time of the tours, and leads one to the conclusion that it can often be determination and tradition, built around a dynamic conductor/leader with a nucleus of loyal ringers, perhaps in conjunction with a well-run committee, which produces and keeps a band at the top.

Almondbury United were a public subscription band, and since 1883, used five different sets of bells.

The G Stockham bells	1883	81 bells
Shelley bells	1884	145 bells
Jubilee set	1887	163 bells
Diamond Jubilee set	1897	163 bells
Last new set (Mears)	1903	145 bells

Replacing old bells with new ones to keep up the standard of the band of course, provided a ready supply of second hand bells for the use of new bands, which helped the movement.

Almondbury's main rivals in the 1880s and 90s were Dewsbury and Liversedge Albert. The Liversedge Albert Hand-bell Ringers were, not only the main rivals to Almondbury, but also to Dewsbury, only a stone's throw away - three miles down the road. Liversedge was a very successful Yorkshire band. "Formed in 1876", said the local newspaper, the Cleckheaton Guardian in 1888, "the band started with 25 bells and by 1888 were using a set of 147 bells."

Liversedge was at the centre of an area of Yorkshire which had towns and villages with long traditions of hand-bell ringing, such as Batley, Dewsbury and Heckmondwike (only half a mile away). These towns all had bands at least as early as 1860, so there would have been no shortage of advice and people with the knowledge of how to form and run a band. How much easier it was to form a band when such people were available locally. Also a point to remember is that these people, at that time, had years of local accumulated experience on which to draw. Most ringers involved in the British hand-bell revival during the 1960s and 70s had very little experience on which to draw, especially for the off table style, apart from the few bands on either side of the Pennines, where a handful of pre-war ringers still existed.

The Liversedge Ringers, as already mentioned, were formed in 1876, and in 1883 Ben Cooke, the former ringer and conductor of Shelley came to live in Birstall, a village about two miles from Liversedge. Shortage of work in Shelley was the reason given for the move. The Liversedge Ringers realised the potential of this man and duly went to see him the day after he arrived in Birstall to offer him the job of becoming their conductor. Birstall itself had a set of hand-bell ringers and Ben Cooke was engaged as conductor there also.

Born in 1840 Ben Cooke was regarded as the finest hand-bell ringer in the country in the 1880s, and many said he was the greatest of all time. Ben got on well with Liversedge and carried on with them where he had left off at Shelley. When Ben took them to Belle Vue in 1883 they were the worst band that competed, but in 1884 they had been really put into shape and won first prize and were placed second in the following two years and first again in 1887. They were hardly out of the prize list at Belle Vue up to 1893 taking first prize in 1889-91-92. In 1894 doctors had to amputate one of Ben Cooke's legs and he was never in good health again,

which seemed to reflect on Liversedge's performance as they were to have a lean time at Belle Vue after 1893 when they came second, only just missing out on being Champion Band of three wins in a row, with rivals Almondbury United taking first prize. Ben Cooke died in April 1897 age 57 and the hand-bell movement mourned the loss of one of its greatest sons. Ben Cooke's record with Liversedge was five first prizes, three seconds and one fifth, and with Birstall his record was one third, two fourths and two fifths.

Just who conducted Liversedge in 1897 and 1898 is at present a mystery, but in 1899 they were conducted by Ben Cooke's son Kaye to third place at Belle Vue. Kaye had always followed his father to the practices and watched the ringing with interest and actually played with Birstall in 1896 under his father's conductorship. The test piece for the British Open that year was "Orphee aux Enfers" (Offenbach). Birstall had worked up the first movement when one of the members, the first tenor, met with an accident, so Ben Cooke called in his son Kaye, who had three bells in the first movement to play, but had 17 bells before he got through the second movement.

Fig. 65: Crowther Street, Stockport by L.S. Lowry 1930. William Gordon operated from 20 Crowther St. (courtesy estate of LS Lowry & Smabs Sputzer)

Fig. 66: William Gordon's final shop, Celtic Street, Stockport (photo Fawcett)

Years after, in an interview, Kaye said the movement in which he had only three bells was the most monotonous of the lot.

A contemporary of Ben Cooke was William Gordon of Stockport, Cheshire, where Gordon kept a shop from which he sold his music - first at 64 Lower Hillgates, then at 20 Crowther Street, and finally an off-licence (liquor store and groceries) in Celtic Street off Webb Lane. Interestingly L.S. Lowry made Crowther Street famous in his 1930s painting.

William Gordon was a highly skilled and dedicated arranger of music for hand-bells and would have known Ben Cooke well. In fact, Gordon adjudicated at a contest at the Drill Hall, Glossop, Derbyshire on Saturday, November 8th 1884, at which Cooke conducted Liversedge to take the first prize of £8.00. 2nd were Dalton Victoria (£5.00) (conductor S. Stead); 3rd St Thomas' Hyde (£3.00) (conductor T. Ashworth); and 4th Almondbury United (£2.00) (conductor F. Littlewood). The other bands who took part were; Howard Brothers, Glossop; Hayfield, Brookfield and Accrington. The test was an own choice of two selections. The report of the contest published in the "Bell News and Ringers Record" said William Gordon's awards were "received by the large audience with great acclamation and evidently gave general satisfaction".

William Gordon, who suffered from sciatica in his later years, was very clever in the way he made his arrangements for hand-bells. He realised that the ringers' hands should fall naturally onto the bells being rung without any awkward movement and that, especially with the tenor and bass ringers, greater precision would be achieved if their notes formed a frequently repeated rhythmical pattern. To achieve this he was quite prepared to move bells around the table and also to move fingers to a nearby group of bells. He made no distinction between treble, tenor and bass ringers, but treated the ringers as a complete band, the ringer of the highest notes being ringer No 1. If however the higher notes only occurred a few times in the tune, he was quite prepared to give these to other ringers, where they were idle at the time or to other ringers where striking one or more of these notes would help to maintain their rhythmical pattern.

Like other hand-bell music arrangers of his time (eg Hyde's arranger, and Daniel Scholefield mentioned earlier), Gordon always arranged the music for the minimum number of ringers, and if he could eliminate a ringer by moving some bells to other parts of the table, he did so. This meant that quite complicated arrangements could be rung by small bands of ringers.

There is always a problem with individual parts for each ringer showing only their own notes. Ringers can get lost, and since they do not have a complete score, it is difficult for them to find their place again. This often happens when there is a change of speed, rhythm, orr time signature in which the ringer does not participate, or when a ringer has several bars rest.Gordon eliminated this problem to some extent by using rests, and by using an indicator of the melody or some other prominent feature of the tune, whichever was the easiest for the ringer to follow. Orchestras also have this problem but it is overcome through practice and a good conductor.

William Gordon's system found favour with the hundreds of smaller bands with straight sets (i.e. no duplicate bells), that were springing up all over the North of England in the 1870s, 80s and 90s in the wake of the British Open at Belle Vue. Many of the ringers from these small non-competitive bands visited Belle Vue each year to look on, and pick up a tip or two, and no doubt William Gordon was there selling his music to them. Gordon arranged music for bands of all sizes, from arrangements for a solo ringer, to arrangements for six ringers on four octaves of bells. He also offered extra bass parts down to 25G, and arrangements for mandolin and bells. Much of Gordon's music was the music of the country ringers, harking back to the early days of Belle Vue, for his arrangements included glees, country dances, polkas, quadrilles and schottische's, but he had excellent arrangements of classical music too, such as "Der Freischütz" by Weber, the Hallelujah Chorus by Handel, and the overture from Don Giovanni by Mozart.

Gordon's earlier arrangements were written for use with the pre-Yorkshire method, before 1867, of trebles "4 in hand" and the rest of the bells standing on their ends, mouth downwards, but his later arrangements were for bells all laid out on their sides on the table.

Some of Gordon's well known arrangements, still in use today are: "The Ashgrove", "March of the Men of Harlech", "The Blue Bells of Scotland" and "Home Sweet Home", all with variations, Home Sweet Home having quite a tricky bass part, which he delegated to one bass ringer, although today many bands share these notes out between two ringers, which rather spoils the visual effect created with just one ringer playing the bass.

Gordon's published music has been found in all parts of England,

Fig. 67: William Gordon, from a Supplement to Bell News C.1895 (courtesy Keith Gordon, grandson)

a few examples being Todmorden (Yorkshire), Moorside (Lancashire), Norbury (Stockport, Cheshire), Wakefield (Yorkshire) and London, and also overseas where emigrating ringers took their bells and music, e.g. Brookhampton in Western Australia and Maryborough in Queensland, Australia.

Gordon's system, or his music, being arranged for "straight sets" was not generally used by any of the big competitive bands who rang on "long sets" with duplicate and triplicate bells. Their conductors wrote their own arrangements to suit the particular configuration of their band's "long set", but there were exceptions. At Belle Vue in 1883 Hyde came in 2nd place and Cheddleton came 4th using copies of the music especially adapted for them by Gordon. A further point of interest about this contest is that Cheddleton had only eight players with only forty nine bells. One year later Gordon himself was one of the adjudicators at Belle Vue, one of the few hand-bell ringers ever to do so. He was described as a "Professor of Music". The other adjudicator that year coincidentally was also a hand-bell ringer, Mr C J Havert, conductor of the Silver Chimes Carillonneurs, London, and also a ringer with the Royal Hand-bell Ringers, Poland Street, London.

William Gordon himself conducted at Belle Vue in the British Open of 1887 taking Whitefield, near Manchester, to third place. The Whitefield Band had only just been formed, although there had been hand-bell ringers in Whitefield before. (In 1857 they entered the Belle Vue Contest). They had only just received their bells, but even so William Gordon did well enough with them, as the band were only two points behind the second placed band, Almondbury. However Whitefield seem to have been a short lived band as I can find no mention of them after their fourth place win at Belle Vue in 1888. Whitefield's main claim to fame is the fact that they were one of the few bands who possessed a low 32G (G2) bell, which now resides along with the rest of the bells in a museum in the town of Bury, Lancashire. Another band which had a 32G is Woodroyd (Honley) Yorkshire, and one of their sets were donated to the William Hartley Memorial Fund and are available for loan to Handbell Ringers of Great Britain members who want to extend or develop their ringing skills. (The other set is still in Honley and hopefully will one day be used again.)

In 1890 and 1891 William Gordon conducted Tintwistle (Christ Church), Cheshire to fifth prize on each occasion, although I think he may have conducted Tintwistle up to 1901 when the church organist Charles Bray took over as resident conductor, but Gordon probably conducted the band after this on odd occasions up to 1915.

The line up and results of the 1891 British Open make interesting reading, and was: First Liversedge Albert (Ben Cooke conductor) 125 marks; second Almondbury United (Ben Lodge) 117 marks; third Woodroyd Victoria (Richard Heaton) 110 marks; fourth

Hyde (Mr A D Keate) 90 marks; and fifth was Tintwistle (William Gordon) 83 marks. Other bands that entered were St Luke's Heywood; Almondbury Juniors, Brookfield, Gorton, Mirfield, Crosland Moor United, Elland, Keighley Parish Church, Whetley Mills (Girlington, Bradford), Northwich, Hopton Congregational, Middleton, Moorside, Congregational Birstall and St Saviour's Birstall. As you can see, one of the bands taking part, although unplaced was probably one of the oldest bands in existence at that time – Middleton.

Fig. 68: Middleton Ringers in their Headquarters, the Top Room Cornwarehouse, Spring Gdns, Middleton, leader Samuel Buckley in 1892

The Tintwistle Hand-bell Ringers were supported by the Sidebottom family who were the owners of big cotton mills in the area, along

Fig. 69: William Gordon with the Tintwistle Hand-bell Ringers - early 1900s (Courtesy Keith Gordon, William's grandson)

the Longdendale valley, Cheshire.

In 1903 Colonel William Sidebottom bought them a new set of 147 bells from the Whitechapel Bell Foundry, London, at a cost of £78.3s.6d. The Sidebottom family were lavish in their support of the established church life in the village which had, amongst

other things, its own orchestra and also an up to date gymnasium. Tintwistle Church became famous for its concerts, tea parties etc; and was the centre around which most of the social life of the village revolved.

The Tintwistle Hand-bell Ringers gained third place in the British Open on two occasions, in 1889 and 1895. In an attempt to win the premier prize at Belle Vue, it would seem that Colonel Sidebottom spared no expense. Several conductors, including William Gordon were engaged. As well as a resident conductor, Charles Bray, there was a Mr T Ashworth (1905) who lived in Nelson Street, Hyde. Mr Ashworth may have been one of the Hyde Hand-bell Ringers. In 1906 Edward Thornley, Mus.Bac. F.R.C.O. was engaged to conduct Tintwistle for the British open. The band was part of the Church Sunday School and continued until broken up by the First World War.

In 1920 an attempt to re-form the Tintwistle Hand-bell Ringers was made by Charles Bray and new ringers were recruited, but this only lasted about two years. A member of this band was Joe Lee, who told me, "There were a few members of the pre-war ringers in the band, but it never really got going, some members left the village and it fell through". Christ Church still has about 30 bells left, so perhaps these will be used again if someone shows interest.

William Gordon was also a tower bell ringer and was conductor of the ringers at St Mary's Parish Church, Stockport. He was associated with the Church as a tower ringer for almost 60 years until his death, aged 77, on June 21st, 1915. After his tea on that day, he read the newspaper, then composed some music and then suddenly passed away. William Gordon was born on the 27th of January, 1838, the son of a book-keeper and was the first of a famous family of bell ringers, whose combined services extended to hundreds of years. There was William Gordon Junior, John Allan Gordon (another son) and his son James Allan Gordon, Allan Samson Gordon (a nephew) and Allan Gordon Clarke and Harold Clarke (grandsons).

During my research I visited Stockport on three occasions to see if I could glean more information on William Gordon. Stockport is a curious town, built on two levels, and is well worth a visit. It was in Stockport that, after many enquiries, I met Mr Keith Gordon, great grandson of William Gordon. Keith told me "All my family over three generations have been hand-bell ringers, including my father Allan James Gordon who died in 1976, I am the only one who has not been a ringer".

However Keith is interested in tradition and is at present a member of Stockport Morris Dancers. He has three sons, Adam John, Matthew James and Daniel Keith Gordon. So let's hope hand-bell ringing is again taken up by this famous family of ringers. Keith Gordon provided me with full details of his great grandfather and the inkphoto reproduced in this book.

As a young man, William Gordon was robust and active. He was educated at Smith's St Mary's Academy, Churchgate, Stockport. He first worked in a cotton mill and then in a hat factory. Meanwhile he developed a strong passion for music and learned to play various string and wind instruments to a good standard, became expert in the arrangement of band and orchestral music and composed tuneful melodies, hymn tunes and part songs.

William Gordon was an energetic man who on one particular tower bell ringing tour rang a long length of Stedman Triples on Sunday morning at Todmorden, a similar length touch of Grandsire Triples at Burnley in the afternoon and the extent of 720 changes of Bob Minor (all the changes available on 6 bells) at Colne in the evening, and still had enough energy to be at Barnoldswick the next morning to instruct a band of hand-bell ringers, and in the evening played for a dramatic performance at Stockport. Phew!

Very early in life he became associated with Stockport Choral Society and from then on he was connected to most musical organisations in the town, including the 4th Cheshire Volunteer Band, the Yeomanry Band, the Excelsior Band, St Joseph's School Band and others. If all that were not enough he conducted various church choirs and the Alliance Orchestra Society, and was also a successful music teacher. For more than twenty years he played the double bass at the Stockport Theatre Royal. He was also at one time one of the organisers of the Vernon Park Musical Festival, acting for a time as librarian. He also found time to write articles for the local newspaper.

133

Fig. 70: Gordon's Golden Wedding Souvenir Programme (courtesy of Metropolitan Borough of Stockport Archives Dept.)

When William Gordon became a music publisher, he occupied premises at 64 Lower Hillgate, Stockport (the shop is still there) where he printed his music by the aid of a lithographic plant, (although his music gave 20 Crowther Street, Stockport as his address – perhaps this was his home address – it was only a few hundred yards from his shop). About 1905 when Gordon was 67 years of age, he and his wife Elizabeth took an off-licence shop

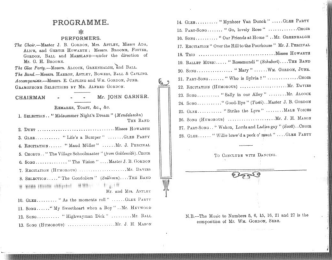

at 44 Celtic Street, off Webb Lane, Stockport (This shop is still in operation as an off licence). From this shop Gordon sold groceries and beer. He also continued to sell his music, mostly by post.

In 1912 the Gordon's celebrated their Golden Wedding. For the celebration a band of tower bell ringers consisting of William Gordon, Senior, treble; Revd A T Beeston, 2nd; G D Warburton, 3rd; James Fernley, 4th; Sidney Hough, 5th; J H Hartley, tenor rang a peal consisting of 720 Grandsire, 720 College Single, 720 Plain Bob, two 720s each of Kent and Oxford Treble Bob, 5040 changes in total. This was rung on the bells of Norbury Church, Stockport on the Saturday.

The following day the bells of Stockport St Mary's were rung. The band of tower bell ringers this time were A G Clarke, treble; H Reynolds, 2nd; J H Mason, 3rd; Peter Brickell, 4th; Alfred Gordon, 5th; William Gordon Junior, 6th; A S Gordon (conductor) 7th; E Edmunds, tenor. A peal of Grandsire Triples was begun but only about 1000 changes were rung.

On the Monday evening Mr and Mrs Gordon held a party at Crossley's Café, Market Place, Stockport, at which a band of six hand-bell ringers, amongst other performers, played.

134

Many of Gordon's arrangements and copies were thought to have been destroyed during the Second World War, as, during the war, a few of the Norbury Hand-bell Ringers visited one of Gordon's relations, realising the value of the music and asked if they could have it, but were told "no", as it was to be given in as waste paper to help with the war effort.

Despite this, quite a lot of Gordon's arrangements have survived to the present day within libraries of music, some of which have now been re-published by the Handbell Ringers of Great Britain, but not in his original style of individual sheets for each ringer with specifically allocated bells to enable smooth "off-table" ringing. HRGB has adopted the Handbell Musicians of America standard which is based on full score piano music and was developed during the middle of the 20th century while hand-bell ringing in England was in the doldrums. This has made William Gordon the most well known Victorian and Edwardian arranger of music for hand-bells. In all things pertaining to music he was an enthusiast and an example to us all.

William Gordon speaks to us today through his music, but he also tells us that many of his musical arrangements were of the popular music of the day. If he were alive today I am sure he would, as then, be arranging popular music of our own day. In my view no band's programme is complete without a William Gordon arrangement, but we should take care not to end up with too much Victorian music. I am certain William Gordon would not want us to.

Another published arranger of the day was W Haney who wrote a booklet of 12 popular airs published by Warner's Bell Foundry in 1898. A copy was discovered recently, and is in the archives of the Handbell Ringers of Great Britain.

One question I am constantly being asked is if there were there any women hand-bell ringers in the old days? Well, until recently I would have answered "no", but in 1984 in "Reverberations", the journal of the Handbell Ringers of Great Britain, there appeared a Victorian photograph of the Walford Family Ringers, with at least two girls in the photo and two others who look as though they were girls, (It's hard to tell as they both have trousers on, but long curls of hair!) the two others on the photo are males - one boy and a man who perhaps was the father of the children.

The name "Walford Family" seemed familiar to me and looking up my records of the British Open I found that they had entered the Contest at Belle Vue on September 24th, 1888.
There were twenty-one sets of ringers who entered the 1888 contest, who according to Belle Vue's advertisement in the

Fig. 71:
The Walford Family -
"The Youngest & Most
Talented Family of
Campanologists in the
World"

Manchester Guardian, included "The following celebrated prize bands - Almondbury United, Cleckheaton Victoria, Liversedge Albert, Dewsbury, Hallamshire, Birstall Congregational, Batley, the Walford Family and co. Admission to Gardens and Contest 6d each. Messrs Dawson's Grand Spectacle of the Siege of Malta at 8.45pm with extra display of fireworks".

I have since read in Anne Doggett and Gwyn Gillard's excellent book "See How They Ring" that the Walford Family began their performing career in 1877 when living in Weston-Super-Mare, Somerset, England. They started with 19 bells and four children and expanded to over 200 Taylor's bells and six children and were still performing in the early years of the 20th Century.

The Walford Family chose a rather unfortunate year in which to take part in the Belle Vue Contest, as the crowd disagreed with the result. The announcement that Dewsbury were first was received with "Hooting and other remarks of disapprobation", as the Bell News and Ringers' Record put it. "The vast audience gave vent to its rage and disappointment by refusing to listen to the extra piece which is always played by the winning band". The crowd felt Almondbury should have been first and Dewsbury last! But such outbursts at the hand-bell contest were, fortunately, rare.

The inclusion of females, even young girls must have raised a few eyebrows in what was a man's world of hand-bell ringing. However fifteen years later there was another female, who to her eternal

136

credit, dared to enter the hallowed hall at Belle Vue as a hand-bell ringer. She was Ida Anderson, a member of the Bingley Hand-bell Ringers, from near Bradford, Yorkshire. When they took part in the British Open on Monday, September 21st, 1903 Miss Anderson was "Loudly applauded for her clever manipulation of the treble bells".

The 12 ringers in the Bingley Band were conducted by Albert Anderson of Dubb Lane, Bingley. The Huddersfield Examiner said the total number of ringers in the fifteen bands who took part in the 1903 contest amounted to 165 men and one woman. Ida Anderson must have had a lot of guts. I bet she was quite a girl! Reasons why hand-bell ringing was a man's world are many, but they must be put into context - first, hand-bell ringing had grown from music making in public houses, which were, even in my childhood regarded as no places fit for women. Also it would have been regarded as unethical for a woman to wish to join what was recognised as a man's organisation, and the wives of the ringers wouldn't have liked other women in a room with their men. It was acceptable if only men were present, but women - no.

Another aspect is the weight of equipment used. Hand-bell cases were large wooden chests and very heavy when filled with bells. There were also mattresses, music stands etc; all of which took some humping about, all of which was thought of as only man's work - unlike today. It was of course a different era with different social standards perhaps born of chivalry, which was to last right up until the Second World War, when women were brought rapidly into the man's world by necessity.

The first woman to become a member of a Yorkshire traditional band in modern times was Dorothy De Salis (nee Lawton) who became a member of the Ecclesfield Hand-bell Ringers in 1948. Dorothy told me she became fascinated watching the ringers at rehearsals week after week at the cricket club, and after a few months a man left the band and she was asked to join, but, said Dorothy "If another man had come forward I don't think they would have asked me to join!"

Dorothy was followed by other women ringers, and today matters have gone to the other extreme with only 2 males out of the 14 members at Ecclesfield at the time of writing. Indeed the situation of having a majority of women over men in a band exists in almost all of the 700 or so bands that operate in Britain today

137

Chapter 4 –
The Yorkshire Hand-bell Ringers' Association – The Second Revival

Fig. 72: William Himsworth Giggle 1873 - 1922 (pronounced Jiggle) c.1906, Founder of the Yorkshire Hand-bell Ringers' Association

In the early days of the 20th Century, bands were having problems recruiting members. Hand-bell ringing was dying out and a decline in the art had set in after the heyday period of the 1880s and 90s when there would be anything between 17 to 25 entries for the British Open at Belle Vue. By the 1900s, entries never went beyond the teens and there was also a decline in the number of smaller bands who didn't compete at all, especially in counties other than Yorkshire.

Something had to be done. Somebody had to do something to stop the rot and provide new impetus, and again the initiative came from independent minded Yorkshire. Mr W H Giggle, the conductor of Horbury (near Wakefield) called a meeting of the principal bands of the county to discuss the state of the movement, its decline and what should be done. This meeting was held on October 10th, 1903 at the New Inn, Littletown, Liversedge, which was opposite the Victoria Tavern, the headquarters of the Liversedge Albert Hand Bell Ringers. Thirteen bands were represented at the meeting. The situation was that although there was still a crop of ten to fourteen crack bands at the top who were as good as any ever seen, there was a distinct lack of bands below this high standard. Because the number of bells required for a band to be in with a chance of winning anything, had increased to between 120 and 190 bells, the cost of starting such a band was prohibitive, unless they had an old set already. Even then, unless they had an experienced ringer to help form a band, it was a difficult task, as who would know how to start with over a hundred bells in front of them? Without anyone to turn to for advice and help there was no point in trying.

The answer to the problem it was felt, was to encourage small bands, as they could be the large bands of the future. The idea was to have a contest for small bands with small sets of 40 to 50 bells, as bands had been, before Shelley introduced duplicate and triplicate bells in the mid 1860s. There was also to be a contest for

138

large bands, and both were to be held annually.

The meeting decided to form an association, the Yorkshire Hand-bell Ringers Association, to promote hand-bell ringing, and to which people could turn for advice. The two contests would be held together in a different town each year with the idea of taking hand-bell ringing out to the people, and the extra publicity would help the art to prosper. A silver challenge cup was purchased for the first section and in 1908 a shield was bought from Fattorini's of Bradford for the second section winners. It was a good idea and it worked. Thus began the second revival of the fortunes of hand-bell ringing, the first being the start of the Belle Vue hand-bell competitions.

The first contest took place at the Armoury Hall in Queensgate, Huddersfield on April 2nd, 1904 with nine bands entering the first section competition for bands with large sets of an unlimited number of bells, and eleven bands in the second section which was limited to between 37 and 49 bells throughout these contests depending on the test piece. (See Appendices 3 and 10)

The winner of the first section was Huddersfield (conductor Lewis Booth), 2nd Almondbury United (conductor Ben Lodge), 3rd Horbury (conductor James Woffenden). The second section winners were Woodroyd (conductor John Moorhouse), 2nd Barnsley (conductor E Stringer), 3rd Birstall (conductor Kaye Cooke). Identical prizes of silver medals were awarded to the successful conductors and each player of the first and second sections, with the second and third bands receiving a silver medal for the conductors only.

The test piece for the first section was the overture from Rossini's "L'Italiana in Algeria". For the second section, a test piece had been written such that it would be within the capabilities of the less experienced ringers. The piece, entitled "Reminiscences of Merrie England" comprised several folk melodies which harkened back to the early days at Belle Vue when bands played simple country tunes. The piece started with a few bars of diatonic descending octaves leading on to a snatch of "The British Grenadiers", after which followed "Cherry Ripe", "Tom Bowling", "The Girl I Left Behind Me", "My Pretty Jane", "Rule Britannia", a snatch of "Home Sweet Home" and "Come Lasses and Lads". The selection presented no real difficulties, but its very simplicity was a pitfall to several of the bands according to the Huddersfield Examiner critic of the contest, who said that wrong notes were common and often the melody was obscured. "A few bands" he said, "mainly in the second section, suffered from having some bells out of tune", (remember an out of tune bell counted as a wrong note every time it was sounded) "and some bands defaulted through ringing bells

139

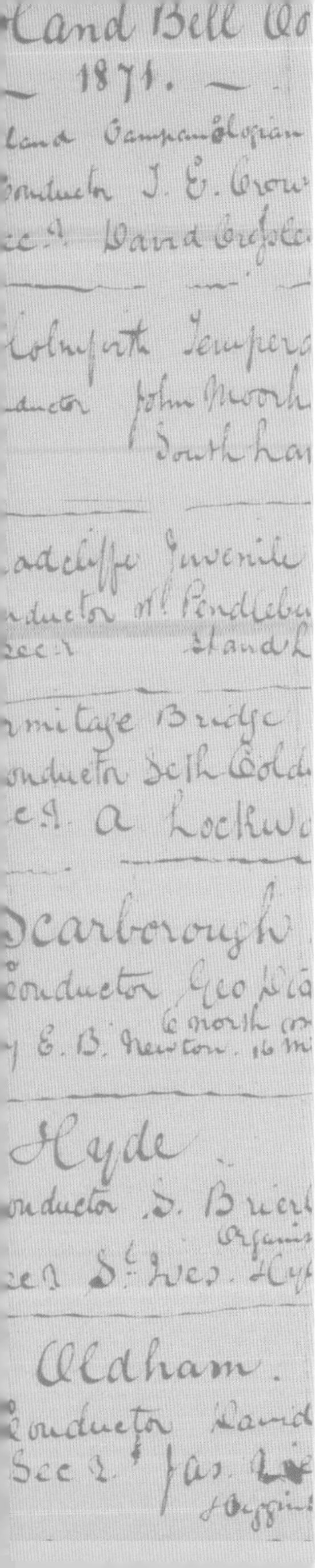

The handwriting in the left margin appears to read:

Land Bell Co
1871. —
land Campanologian
Conductor J. E. Crow
Sec.y David Cripsle

Holmfirth Temperance
...ductor John Moorh...
South Lan...

...adcliffe Juvenile
...ductor W.ᵐ Pendlebu...
Sec.y ...land...

...mitage Bridge
...onductor Seth Gold...
Sec.y A. Lockwo...

Scarborough
Conductor Geo W...a
...y E. B. Newton. 16 m...

Hyde
...onductor S. Brier...
...Organis...
...ec.y St Ives. Hyd...

Oldham.
Conductor David
Sec.y Jas. L...

with too much force, the worst offenders being Low Moor and Sheffield Hartshead." The Examiner correspondent criticised Kaye Cooke's conducting and said his band "Suffered from his eccentric and excited conducting, as he adopted the plan of giving two beats where he should have given one, and thereby got unsteady playing and want of smooth and broad phrasing".

I think the correspondent must have been a hand-bell ringer, as reports of contests, even of Belle Vue were never so personal. I have a theory that the Examiner correspondent could have been former Shelly ringer, Fred Shaw, who was still around and had strong views on the modern hand-bell ringers of the day.

"The first section bands" said the Examiner correspondent, "Played generally with remarkable accuracy and excellent style". Other bands who took part were: Liversedge Albert (conductor K Cooke); Birstall St Saviour's (conductor K Cooke); Thurlstone (conductor E Biltcliffe), Clifton (conductor A Sales). Royston United failed to put in an appearance but had entered. Second section: Heptonstall (conductor W Sunderland); Lightcliffe (conductor A Wheeler); Brighouse Park Church (conductor P Marshall); Holmfirth Lane Congregational (conductor J. Moorhouse) (who also conducted the winners, Woodroyd), Sheffield Hartshead (conductor J A Ironside) and Low Moor (conductor K Cooke).

The report says Darfield and Yorkshire (Sheffield) bands also entered for the second section, but did not put in an appearance. The last named band "Yorkshire (Sheffield)" I cannot place or put into context. Perhaps the correspondent did not identify it correctly.

However the event was a qualified success. The audience for the second section contest, held in the afternoon, attracted only a few people beyond band members and friends and relations, but for the first section competition in the evening there was a very much larger audience though not all seats were filled.

Because of the Yorkshire Association's decision to hold the contest in a different place each year, the second annual competition took place at Barnsley on April 1st, 1905. The regrowth of interest in the art, for which the Association had worked hard to achieve, produced twenty bands entering for the two sections, with a better all round standard of performance in both sections and a better level of attendance by the general public.

Flushed with their success the Association went on to hold their annual contest in other towns. In 1906 it was held at Dewsbury Town Hall. In 1907 it was back at Barnsley Public Hall, which, one week later, was burnt down with much loss of life. In 1908 the event was held in the Victoria Hall, Batley.

The event had now attained a good following and, at the May 1908 meeting of the Association, the secretary and founder, William H Giggle, submitted a scheme for the rearrangement of the date and conditions of the annual contest, which met with the approval of the delegates, and after some discussion it was decided "that the secretary write to the proprietors of the various places of amusement in several pleasure resorts asking on what terms they would be willing to allow the contest to be held in the halls belonging to them".

In January, after some discussion, it was decided to accept the offer of Mr Joseph Bunce to hold the contest at Sunny Vale Pleasure Gardens, Hipperholme, near Halifax. A deputation was chosen to meet Bunce. The outcome was that the contest took place at Sunny Vale for the first time on Easter Saturday, April 10th, 1909.

There was a big holiday crowd for the contest, "which" said the local newspaper, the Brighouse Echo, "was distinct evidence that the popular northern revival of hand-bell ringing, was no flash in the pan, but a revival that possesses every possibility of lasting".

The first Sunny Vale contest had been a success and Sunny Vale was chosen again as the venue for the 1910 contest. At this contest Crosland Moor Public won the first section contest with 95 marks out of a possible 100. The test was a selection from the Mikado (Sullivan). Lepton United were the second section winners with 94 marks for their performance of Maritana (Wallace).

The adjudicator, Mr A Jowett Mus, Bac(Oxon) Leeds, in his public summing up, made some useful comments which are still of relevance today and underline the benefit of competition when he said; "There was one band in the second competition inclined to force a little too much out of the bells in respect to tone. That was just the same as shouting in singing, which, as all know, did not make singing. It (the band) very often forced the bell out of tone. With regard to the other extreme - piano and pianissimo passages, in some of the performances there was a sort of blur; that did not make tone. There should be a distinctness in the notes, even if the bass be soft. Rhythm made music and should be there". He went on to say that if the bands would follow his advice tendered on the remarks sheet, he could name two or three in which he would expect an improvement of 25% next year.

The weather for this contest was wretched all the afternoon, and at one point the contest had to be stopped for half and hour, owing to the noise made by the rain and wind on the iron roof of the contest hall. But despite the bad weather about 1,000 people attended, which was an excellent turn out on such a day. Without the contest, there would have been very few people at Sunny Vale Pleasure Gardens that day.

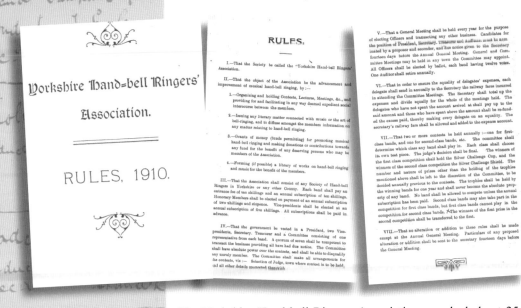

The Yorkshire Hand-bell Ringers Association now had about 25 member bands, each band paying an entrance fee of 10/- (50p) and an annual subscription of 10/- (50p). Honorary members were elected on payment of half-a-crown (12½p) per annum. Vice-presidents were elected at an annual subscription of 5/- (25p).

After the inaugural meeting at the New Inn, Liversedge in 1903, the Yorkshire Association meetings were held in various parts of the County. But from 1906 to 1921 The Old Hat Hotel, Huddersfield (which still exists) was the headquarters as the proprietor, Mr Ben Brierley used to be a hand bell ringer himself. In 1921 the headquarters were transferred to The Railway Hotel, Berry Brow, nr Huddersfield then in 1928 the headquarters were again moved to The Plough Hotel, Westgate, Huddersfield.

In the room where the meetings were held was a piano organ, a mechanical instrument similar to a barrel organ, but without pipes. Notes were produced by hammers striking strings. When test pieces for contest were received, they were played on this instrument for the delegates, so they had a better idea of how the piece should be played. The test pieces were selected from pieces which had been put forward by delegates. They were then played on the piano organ and voted in by the members. The organ was played by the organist of Huddersfield Parish Church. Walter Toulson, the only surviving ringer from the pre 1915 Clifton band told me in 1978 that he remembered hearing the instrument. I visited the Old Hat and asked if it was still there, but the landlady said that it had been, but she had had it taken out.

The Old Hat was also the venue for the Association's annual dinner and meeting, held usually a few weeks after the Association's contest. The Association had strong support from member bands. At the annual dinner and meeting in 1907, every band in the Association at the time was represented. They were: Almondbury, Barnsley, Crosland Moor, Clifton, Dewsbury, Darfield, Huddersfield, Horbury, Holmfirth, Heptonstall, Liversedge, Low Moor, Lightcliffe, Lindley, Royston, Sheffield, Thurlstone, Mirfield, Woodroyd, St Aidan's Ossett and Higher Walton. The last named band, Higher Walton is a Lancashire organisation from near Preston. The Higher Walton ringers were said to be very enthusiastic and determined that even though hand-bell ringing in Lancashire had declined to only a handful of bands at the time, they would do all they could to foster the art in Lancashire, and with this view in mind they applied for admission and were accepted as members of the Yorkshire Association in April 1907. Unfortunately the enthusiasm of the Higher Walton members seems to have been rather short lived, as by 1910, the band had stopped coming to Yorkshire Association meetings. However they still existed in the 1960s and played in several early HRGB rallies. The band entered the second section of the Yorkshire Association Contest in 1908 and 1909. In 1908 the band's conductor was Mr H Brearley and in 1909 they were conducted by Mr W North.

The "British Bandsman" spoke quite well of Higher Walton, saying they had a nice set of bells with a fine tone. The band purchased their 123 bells from the Whitechapel Bell Foundry in 1907, and these bells were still in use at Higher Walton at the time of writing. Prior to the 1907 set, the band had an older set of about 87 bells. Local knowledge says the Higher Walton band began around 1880 but went into recess for a period in 1914.

Fig. 74: Higher Walton HBR 1908 or 1909

In the 1908 Yorkshire Association Championships held at Batley, the Higher Walton band only just arrived in time to take the platform, through missing their train connection. They lost no time when getting ready and, according to the British Bandsman, they rang "with freedom - a very promising band". They were not disgraced in the points table, gaining 72 marks, which was 2 marks more than Liversedge (who were to go on and win the second section in 1911) and 9 marks ahead of Mirfield.

Other Lancashire bands were to follow Higher Walton's lead and join the Association - Newchurch, Lees St Agnes (near Oldham), Pendlebury and Bolton Parish Church. All these bands became members between 1907 and 1913 with the exception of Lees who joined about 1920. At the 1907 Annual General Meeting which followed the dinner, the then secretary and founder, Mr W H Giggle read out the accounts, which showed that the Association's turnover amounted to £38.16s.10d. (£38.84) and after expenses there was a balance of £14.14s.5d. There was also correspondence between the secretary and Jennison's, the owners of Belle Vue, in regard to the prize money for the British Open. After much discussion it was agreed to recommend that the £50 prize money be divided into seven prizes instead of five as before. It was also decided that the rule which sent the lowest placed band in the Association's first section competition down to the second section be suspended, which meant the previous year's first section would remain as it was, but that Lindley, who were the winners of the second section contest would still join the premier first section.

These Yorkshire ringers, when in competition, were the keenest of rivals against each other, but there was a close-knit comradeship between them, which even extended to the lending of sets of bells to one another to compete if they were required. At the British Open in 1900 Crosland Moor United borrowed the Liversedge bells to compete. In 1912 Bradford (Tennyson Place) borrowed bells from the Mirfield hand-bell ringers to compete in the Yorkshire Association's contest, at a charge of 10 shillings (50p), but 5 shillings (25p) of this was returned to the Bradford band as a donation to their bell fund.

Mirfield was a pub band which practised in a number of public houses in the village, including the Plough Inn, and Shepley Arms whose landlord was a member. In 1909 the band's committee made the momentous decision to present a cigar to Mr J.E. Cartwright for his trouble in buying their old bells for £4.2s as scrap. The band's accounts book for the period contains amongst other things, regular payments for beer for the ringers at each practice. The Mirfield band had taken third prize at Belle Vue in 1886, (my first record of them) and had their best run of success in 1888 and 1889 when they came second on each occasion. The Mirfield band became a casualty of the first World War and never recovered.

Three of the Mirfield ringers formed a hand-bell trio after the war,

144

Fig. 75: Mirfield Hand-bell Ringers, outside their headquarters - The Shepley Arms 1887

using William Gordon's music as well as arrangements by their leader Fred North, a competent all round musician, who played concertina and piano accordion. He also played drums with an orchestra after the decline of hand-bell ringing, but never gave up the fight to keep the art alive. Even in the early 1950s he was still trying to establish a band of ringers in the Little Duck Private Club in Mirfield. The Mirfield bells are still in the village and are protected, so one day we may see a revival of hand-bell ringing in the village.

In the early 1980s, during my research for this book I inspected Mirfield's bells. They were still in Mirfield with a lady I only knew as Miss North. She lived in a cottage off Greenside at the rear of the Co-operative store. She must have been at least 75 then. There was a box of at least a 100 bells under her bed, I said to her "what will happen to the bells when you go?" "Well something will happen won't it" was her reply. Her father was Fred North. I wonder what did happen to the bells?

Another Mirfield band was Gilder Hall who were set on their way, it is thought, by sponsorship from local colliery owner Miss Robinson. The Gilder Hall itself was a youth club. The Gilder Hall Band appeared on the contest scene at the Yorkshire Association's championships held at Ecclesfield in 1911 when they won first

145

GILDER HALL HANDBELL RINGERS, MIRFIELD.
1912 - 1913.

H.Singleton, H.Naylor, W.S.Holt, A.Cartwright, F.Weldrick, G.Brearley, J.Holt, W.Beaumont, G.Butterfield, G.A.Holt, H.Hirst, F.Barrowclough.

Fig. 76: Gilder Hall Hand-bell Ringers, Mirfield 1912-1913 Freedom Barraclough (extreme right) was Grandfather to his famous Shakespearian actor Grandson, Sir Patrick Stewart who began his acting career at the Gilder Hall.

prize in the third section contest, which they won again in 1912. In 1913 the band competed in the second section and the first section coming in third place. Gilder Hall also went to Belle Vue, where they took second prize in 1912 and 1913, so their standard must have been very high. They had a very good conductor and leader, Mr Gill Brearley, who also taught sword dancing in the village. He is remembered today in the area, as conductor of the Mirfield Military Band. He was also the type of man who took an active interest in the community in which he lived. Such people are in short supply these days. The Gilder Hall Band Bell Ringers did not compete after 1914 - another victim of the 1914-1918 war.

With the Yorkshire Association's 1910 championships at Sunny Vale being such a success after attracting over 1,000 on a cold rainy day, the Association's committee decided that the time had come for the proprietor of Sunny Vale Pleasure Gardens, Joseph Bunce, to give more money towards the prizes and cost of the medals for the contest. So far Bunce had contributed only £2 10s(£2.50) towards these costs. The Association asked for more. This Bunce refused to give. The result was that the contest went on the road again, this time to Ecclesfield near Sheffield. One of the Ecclesfield ringers Arthur Sorsby had gone round pubs in the village and collected £5 to bring the Yorkshire Association's Championships to Ecclesfield. Interestingly this was in the same year that the beer drinkers of Burnley, Lancashire picketed public houses because the price of beer was raised by a halfpenny.

In 1912 the Yorkshire Association took the Championships back to Sunny Vale, the proprietor Joseph Bunce no doubt coming up

146

with the extra cash the Association required. The third section was again included, but after 1912 the section was discontinued for some unknown and unexplained reason. It had been well supported so why abandon it? Sunny Vale Pleasure Gardens was a popular place for a day's outing, not only for people in the Halifax district, but it also attracted visitors from a wide area of the North of England. Joseph Bunce, the founder was born in 1850 and arrived at the site at Wood Bottom Farm, Hipperholme in 1880, to set up a market garden on the two acres of land, but saw the potential of pleasure gardens, especially as there was a railway station nearby. He built lakes, a maze and purchased from the Bradford Exhibition, the Palace of Illusions, which he re-erected at Sunny Vale.

The Yorkshire Association's contests were to remain at Sunny Vale until 1929, when they were moved to the rival Hope Bank Pleasure Grounds, Honley.

Fig. 77: Yorkshire Assoc 1910 Sunny Vale Handbell Competion Flyer

In 1982 I spoke to Albert Braybrook, who was only a lad at the time of the 1911 contest at Ecclesfield, but remembered the event well. "Me and another lad were given the job of meeting the bands at the railway station. The Saddleworth ringers missed Ecclesfield and got off the train in Chapeltown, and they had to hire a horse and dray to bring them back to Ecclesfield, but we took the bands to the West End Chapel Hall where the contest was to be held. Then the committee, Arthur Sorsby and my father (George Braybrook) took the bands and their supporters to the pubs to which they were allocated. There were a few bands in each pub at dinner time before the contest. The first round in the 'Black Bull' was for 21 pints. They always enjoyed a good "Booze up" at a contest. Ecclesfield were known as the Ecclesfield Ale and Bacca Band at the time", said Albert. Ecclesfield had joined the Yorkshire Hand-bell Ringers' Association in 1909. Albert Braybrook told me the Ecclesfield hand-bell ringers were formed after the landlord of the Greyhound in the village went on a "Boozing excursion" one weekend and brought back 14 or 15 bells, and it built up from there. The landlord, Billy Hirst, was a champion concertina player. They then collected more money round the pubs and bought 50 bells from Girlington (Whetley Mills) Hand-bell Ringers, Bradford.

Hazel Bradey, the present conductor of Ecclesfield said that Ken Gregory, a contempory of Albert in the band had had a similar

147

but slightly different recollection of the event - George Hirst (actually Billy Hirst) along with Tom Kitson (Junior) and Freddy Whitham formed the Ecclesfield Hand-bell Ringers after having a go on a small set of only 12 – 14 bells, probably owned by the Kitson family. George Hirst then went to Bradford in 1904 to attend a hand-bell competition there and came back with a set of hand-bells, mainly cast by Shaws of Bradford, although there were some 1840's Mears bells that had been chip-tuned rather than tuned on a lathe. He had bought the bells from the Girlington Hand-bell Ringers, who had just purchased a new long set of 5 octaves (with duplicates). Thomas Kitson Senior, with his three boys, including Thomas junior and his two step sons used to ring as a family during the 1880s and 90s. Indeed the 'Kitson Brothers' performed for Queen Victoria's Diamond Jubilee Celebrations at Bradfield Church in1897.

Fig. 78: Kitson Family about 1880 (courtesy Hazel Bradey)

Fig. 79: Ecclesfield Hand-bell Ringers 1911: L to R Ernest Flathers, George Stringer, Ernest Greaves, Frank Clarke, Freddy Whitham (Cond), George Higgins, Walter Hague, Frank Kay, Albert Bradshaw, Arthur Sorsby, Ernest Whitham (courtesy Hazel Bradey)

The band's conductor in the Yorkshire Association contest in 1909 and 1910 was Edwin Biltcliffe who had conducted Thurlstone at Belle Vue in 1899. Edwin Biltcliffe lived at Nestfield Terrace, Penistone and had conducted the Penistone Ringers at Belle Vue, as early as 1874. There was also a John Biltcliffe of the same address, who conducted Penistone in 1877 at Belle Vue. I wonder if he were Edwin's father or was it perhaps his brother?

In the 1909 Yorkshire Association contest in which Edwin Biltcliffe conducted Ecclesfield, it was stated that Biltcliffe marred their performance by "Stamping and counting loudly",

In 1911 Fred Whitham became Ecclesfield's conductor and remained so for many years. He was a local man who lived in Yew Lane in the village. Albert Braybrook remembered him with admiration "Fred wasn't all that musical but he would always listen to advice, that's why he was so good", said Albert.

The Yorkshire Hand-bell Ringers Association held its eighth championship contest at Ecclesfield on Monday, April 17th, 1911. This was the first occasion at which there had been three sections of contests. There was the first section for bands with an unlimited number of bells as before, and the second section contest which was restricted to 49 bells (or under) and no duplicates to be used. There was also a third section for which I have been unable to find out any specification. The test piece for the first (championship) section was Mozart's "Don Giovanni". The test piece for the second section was "Les Cloches De Bridal" a fantasia arranged by Kaye Cooke (then Vice President of the Association). The piece was full of beauty and included Wagner's "Bridal Chorus" from Lohengrin,, Mendelssohn's "Wedding March" from a Midsummer Night's Dream and the "Church's One Foundation". The change from the one to the other was one of the principal features of the selection, which concluded with a Westminster peal.

Competing in the second section were the host band Ecclesfield under their new conductor Fred Whitham. Ecclesfield did very well gaining 107 marks, but 3 marks ahead of them were Liversedge Albert, who had made a come back to win the Yorkshire Shield gaining 110 marks. In third place, a long way behind, were Clifton Juniors who gained 77 marks. Other bands who competed in this section were; Mirfield, Thurlstone, Royston United, Saddleworth, Sheffield Hartshead Friends.

Fig. 80: Liversedge Albert Hand-bell Ringers with the Yorkshire Shield won at Ecclesfield in 1911. The photo was taken in their rehearsal room at the Victoria Tavern, Knowler Hill, Littletown, Liversedge.

The new third section was won by Gilder Hall, Mirfield, who gained 103 marks. Second were Bradford Tennyson, 101 marks and third were Cleckheaton Adult School, 95 marks. The first section (championship) was won by Dewsbury, another band who had had to change their style of ringing in order to compete with Crosland Moor United's new wave, chippy choppy style, of which we shall hear more. Dewsbury had also introduced new young ringers into the band, so it was more to their credit that they gained 125 marks, putting a new "spin-off" from Crosland Moor United, Crosland Moor Public, into second place. The Public Band gained 121 marks. Lepton United were third, gaining 114 marks.

The British Bandsman reported on the competition on p. 373 of its 22nd April 1911 edition.

The eighth annual contest of the Yorkshire Hand-bell Ringers Association was held on Monday at Ecclesfield, near Sheffield. Hand-bell Ringing which flourishes more in Yorkshire than in perhaps any other County has become increasingly popular of late years. The Yorkshire Association includes 25 bands, and from simple tunes the test pieces have advanced to difficult concert pieces and operatic selections. There were three competitions on Monday, and nineteen bands competed. The test piece for the first section was a selection from Mozart's "Don Giovanni" (rung from the ordinary pianoforte score), for the second section "Les Cloches de Bridal", for the third section "Martha". Mr John Rigg adjudicated; the maximum marks in each competition were 140.

The first section test piece, Mozart's "Don Giovanni" had been specially adapted for hand-bells, but in the main, only the repeats were taken out. The climax of the piece was a series of full chords. The music before 1939 was heavily chorded. Some hand-bell historians today say this was done to cover up defects in the tuning of the bells, which were tuned by ear and often were not as accurately tuned as bells are today.

Having spoken to old ringers I would say that it was simply that the old bands liked a full bodied chorded sound with plenty of tenor bells ringing - as many as 16 on average.

The Dewsbury band played from the ordinary pianoforte score, as did most of the other bands which competed, this practice being widely used by the Yorkshire bands instead of playing from orchestral parts, first and second violins and tenor violin (approx half way between the modern 'cello and viola, tuned an octave lower than a violin) for some middle parts, as bands had done in the 19th century.

Old ringers, such as Shelley's Fred Shaw didn't like this new trend of playing straight from piano scores. Nor did they like other new trends and big changes that had taken place since the death of Queen Victoria in 1901.

The band which started many of these trends had the greatest record of any band in the annals of musical contests at Belle Vue (including the brass band contest). The band was Crosland Moor United. The band had its origins back in July 1890, when a group of local worthies set up the band to keep lads off the streets.

The band's founder was also their first conductor and instructor. He was a Huddersfield solicitor called Thomas Cartwright, a former member of the Holmfirth Temperance Hand-bell Ringers in the mid 1870s when the band narrowly missed winning the championship in 1876.

Rehearsals began in July 1890 using a set of 50 bells. The band's biographer, Jimmy Ellis gave the following account of the band's first set of bells.

"The first peal of bells was a second-hand one, which must have been in use a large number of years, judging by the condition of the handles. No one appears to know the maker's name, but each dome was stamped with a letter "D". It was a very small peal, as it contained about fifty bells only, ranging from 25G to 03A treble, all single bells, without any duplicates whatever. They were a good set of bells, rich and mellow in tone and during the whole of the fourteen years the band had them - and some were in constant use practically all the time - not a single bell ever cracked. Each dome was thicker and had more weight of metal in it, than is the case with peals at the present time (1906). In fact when we ordered a new peal of bells in 1901, we should certainly have communicated with the makers of that peal, had we known the name of the firm, with the view of placing our order with them."

I wonder if the bells were made by George Dalton of York? Were his bells marked "D"? The set was small by Northern standards. Other bands at the time would be using up to 150 bells.

Notices were given out at the Sunday Schools in the district that a band was being formed, asking for young men interested to give in their names. There were a good number who wished to join, but when some of them found out that hand-bell ringing was not so easy as they thought, but needed effort, perseverance and constant practice, some of them gave it up. Mr Cartwright made great efforts to make the band a success, little did he know at the time, what success was in store for his band.

The first rehearsal room was known as "Th'owd Killin hoil", the name derived from the place having been a slaughterhouse.

The ringers persevered and a band was finally put together, with four treble, four tenor and three bass ringers. The average age of the band was about fourteen years. The ringers thought they could do something exceptional when they could play the "Blue Bells of Scotland". By 1891 the band had a new set of bells bought through public subscription. These were purchased from Shaws of Bradford at a cost of £56. The range of the set was: 5½ octaves, from 29C (C3) to 003A (A8) inclusive….70 bells, 3 octaves from 22C (C4) to 1C (C7) inclusive as duplicates…37 bells - total set 107 bells.

Crosland Moor United made its first appearance at the British Open at Belle Vue, only thirteen months after being formed, which in itself shows how much progress had been made in such a short time. The test piece was von Flotows "Martha" which was a difficult selection for such a young band to attempt, and they put up a creditable performance against such redoubtable bands as Liversedge Albert, Almondbury, Dewsbury, all of which were composed of men many years their senior. Here was a group of 15 year old boys who had the pluck to learn how to ring hand-bells and then tackle a difficult piece of music and enter the British Open Championship, after being together for only thirteen months.

On their appearance at Belle Vue, the audience, seeing their youth and coming from Crosland Moor, named them "Wark'us lads" (Workhouse lads), a name which stuck. Even years later in 1903, a wag in the audience at Belle Vue shouted "Good owd wark'us lads" recorded the band's biographer. The band did not win a prize at the 1891 contest, but the ringers were by no means discouraged and their appearance at the contest "did them a world of good". It must have done so, as the band gained joint third place at the 1893 British Open, along with Dalton Victoria, which was another well established band from the Huddersfield district. The tie strangely enough was the only tie of the whole 67 years of the contest. There had been occasions in past contests when the adjudicators could not decide which band merited the higher place, but this was sorted out by asking each band to play again, so it seems strange that the adjudicators declared a tie.

The band now erected a wooden building 15 feet wide and 13 feet high at the ridge, next to where the Liberal Club still stands, as a rehearsal room, but this was later removed in one piece to another site in Barton Road.

By 1895 "The bells were getting into a rather bad condition, as they had been in constant use for nearly five years. They were inferior in many respects, especially in tune and tone, to the sets that other bands were using", said the Band's biographer. An effort was made to get new bells and a printed appeal for subscriptions was made, but this was not a success and the band had to carry on using the "old" set.

The band lost members. However, the remaining members were determined to keep the band going at any cost. Again notices were sent round the village asking for new members, the result was four new members.

Thomas Cartwright, the band's founder and conductor, was elected to the town council in 1896 and resigned as conductor in early 1897. He later became the first and only hand-bell ringer to become Mayor of Huddersfield. One of the ringers then conducted and played in the band, until a new conductor, a local violin teacher, Albert Townend was appointed in 1899. Mr Townend was new to hand-bell ringing, but the band's members knew how to ring a bell in the correct way having been taught by Thomas Cartwright, who being an old hand-bell ringer himself, knew all the tricks of the trade, which is half the battle. Subsequently any new members who joined, would have Mr Cartwright's tricks passed onto them by the ringers - traditions, which remember, Mr Cartwright himself had learnt from Holmfirth. This is something which we today, must do also.

For the 1896 British Open the band borrowed the Liversedge Albert bells as their own were so bad. "The band was now in very straitened circumstances and it was all members could do to keep its head above water" but still they persevered.

The band gave many concerts around the district, one of which led to a funny episode, which I am sure wouldn't be out of place in a television comedy of today. The band had an engagement in Milnsbridge which is a village at the bottom of Crosland Moor. The band had hired a donkey and cart to take and bring back the bells and equipment. The return journey took them up Pinfold Hill, which is at least a 35% incline. "Moko", the donkey refused to move and nothing would make him go up the hill, and the ringers had to push both the donkey and cart up, which was a struggle, as several times the animal attempted to lie down in the road. "Needless to say" said the band's biographer, "Moko was not engaged again"!!

As they still had their bad set of bells, Crosland Moor United entered the British Open in 1900 with another set borrowed for the contest, this time from the Woodroyd band from about 3 miles down the road. This act of kindness shows that although rivalry was keen, there was still a bond between rival bands - what mattered was the tradition of hand-bell ringing.

The test piece was "Czar and Zimmermann" by Lortzing. At this stage, six of the band's ten members had been with the organisation from when it began in 1890. Every effort was put into practising the test piece and the ringers were "confident they would be in the prize list". The contest day came and they gave a "Capital performance", and they were delighted to find they had been placed second. The adjudicators remarks said: "A trifle slow, otherwise an excellent performance and would have taken first prize but for the bells, had they been better in tune. We regret this very much".

In fact the band had only had loan of the bells for a fortnight in which to get used to them, and as we know today it takes time

Land Campanologian
Conductor J. E. Crow
Sec David Drufsler

Holmforth Tempera
ductor John Moork
South han

adcliffe Juvenile
nductor M. Pendlebu
Sec Handel

rmitage Bridge
Conductor Seth Cold
ec a Lockwo

Scarborough
Conductor Geo Dia
y E. B. Newton *north co*

Hyde
onductor S. Brier
Organis
ec S. Ives. Hy

Oldham
Conductor David
Sec Jas. L

to get the feel of a set of bells and would have especially been difficult at that level of play.

The number of points awarded was first; Almondbury United 96, who now became Champion Band and Crosland Moor United 95, which shows the band had made real progress under their new conductor Albert Townend.

The down pointing by the adjudicators for having bells out of tune (although they can't have been very much) may seem harsh, but bands were judged by the "music" produced and even if only one bell is out of tune, if it can be heard, then to the critical ear, it will not make as good music as bells fully in tune with one another, and as stated before, down pointing for out of tune bells had a spin-off effect of putting second hand bells on the market for new bands to buy, therefore increasing the potential for new bands to be formed.

After the 1900 result, the members of the band were convinced they could make no further progress without a new set of bells, but their funds were low. They only had £5 in the bank, but for gaining second place, their prize was £12, which was added to the account.

A new effort was now made to raise money for new bells, which was successful. Subscriptions had raised enough for the band to be confident enough to order a set of 172 bells only 2 months after the 1900 contest, and after correspondence with other bands on the subject of which bells were the best, it was decided to buy them from the Whitechapel bell foundry of Mears and Stainbank. The range of the set was 70 bells from 29C to 003A inclusive. 59 bells as duplicates from 25G to 005F inclusive. 42 bells as triplicates from 19F to 03A# inclusive. 1 bell extra 22C.

The secretary and treasurer travelled to the foundry in London to make sure everything was in order and that there could be no mistake. The bells had to be the best. Every bell was warranted and the whole set guaranteed in perfect tune.

The old set of 107 bells, which was by the standards of the day "a small set", was kept for practising. These were sent for refurbishing and new bells were added to make an identical set of 172 bells. This is a practice which all the top bands of the day employed. They kept a perfect set "as new" for contest and concerts, and usually an older refurbished set for practice only. The contest and concert bells were kept in their boxes permanently, except when used at contests and concerts.

Some bands like Crosland Moor took this a stage further and also had a second set of tables and mattresses which were also only used for contests and concerts. The band could then leave the practice set of bells on the table permanently, so no practice time was wasted in taking down and putting back the bells and tables, and this saved wear and tear on bells, mattresses and tables. Above all this ensured that the band had near perfect bells for contesting.

The fact that the other bands had recommended bells from the Whitechapel Bell Foundry, demonstrates the popularity which Whitechapel now enjoyed, with the Foundry taking over the number one spot from Shaws of Bradford. Although some bands such as Horbury and Dewsbury stuck with Shaws and continued to do so.

Crosland Moor United Hand-bell Ringers, with their new bells, were now set to take the hand-bell world by storm.

The bands of those days made a really big splash when they bought a new set of bells and Crosland Moor were no exception. They held a public opening of the new bells, and anyone who was anybody was present. Thomas Cartwright started the first tune to be played on the new set of bells by ringing the first note of the tune on a silver hand-bell (which still exists).

There were also Glee singers. Fred Shaw of the old Shelley Band was there, as was a Colonel Carlisle. The Methodist School Room was crowded. The opening ceremony was a big success both financially and socially. The band had a debt of £15 owing to the five founder members which was now settled. The band's concert programme included usually whatever overture had been learned for the British Open as well as the "Kyrie and Gloria" from Mozart's twelfth mass (arranged by T Cartwright), which in fact was a favourite arrangement of many bands from then until the present day. Another favourite was Fred Shaw's arrangement of "Auld Lang Syne", with variations, an arrangement which is still in the libraries of a few Yorkshire bands today.

After their second place success in the British Open in 1900, the band, now with a large set of new bells, were looking forward to the 1901 contest for which the test piece was a selection from Planquette's opera "Les Cloches de Corneville", arranged by Lieutenant Charles Godrey, R.A.M. Bandmaster of the Royal Horse Guards, London. This was, according to the band's biographer, "One of the most suitable selections ever made for the hand-bell contest". The writer remembers well being at the 1977 Handbell Ringers of Great Britain's tenth festival, held at the Wembley Conference Centre, London, when "Les Cloches de Corneville" was performed by the "Sound of Brass" hand-bell ringers, from Chelmsford, Essex. Sound in Brass' origins date from 1960 when three young towerbell ringers, Andrew Hudson, Jeremy Branden

155

and Howard Egglestone formed a "4 in hand" band using Jeremy's 12 bells. After attending the revival hand-bell rally at Norbury, Cheshire in 1966 and then the inaugural HRGB Rally at Ashton under Lyne, Lancashire, in 1967, and seeing northern teams playing "off table" on "long sets" of bells of up to 200 hand-bells Andrew Hudson bought a straight set of about four octaves of second hand bells, recruited a band of new ringers, took the name "Sound in Brass" and adopted the highly developed Yorkshire off table method of playing.

In 1977 Andrew acquired the Crosland Moor United concert/contest set (Woodroyd had the practice set) which had been stored for many years at the Brocks firework factory in Half Moon Street, Huddersfield. Sound in Brass, thus using the Crosland Moor United's concert/competition bells performed "Les Cloches de Corneville", the piece with which Crosland Moor United won first prize in the British Open, 76 years previously. I am sure the Crosland Moor men would have been as pleased as I was with the performance of the piece by the Sound in Brass ringers.

There were sixteen entries for the 1901 contest and Crosland Moor United's win was the start of a record run of success for the band, which has never since been equalled by any band in any Belle Vue contest - Concertina, Brass Band or hand-bell.

The United band took the first prize in the contests of 1901 and 1902. The entry form for the 1903 British Open arrived just before Easter and the band entered immediately. The test piece was a grand selection from Offenbach's opera, "Geneviève de Brabant", which contained several airs familiar to the ringers. One was the gendarmes' duet "We'll run 'em in".

The prospect of a third and Championship win brought scenes of almost hysteria to Crosland Moor. Twelve hundred people were estimated to have heard the band in its final rehearsals. Every person in the village, old and young, was greatly interested in the progress of the band.

On the contest day, a great number of supporters travelled with the band to Manchester. The train was so packed, some of the ringers had to travel in the luggage van.

At Belle Vue, the ballot to decide the playing order placed the band at number 13, but it was their lucky number as it turned out, as the band won first prize and the Championship.

The band's homecoming was a triumph. On their arrival at the Liberal Club the ringers were greeted by a massive crowd who cheered and lustily sang "See the Conquering Heroes Come".

After being debarred for one year, Crosland Moor United came back to Belle Vue to win the contests of 1905, 06 and 1907, which completed a double hat-trick - an all time record. No other band of any kind had accomplished a double hat-trick in any British Open Competition. The only band to approach equalling this feat was Black Dyke Mill Brass Band, when they only had to win the 1978 British Open Contest at Belle Vue to complete a double hat-trick.

Fig. 81: Sturdy and True, Crosland Moor United, as Proud as Punch after their first win in the British Open in 1901. Standing on the extreme left is Jimmy Ellis, one of the finest hand-bell ringers of all time. Seated on the left is the band's founder, Thomas Cartwright. Seated on the right is conductor Albert Townend. (Image Courtesy of the Kirklees Image Archive: www. kirkleesimages.org.uk)

The writer was in the audience at Belle Vue in 1978 to see if Black Dyke could equal Crosland Moor United's record. The result of the contest was announced, the winners - Brighouse and Rastrick! Everybody jumped a yard into the air, including the writer, who was the only one out of the 3,000 or so people in the King's Hall who was cheering not only Brighouse and Rastrick Brass Band, but for Crosland Moor United Hand-bell Ringers - whose record still stands to this day.

The only other ringers to get anywhere near a double hat-trick was Crosland Moor Public who won 1911-12-13, debarred in 1914 and winners again in 1915, and had it not been for the intervention of the Great War, would have gone on, I feel, to complete a double hat-trick as well.

A team with a link to Crosland Moor United was the Huddersfield Band. In 1899 the Huddersfield band were lent a set of bells by the Hyde Ringers of Cheshire, but the strikers "Were too hard" which spoilt their performance in the British Open that year. To overcome this problem the band bought a brand new set of 164 bells in early 1901. This investment was well worth while as they then went on to win the Yorkshire Association Championshire under their young conductor, Lewis Booth followed by the British Open Championship in the same year – 1904 - for which they once more brought in J. B. (Wick) Lodge to conductor to ensure that there was no mistake – which there was not as they won it.. This was hardly surprising as the band were the runners up to Crosland Moor United in 1902 and 1903. Huddersfield's headquarters were in Battye's Yard, which still exists, off the market place in the town.

J. B. Lodge should not to be confused with Ben Lodge of Almondbury, who was not related. J. B. Lodge was also a tower bell ringer at Huddersfield Parish Church.

I was given a newspaper cutting which showed a picture of the medal which had been presented to J.D. (Wick) Lodge when the Huddersfield Band won the Belle Vue Competition in September 1904. The cutting said that Mr Lodge's ability to conduct and ring the bells of the Huddersfield Band was legendary. After a lot of digging around I managed to track down some of the Belle Vue medals and I have to thank the Kirklees Image Archive for letting me see, and have photographs of them. Although the medals were not Mr Lodge's, perhaps it is appropriate that they belonged to Albert Townend, as his band, Crosland Moor United took over the Huddersfield bells and music after they disbanded.

One other medal which the Kierklees Image Archive had from Albert Townend's decendants was the medal he was given when Crosland Moor United won a 'one-off' competition at the Tong Carnival Contest. For the sake of completeness here it is:

Lewis Booth, Huddersfield's young conductor lived at Golcar, but later removed to Bradford and was adjudicator of the Yorkshire Association's contests at Barnsley in 1907, by which time Lewis Booth's brother William Booth, who had conducted the band at Belle Vue in 1900, took over.

William Booth, who was a weaver by trade, had been a member of the band for over thirty years, since 1873..Shortly after the formation of the Yorkshire Association he was elected Treasurer, the position he held until his death in June 1908 in his forty-ninth year, after which I think the Huddersfield Hand-bell Ringers went out of existence, as we hear nothing of them again, and their bells were bought by the Crosland Moor Public Hand-bell Ringers in 1909. Indeed the Crosland Moor's library still contains

Fig. 82: The Armoury, alias The Hippodrome, alias The Classic Cinema, alias the Alias Che Nightclub, Huddersfield where the first Yorkshire Hand-bell Ringers Association Contest were held in 1904 (courtesy Huddersfield Examiner)

Fig. 83: (Above) Belle Vue Competition Gold Medal presented to Albert Townend in 1906

music, stamped "Huddersfield Hand-bell Ringers". Members of the Booth family still live in Huddersfield. .

The name of Huddersfield is one of the oldest in the book, as already mentioned. However the band was rather late in entering the British Open, which it did for the first time in 1873, securing third place under their conductor Charles Broadbent.

The fantastic success of Crosland Moor United had not come overnight. It had taken them ten years to get to the top. Their success on the contest platform brought them equal success on the concert platform. Many concert engagements were undertaken, which took them to the Birmingham Exhibition for 3 days, the Palace Theatre Blackpool for 4 days - and Blackpool only engaged the best! Also Blyth in Northumberland for 2 days and such places as Manchester, Bolton, Blackburn, Droylsden and other Lancashire towns, and also in Yorkshire, such as Leeds, Sheffield and Dewsbury. The band even played at the London Hippodrome and made an 80rpm recording in 1911, the first hand-bell ringers to do so.

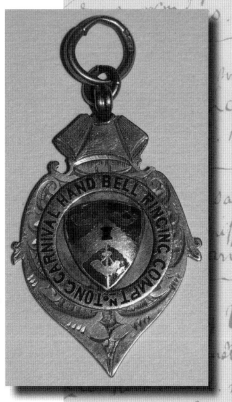

The band brought hand-bell ringing to a level of popularity during the period between 1901 and 1915 which the art had never enjoyed before nor since in Great Britain. A good example was a concert at the Halifax Victoria Hall, 6 miles from Huddersfield, in March 1909. The hall seated 3,500 people, which proved too small. It was estimated that as many people were turned away as there were in the hall. The concert had to be delayed for half an hour, as the band could not get on stage because of the crowds. The police had to be called in to clear the corridors and exits before the concert could begin.

As stated before, in the run up to the 1903 British Open, it was estimated that twelve hundred people came to hear the band in final rehearsals. Everybody in Crosland Moor old and young became interested in the band's progress.

In August 1911, the band set off on a tour of New Zealand and Australia returning in May 1912 after travelling 34,510 miles.

But why had Crosland Moor United been so successful? The reasons were many. To begin with the band had been given good training on how to handle the bells in the relaxed Yorkshire way, the idea being that hand-bell ringing, when practised at its best is perpetual motion without a hint of stiffness in the arm movements, with the bell worked from the wrist making use of both the "up stroke" and the "back stroke". The band had been given these tips

Fig. 86: The Huddersfield Prize Hand-bell Band having won both the first Yorkshire Association Contest's First Section and the British Open at Belle Vue in September 1904 outside their headquarters in Battye's Yard, Huddersfield (Now a coffee shop)

by Thomas Cartwright who had all of thirty years experience in the art.

So when Albert Townend became conductor in 1899, he inherited a band who knew all about handling the bells and how to play any sequences of music, which is half the battle in hand-bell ringing. Albert Townend could also seek the advice of Thomas Cartwright on how to arrange the music. But Albert Townend, a violin teacher of considerable standing, had his own ideas as to how hand-bell music should sound.

In 1977 I spoke with Mr Harold Godward the son of George Henry Godward who was one of the Almondbury champion ringers who

went on tour to the USA in 1901 and kept the diary.

Harold Godward made his first public performance with Almondbury Juniors on January 19th, 1907 at the age of 15, so he was well versed and knowledgeable on the development of hand-bell ringing.

Mr Godward told me, "Before Crosland Moor United came along in 1901, the old Almondbury and all the other bands didn't damp their bells so much. They did damp them, but they didn't damp them as clean cut as Crosland Moor United did. Crosland Moor United carried the damping further, they were the first to damp their bells in between, up to then bands hadn't bothered damping so much, they played the bells like a piano with the pedal down all the way through, instead of changing the pedal as different harmonies came along", and added that "Crosland Moor Public (more of whom we shall learn later) took the damping even further".

So under Albert Townend, Crosland Moor United harnessed the "whoop" sound, made when bells, especially in the middle and lower ranges, are replaced on the table during "off table" ringing and used it to create a rhythmical effect, whereby the damping of the bells was used like an extra note. (American hand-bell ringers now call this 'echo' ringing Ed.) This style of playing created by Crosland Moor United is widely used by the "off table" bands of today (See Appendix 8), and as now, not everybody in the first years of the twentieth century agreed with this heavy accentuated damping of bells. Correspondence appeared in the Huddersfield Examiner criticising the practice as "Chippy-choppy" and as to whether chippy choppy ringing as Crosland Moor's style was called, was the kind of ringing to be expected in the future.

Fig. 87: Albert Townend, Conductor of Crosland Moor United c. 1905

The band's secretary and first treble ringer Jimmy Ellis replied that nevertheless, nearly all bands had attempted this kind of ringing since Crosland Moor United had done so. We today of course, know the answer to the question - Yes, chippy-choppy was the kind of ringing to be expected in the future and "off table" bands of today are still following Crosland Moor United's chippy-choppy style, which is deliberately used in faster pieces of music and marches.

There was also another development in ringing style, again brought in by Crosland Moor United in the early 1900s. These were changes in the way the bass bells were played.

Before 1900, the bands didn't usually attempt runs on the large bells from 25G to 29C. Indeed such large bells were uncommon at the start of the Belle Vue contests in 1855.

Information on when such bells were first used is at present rather hazy, but the Honley Temperance bells which were cast in 1876 by George Stockham and Company, London, do included these bells,

25G to 29C. Interestingly, like Shaw's bells, they are smaller in size and weight than Whitechapel bells from the turn of the century and later, and therefore were easier to ring than their heavier counterparts. However bass runs did not make a public appearance until Crosland Moor introduced them in their performances.

John Terry told me that Crosland Moor were the first band to do so, "They made the bass just as important as the trebles, by putting in bass runs and creating a more balanced sound". This of course is another practice which is still a popular feature of hand-bell ringing today.

But the practice was not liked by some of the old ringers who resented the new indulgence. They hadn't done it so why should anyone else? Fred Shaw, formerly with Shelley Hand-bell Ringers, did not like these new trends at all.

In 1907 there was a contest at which Fred Shaw was adjudicator, held at the Linthwaite District Nurses Association carnival, which took place in the Spa Pleasure Grounds, Slaithwaite, near Huddersfield.

I touched on this contest in the chapter on Shelley, but the details are relevant to what I am saying about bass bell runs, so I feel it will be useful to give them again along with a few more of Mr Shaw's comments.

In his remarks on each band, amongst other grumbling, he said "Bands should not attempt runs on the big bass bells such as G, size 25, or G in the bottom line in F clef. This bell is about eight inches in diameter, weight 6lb, length about 15 ins. Compute how far this has to travel to get a stroke. This octave is too heavy in tone for quick passages. From G11 to G18 is the best part to put in some good harmony and runs. Bands should only show score copies of what they intend to play".

There were nine bands in the competition most of whom Mr Shaw advised to get a better test piece. He also criticised the bands for a number of other developments which had been taking place, including playing straight from piano music, a practice that was to remain popular right up to the Second World War. Mr Shaw went on, "I am disappointed at bands not having a better selection of test pieces, especially at an open contest. I am also surprised at ringing having deteriorated during the last thirty years so much" - since he had given up ringing! Mr Shaw went on: "I would advise bands not to take piano pieces, but write from orchestral parts, first and second violins and tenor violin, for some good middle parts". The contest was won, ironically, by the band who had started using bass runs in the first place - Crosland Moor United.

162

There had been developments in the design of hand-bells, by Mears and Stainbank at the Whitechapel Bell Foundry. One of these developments made bass runs easier to play than they had been in Fred Shaw's day. The top flight bands were always on the look out for any new innovations which would improve their standard of performance. Bell foundries were eager to meet this demand. One of these innovations was an improved deluxe striker mechanism, developed by Whitechapel. This was the "split ball striker". With this form of striker the ringer had a greater control over the volume of sound produced, which was also of a better tonal quality and there was a much quicker response, especially when quick bass runs were played.

The fitting of these strikers was a bit like installing power assisted steering on a motor vehicle. The split ball strikers made it possible for more complicated arrangements to be played. All this is a direct result of having a much heavier type of striker, but the sheer weight of the clapper leads to complications in the design of the whole staple assembly.

The bell had to be struck by something softer than a leather peg covered with felt, otherwise the sound produced is harsh. The problem was overcome by having a felt disc in two sections to strike the bell.

Also, different springs were required to prevent the heavier striker giving a double ring. So instead of flat springs, curved "T" shape springs bound around with leather were fitted, (Whitechapel used the leather from old army boots for this!). The hole created between the leather bindings and the spring was filled with felt to support the leather binding.

Recent tests have also shown that the reason two felt discs were fitted to the striker, is because the discs separate and spread out on impact, producing a better tonal sound than one disc.

These strikers were fitted to the bass bells from 20E to 29C, but only the top flight bands had them. These can still be seen fitted on bells today, still in use by bands such as Clifton, Ecclesfield and Sound in Brass on the Crosland Moor United bells.

Today Whitechapel only fit split ball strikers to the very bottom bells D28 and C29 as standard, but can supply split ball strikers and curved springs for the bells up to E20, but they have to

Fig. 88: A Split-ball Striker c.1908 (illustration courtesy John Teal)

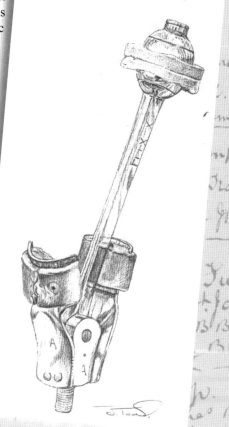

163

be specially manufactured and therefore are more expensive than the standard fittings, but if the best is required, the better results are well worth the extra cost involved.

The result of Albert Townend's innovations, helped by Whitechapel's own innovations, was that Crosland Moor United, became the band, the balance, and the sound, that everyone else wanted to emulate.

On September 23rd 1907 there was an article on Horbury Hand-bell Ringers in the "Leeds Mercury", entitled "Champion Hand-bell Ringers", with a photograph of the Horbury band. In the article it was claimed that Horbury were "the most proficient hand-bell ringers in the country".

This claim brought an immediate flurry of indignation from the Crosland Moor United band, who only a few days before, had become Champion Band for the second time in the last seven years.

Two days after the article, an article on Crosland Moor United appeared, this time in the Daily Despatch, a national paper, entitled "The Champion Hand-bell Ringers". There was a sharp exchange of letters in the Ossett Observer (Horbury's local paper) between Jimmy Ellis, the secretary of Crosland Moor United and W H Giggle, the conductor of Horbury, on the respective merits of each band. W H Giggle accused Crosland Moor of being jealous, because Horbury had been chosen to play at the National Band Festival at Crystal Palace on September 28th. This was denied by Jimmy Ellis. However Crosland Moor was the Champion Band, of that there could be no argument, and the long correspondence ended with Jimmy Ellis advising Horbury to "do like they did in Birstall" and "Kar quiet" until Horbury had something to boast about.

There was a similar occurrence in 1981 when a feature on hand-bell ringing in a woman's magazine, stated that Thurlstone were the premier band in the country. However there was no further correspondence on this rather brash statement by other bands in the country, including several other neighbouring Yorkshire bands. They preferred to take the claim with a pinch of salt, and in any case there was no British Open Championship to settle things, so the matter was never resolved.

However it must be stated that Thurlstone were one of the country's top bands of the 20th century, but after the death of their director Alec Dyson in August 1995 (aged 77) the band went into decline and ceased ringing altogether in 2000.

(Hazel Bradey, current director of the Ecclesfield Hand-bell Ringers told the Editor, Philip Bedford, of an eerie follow-up to Thurlstone's demise. Some years later she had been given permission to use the Thurlstone bells and the practice hall when the Ecclesfield bells were sent to Whitechapel for overhaul.

"It felt very queer, almost ghostly. The practice room had an old, heavy, early Victorian door." She said "We unlocked it. It creaked open; and we crept inside. The practice room was untouched since the Thurstone ringers had walked out and locked the door for their last time in 2000. The bells were still set out on the table ready for practice. The trophies and other memorabilia were still in their glass cabinets around the walls – and there were mice droppings and festoons of cobwebs everywhere. We cleaned the place up and held our weekly practices there for 8 weeks until our own bells returned. Then, leaving the bells set out on the tables as before, we also walked out of the Thurstone practice room for the last time – and locked the door. It was very eerie, very spooky"

Hazel went on to say that she has since heard that the room is now being used for a playgroup and that the bells and other memorabilia have been stored for safekeeping until such time as someone with the knowledge and enthusiasm wants to get the band going again. When that happens a practice room will once again be made available to them in the village. Ed.)

In 1904 when Crosland Moor United were declared Champions and debarred from competing in the British Open, the band kept itself busy playing at concerts.

The band visited Sheffield (Yorkshire) for 2 days, Bolton, Darwen, Blackburn in Lancashire and other places. At Blackburn the large hall was packed an hour before the concert began.

On their return to Crosland Moor the band arrived at Exchange Station in Manchester, but found there was only one train to Huddersfield, which was from London Road Station, at midnight. Outside Exchange Station they asked a "Cabby" (horse and cab) if he would take the luggage (two large boxes containing 172 bells), which were a tremendous weight, across the city to the station. The band's biographer takes up the story: " The cabby replied, "Yes anything". He was evidently wanting a job, for no other cabby in Huddersfield could have been persuaded to take one of the boxes. One was hoisted onto the "Dickey" and another on top of the cab. Get inside shouted the cabby, but no-one desired to risk his life. No-one would have been surprised to see the bells in the street any minute. The cabby whipped up his horse and the ringers chased after their things and arrived at London Road Station just

...and Bell Co
~ 1871. ~

...and Campanologian
Conductor J. E. Crow...
...ec... David Crofts...

Holmfirth Temper...
...ductor John Moor...
...South Ha...

...adcliffe Juvenile
...nductor N. Pendlebu...
Sec... ...and L...

...rmitage Bridge
...onductor Seth Cold...
...ec... a Lockwo...

Scarborough
Conductor Geo Dia...
...y E. B. Newton. ...north (o...
...16 m...

Hyde
...onductor S. Brier...
...ec... S. Ives. Hy... Organis...

Oldham.
...onductor David...
Sec... Jas. ...
...Huggin...

in time to see the train depart". They did get home eventually.

A total of twenty six engagements were fulfilled during 1904. One of these was at Blyth in Northumberland for three days. During the ringers' absence at Blyth, some boys had hidden pieces of wood and baskets behind the band's rehearsal building in readiness for bonfire night and three boys aged about ten, discovered the wood and baskets and set fire to them. The result was the practice room caught fire. Seeing the blaze was getting bigger the boys became alarmed and tried and failed to put the fire out. Someone called the fire brigade but it was too late and the building was entirely gutted. This event is still remembered in Crosland Moor today. The fire was on September 10th, 1904. In the building there were 516 bells in three sets, only 100 were recovered and were damaged beyond repair. The only repairable article left was the collapsible wrought iron table. The value of the bells alone was £280 and along with other articles the total damage amounted to £350 at least, and by today's comparable values (2011), the band had lost property worth over £180,000. The property was not insured as insurance was not available on a wooden building.

This event would have discouraged most bands into giving up, but not the Crosland Moor men. Within forty eight hours from the fire starting, another set of 165 bells had been ordered from Shaw's Bell Foundry of Bradford, at a cost of £65. The band asked for public support and got it. The week following the fire the sum of £70 was brought to the Treasurer by the ringers. The secretary sent appeals to "gentlemen in the town" and received about £120, a considerable amount of money in those days.

All the music was destroyed in the fire, which Albert Townend, assisted by founder Thomas Cartwright had to rewrite.

The band had engagements already booked for the coming winter, the first being at Sheffield in seven weeks time and this was the first engagement which the band had ever taken at which it was bound by contract to appear, which it was able to do, using its new set on Saturday, October 29th, 1904 - how's that for a comeback? - and we today worry about trifling little problems and wonder if we should carry on. All should take heart from Crosland Moor United's example.

As I have already said, the band's biographer had stated that it was "absolutely necessary" that the band should have two sets of bells, one for engagements and contests, and the other for practice. This was something which all the top bands did, to make sure that they had as near a perfect a set of bells as possible for contesting, in order to gain the maximum number of marks. This also meant the public didn't have to listen to out-of-tune bells at concerts, so a higher standard was kept up.

Accordingly another set of 165 bells was ordered from Mears and Stainbank at the Whitechapel Bell Foundry, London at a cost of £95. The set was identical to the one bought from Shaw's and was as follows: 5½ octaves, from tenor 29C to 005F inclusive, 66 bells, 4½ octaves from tenor 25G to 01C inclusive as duplicates, 54 bells, 3½ octaves from tenor 19F to 03A sharp inclusive as triplicates, 42 bells, 3 extra bells 11G, 4G and 10A, total in the set 165 bells, which were christened "Nil Desperandum" by the band. This was the standard hand-bell "long set" used by the top class bands, and was the number used by many other bands, although some used more bells than this. The ringers at Clifton used a set of 193, while the Elland Band had a set of 172 bells bought in March 1914.

Other neighbouring bands came to help raise funds, so the Crosland Moor ringers could meet their liabilities. A benefit concert was organised by the Almondbury and Huddersfield Hand-bell Ringers, both fierce rivals in competition with Crosland Moor, but friends nevertheless. The concert was held on Christmas Eve 1904 at Huddersfield Town Hall. All three bands took part as well as Linthwaite Brass Band, Crosland Moor Wesleyan, Crosland Hill Wesleyan and the Huddersfield Co-operative choirs, along with Harry Horner, a baritone singer and Herbert Leeming, humourist.

As a result of many fund raising events the band was able to pay for the bells and build a new purpose-built brick band room, on the site of the old wooden one.

The band bought the freehold upon which the old band room stood (177 square yards). The new building was 22 feet long, 16 feet wide, 13½ feet high (to the ridge) and on the outside 8½ feet to the eaves. The total cost of the room and freehold was nearly £150.

I took a look at the building in 1982. It had been used as a workshop since being sold by the United band in 1935 and was full of junk. There was bench seating on three sides for the ringers, and more significantly a small gas heater in the centre of the floor. I wondered why the heater was in the middle of the floor as it would have been underneath a standard oblong bell ringing table, as specified by the Belle Vue authorities, which was 13 feet by 6 feet 6 inches. This was the size of table used by all the competition bands, because at Belle Vue, all the bands in the British Open used the same table, on which they placed their own paddings, cover and bells.

I knew the band used a three sided "U shaped" table as early as 1912. This type of table is used by most 'off table' bands in Britain

...and Bell Co
1871. —

...and Campanologian
conductor J. E. Crow...
...David Crofol...

Colnforth Temper...
...ductor John Moork
...South ham

...adcliffe Juvenile
...ductor Mr Pendlebu...
...ec... ...Hand L...

...mitage Bridge
...nductor Seth Gold...
...c... a Lockwo...

...carborough
...onductor Geo Pia...
E. B. Newton. 16 m...

Hyde.
...nductor S. Brier...
Organis...
...c... St Ives. Hy...

Oldham.
...onductor David
Sec... Jas. L...
...ippin...

today, but inside the United band room, I noticed the gas heater was in a central position, and because of the limits of the size of the building, a central position was the only place where the heater could go. If it had been next to a wall, the heater would have burnt either the ringers legs or set fire to the table, as there was only just enough room for the ringers to walk round the table to their ringing positions. So by design there was only one place where the heater could stand - in the centre of the room. It was then that I realised I had discovered the origins of the "U shaped" table. Its introduction by Crosland Moor United had little to do with having ringers on three sides so they didn't have their backs to the audience, but it was because of the gas heater. The band's biographer did say space had been cleverly utilised to the best advantage. I have a photograph of the band, taken in 1912, standing around their "U shaped" table. So this I feel is the origin of the "U shaped" table - another innovation from Crosland Moor United.

I had been hopeful of getting the use of the old United band room, for a revival of hand-bell ringing in the village, and Cyril Clay, one of the former Crosland Moor Public ringers, and I made enquires about the building to the owner, but a few weeks after our visit, I received news that the building had been severely damaged by fire and again with remarkable repetition, children were thought to be responsible. This fire was on October 7th, 1982 and within a month of the anniversary of the 1904 fire.

However, like the ringers of 1904, I did not give up and another rehearsal room was found at the Liberal Club, when a new band was formed in April 1983 and in a remarkable repeat of history the band, conducted by Richard Sigsworth, won the 3.5 octaves and under class, at the 1985 Mrs Sunderland Musical Competition in Huddersfield at their first attempt.

So Crosland Moor United, under their conductor Albert Townend, had brought the art of hand-bell ringing to a high level. The band had introduced new innovations of style, technique and musical expression, the latter an area in the art of hand-bell ringing which is often overlooked - and most other northern bands had taken up these innovations.

The correspondent of the Manchester Evening Chronicle, reporting on the 1907 British Open, said, "The number of bells generally has shown a tendency to increase of late years, so that many of the notes were duplicated to facilitate execution in playing the more difficult pieces". The correspondent then quotes "There was a time' declared one veteran ' when all that was required was that each note should be clearly sounded, but now, not merely the technique, but something of the expression demanded of the pianist is essential to success. Indeed, the performers are all provided with the piano score, all the markings of which must be faithfully observed'".

So standards had risen, but in contradiction to the evidence, Shelley's Fred Shaw, in an interview with the Huddersfield Examiner correspondent in 1913, contended that the pieces which Shelley had played back in the 1870s were as difficult as any yet mastered. In Shelley's case this was probably true, but it was the way in which pieces were played that had improved, and of course the bass had been given more prominence.

In his book on Crosland Moor United the band's biographer, Jimmy Ellis outlines the method of arranging a British Open test piece. "In the first place the selection sent is an ordinary piano score, with the metronome times inserted on each movement. The music is now sent, (1906) without any metronome marks whatever. The notes in the treble clef are written in the treble book and the notes up to about top F in the bass clef are written in the bass book. All notes from the bass F to, say, the G on the second line in the treble clef are written in the tenor book. All the music is written out in the treble clef so as to be uniform. Then we go carefully through the selection and the bass ringers take as their bells whatever they think they can manage, say up to bass F (top line in the bass clef). The tenor ringers would then have all from bass F to bottom treble F#, about one octave and the treble ringers all above this. Each section would then arrange its own part. For instance in the treble, the bottom ringer would have as his ordinary bells G and A, the next B and C, next D and E and the top treble ringer F and G. Also each ringer would probably have the accidentals and octaves to these bells. All other notes would be shared out to the best advantage and if a ringer could not put a certain note in he would arrange with one of the others to do so. It will therefore, be readily seen that a good arrangement of a piece is half the battle".

This was the system used by most bands right into the 1930s, and is still the basis of most Yorkshire-type bands today. It is a good description of the Yorkshire method of playing.

Chapter 5 –
Other Influential Bands

At this stage I think we should take a look at some of the other influential bands who made up the pre-first World War hand-bell scene.

One of these was Horbury (near Wakefield, Yorkshire) who had been the only band to break the domination by Dewsbury, Liversedge and Almondbury, of the British Open in the 1880s and 90s. Between them these three bands had won every contest between 1883 and 1900 apart from 1896 when the winners were Horbury, under conductor James Woffenden. Horbury became a different kind of band and were probably unique in the world of hand-bell ringing in England. Just when hand-bell ringing began in the village is not known, but there was a set of twelve bells in existence in 1853 and probably long before that. These belonged to the change ringers and were used only for tune ringing at Christmas and on other festive occasions. In 1855 or 1856 twelve or fifteen additional bells were purchased, each member contributing to the cost. Only simple tune playing was attempted. In 1869 when the change ringers broke up, several of the members took some bells as their share. A few of these bells were bought by shopkeepers and used as door bells. The original peal of twelve was left intact. The tenor bell was said to have been cast by Henry Carter, a local blacksmith and was noted for its unusual thickness. I decided to go to Horbury to see if this bell was still there. It was not.

A new era at Horbury began in 1871 when the hand-bell ringers became independent of the change ringers, having officers and practices of their own. This band was formed by several of the church choir boys whose voices were breaking.

In late 1872 a fund raising concert was held. The artists were Horbury Brass Band and the Shelley Hand-bell Ringers. The profit was £20, with which a set of 56 bells were bought from the Darton Hand-bell Ringers (near Barnsley).

This set was used for a few years and then sold to another Wakefield band, Chapelthorpe, who were members of the Yorkshire Association up to the 1914 World War. The Horbury band then bought 111 bells in 1876 for £50 from Stockham's Foundry, London. This band flourished until 1882, when they lost several members and the band broke up, to be re-formed in 1889.

The Stockham bells were replaced by a new set of 148 Shaw bells in 1895, which cost £57. It was with these bells that the band won first prize and a gold medal in the British Open at Belle Vue in 1896. In July 1899 the band was engaged for a week in Scotland. In 1901 the tower bell ringers resolved that no member of their band should be active members of the hand-bell ringers, which "crippled the Society for some time". However the band recovered from this setback and another set of 171 Shaw bells were bought in 1903, and the old set sold to the newly formed Lindley Parish Church Hand-bell Ringers (Huddersfield) who won the second section of the Yorkshire Association's 1907 contest. The Lindley band was sponsored by several local pubs, who all contributed to buy the bells, but the band broke up at the outset of the 1914 war. There was a short revival in the 1920s, after which the bells remained unused until 1986.

Fig. 89: Lindley Parish Church HBR 1907: L. Stansfield (Cond)

But back to Horbury. The band's most well known conductor was Mr William Giggle, who took over in 1904. It was he who had founded the Yorkshire Association the year before.

Under Giggle, Horbury became a different sort of band from the rest. Concentrating on concerts rather than contests, they formed a party of Glee singers amongst four of the band members. This enabled the band to supply a concert programme without any outside help. The glee singers sang, accompanied by the hand-bells, "Alone on the deep" and "Battle Eve". The tenor singer also sang solo with hand-bell accompaniment, "My Pretty Jane".

The band's repertoire included the usual overtures being performed at the time, such as "Poet and Peasant" and "Der Freischutz". There were also such items as the intermezzo from "Cavalleria Rusticana", "These Evening Bells", "Merry Bells", the march from "Tannhauser", and the glee "Farewell the Parting Hour is Nigh" which was used to close their concerts. There was also a selection "Maritana", and one of Mendelssohn's "Lieder ohne Worte".

As the band's fame spread, the band fulfilled engagements in areas as far apart as London, Scotland, the Isle of Man, Wales and the USA.

In 1907 they played for ten days in North Wales where the band based themselves at Menai Bridge on the Isle of Anglesey, where concerts were given in Beaumaris and on board steamers. The band returned to Wales at Whitsuntide 1908 playing at Colwyn Bay for four days, giving two performances each day. A few weeks

Fig. 90: The Horbury Glee Party - early 20th Century, L. to R. W Wain - tenor, J E Jessop - bass, C Dawson - baritone, E Charlesworth - Alto.

before that, saw them at Middlesborough at Easter and on January 2nd, 1909 they were at Paisley in Scotland. With all this travel it's hardly surprising the band's contest work fell off considerably.

Here is a promotional cutting from Jimmy Ellis' Scrap Book:

There was excitement amongst all hand-bell ringers in 1907 when Horbury were asked to play at the National Band Festival at Crystal Palace on the 28th of September, the first time hand-bell ringing had been seen at Crystal Palace since Enderby Jackson's experimental hand-bell contest back in 1856. It was ironic that again, the appearance of Horbury was seen as an experiment, which, had it been successful could have led to a hand-bell ringing contest at the Palace in 1908.

The festival already had contests for Brass Bands, (its mainstay) and for concertina and reed bands. The festival was started in 1900 by a gifted entrepreneur who did a lot of good for brass bands, but did the hand-bell movement very little good at all. Remember his name as he comes into our story later. He was John Henry Iles, who, with nothing to do while on a business trip in Manchester, wandered into Belle Vue in 1898 to see the British Open Brass Band Contest and was instantly taken with the sound of brass.

On Iles' return to London he continued his new found interest and within three months he had met Samuel Cope, the founder, editor and owner of the "British Bandsman" newspaper. Iles immediately bought the paper from Cope but kept Cope on as editor. Iles' one action which did the hand-bell movement some good was that he allowed a portion of the British Bandsman for the publication of hand-bell ringers news, which was first included on November 17th, 1906. Sometimes there would be a few column inches and on other occasions there would be a whole page.

The articles were a regular feature up to 1910, but became few and far between after 1910 and faded out altogether around 1913.

Fig. 91: Horbury Hand-bell Ringers - promotional advert

A student at Bradford University, tipped me off about the articles, saying he'd seen them at the British Newspaper Library, Colindale, London.

I set off to London and spent five days at the Library, from opening to closing time each day, researching the articles - very tedious work, but the articles give a vivid picture of the day to day workings of the bands of the era, and I'll never forget going back to my lodgings dog-tired, but hardly able to sleep, being so excited at what I had read.

The Yorkshire Hand-bell Ringers Association adopted the British Bandsman as its official organ. The news was complied by an association member who wrote under the alias of "Codon".

Iles, inspired by Enderby Jackson's legendary contest at the Crystal Palace, began to think how he could arrange a contest at the Palace.

His chance came during the great patriotic wave, which swept over the country with the outbreak of the Boer War. Iles organised the British Bandsman War Fund to be run in conjunction with a campaign in the "Daily Mail" to raise money to help relatives and

Fig. 92: John Henry Iles

173

dependants of soldiers fighting in South Africa. Subsequently, with the Daily Mail's help and massive publicity, the Royal Albert Hall was hired and a great Grand Patriotic Brass Band Concert was held to help the fund. The line up of ten bands included three of the Northern "Crack brass bands" - Wyke Temperance, Besses O'th' Barn and Black Dyke Mills Brass Bands.

Iles' "rabbit-out-of-the-hat" was to persuade a reluctant Sir Arthur Sullivan (of Gilbert and Sullivan fame), to conduct the massed brass bands in his arrangement of "The Absent-minded Beggar". So on a night of bad weather on January 20th 1900, the Hall was full, with 10,000 folk taking their places.

Sullivan picked up his baton and Mme Bertha Flotow sang "Onward Christian Soldiers" accompanied by the Albert Hall organ and the brass bands' two hundred and fifty players - and a tide of pent-up emotion was released and the whole concert was carried along on a flood of patriotism. The distinguished conductor, on the brink of tears, turned to Iles and asked, "What can be done for these fellows?", and who was one of the directors of the Crystal Palace Company? None other than Sir Arthur Sullivan. The National Band Festival began life six months later in July.

The festival was to remain at the Crystal Palace, the central showpiece of the 1851 Great Exhibition, until this magnificent building was destroyed by fire in 1936. I did hear recently that a replica of the Crystal Palace is being built at Dallas, Texas, USA - I would love to see it!

"Horbury Hand-bell Ringers contribution to the 1907 National Band Festival at the Palace", said the British Bandsman, "came as a great surprise to many of the London audience and the band were the object of much interest and their dexterity in handling such a large number of bells. The Bandsman added "Their rendering of Suppé's overture 'Poet and Peasant' was excellent, but in such a large hall, a hand-bell combination, however excellent, does not show to its best advantage. Not a very encouraging report for the country's hand-bell ringers who wanted a contest along with the other bands of brass and concertinas.

Rumours about the proposed Crystal Palace Hand-bell Ringing Contest rumbled on for months among the hand-bell movement. Kaye Cooke, a vice-president of the Yorkshire Association, commented in the British Bandsman in January 1908 and thought it would be a good idea and that, "We ought to have one, for, like the other bands, it would be a higher ideal to aim at, and would let the vast number of people there see what beautiful music the hand-bell band can produce". In May there was a rumour that the proposed contest at the Palace had been abandoned for the

174

year. The British Bandsman denied the rumour, saying, "Mr Iles is doing all he possibly can with the Crystal Palace Management to bring about such a contest in connection with the National Band Festival and he hopes to be in a position to make an announcement very shortly". When Iles did make a statement, it was that the idea for a hand-bell contest in the National Band Festival was not to be proceeded with for the year 1908.

The idea was never brought up again. What its effect could have been on the future of the hand-bell movement can only be imagined, but it could have helped bring the spread of hand-bell ringing in its highly developed Yorkshire method form to the South of England in the first decade of the twentieth century, which would have strengthened the movement and thus it would have been in a much stronger position to withstand the decline of the art when it arrived.

The idea of spreading the movement to the rest of the country was mooted as early as 1906, with the arrival of the "Hand-bell Ringers News" in the British Bandsman. In the issue of February 2nd, 1907, the British Bandsman said how well hand-bell ringing was doing in Yorkshire and that the ringers there were getting much enjoyment out of their hobby, as well as bringing their art to a higher state of perfection - a state of affairs which had come

about "Through being united and working together in harmonious spirit. It was the formation of the Yorkshire Hand-bell Ringers Association which has put life into it". "Why" said the Bandsman, "then, do not the other counties follow suit? If we had several such associations formed in different places, inter-county contest would be very interesting and attractive. Why, then, don't other counties where hand-bell ringers are fairly strong make a move towards forming such an organisation?"

175

The Bandsman invited people in sympathy with such a movement to write in, and then it could be organised. Of course no-one did write in, the reason being that by 1907, the only county, where hand-bell ringing was strong, was Yorkshire. But the appeal was worth a try.

If the movement as a whole didn't benefit from the appearance by Horbury at the Crystal Palace, the Horbury Band did. After the Palace appearance the band was inundated with enquiries for terms, and were the chief attraction at the reopening concert of the Alexandra Hall, New Brighton on October 10th, 1907, as well as places aforementioned, but the best was yet to come. In January 1909 the band signed a contract for a tour of the United States in the following summer. The band of seven ringers plus Giggle, the conductor, sailed on Wednesday the 9th of June 1909 on the S.S. Haverford. The members of the band were: W Wain, T Mountain, W H Schofield, G Hunt, E Charlesworth, A A Fothergill and E Jessop.

The first performance of the tour was on June 28th and the last, in New York, on December 15th. The first twelve weeks of the tour were in the districts west of Chicago.

The British Bandsman gave regular details of the tour and the towns and cities where they played, all too numerous to mention here. The band performed at Ottumwa, the capital of Wapello County, Iowa State. The concerts there met with great success. The audience went wild with enthusiasm and so many encores were demanded. The concert lasted three times longer than arranged, but at the next town, Boone, the audience was just the opposite "Being very undemonstrative".

Their concert at Montezuma attracted a very large crowd and there were two hundred carriages waiting outside at the close of the concert. At this concert there was an interesting incident. Somehow it became known amongst the audience that one of the ringers, Tom Mountain, had been an English soldier in the Boer War, and he was besieged with people who wished to shake his hand.

When at Anamosa, the members of the band met the Governor of Nebraska, with whom they dined in the evening.

The band found the Summer heat difficult to cope with. At times the temperature ranged from 100 - 113 degrees F in the shade. At Charlton the heat was "almost unbearable" and their conductor W H Giggle (who had never been in the best of health most of his life) was completely overcome by the heat at the afternoon concert, a doctor forbidding him to appear at the evening concert, but he was well enough to conduct again the next day.

Perhaps the decision to tour in the summer months had been influenced by the experiences of Almondbury's winter tour, eight years earlier, when the ringers seemed to be frozen stiff most of the time.

The band sailed home from New York on the S.S. Campania on 15th December 1909. Mr Giggle was approached for a return visit in 1910. There was also an offer to tour Australia, which was not taken up. The Horbury Ringers did make a second tour of the USA and Canada in 1912, but it seems that W H Giggle did not go with Horbury and that their conductor for the 1912 tour may have been Mr Arthur Fothergill, one of the ringers on the 1909 tour, or Giggle's predecessor and successor, James Woffenden.

In the USA the Horbury Band was billed as "The Royal English Hand-bell Ringers, of Horbury", something the band did not publicize back in Britain. If they had, there would have been a chorus of laughter and derision from the other bands, especially in Yorkshire, where they show no mercy over such matters. The name "Royal" was of course a throw back to when Uttoxeter, Shelley and the Poland Street Hand-bell Ringers had used the title.

One member of the 1912 touring band, Jack F Jessop, never returned to Horbury. He sent for his fiancée, Lilian Schofield and they were married in the USA.

The band did no more concerts after the second tour; one of the reasons being that several of the band's members didn't return to England until the War in Europe had ended.

After the War the band re-formed including some new members, and returned to contesting again, under the conductorship of Arthur Audsley Fothergill, with whom they had won fifth prize in the British Open in 1923. The year before, the band had taken first prize, in the second section of the Yorkshire Association Championships.

Arthur Fothergill made his living selling pots, pans and oil lamps, from door to door, for which he was nicknamed "Old Lamp Oil" by the locals.

William II Giggle made a living selling yeast and flour for baking, while his wife kept a millinery shop in the village. He began his musical career as a chorister at St Peter's Church, Horbury in 1882. In the early years of the century he was organist and choirmaster at St Aidan's Church, South Ossett, where he conducted another band of hand-bell ringers. The St Aidan's Hand-bell Ringers seemed to have begun life around 1907 when they entered the Yorkshire Association's contest at Barnsley Public Hall. The band took part in those competitions up to the 1910 contest when the band entered with Giggle listed in the programme as conductor, but they did not compete. In February 1908, the Ossett band bought a set of bells from the Crosshill's Hand-bell Ringers from near Keighley, Yorkshire. The Crosshill Ringers didn't seem to be a particularly active band and I can only account for their entry in one contest, which was the 1901 British Open when the 10 ringers in the band were conducted by Mr R Redmond. The Ossett St Aidan's band don't appear to have lasted much longer after 1910, as we never hear of them again after this date. First mention of hand-bell ringing in Ossett is in 1867 when a band from Streetside, Ossett, with 10 ringers, were conducted at the British Open by Joseph Smith.

When Giggle went with Horbury to the USA in 1909 Ossett engaged Giggle's predecessor at Horbury, James Woffenden, as their conductor while Giggle was away.

Horbury also entered the 1910 Yorkshire Association contests, but the band did not compete and no name was given as their conductor in the programme, only the names of the ringers were given, all of which, along with other evidence leads me to think that Mr Giggle's relations with the Horbury Ringers may have become less than ideal during the 1909 tour of the USA, which could have been one of the reasons for his sudden departure from the Horbury Band.

Mr Giggle presented the prizes at the Yorkshire Association's 1910 contest in his capacity as President of the Association. Before 1909 he had been Secretary, and had also been Secretary of Horbury Change Ringers (their towerbell ringing society), until they ruled that their tower bell ringers should not be active members of the hand-bell ringers. Giggle's ringing career began in 1889 when the Horbury band was re-formed using the old Stockham bells.

Another reason why I think Giggle's relations with the Horbury ringers became less than perfect, is because around the time when Horbury went back to the USA for their second visit in 1912, Giggle formed the Imperial Hand-bell Ringers - a professional band. The band was put together specifically in order to tour Canada and the USA. The Imperial was the only hand-bell band formed in England, to be purely professional hand-bell ringers. (There had been such bands in the USA on Vaudeville for years, but not in England) Bands like Shelley and Crosland Moor United were only semi-professional.

Up to 1982 all I knew about the Imperial Hand-bell Ringers was

178

just a few lines and a photo printed on a poster used to promote their concerts in Canada, but this said nothing of the band's origins, although I had recognised W H Giggle on the poster. I also found a photo of the band, taken in Canada, at Horbury. In 1982 when interviewing Ecclesfield's veteran ringers Albert Braybrook and Kenneth Gregory, I was amazed to discover they had knowledge of the Imperial Band. Albert also produced more photographs of them and told me of the band's origins and adventures.

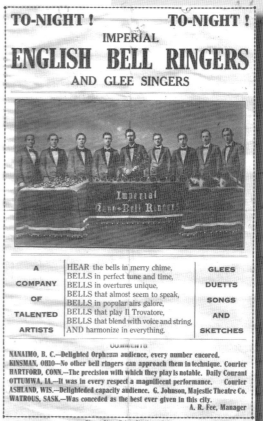

Fig. 94: Imperial Hand-bell Ringers c.1912

"The Band included two Ecclesfield ringers, my Uncle Ellis and Arthur Sorsby. They went to rehearsals every Saturday at Horbury or Ossett. All they had was five weeks' practice. The other seven members of the Band were all new to hand-bell ringing, but they were already musicians, they practised full time during the five weeks' preparation."

"Giggle selected people to be in the band who could do something else, so they could provide a full concert without outside help. My Uncle Ellis and Arthur Sorsby were good singers, another young lad called Francis played the cello as well as the bells in the programme."

"The Band performed at a concert in Chicago, the famous tenor Caruso, was in the same programme."

"The ringers had a dispute with Giggle. He took his wife with him, and made her a member of the Band and took money from the wages of the others to pay her, which was not part of the agreement. So Giggle was going to let them down. The Police were called, who sealed the boxes of bells until the dispute was settled."

"Each ringer was paid £2 10 shillings a week, which the two Ecclesfield men spent mostly on booze" said Albert with a smile.

After the 1912 Imperial tour William H Giggle who had been one of the leading lights of the hand-bell scene for so long, fades from sight and we hear nothing of him again, except in a passing reference in the Huddersfield Weekly Examiner May 20th 1930 (page 8 – Col 2). The Examiner, which was reporting on the Yorkshire Hand-bell Ringers Association's 'Coming of Age Gathering – A review of progress since 1904', said that the founder, W. H. Giggle did not live long enough to see the full fruits of his secreting (sic) work.

I took a trip to see if the Horbury bells were still there - they were not. The band's last rehearsal room was a wooden building in Chepstye Road, used until recently by Horbury Brass Band. Before this, several rooms had been used, including the Temperance building and a room over a bake-house in Ranters Fold.

The Band became inactive in the late 1930s, probably after the death of long-standing ringer and conductor Arthur A Fothergill in January 1939 age 63, after which the 170 bells were taken to St Peter's Church for safe keeping until needed again, something which many subscription bands did when inactive, this has led many people to believe that hand-bell bands were always Church bands.

In around 1968, the bells, of which there were about 100 or so left, were sold for 4 shillings (20p) and 5 shillings (25p) each in a Church bazaar. The sale was instigated by the vicar at the time, who wanted a clear out. The sale raised about £28 I was told, a paltry sum for over 100 years of Horbury's heritage and culture. One of the old ringers, Mathias Yelland objected to the sale, as did relatives of other past ringers and there were letters of objection in the Yorkshire Post newspaper. The vicar (who was only at Horbury 3 years) replied that the bells had been at the Church for nearly 30 years, so the Church could do what they liked with them and the sale went ahead. Two of the largest bells were sold to a farmer's wife at Grimethorpe who wanted them for calling the workers from the fields for their meals.

The bells were not even sold as a set - one of the worst acts of irresponsibility I have encountered during my research.

The bells of Christ Church, Tintwistle, William Gordon's old band, suffered a similar fate in the early 1980s when their set of 147 Whitechapel bells was divided up and sold here and there to other bands all round the country, although a three octave single set was kept.

Also, bells have been sold as "Sets" by other Churches, who seem to look upon hand-bells as short-term cash, rather than instruments of value to the heritage, culture and tradition of their locality. Even if such bells are not being used, there is always the chance that they will be used in the future - if they are kept for such an occasion. The fact that bells have been unused for many years is no reason to dispose of them. Tradition is subject to decline and revival. The decline may last years, in some cases only a few years, in others the decline may last for as many as sixty years or more, as at Clifton, but, when the right conditions return, like a seed in a desert, when the rains come - the tradition will grow and bloom again.

180

So I urge all custodians of hand-bells, to preserve and care for them, for use in their own locality by future generations.

However, the short term lending of bells to someone in another area, to enable them to start a band, is good for the art and can often stimulate interest locally, but proper provision should be made for their return. One successful loan arrangement was between Elland and Beverley Town (Yorkshire) in 1982 when Beverley borrowed unused bells from Elland and raised enough money, using the Elland bells to buy a new set of their own. After the borrowed bells were returned to Elland, interest had been aroused and a new band was formed in 1985. So the result of the loan, was that two bands were formed. If the bells had been sold, the result would have been one band. Which is the better situation?

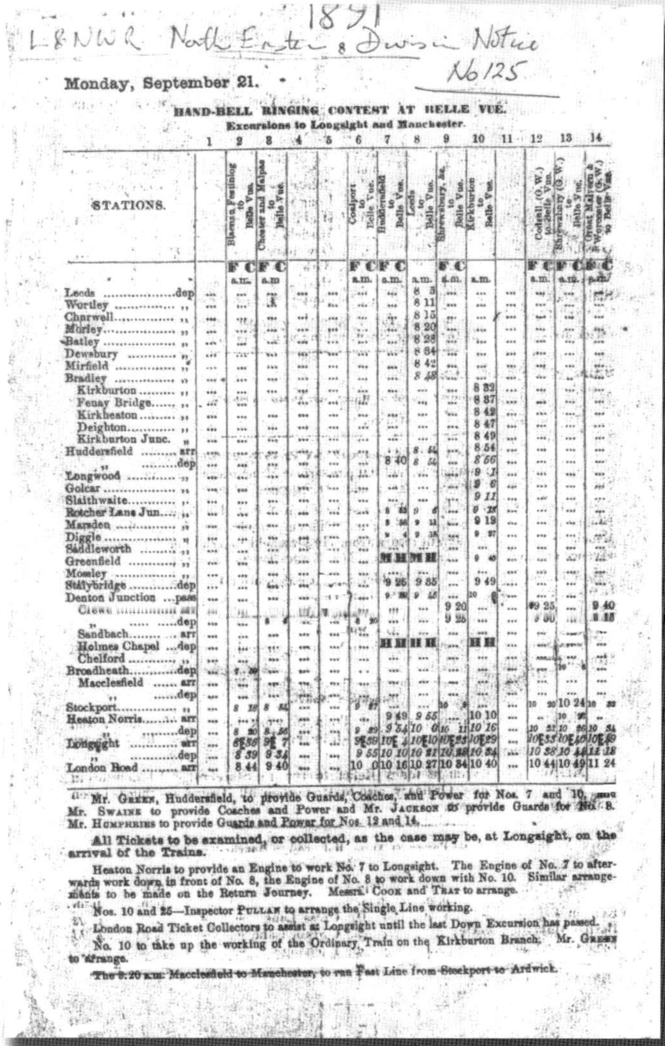

1891
L&NWR North Eastern Division Notice
No 125

Monday, September 21.

HAND-BELL RINGING CONTEST AT BELLE VUE.
Excursions to Longsight and Manchester.

STATIONS.	1	2	3	4	5	6	7	8	9	10	11	12	13	14
		Blaenau Festiniog to Belle Vue.	Chester and Malpas to Belle Vue.			Coalport to Belle Vue.	Huddersfield to Belle Vue.	Leeds to Belle Vue.	Shrewsbury, &c. to Belle Vue.	Kirkburton to Belle Vue.		Codsall (G.W.) to Belle Vue.	Shrewsbury (G.W.) to Belle Vue.	Great Malvern & Worcester (G.W.) to Belle Vue.
		F C	F C			F C	F C		F C			F C	F C	F C
		a.m.	a.m			a.m.	a.m.	a.m.	a.m.	a.m.		a.m.	a.m.	p.m.
Leeds dep	...	...	...	...	...	...	...	8 5	...	...	...	...	...	...
Wortley ,,	...	...	...	...	...	...	...	8 11	...	...	...	...	...	...
Churwell ,,	...	...	...	...	...	...	...	8 15	...	...	...	...	...	...
Morley ,,	...	...	...	...	...	...	...	8 20	...	...	...	...	...	...
Batley ,,	...	...	...	...	...	...	...	8 28	...	...	...	...	...	...
Dewsbury ,,	...	...	...	...	...	...	...	8 34	...	...	...	...	...	...
Mirfield ,,	...	...	...	...	...	...	...	8 42	...	...	...	...	...	...
Bradley ,,	...	...	...	...	...	...	...	8 48	...	...	...	...	...	...
Kirkburton ,,	...	...	...	...	...	...	...	...	...	8 32	...	...	...	...
Fenay Bridge ,,	...	...	...	...	...	...	...	...	...	8 37	...	...	...	...
Kirkheaton ,,	...	...	...	...	...	...	...	...	...	8 42	...	...	...	...
Deighton ,,	...	...	...	...	...	...	...	...	...	8 47	...	...	...	...
Kirkburton Junc. ,,	...	...	...	...	...	...	...	...	...	8 49	...	...	...	...
Huddersfield arr	...	...	...	...	...	...	...	8 54	...	8 54	...	...	...	...
,, dep	...	...	...	...	...	...	8 40	8 54	...	8 56	...	...	...	...
Longwood ,,	...	...	...	...	...	...	...	...	...	9 1	...	...	...	...
Golcar ,,	...	...	...	...	...	...	...	...	...	9 6	...	...	...	...
Slaithwaite ,,	...	...	...	...	...	...	...	...	...	9 11	...	...	...	...
Rotcher Lane Jun. ,,	...	...	...	...	...	...	8 [illegible]	9 6	...	9 15	...	...	...	...
Marsden ,,	...	...	...	...	...	...	8 56	9 11	...	9 19	...	...	...	...
Diggle ,,	...	...	...	...	...	...	9 4	9 18	...	9 27	...	...	...	...
Saddleworth ,,	...	...	...	...	...	...	...	...	...	...	...	...	...	...
Greenfield ,,	...	...	...	...	...	...	H H	H H	...	9 40	...	...	...	...
Mosley ,,	...	...	...	...	...	...	...	...	...	...	...	...	...	...
Stalybridge dep	...	...	...	...	...	...	9 25	9 35	...	9 49	...	...	...	...
Denton Junction pass	...	...	...	...	...	...	9 [illegible]	9 45	...	10 [illegible]	...	...	...	...
Crewe arr	...	...	...	...	...	...	...	...	9 20	...	...	9 25	...	9 40
,, dep	...	...	8 [illegible]	...	...	8 20	...	...	9 25	...	...	9 30	...	[illegible]
Sandbach arr	...	...	...	...	...	...	...	...	...	...	...	...	...	...
Holmes Chapel dep	...	...	...	...	...	...	H H	H H	...	H H	...	...	...	...
Chelford ,,	...	...	...	...	...	...	...	...	...	...	...	...	...	...
Broadheath dep	...	7 [illegible]	...	...	...	...	...	...	...	...	...	...	10 [illegible]	...
Macclesfield arr	...	...	...	...	...	...	...	...	...	...	...	...	...	...
,, dep	...	...	...	...	...	...	...	...	...	...	...	...	...	...
Stockport ,,	...	8 18	8 54	...	...	9 27	...	...	10 [illegible]	...	...	10 20	10 24	10 [illegible]
Heaton Norris arr	...	...	...	...	...	...	9 49	9 55	...	10 10	...	...	10 [illegible]	...
,, dep	...	8 20	8 56	...	...	9 [illegible]	9 54	10 0	10 11	10 16	...	10 [illegible]	10 26	10 [illegible]
Longsight arr	...	8 36	9 7	...	...	9 59	10 4	10 10	10 23	10 29	...	10 35	10 40	10 [illegible]
,, dep	...	8 39	9 34	...	...	9 55	10 10	10 21	10 [illegible]	10 34	...	10 38	10 44	11 18
London Road arr	...	8 44	9 40	...	...	10 0	10 16	10 27	10 34	10 40	...	10 44	10 49	11 24

Mr. GREEN, Huddersfield, to provide Guards, Coaches, and Power for Nos. 7 and 10, and Mr. SWAINE to provide Coaches and Power and Mr. JACKSON to provide Guards for No. 8. Mr. HUMPHRIES to provide Guards and Power for Nos. 12 and 14.

All Tickets to be examined, or collected, as the case may be, at Longsight, on the arrival of the Trains.

Heaton Norris to provide an Engine to work No. 7 to Longsight. The Engine of No. 7 to afterwards work down in front of No. 8, the Engine of No. 8 to work down with No. 10. Similar arrangements to be made on the Return Journey. Messrs. COOK and TEAT to arrange.

Nos. 10 and 25—Inspector PULLAN to arrange the Single Line working.

London Road Ticket Collectors to assist at Longsight until the last Down Excursion has passed.

No. 10 to take up the working of the Ordinary Train on the Kirkburton Branch. Mr. GREEN to arrange.

The 8.20 a.m. Macclesfield to Manchester, to run Fast Line from Stockport to Ardwick.

Fig. 95: Special Excursion Trains were always provided for the British Open. (no fewer than 40 trains in 1913)

Another interesting band was based at Lane Bottom Congregational Chapel, Holmfirth, (Yorkshire). Known as Lane Hand-bell Ringers, Holmfirth, the band was only short lived, beginning in 1901 among members of the Sunday School, although Holmfirth is one of the older names associated with the art, having taken part in the first British Open at Belle Vue in 1855. The Lane band's best performance in the British Open was in 1904 when they came third. The following year, they competed in the Yorkshire Championships held at the Public Hall, Barnsley. Lane and all the Huddersfield bands, Lindley and Crosland Moor United, travelled to Barnsley on a special hand-bell ringers express, along with the Huddersfield Examiner correspondent, who reported, “The special train to Barnsley left Huddersfield at 1.15 pm and reached Barnsley at 3.30 pm, ten minutes after the stated time for the competition to begin! The whole journey could have been done in a good train in the time the special train was

Figure 96: Lane Hand Bell Ringers, Holmfirth after their win in the 1904 Yorkshire Association Championships at Barnsley. Conductor John Moorhouse is on the right of the picture

late", said the bemused reporter.

The day was however a good one for Lane who won the first prize in the second section contest. The day was also a good one for Almondbury United. The late night eleven o'clock tram car to Almondbury contained sixty-nine passengers and the Challenge Cup for the first section winner and the change ringers of All Saints then went up the tower and rang a peal in honour of Almondbury's success. How many ringers would dare do that today I wonder?

But fortunes in hand-bell ringing can quickly change and at the beginning of 1907, the Lane band had only four members, and up to 1908, it had "been a hard struggle to keep going at all".

March 1908 saw them in third place in the first section of the Yorkshire Championships and fourth at the British Open when they were probably the youngest band in the country at that time. Youth was on their side but not fate because after the 1909 contest the band faded from the scene never to be heard of again, very unusual, for a new pre-first war band, to break up before the war had even been envisaged. The band's conductor, John Moorhouse, who lived in South Lane, Holmfirth, also conducted another band at the time, Woodroyd, just a stone's throw up the road at Honley. From his photo, Mr Moorhouse looked a seasoned campaigner and was conductor of Holmfirth Temperance back in 1875 when the band won first prize for the second year running. Mr Moorhouse was probably one of the Holmfirth ringers.

Almondbury United had one more Yorkshire Championship win in 1907 with a masterly performance of a selection from "Il Travatore" (Verdi). After the band's return from their adventures in the USA they did their best to regain supremacy at Belle Vue and came second in 1904, 1905 and 1906. Like the other bands, they had had to change their style, to keep up with Crosland Moor United.

In December 1907 Almondbury United decided to call it a day, going out as "Yorkshire Champions", they organised a Grand Final Concert in Huddersfield Town Hall on December 14th.

Their guests were the Huddersfield Hand-bell Ringers, Miss Emily Cox (soprano), Master Harry Idle (violinist), Crosland Moor United Hand-bell Ringers, the Carlton Quartet, Mr J C Dyson (cornet) and Almondbury Juniors who had been formed to continue the tradition and gave their first performance on January 19th, 1907 aged between 13 and 17. After the retirement of the senior band, they dropped the word "Juniors" and were known simply as "Almondbury".

Also in the Town Hall concert were the famous Heckmondwike Concertina Band, 20 performers all in evening dress.

The concert was closed with Almondbury United playing "Auld Lang Syne" with variations, the close of one of the most brilliant careers in the annals of hand-bell ringing.

The concertina bands were also very popular in the North of England and had their own contest at Belle Vue. The concertina contest at Belle Vue began in 1905 after a conversation between Belle Vue's owner, James Jennison and a concertina buff, who asked Jennison if he would run a contest, but was told it would not be a draw. At that point a big man on the brass band scene, John Gladney, came along. Jennison asked him if he knew anything of concertina bands. "Yes", said Mr Gladney, "I have heard them play, they can get splendid effects, the tenor and bass parts coming out just like a brass band. I think they will gain a preference over the hand-bells". Well, Mr Gladney was a giant in the brass band world, but he certainly got that one wrong.

While Horbury toured the USA, Shrewsbury, in Shropshire, was the venue for a one-off special contest held on Whit Monday, 1909 at the famous flower show. The competing bands were Clifton Seniors; Birstall St Saviours; Clifton Juniors and Ossett St Aidan's. Crosland Moor United had entered but pulled out beforehand.

183

Fig. 97: Clifton Hand-bell Ringers in 1895 shortly after receiving their new bells (Is that a 32G in front of the bass ringer?)

The adjudicator was Mr J Ord Hume, who had arranged the test piece for John Henry Ile's first brass band contest at Crystal Palace. Mr Ord Hume had also been one of the adjudicators of the British Open Hand-bell Ringing Contest back in 1899. I don't think he was very popular as he wasn't engaged again.

Before announcing his decision at the Shrewsbury contest Ord Hume complained that one of the bands had caused him some annoyance because they had taken twenty minutes to get ready. He then gave his awards - first prize £7 Clifton Senior, second £5 Birstall St Saviour's, third Clifton Juniors and fourth to Ossett St Aidan's.

Ord Hume's remarks caused quite a stir at the time. The blame for not getting ready was attributed to Birstall, when it should have been Clifton Seniors, who played just before Birstall, and though they had a larger number of men, it took them a long time to clear their bells away. Birstall had a smaller number of men and therefore legitimately took some time to set up their bells, thus adding to the delay caused by Clifton Seniors. It was thought that the decision was prejudiced as a result. The British Bandsman correspondent "Codon" commented that it took time to get hand-bells ready for a performance and the adjudicators should be experienced enough to know that it wasn't wise to fluster men by hurrying them.

Mind you, J Ord Hume was a bit of a lad. He once gave a very poor tenor horn player the medal for the best trombone!

The winners of the Shrewsbury competition, Clifton, returned to

184

their hill top village, near Brighouse on the edge of the Pennines, with their prize, amid great rejoicing. After all, the band had had an unfortunate record of being one of Yorkshire's "crack" bands without actually winning a first prize. They had always been among the best bands since their fifth place at the British Open in 1894 with their highest placing being second to Crosland Moor United in 1901.

The band rose from small beginnings with 24 bells in 1890.

The band was composed of members of Clifton Parish Church, to which the 24 bells belonged. Their leader was Mr James Fearnley, a Clifton joiner.

In those days they played just a few simple tunes, but membership grew. Their efforts became more popular and a larger set of bells was bought by public subscription. The original 24 bells would have been returned to the Church as at Horbury, although in Horbury's case the bells did not belong to the church. They were only put there for safe keeping after the band disbanded!. This was done by many bands who quickly broke their ties with the church and became public subscription bands   Their rationale was to return to the Church its property and start afresh, as an independent organisation with command of its own rules and constitution and above all, ownership of the bells. The public subscription method of running a band, has proved itself to be the best way of providing continuity of the tradition, within a particular town or village. (At Clifton in 1919 (when the bells were not in use) an offer was received from a neighbouring town to buy the bells for £80, but this was declined - the bells belonged to Clifton.)

At the British Open at Belle Vue in 1898 and 1899, the village fielded two bands Clifton and Clifton Juniors, the Juniors being conducted by Mr H Evans, one of the senior ringers. But after 1899, Clifton Juniors didn't enter any competitions, so perhaps the Juniors didn't last long, with one or two of its members joining the main band. In 1906 another junior band was formed, again under the conductorship of Fred Squire, a member of the senior band, who was elected Treasurer of the Yorkshire Hand-bell Ringers Association in December 1908, a post he was to hold many years.

The new Clifton Juniors did quite well and attracted a good number of members, until they entered their last competition at Belle Vue in September 1911.

The Junior Band must have collapsed in 1912 as we hear nothing about them at all after 1911. The reason for the collapse hadn't much to do with hand-bell ringing, according to the late Mr Walter Tolson, to whom I spoke in 1978. Mr Tolson, who was a member

185

Fig. 98: Clifton Juniors HBR - 1909 Conductor, Fred Squire.

of the juniors at the time, told me that many of the junior band were (including himself) enticed into joining Clifton St John's Church cricket team, after a pitch was newly put down not far from the band's rehearsal room at Clifton Conservative Club. The pitch also bordered onto the village school.

Mr Tolson recalled Christmas carolling, when they began a tour of the village from Kirklees Hall, the home of the band's President, Sir George Armytage. "We began playing after midnight at the Hall, when the tower bells of Brighouse Parish Church stopped ringing. We then played at intervals all through the village until dawn, people would leave their windows open so they could hear us. A few years later we began to start from the 'Ring O' Bells' public house in Brighouse and played our way up from the other end of the village".

The band also performed carols at other places by request. One story is that when carolling outside a Brighouse clothing mill, the mill owner asked the band's conductor why one of the ringers wasn't wearing an overcoat on such a cold night. The reply was, "Well, he must not have one sir", whereupon the mill owner instructed one of his workers, "Go into the mill and get that man a new overcoat". So the ringer without an overcoat went home with the best overcoat in the band.

It was with Clifton that the writer became a hand-bell ringer in 1976, and in 1977 and 1978 the practice of playing carols at Christmas, from midnight until dawn, was again carried out in the village, and was well received by everyone except a few grumblers, who said it woke them up, but what better way of waking up to Christmas, than by the sweet sound of hand-bells?

Mr Tolson also recalled the band's annual concerts held at the Albert Theatre (now a bingo hall) in Brighouse, "We had various guests, Heckmondwike Concertina Band, the tenor Walter Widdop and a joint concert with Clifton Brass Band with guest John Shaw, a blind concertina soloist. We also had the Mayor and his guest in the audience, we performed to two full houses, afternoon and evening. We also held a dance on New Year's Eve, at our headquarters at Clifton Conservative Club".

Clifton could not enter the Yorkshire Association Championships in March 1905 as their new set of bells on order, had not arrived, and their practice set wasn't up to contest standard. However when the new bells arrived and were used in competition they received poor marks for tone and tune of the bells. Mr Tolson told me, "The band complained to the Founder and Vice-Presidents of the band, John Mallett and Mr W H Benskin dealt with the matter over which there was nearly a court case". Both of these men were of considerable standing in the village and would have spared no cost in seeing that justice was done for the band, but evidently the problem was overcome.

Another set of 180 bells were cast by the Whitechapel Bell Foundry in 1908, at a cost of £102 5 shillings delivered, 155 of which the band still uses today.

The 1908 set comprised five octaves fully chromatic from 29C, plus four and a half octaves chromatic as duplicates from 25G, four octaves chromatic as triplicates from 22C, and sixteen extra bells. There was also a sixth octave of very small 00 bells ("Whistles" is the name by which old Yorkshire ringers refer to these small bells which are not very tuneful and were not widely used, even at the turn of the twentieth century. Some of Clifton's very small bells were cast by Shaws of Bradford).

By 1914 the band had a set of 193 bells, which were always known to be of a very sweet tone, but low in volume.

Before a contest, the final rehearsals were held in a local public house, the Armytage Arms, which was, like the whole of the village, owned by the band's President Sir George Armytage.

Albert Sayles was the conductor of Clifton Seniors. On the

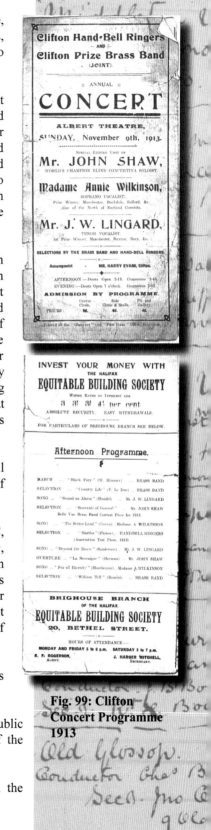

Fig. 99: Clifton Concert Programme 1913

Fig. 100: Clifton HBR with their replacement long set 1910

retirement of Albert Sayles in 1912 hand-bell ringing in Clifton was in a very good condition, having a good band of juniors as well as a senior band. But twelve months later the junior band had collapsed, for the reasons already given. This must have been a

Left to right back: Dickson, Willie Sykes, Richardson Sykes, Arnold Sykes, Cliff Wood, GeorgeSmith. Front: Walter Harrison, Harry Smith, Albert Sayles, Alfred Schofield, Ned Fearnley.

great disappointment for the Clifton organisation, to have taught the music and technique of the art to so many young lads, only to see them poached away to cricket.

The conductor of the juniors, Fred Squire, whilst still being a member of Clifton, became conductor of another band, Elland, only three miles away, taking over in 1912. He was to remain with Elland right into the 1920s with much success.

But for Clifton, the loss of the juniors was the beginning of the end - almost.

Clifton competed in the British Open of 1912 and came fourth in 1913, so the band's standard was very high.

But in February 1915 the Clifton ringers decided to disband. The reason given was lack of interest. The bells, table, cover and music etc. were handed over to the Parish Council, so that if anyone wished to use them again the bells would be there. On behalf of the band Richardson Sykes, one of the ringers, said the conditions were "That if any set of young men in the village were desirable of using the bells they should call themselves the Clifton Hand-bell

188

Ringers and before taking over they should find two householders to be responsible". Mr Sykes went on to say the bells "should be kept in a dry room". By this time the band had been together for 25 years.

On the close of Clifton Council Offices in 1935, the bells etc., were transferred to a small ground floor store at the wire works of Mr Ernest Lister in Clifton Road, next to Clifton Beck, which I'm sure you've already guessed, overflowed into where the bells were stored, on at least two occasions. Fortunately one box containing the cover, music and a few bells rested on a table and escaped damage.

The bells sat unused for 60 years until discovered by the writer in December 1974, although a few bells had been used from time to time. (In fact I had not been looking for hand-bells, but was carrying out research into morris dancing, starting a morris dancing group in the neighbouring village of Hartshead in 1978 in conjunction with the Hartshead Tradition Society founded by the writer in 1977.) But there had been no band organised under the terms left by Richardson Sykes. It was not until November 1975 that I decided to take any action and after contacting householders in Clifton, a new band was formed in March 1976.

On discovering the Clifton bells I had expected to find about a dozen small bells, so you can imagine my surprise at finding over a hundred bells with a range of five octaves. About 50 bells were found to be missing. During the floods mud had been washed into and among the bells, some of which lay on the stone floor with grass growing out of them, handles broken and strikers missing.

Our bunch of enthusiasts cleaned and washed the bells out and within a week my father Dick and I had assembled a ringable single set of 25 bells.

We were lucky to be able to engage Mr Geoffrey Lee as conductor, who had previously been a hand-bell ringer at Norbury in Cheshire and conductor of Liversedge. Under Mr Lee the band attained a high standard.

In 1977 I met, during my research, an ex-Almondbury ringer, Arnold Calvert, whom I invited along to Clifton. It wasn't too long before he was a member of the band. Mr Calvert brought important experience into the band especially in traditional techniques of how to handle and ring the bells, the main one being the use of the up and back-strokes when ringing. This was of great benefit to the band. Mr Calvert had one of the most beautiful styles of ringing a bell I have ever seen.

189

Fig. 101: Clifton Village HBR in March 1987 after winning the Harrogate Musical Competition Hand-bell Class. The Band has brought new standards to the movement in the 1980s (Bass ringer & conductor, David Sunderland, is fourth from the left) (Photo: Fawcett)

In August 1978 the writer and Mr Calvert formed another junior band at Clifton, which also achieved a high standard.

My one regret is that I never met Mr Richardson Sykes, to tell him we had re-formed the band - he died in 1974. We missed by only two years.

Clifton became the most successful of the competition bands of the 1980s. In 1983 the band were the winners of the over 3½ octave class at the Mrs Sunderland Musical Competition, under conductor Mr Geoffrey Lee. It was the first occasion on which hand-bell ringing had been included in the competition held in Huddersfield each February. (The first winners of the under 3½ octave class at

the Mrs Sunderland were Hope Hand-bell Ringers from Hebden Bridge under conductor Julie Ming).

Another of the bands that entered the 1909 contest at Shrewsbury was Birstall St Saviours, from the village of Birstall, near Batley, in Yorkshire. The band's rehearsal rooms included a room at Sheard's Mill in Bradford Road, and a stable at the rear of the public house at Smythies in the village.

The band was formed in 1879, when a set of 37 bells was given to them by the local Earl of Wilton's agent, Mr Michael Sheard (a local mill owner). The members belonged to St Saviour's Church Sunday School. The Church has no tower bells.

A start was made under Mr Pickles of Dewsbury, which is about four miles from Birstall. In 1882 the set was augmented to 85. Following the pattern of other bands that began life in the Church, Birstall became an independent organisation, probably when the set of bells was enlarged to 85, but the name St Saviours was kept on.

In 1883 Ben Cooke (formerly conductor of Shelley) was engaged to take them to the British Open, where they were "the worst band that competed", but the following year they took fourth prize and fifth in 1885 and in 1893, third place.

Cooke's son Kaye, took over as conductor in 1898, when they bought a new set of 145 bells.

From 1900 to 1905 "the band was down". The reasons given were, the loss of several members, some through work and some through death. Even though living conditions had improved, a look at the burials register shows that people could still fall ill and die at any age, so there was always the threat of death at an early age, something that was to continue right into the 1930s. Kaye Cooke's eldest child died young on January 14th, 1908.

In 1905 they bought the bells of the Royal Poland Street Hand-bell Ringers of London. Made at Whitechapel, they were said to be the best the Birstall ringers had ever had, and it was with these bells that they won the second section in the Yorkshire Association Championships of 1906, and after being promoted to the first section, the band won the Yorkshire Challenge Cup in 1908.

In 1907 and 1909 Birstall St Saviours came second in the British Open. Surprisingly the Bell News and Ringers Record of Nov 9th 1912 carried an article advertising for sale Birstall St Saviours' 230 bells, together with tables and other paraphernalia - but they did not sell them at that time. They entered the Yorkshire Association contests of 1913, 14, and 15, and came back again in 1920 and 1921. However, as the History of St Saviour's Church (1971) said, they disbanded sometime after this, probably about 1925. A 1939 article from the Dewsbury Reporter said the bells were sold to "a party in Bradford and nothing has been heard of them since". After winning the Yorkshire Championship in 1908, the band and about eighty others held a celebration tea in the Sykes Assembly Rooms, Birstall, when several songs were sung and "solos on the gramophone were given at intervals". An annual concert was also held in the Temperance Hall, Birstall.

Kaye Cooke also conducted Liversedge Albert as aforementioned, but he also conducted two other bands at various times, Low Moor and Tennyson Place, both Bradford bands.

The first mention I have found of Low Moor is when they entered the second section at the first Yorkshire Association contest in 1904 when the conductor was Kaye Cooke who was conductor in the 1920s, when my friend the late John Terry was a member of the band. John recalled crossing swords with Kaye Cooke in the band room. "He would always insist on playing the music as written, without any regard to phrasing, or what the particular piece was supposed to portray, he charged us 10 shillings (50p) per rehearsal plus expenses from his home in Leeds. We could only afford him for a few rehearsals prior to the contest. Sometimes, if we needed an extra rehearsal we had to take the bells to his house in Kirkstall, Leeds. He would still charge us 10 shillings though. I remember travelling somewhere with him on a tram when I found I was a ha'penny short of the fare (less than half a new penny) Kaye Cooke put a ha'penny in my hand. Six months later when the contest season came round again, he added the ha'penny fare to our bill" - Kaye Cooke was a bank manager.

The Low Moor bells were cast by Shaw of Bradford. Local knowledge says that gold and silver jewellery, collected in the village, were thrown into the vat of molten bell metal to make the set of 56 bells. Gold and silver was thought to be lucky and items such as gold or silver watch chains were sometimes hung on rush-carts, mentioned earlier, at the time of the wakes, although this is the only example of which I have heard in connection with hand-bells.

The hand-bell ringers in Yorkshire were very superstitious; one of the main superstitions being that the number thirteen brought bad luck. The bands would never use the number 13 on their music and of course no-one wanted to be drawn at that number in the playing order at a contest. This fear even extended to its non-usage on the bells. Each bell had of course a cast number cast into the top of each bell underneath the collar. These numbers extend from one to twenty nine, but in every set of bells that I have inspected which were used by the Yorkshire competition bands, the number thirteen has not been cast on the bell - the bell has no number at all, just its letter "E" on the handle.

Another Bradford band was formed about 1912 at the Tennyson Place Methodist Church, Bradford Moor, under the conductorship of Charles Cawley, who also arranged test pieces for the Yorkshire Association. This band went under the name Bradford (Tennyson).

In 1915 a second band was formed called Tennyson Place P.M. Both bands did very well in the second section competition of the 1915 Yorkshire Championships, with Bradford (Tennyson) coming in first place with 78 points and Tennyson Place P.M. second with 76 points. Kaye Cooke conducted, though Tennyson Place won the contest in 1926 with Charles Cawley as conductor. The band had a small set of 57 bells, which were sold for scrap when the Church closed.

Fig. 102: Tennyson Place, Bradford 1926, Conductor Charles Cawley

Another band that was very active before the first World War was Barnsley, a pub band that was based at the Windmill Inn. This band seems to have begun in 1900 with Mr E Stringer as conductor until 1905 when Mr T Fleetwood took over. The band continued to compete until September 1909, but after this I can find no mention of them. The name of Barnsley first appeared at the British Open of 1857 when their conductor was Samuel Wilkinson of Park Row, Barnsley. The band was active in the 1870s and the 1880s competing in the British Open. However I did see a report in The Ringing World for April 9th 1943 which said "At a meeting of the Barnsley and District Society the chief item of interest was 108 hand bells which had been stored at the King George Hotel, Barnsley and had been with out an owner for over 30 years. After consultation with the building manager of the Barnsley Brewing Company, they were handed over to the Society for safe keeping in the Royal Hotel, the Society's Headquarters" I wonder where they are now? I have asked the current Secretary of the Society, but other than the minutes of the meeting referred to they have no other record of them.

Other bands in the Barnsley district, Darton, Darfield and Royston United were members of the Yorkshire Association. Darfield had 120 bells which were sold in the early 1960s to a man in nearby South Hiendley, and were subsequently sold to a Kettering school master, who advertised for a set in a national paper. Darfield seemed to be active from 1903 to 1907. During this period they entered every Yorkshire Association Contest and the British Open of 1903 and 1907, but hold a unique record of not competing in any, with the exception of the 1903 British Open, when the conductor was Samuel Woodcock of Vicar Road, Darfield.

Darton entered the British Open in 1898 and 1899 under the

193

Fig. 103: Brighouse
Park (Methodist)
Church HBR 1904

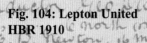

Fig. 104: Lepton United
HBR 1910

conductorship of E C Stratford. The last mention of them is in the 1903 contest. Their conductor that year was Mr G B Mellor of Darton. In 1985 the bells were found and an attempt was made to form a band, but nothing came of it.

Royston United first appeared on the scene at Belle Vue in 1899. After this the band entered the British open and the Yorkshire Association Championships regularly until 1911, but after 1911 I cannot find any mention of them. The band bought a new set of bells in 1908 with which they gained their greatest prize, second position in the British Open of that year, under conductor James Watson of Royston. Their prize was £10. The adjudicator in the 1908 contest was George Pritchard of London. He gave Royston high praise for their performance with the new bells, but in the same contest one year later, the same adjudicator said in his remarks, that their highest bells seemed flat and out of tune; and the band won no prizes - all very strange?

The Yorkshire Hand-bell Ringers Association's efforts to revitalise the hand-bell scene included encouraging the formation of junior bands. The

194

BRIGHOUSE CHURCH INSTITUTE HAND-BELL RINGERS.

Figure 105: Brighouse Church Institute HBR 1929

Association were not slow to realise they had to expand and encourage youth if the art was to flourish.

As a result many of the established bands formed juniors.

Amongst the bands who formed juniors were Almondbury; Clifton; Thurlstone; Bradford Tennyson; Crosland Moor United and Elland. Also new bands were formed, encouraged by the Association's contests. Among these were Lindley Parish Church (Huddersfield); Mirfield (Gilder Hall); Brighouse Park Church (Methodist); Brighouse Church Institute (C of E), Sheffield Hartshead; Holmfirth (Lane); Sowerby; Thornhill; St Aidan's Ossett; Saddleworth; Lepton United; Sowerby Bridge and Heptonstall near Halifax.

New life was also put into old names such as Armitage Bridge and Penistone.

The revival even spread in a limited way to Lancashire. New Church, near Warrington, joined the Yorkshire Association and entered the third section contest in 1912 at Sunny Vale, under conductorship of Mr J Orme. They also entered the second section in 1913. New Church had entered the British Open in 1862 when their conductor was John Warburton.

Bolton Parish Church (St George's) joined the Association one year after New Church, in 1913. The band entered the second section in 1913, 1914, 1915 and 1921. Bolton entered the British

195

...and Bell Co
— 1871. —

...and Campanologian
...nductor J. E. Crow...
...c... David Crofie...

...olnforth Temper...
...nctor John Moorh...
...South Ha...

...adcliffe Juvenile
...ductor M. Pendleb...
...ec... ...tand...

...mitage Bridge
...nductor Seth Gold...
...c... a. Lockw...

...carborough
...nductor Geo Dic...
E. B. Newton. 16 m...

Hyde.
...nductor S. Brier...
...organis...
...c... St. Ives. Hyd...

Oldham.
...nductor David
...ec... Jas. L...
...Oggin...

Open of 1836 when the conductor was Edward Lee of 68 Chapel Street, Little Bolton.

Other Lancashire bands joined the Yorkshire Association, including Pendlebury; Church (Accrington); Lees St Agnes (near Oldham); Higher Walton (near Preston) and Friends Adult School, Oldham

The Yorkshire Hand-bell Ringers Association's efforts are significant. If they had not made their move when they did, then the art might not have survived the effects of the 1914 -1918 war, in its highly developed form and thus may not have survived in a strong enough form until the modern revival which began in 1966. We today should be thankful for their efforts and must make sure we do as much as they did for the art.

Lepton United was a band made up of miners, and first competed in the British Open at Belle Vue in 1898. However, after competing in the British Open again in 1899, a lull in interest saw the Lepton band sell a practically new set of 160 Whitechapel bells to Crosland Moor United in 1903. The band then enjoyed a revival when an ex Almondbury United ringer, Joshua Haigh Dawson, who was one of the Almondbury ringers who toured the USA became conductor in 1910. They achieved considerable success in the contest field winning the Yorkshire Association second section in 1910, and the first section Yorkshire Challenge Cup in 1913 and 1914. They also built their own band room in the village near Huddersfield. The band room is now a cottage. In 1910 and 1911 the band came second in the British open, great success for the renewed band. Lepton came second in the first section of the Yorkshire Championships held in June 1915, but were absent from the British Open the following September. The band was another casualty of the first world warbecause, although there was an attempt to revive the band after the war it had disbanded by 1920. The band's 166 bells, cast by the Whitechapel Bell Foundry at a cost of £97 10shillings, were sold in 1938 by the Lepton band's trustees to the Norbury Hand-bell Ringers from near Stockport, Cheshire, where they are still used.

The Norbury band itself is an old one. There was a band in existence in 1885 when their leader was Mr S Penney. In April 1895 they gave a performance at the Queen's Street Institute in Manchester when they were conducted by James Fernley, who owned the 60 bells the band then used. Mr Fernley was one of the tower bell ringers at William Gordon's golden wedding celebrations in 1912, mentioned in an earlier chapter.

In 1895 the local paper, the Stockport Advertiser, urged the Norbury band to enter the 1895 British Open at Belle Vue, but present evidence suggests that they did not enter any contest at all.

Norbury's practices were held at Mr Fernley's home. In the early 1930s James Fernley Junior took over as conductor.

In 1937 the Norbury ringers made contact with John Thomas Wilson, of Elland, Yorkshire, who was the Secretary of the Yorkshire Hand-bell Ringers Association, after which, the Lepton bells were purchased. The Norbury ringers asked Mr Wilson for his advice on how to ring the bells, and he invited them to Yorkshire to see the Elland M.O.B. (Men's Own Brotherhood) hand-bell ringers.

John Thomas Wilson also visited Norbury where he told the members they were doing things all wrong, and gave advice on how to improve their methods. This advice was taken. Now here lies a little story. You may recall that Fred Squire, a Clifton ringer, went to Elland to conduct. It was he who taught John Thomas Wilson, who in turn taught Norbury. In 1949, Geoffrey Lee while working in Stockport was introduced to hand-bell ringing at Norbury, and in 1976 Geoffrey Lee became conductor of the new Clifton Hand-bell Ringers, thus completing a full circle!

Elland is another Yorkshire Pennine town with a long association with the art of hand-bell ringing. The band scored a hat trick of wins in 1920, 1921 and 1922, winning the Yorkshire Hand-bell Ringers Association's Challenge Cup for the first section bands. The only other band to achieve this was Thurlstone Public.

The first mention of Elland hand-bell ringers is in 1870 when they entered the British Open at Belle Vue for the first time. The conductor was Mr T E Crowther who held the post until 1873 when Walter Spencer of Ainley Bottom, Elland took over. Secretary at the time was David Copley of Northgate, Elland.

However, I can find no mention of Elland again until 1911 when the band took part in the third section Yorkshire Association contest held at Ecclesfield.

This band was formed from members of Elland Church of England Men's Society, hence the name of the band, Elland C.E.M.S. The C.E.M.S. band came to prominence in 1913 when they won the Yorkshire Association Shield for the second section winners.

At the outset in 1911 their conductor was Mr C H Waddington who also took the band in 1912, but with Fred Squire of Clifton as adviser during final rehearsals. But from 1913 Fred Squire was appointed as conductor and remained so until 1925 when the band's name was changed to Elland Church United after a disagreement, but with Mr Squire still as conductor.

For their final rehearsals before a contest the C.E.M.S. band often

197

Fig. 106: Ben Cartwright - ex Thurlstone HBR in 1988

engaged Mr S W Garside of Elland, who was president of Huddersfield Choral Society to advise them on the finer points of performing the test piece.

A member of Elland C.E.M.S. hand-bell ringers was the late Mr Roland Walton to whom I spoke in 1978. Mr Walton told me he joined after the 1914 - 18 war as a treble ringer. He recalled their conductor Fred Squire, "Fred was a very good conductor. He would work for hours with us, but if he felt we weren't trying hard enough, he would throw his baton across the bell table and walk out, but he always came back at the next rehearsal".

About 1930 another society, Elland Men's Own Brotherhood took over the bells. This band was conducted by a former member of the C.E.M.S. and Church United, John Thomas Wilson, mentioned earlier. This band went under the rather unlikely name of Elland M.O.B. Hand-bell Ringers.

In addition to Elland C.E.M.S., Thurlstone Public Hand-bell Ringers were the only other band to score a hat trick of wins in the first section of the Yorkshire Hand-bell Association contests. This was in the years 1930, 1931 and 1932.

The latest band at Thurlstone, a small Pennine village near Sheffield, began with a re-formation, including former pre-World War II ringers, around 1962. The band had re-formed after the Second War but disbanded in 1950, the reasons given being the National Service and television. However this latter reason is very unlikely as there was no television in Sheffield until the Sutton Coldfield transmitter went live in December 1949, and even then reception was very poor until Holme Moss started transmitting in October 1951. Privately owned TVs were still rare, even at the time of the Coronation in 1953. Around 1962 the band was re-formed by Mr Reg Proud, who had been a member in the 1920s and 30s. Mr Proud was prompted to re-form the band by another former ringer, Roy Armytage.

Mr Proud told me, "Six or seven of the eleven members of the new re-formed band were old ringers". One of these old ringers was Laurence Sykes, whose father, Tom, had also been a prominent member. Laurence Sykes was very highly regarded as one of the best Thurlstone hand-bell ringers ever, and he put a lot of work into training the new members in the 1960s after Reg Proud rallied round pre-war ringers and recruited some new ringers and re-formed the band.

In 1988 I spoke to one of Mr Proud's fellow ringers in the 1930s, Mr Ben Cartwright, who lives in Penistone two miles from Thurlstone. Mr Cartwright paid tribute to Mr Proud as the saviour of hand-bell ringing in the village, "It would have died out if it hadn't been for Reg. He kept the band going through the 1930s when times were bad and was the driving force behind the revival of the 1960s".

Mr Proud was conductor at Thurlstone until 1969, when Alec Dyson, who first became a member of the band in 1938, took over as conductor. "But friction arose immediately" said Mr Cartwright. "One night at rehearsals Laurence Sykes was instructing a new member when Alec shouted to Laurence 'I'll show him how to do it, not you. I am conductor'. Laurence walked out of the room never to return. That night he got all the collection of Thurlstone's music, which had been under his bed for years, and set fire to it in his garden, shouting at the top of his voice 'Dyson will not get his hands on this.'"

Thurlstone also produced several long-playing records, and were well known for their playing of "Themes from Famous Overtures". My own favourite tune from their repertoire is "El Relicario", (J Padilla/Masters) but they were most well known for their signature tune "Cubley Brook" composed by Edwin Biltcliffe, their conductor at the turn of the century. Biltcliffe also took the tune to Ecclesfield where the tune is still in the band's library. (Alec Dyson also gave a copy of the tune to the Mount Torrens Ringers for their joint concert with Thurlstone in 1986. Ed.)

In the 1970s and 80s the band toured Germany, and the USA twice (Video-clips of the Band during their 1983 tour playing "Entry of the Gladiators" by Julius Fucik can be found on YouTube at www.youtube.com/watch?v=kejMrE9X4ug), and became very popular giving concert performances all over Britain, but there was consternation amongst the old Thurlstone hand-bell ringers when the band changed their name to "The Thurlstone Bell Orchestra" in the early 1970s. Laurence Sykes was said to be furious.

The people of Yorkshire staunchly keep their traditions and any attempt to tamper with them is viewed as sacrilege, and in a county which prides itself on calling a spade, a spade, the change of name would appear to be totally out of character.

The name did however have its precedents. At the British Open in 1857 a band from Ashton-under-Lyne competed under the name of "Hurst Brook Campanologian Band", others followed Hurst Brook's lead, Heckmondwike (1860); Loughborough (1865); York (1861); Glossop (1869); Royal Albert, Birmingham (1869); Elland

199

Fig. 107: Thurlstone Public with the Yorkshire Shield which they had just won at Sunny Vale Pleasure Gardens, Hipperholme on June 8th 1924. The Shield was for the winners of the Second Section Contest of the Yorkshire Hand-bell Ringers Association. The test piece that year was an arrangement of Weber's Opera 'Oberon'

(1871) and Madeley also in 1871. Fortunately this fashion was short lived.

The word "campanologia" actually appeared 200 years before this when in 1677 Fabian Stedman used it as the title of his treatise on towerbell change ringing, and is derived from the latin 'campana' meaning 'bell', 'Nola', a town in Northern Italy where bells are said to have been first rung in public to call people to worship when the persecution of Christians ceased under the Emperor Constantine, and the Greek 'logia' literally meaning 'sayings, utterances, or oracles' The Victorians were very fond of using fanciful scientific sounding names. However the name is generally avoided by bellringers who refer to their art as 'bellringing'.

But back to Thurlstone. The band has an old copy of the Penistone Almanac which states that the band was formed in 1855 though the first mention I have found of Thurlstone is of the band's first entry in the British Open in 1869, which is listed in the Jennison Ledgers. The Secretary at the time was given as Herbert Rusby and the conductor Joseph Kenworthy and there were 12 members in the band. In 1870 Thurlstone again entered with the same conductor but a W Marsh was now Secretary. They entered again for the British Open of 1873 when their own-choice test piece was the "Overture to the Caliph of Bagdad". In 1899 Edwin Biltcliffe was conductor before leaving in 1905 to conduct Ecclesfield. Biltcliffe was replaced at Thurlstone by Ben Lodge who was the regular conductor of Almondbury. Lodge conducted Thurlstone at both the British Open and Yorkshire Association contest in 1905, 1906 and 1907.

It was in 1908 that Fred Taylor, Thurlstone's most famous and longest serving conductor took up the baton, although in that year the band did not compete at all, but they did put in an entry for the Yorkshire Association's championships, but did not compete. Perhaps their new conductor thought some reorganisation was required and more practice in their rehearsal rooms in the basement of the local school, which the band still used until recently, free of charge, under a very old agreement with the local council. The room now has electric lighting etc., but in the old days before the 1950s the room had to be lit by oil lamps, "It was a decrepit hole" said Ben Cartwright.

Fred Taylor, a violin teacher, was a well known character on the Yorkshire hand-bell scene and was Thurlstone's delegate on the Yorkshire Hand-bell Ringers Association's committee.

Fred Taylor is still remembered by Yorkshire veteran ringers for the way he conducted, stooped over, jarring his hands jerkily up and down in a comic fashion. One of the old Woodroyd (Honley) hand-bell ringers, Norman Webster, told me "Once Fred got his head down, he never looked up until the band had finished ringing".

Thurlstone had a good contest record, their highest position in the

Fig. 108: Thurlstone Public Hand-bell Ringers c.1930 with the Yorkshire Challenge Cup. Back Row L. to R: L. Sykes, C. Mitchell, N. Crossland, M. Walshaw, E. Wood, Front Row: T. Sykes, M. Beard, R. Lees, F. Taylor, C. Latimer, H. Beard, J. Beever

British Open being second place, in 1915, 1925 and 1926 when the winner each time was Crosland Moor Public. Thurlstone also won prizes in the Yorkshire Association's contests, winning the second section shield for the first time in 1924. In 1930, 1931 and 1932 the band won the first section challenge cup. For this hat trick the Yorkshire Hand-bell Ringers Association awarded each member of the band a special gold hand-bell shaped medal. They also received a silver medal each.

Fred Taylor was a strict disciplinarian, Ben Cartwright told me. "One day he threw out two members of the band for being naughty boys. The two lads had arrived late for rehearsals, with the excuse that they had been playing tennis, at which Fred ordered them out", I shall not name them as the two naughty boys are still playing tennis.

Fred Taylor remained conductor until 1931, when he got married and moved away from the area and was never seen again. After this Tom Sykes, who had conducted a short-lived junior band, took over as resident conductor and remained so until 1939, but for the 1932 Yorkshire Association contest the band hired the services of Arthur Jenkinson, who had previously had a lot of success as conductor of Woodroyd, Honley.

I also spoke to Harold Beard who was another member of Thurlstone in the late 1920s and early 1930s. Mr Beard explained to me the band's basic method of ringing the bells, "When ringing the bells we used the up stroke and the back stroke - say for two notes we would ring the first note on the up stroke and the second note on the back stroke. It was the same when ringing four notes, up, back, up and back to the table on the fourth note, but we used only the up stroke for staccato".

The above method was used by all the old bands before 1939, but is not so widespread among the 'off table' hand-bell teams today. The benefits of the method is that the bell is rung in a constant natural movement from the wrist, and when ringing two or four notes the bell is already on its way back to the table to be damped, leaving the hand free to pick up another bell more quickly than if the bell was rung using all up strokes, as when at the end of the up stroke hand movement, the bell is still in the air at the finish of the note.

The use of both the up and back strokes enabled the ringers to play at a greater speed, which was essential in order to be able to play music of the complexity achieved during the early years of the twentieth century.

Some ringers such as those from Crosland Moor took things a stage

202

further and used both the up stroke and the back stroke selectively within a particular piece of music, so at one point could be using all up strokes and synchronised up and back strokes in other parts of the music. The visual effect could be stunning. (I remember the 5 beefy and muscly Thurlstone Tenor ringers synchronising their up strokes during a performance of Offenbach's Can-Can - just like the legs of the Can-Can dancers themselves, except rather beefier and musclier – Ed.) None of the top flight old bands I have investigated used only up strokes. This fashion seems to have begun with the revival of the late 1960s and is not, in my view as entertaining to watch as an off table band using both up and back strokes.

The British Open of 1906 marked a milestone for Shelley's Fred Shaw. He had now made forty-three annual trips without a break to Belle Vue for the great hand-bell contest "and there were many present", said the Huddersfield Examiner, "who followed Shelley and Dalton in the 1860s", which demonstrated the remarkable following the British Open attracted throughout its existence.

If the monumental success of the Crosland Moor United hand-bell ringers could be described as remarkable, then the emergence and rise of the Crosland Moor United Junior Band could only be described as sensational.

The Junior Band began after a feeling amongst the members of the United Band (inspired by the Youth policy of the Yorkshire Hand-bell Ringers Association) that the band should have youngsters coming along to keep the band up to strength in the future. The band's official name was "Crosland Moor Junior Hand-bell Ringers", but in order to keep records straight we will refer to them as the United Juniors.

But little did the United Senior ringers realise that they had spawned an aggressive rival. Within a year of their formation, the Juniors split away from the United organisation after a bitter dispute and formed their own society - Crosland Moor Public Hand-bell Ringers - who subsequently beat their United seniors in the British Open of 1909.

The United Juniors got off to a flying start, for within ten months of their formation the band went to Belle Vue, Manchester and actually won first prize in the 1908 British Open! - the most sensational win in the whole of the contest's 67 year history, all this when the average age of the ringers was only 16½ years, way below that of most of the other competing bands. There is no substitute for youthful enthusiasm!

The Crosland Moor United Juniors were formed in November

Fig. 109: James Hobson Ellis (Jimmy)

1907 under the conductorship of the United Band's hugely talented first treble ringer, James Hobson Ellis who was destined to become one of the most charismatic figures that the hand-bell movement has ever known, and it was his capacity to inspire everyone who came into contact with him, with devotion and enthusiasm, which was the key to the rapid progress of the United Junior ringers.

In his book on the history of Crosland Moor United up to 1906, James (Jimmy) Ellis recalls one of his first encounters with the sound of hand-bell ringing on Christmas Day, 1890. "I well remember the ringers coming to the Wesleyan School at Crosland Moor. The peal and Christmas hymn were the two tunes played and I at the time thought the performance was marvellous".

The hearing of Christmas bells must have stirred ambition in the mind of the young Jimmy Ellis to become one day, a hand-bell ringer himself, because in 1898 he applied to become a member of the United Band, after reading a notice in his Sunday School asking for applicants to give in their names. Response was good as "A great number complied with the request" and, after various trials, Jimmy, along with three others was accepted as a member of the band.

Jimmy Ellis was born at Crosland Moor in 1880 and at the age of nine his parents realised he possessed the "bump" for music, as "Codon", writing in the British Bandsman's Hand-bell Ringers News in 1909 put it. "So they placed him on a piano stool with a teacher by his side. He made rapid progress, under various masters and his "bump" developed wonderfully, having gained a mastery over the pianoforte and thorough knowledge of music".

During the whole of Jimmy's career with the United he played the first treble bells. In a 1909 article in the British Bandsman, Codon quoted a local Huddersfield paper as stating - "He (Jimmy Ellis) is probably the finest treble ringer in the country, I believe he has assisted in winning the first prize at Belle Vue oftener than any other individual ringer". However this brought a letter to the British Bandsman by someone calling himself "Campan" in which he disagreed with the statement by saying - "That honour stands to the credit of the late Mr Ben Cooke of Shelley". Of course Ben Cooke and Jimmy Ellis were of different generations, and by 1909, ringing had changed since the days of Shelley in the 1870s, and both men today stand high in the hand-bell ringers' hall of fame.

The first signs the ringing world had of the rapid progress being made by Crosland Moor United Juniors came at the Yorkshire

Association's annual contest at Batley in March 1908 when the Juniors won the Yorkshire Shield for the first prize in the second section contest. The test piece was a Fantasia from the works of Mendelssohn and the United Juniors gained 95 marks out of a possible 100. Second was Almondbury United with 89 marks, third Dewsbury with 83, then came Clifton Juniors and St Aiden's Ossett who both had 75 marks each, Holmfirth 74, Higher Walton 72, Liversedge 70 and Mirfield 63.

All of the above were young bands, but nevertheless the United Juniors had only been formed five months before the contest.

Even more startling events were yet to come. The test piece for the British Open the following September was a selection from Verdi's opera "La Traviata", the United Senior Band having completed their second hat trick of first prize wins the previous year, were not eligible to enter, but this did not apply to the United Juniors, who along with ten other bands, competed for the Mears Challenge Trophy on the 21st September. The result was a victory for the juniors.

News of the win reached Crosland Moor long before the arrival of the ringers themselves, who, on arrival home at about half past ten at night, were met by large crowds of people - cheer after cheer went up as the ringers and supporters made their way to the Conservative Club, where speeches and a toast were given. Following this, the celebration continued when the band visited the Liberal Club. Such outbursts of civic pride always followed any local successes and spurred people onward to better their efforts and keep their organisation in the public eye.

Fig. 110: Belle Vue British Open - Mears Challenge Trophy

The local press was ecstatic about the United Junior's success. The Slaithwaite Guardian in its report began: " 'What's bred in the bone comes out in the flesh' is an old adage. It was never more true than in the case of the musical fraternity at Crosland Moor. Musical talent is born, bred and nurtured in the locality to a surprising degree". The Crosland Moor Wesleyan Choir had also had its share of success at Belle Vue, winning the choir competition. The Guardian went on - "Everybody knows of the success achieved on the contest platform by the local Wesleyan choir and of the famous Senior Hand-bell Ringers, now a new star has arisen on the horizon and bids fair to shine as bright as any of its precious rivals. We refer to the Crosland Moor United Junior

Hand-bell Ringers". The Guardian correspondent continued in his excitement, "Here are the names of the youths destined to make history: Harold Inman, Harold Jebson, Norman Walker, Vernon Priestley, Tom Ellis (who was Jimmy's brother), Harry Armitage, Ernest Lunn, Joe Sykes (who died after a lingering illness two years later in March 1910, aged 17), Willie Hanson, Victor Smith, Joseph Walton, Lewis Mellor with Mr J H Ellis, one of the senior ringers as conductor". The above report demonstrates the esteem in which the United Senior Hand-bell Ringers were held. This is also a clue as to why the Juniors achieved so much so quickly - because the Senior Band was so successful and famous and were the British Open Champions of Great Britian.

There was no shortage of young men wanting to become part of this famous band when the Juniors were being formed, so Jimmy Ellis could pick and choose whom he wanted, to begin the new band. They were told what they had to do if they also wished to be successful and they did it, duty was accepted, understood and unquestioned in the days before the Great War of 1914 - 18. Today the word 'duty' hardly exists.

The United Juniors did have luck on their side on the day of their first British Open win, as Birstall St Saviour's, the runners up to the United Seniors the previous year, were, according to "Codon", writing in the British Bandsman, "In great form and it is evident that they would have won easily but for the accidental misplacing of a bell, which upset the whole show", which brought an old adage from the pen of Codon, "there's many a slip betwixt cup and lip".

The previous March, Birstall had won the Yorkshire Association Challenge Cup for winning the first section contest, but a few weeks before the British Open they expelled two members, J Halliday and A Bellis from the band, a fact that was made public in the British Bandsman. The reason given was: "Acting foolishly and not conforming to the wishes of the majority", so Birstall's runners-up position to Crosland Moor United Juniors, was in itself a remarkable feat.

Nevertheless the United Junior Ringers did win the British Open that year,though this was not to everyone's liking on Crosland Moor–. Seeds of discontent were growing and, within two months after the British Open, the United Senior and United Junior Ringers were in public dispute with each other.

The juniors convened a public meeting to "Consider the unfortunate position which has arisen between the Senior and Junior hand-bell ringers", - 400 people attended this meeting, which shows how much people cared about their hand-bell ringers.
The meeting came about like this. There had been murmurs of

dissatisfaction throughout the Summer of 1908 according to the Juniors, ever since their winning of the Yorkshire Association's Challenge Shield in early March. The matter came to a head shortly after their win at the British Open. The Juniors were offered a concert engagement, but subsequently found that they were not able to accept the invitation, because the Senior ringers refused them use of the bells on the date in question.

The result was uproar. It was the last straw. The United Senior Ringers, had already realised that a year hence they would have to compete with the Juniors in the British Open Championship so had hurriedly and perhaps clumsily redrawn the rules which the Seniors themselves had previously made to govern the Juniors. It was one of these new rules, rule number 7, which was the subject of the Junior's main grievance, "That the Junior band shall not enter into competition with the Senior band at any contest".

At this stage I think it would be appropriate to list the new and old rules, so that the reader may be able to understand more fully some of the complexities of the dispute because if I gave here all that was said and written on the matter, it could take a whole book up itself!

RULES FOR JUNIOR TEAM, OCTOBER 1907

1. **That the band be called the Crosland Moor Junior Hand-bell Ringers.**
2. **That the Juniors shall consist of as many members as the Senior band deem necessary**
3. **That the entrance fee be 1 shilling and a subscription of 2d a week at present.**
4. **That the band shall appoint one of their number a secretary, who shall undertake duties**
     appertaining thereto and also keep account of all monies received and paid. All monies
      to be handed over to the treasurer of senior band, who shall keep an account of the
       same.
5. **That the band pay a standing charge of £2.10s for working expenses.**
6. **That any member found guilty of misconduct shall be liable to be expelled.**
7. **That in the event of any member being expelled, he shall forfeit all claims on the band of**
     any description.
8. **That this band shall be a reserve for the Senior band**
9. **That all additions and deletions to the rules shall only be made by the Senior band.**

1. That the band shall be called the Crosland Moor Junior Hand-bell Ringers.
2. That the Junior band shall consist of as many members as the Senior band shall from time to time deem necessary.
3. That the entrance fee for new members be 1 shilling.
4. That the Senior band shall have full control of the Junior band and that the Senior band shall pay and receive all monies in connection with the Junior band.
5. That any member found guilty of misconduct shall be liable to be expelled.
6. That in the event of any member being expelled for any cause whatever, he shall forfeit all claims upon the band of any description.
7. That the Junior band shall not enter into competition with the Senior band at any contest.
8. That the Junior band is for the sole object of reserves for the Senior band and if at any time the Senior band deem it necessary to require a ringer from the Junior band, they have full power to choose whom they (the Senior band) think fit.
9. That the conductor of the Junior band shall be elected annually by the Senior band.
10. That any additions or deletions to these rules only be made by the Senior band.

The public meeting convened by the Juniors was so volatile and so many statements were made in anger, all of which were reported in full in the local newspapers, that I'm sure if the same meeting were held today, there would be a court case for defamation.

The Huddersfield Chronicle in its Editorial commented: "Every effort should be made to restore peace. It would indeed be a lasting pity if an organisation built up by years of hard work and remarkable self-denial should now be wrecked. It is absurd in the extreme to use such words as "murder" and "manslaughter" in connection with a dispute of this kind".

The above words had been used by the Chairman of the meeting, Mr J D Priestley, (father of one of the Juniors) who said that the Seniors had become jealous and had made up their mind that they would murder the Juniors and had tried to manslaughter (laughter at this crack) them with new rules.

The five founders, led by Thomas Cartwright, founder and former conductor of the Seniors and later mayor of Huddersfield, had previously attempted to settle the dispute by diplomacy. Mr Cartwright had written to Joe Kaye, the Secretary of the Seniors, asking if the Seniors were willing to meet the five and himself, with a view to arriving at an amicable settlement. However Mr Kaye replied that his band could not agree to receiving any deputation from the public, as the matter was not one for public interference.

The Senior Band regarded themselves as a private enterprise, set up for the benefit of its members.

At the public meeting Thomas Cartwright said, "The public having given about £500 with which the property and bells were purchased; they did not provide it for a private hand-bell company, but for public purposes, to be managed by the public". He went on to say it would have been better if the Seniors had themselves proposed the appointment of trustees, (He had done so at the meeting following the fire in 1904 which destroyed so much of Crosland Moor's bells and equipment.), but instead, after the fire, they had made themselves into a private company, with the sole purpose of making as much money out of it as possible. Mr Cartwright continued, saying profits had gone into the ringers' own pockets, at which point someone shouted "To build houses with". There was then laughter.

That the United band was semi-professional was true, and was not denied by the band in their reply to the report of the meeting - a long prepared statement, sent out to the local papers. The statement took up two full length broad sheet columns in the Huddersfield Chronicle, the first half of which contained a history of the band, and the second half giving their side of the argument in reaction to the public meeting. In fact, not one member of the Seniors attended the meeting, but three of their wives did and it turned out later that the Seniors had hired a private reporter to let them know what had been said.

In their long statement the Seniors said they had considered contesting with two teams, but had come to the conclusion that only one band should enter any one contest and the position was that which ever band was elected to compete at a contest would have all facilities for practice and use of bells, etc., and that the other band would stand down altogether. They went on to say that the Juniors had not tried the arrangement, and had they given the scheme a trial they may well have been the band to be chosen to compete.

But the Seniors had not inspired the Juniors' confidence with their actions. After all, had not the dispute been sparked off by the Seniors' actions in disallowing the Juniors the use of the bells for a concert, even though (according to the Juniors) the Seniors didn't have a concert on the same day a fact which the Seniors never publicly denied. However in a letter to the Huddersfield

Fig. 111: James Hobson Ellis (Jimmy)

Examiner, a correspondent on the side of the Seniors, calling himself "Crosland Moorite", claimed that the Seniors did have a concert on the date in question, however Moorite did not by his own admission, attend the public meeting. The Juniors' reply to Moorite's letter, reiterated that the Seniors had had no engagement booked for the said date. It is difficult after the passing of a hundred years to judge who was telling the truth. However one thing is certain. – It was that incident which was the spark which lit the fuse which led to the dispute.

In one of several long letters from supporters of both teams, published in the Huddersfield Examiner, the Chairman of the public meeting, Mr J D Priestley said he did not believe the Juniors would have been the chosen band to compete in the British Open the following year (1909). A rather exasperated editor of the Examiner added that the letters would not appear in the weekly edition of the paper!

Fig. 112: Crosland Moor United Juniors after their second section shield win (c.1908) at Batley in the Yorkshire Association Championships

There was another grievance between the bands, the Juniors' conductor, Jimmy Ellis. Although not named in the Seniors' statement to the press, the statement contained the following words which made Jimmy Ellis' position quite clear: "We may say without fear of contradiction that it is not possible for a ringer to ring with the Seniors and conduct the Juniors and do both satisfactorily. The time required would be too much for one person to do justice to either band".

So Jimmy Ellis now knew it was "Us or them!" He had to choose. But to the credit of both Jimmy Ellis, the conductor of the Juniors, and Albert Townend, the conductor of the Seniors, neither man made any public comment on the dispute and remained friends throughout, and after.

Harsh words had been spoken and there was to be no compromise, but remember these were the days when "men were men" and this was Yorkshire where they call a spade, a spade.

The result was that the Juniors called a second public meeting fifteen days later. Leaflets were again distributed round the district, giving details of the meeting "When the question of forming a PUBLIC band of hand-bell ringers will be discussed".

At the second meeting, the Chairman, Mr J D Priestley said that the lads had had an offer of "a complete outfit" for a little over £100. They had £12 and at a meeting earlier in the week had decided to contribute 10 shillings (50p) each. The offer of a complete outfit probably came from the Huddersfield Hand-bell Ringers as I can find no mention of the band after 1908, and the band had fallen on bad times after the death of their conductor William Booth in June 1908 and they did not enter the 1908 British Open.

The proposal to form a new band was put to the meeting, "Mr Richard Morley formally proposed and Mr Sidney Gay seconded, that a Junior Public Band be formed, the resolution was then put and carried unanimously, amid enthusiasm".

Great emphasis was placed on the new band being a PUBLIC band, controlled by the public, with trustees appointed by the inhabitants of the district. It was stated, quite correctly, that "the Seniors could sell their effects tomorrow and no one could interfere". At a meeting two years later in February 1910, trustees were elected and a trust deed prepared, the principal clause being "that all the property of the band would be vested in the trustees for the inhabitants of Crosland Moor for ever". This principal clause has been honoured to the present day, even though by only a thin red line at times. The tradition has been maintained more or less intact.

The gentlemen elected as trustees were: R Morley; J D Priestley; H Lunn; J E Crosland; J Avison; Councillor T Cartwright; J Baxter; B Ibeson and James H Ellis, who was also invited to become the new band's conductor, an invitation he accepted. Jimmy Ellis knew that in becoming the new band's conductor, he would not be allowed to continue as first treble ringer with Crosland Moor United.

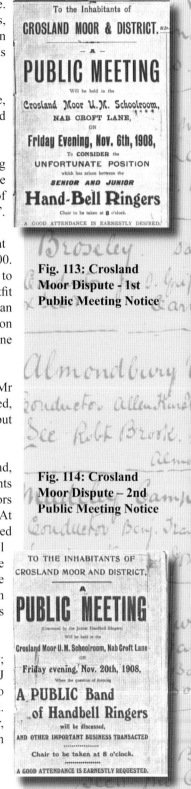

To the Inhabitants of

CROSLAND MOOR & DISTRICT.

— A —

PUBLIC MEETING

Will be held in the

Crosland Moor U.M. Schoolroom,

NAB CROFT LANE,

ON

Friday Evening, Nov. 6th, 1908,

To CONSIDER the

UNFORTUNATE POSITION

which has arisen between the

SENIOR AND JUNIOR

Hand-Bell Ringers

Chair to be taken at 8 o'clock.

A GOOD ATTENDANCE IS EARNESTLY DESIRED.

Fig. 113: Crosland Moor Dispute - 1st Public Meeting Notice

Fig. 114: Crosland Moor Dispute – 2nd Public Meeting Notice

TO THE INHABITANTS OF

CROSLAND MOOR AND DISTRICT.

A

PUBLIC MEETING

(Convened by the Junior Handbell Ringers)

Will be held in the

Crosland Moor U.M. Schoolroom, Nab Croft Lane

ON

Friday evening, Nov. 20th, 1908,

When the question of forming

A PUBLIC Band of Handbell Ringers

will be discussed,

AND OTHER IMPORTANT BUSINESS TRANSACTED

Chair to be taken at 8 o'clock.

A GOOD ATTENDANCE IS EARNESTLY REQUESTED.

In keeping with its principles, the new band was named Crosland Moor Public Hand-bell Ringers. The necessary cash was raised to pay for the complete outfit offered to the band, but fund raising went even better than anyone expected and by February 1909 the Public Band was in a position to order a new set of 165 bells from the Mears and Stainbank at the Whitechapel bell foundry, ready for the British Open the following September. In 1914 the Band purchased another identical set of 165 bells, again from Whitechapel.

The Public Band's rehearsal room and headquarters were in an upstairs room at Crosland Moor Working Men's Club. The room now contains a snooker table.

So there were now two rival Crosland Moor Bands and the scene was set for the big showdown at the Queens Hall Ballroom, Belle Vue for the 1909 British Open Championship of Great Britain. Both bands put in all the spare time they could in rehearsal of the test piece, which was a selection from Balfe's overture "Bohemian Girl".

The day finally arrived for the 55th Annual Contest, Monday September 27th, "when great interest was taken in the event. Excursion trains, of which a vast number of people availed themselves, were run from all parts", said the British Bandsman, who had its correspondent Codon and friend to report on the year's great feast of hand-bell entertainment, and it is thanks to the Bandsman's published account that we can now go (with a little imagination) with Codon and his friend, back in time to the day of the contest. (Incidentally I have undertaken this same train journey from Huddersfield to Manchester many times while carrying out my research, and often I would ponder on the fact that I was walking over the same platforms and travelling on the same routes as countless hand-bell ringers and their supporters had done before me.)

We have probably made the journey on one of the excursion trains (I hope you remembered to go to the loo beforehand, because the carriages are enclosed, with no W.C.s). We disembark at Longsight Station and a short walk takes us into Hyde Road where the entrance is. We pay our 6d admission at the turnstile and walk straight forward for about 50 yards, passing the Museum on our right and the Aviary to our left. On reaching the Leopard House (part of the world famous zoo) we turn right, and the Music Hall (called the Queen's Hall) where the Contest is being held, stands right in front of us.

We are however, late for the start, did Codon and his friend buy us a drink in Jennison's Bar which stands just inside the entrance? (a public house still open today). At the entrance we are sold a programme, which contains the names of the bands taking part and the names and addresses of each of the ringers in each band.

The stage where the bands perform is at the far end of the hall in front of the orchestra. At this point I will hand over to Codon to take up the story.

"We were not as punctual in taking up a position in the Hall as the management were in starting the Contest, which was timed for two o'clock. The first band, Dewsbury, who were conducted by Mr Arthur Fearnsides, had actually concluded their performance when we entered the hall. Therefore we can offer no criticism but it was said they had given a fair performance.

The board now announced Almondbury as the next band, Mr J A North was the conductor. The performance was somewhat tame, but of fair merit.

Royston United were conducted by Mr Jas Watson. The men rang with confidence, though occasionally we get a few bells out of tune and some parts were indistinct, but on the whole it was a fairly good performance.

Birstall St Saviour's were now announced, Mr Kaye Cooke being in command, but they are small in number, having only eight ringers, whilst others have ten and even eleven. The quality of tone was good, character of the music nicely displayed and everything is clean and distinct. One or two places, however allow for a little more freedom. A good finish to a capital performance.

The board now announces Barnsley, who are conducted by Mr T Fleetwood. There is merit in their ringing, but the bells are very much out of tune.

Thurlstone now come on the scene conducted by Mr Fred Taylor. They open better than the previous band, some parts of the performance are very good whilst in others there is a stiffness which does not give a good effect. Just a fair performance.

There is excitement now when the board announces Crosland Moor United. Mr Albert Townend conducted, they start, sounding masterly. There are a few misses, which has a bad effect. At times the ringing is fine, but the last few chords in the piece are untuneful.

Clifton Juniors are next on, Mr Fred Squire being the conductor. They are very nice at times, but hardly up to the standard of some previous bands.

Saddleworth come on the scene next, Mr William Pawnall being in charge. They are evidently a young band, who with care and practice may do well, but today they are outclassed.

Lepton are conducted by Mr J H Dawson. They are not so precise as some of the other bands and the treble bells are sharp. A fair performance on the whole.

Crosland Moor Public is the next up, and excitement runs high as they are getting ready. Mr James H Ellis conducts. From the first note it is interesting, the performance throughout is excellent, for besides being clear in tone the effects produced are excellent. Best so far.

Clifton, who are conducted by Mr A Sayles, invariably gives a good performance at Belle Vue and they are no disappointment this time. It is a nice performance in every respect.

Pendlebury brings up the rear, Mr A Royle wielding the baton. They have a large band, but they have a little way to go yet before they are equal to a few of the others. The top octave bells are sharp.

After about twenty minutes of anxious waiting, the decision announced:
First prize, Crosland Moor Public;
Second prize, Birstall;
Third prize, Clifton;
Fourth prize, Dewsbury
Fifth prize, Crosland Moor United

The next four in order of merit for the consolation prizes are Pendlebury, Thurlstone, Almondbury and Clifton Juniors. The decision is considered a good one with the exception that Royston might have occupied the sixth place instead of Pendlebury. Mr George Pritchard of London and Mr Fred Owen of Manchester adjudicated.
Well, it's over for another year, we can go home now, or would you like to stay for the firework display?"

Back in Huddersfield, the Public Band's return at about 11.30 pm was met by "scenes of the wildest enthusiasm", said the Colne Valley News. A huge concourse of people greeted them as they stepped onto the platform. Two special tram cars were in waiting and the party made a triumphal ride to Crosland Moor where hundreds of people cheered. Flags and bunting had been put up. Speeches were made, including one from the founder of the United Band, Councillor Thomas Cartwright, who now supported and had helped in rehearsals of the new Public Band.

The United had been beaten by their pupils, said the Colne Valley News, but added that, "In fairness to Crossland Moor United, it should be stated that an unfortunate hitch occurred during their playing of the test piece. One of the treble ringers in passing a bell to his neighbour touched another bell which was turned completely round in consequence, causing both ringers to become flurried".

However, undaunted by this defeat, one year later the United Band returned to Belle Vue and won first prize. The Public Band were not even in the first five.

There were several bands in the area who were connected with the Quaker movement. One of these, Hartshead Hand-bell Ringers, was based at Friends School in Hartshead in the Sheffield city centre. There was another Quaker band in Bradford with the rather large name of "Friends First Day School Otley Road Hand-bell Ringers". I had no knowledge of this band at all until a photograph of the band, dated 1901, appeared in the Bradford Telegraph and Argus in 1988. I have no other information on the band but it did not enter any contest I am aware of.

In Lancashire there was a Quaker band at Oldham. The band was based at the Friends School, Greaves Street, in the town.

Although Hartshead was the most successful of the Quaker or Friends bands they never reached the top flight of the hand-bell world and only took part in one British Open, in 1903 which is the first recorded mention I have found of the band. They only had a small set of about 80 bells, which were, according to people who remember them, not all that good a set, which is probably why the band didn't go in for the British Open.

Hartshead would have been at a disadvantage, using such a small set of bells in less than top class condition. However Hartshead competed regularly in the Yorkshire Hand-bell Ringers Association Championships, and a Hartshead ringer, Mr W Dyson was Yorkshire Association President from 1907 to 1911, and the Association's Secretary for 15 years, from 1910 to 1925, after which he relinquished the position on "suffering the effects of severe illness".

(Incidentally the Barnsley Independent on Sept 24th 1932 (Page 6- Col 2) pointed out "In 1870-80 expectation of life at birth was 41 years for a boy and 44 for a girl. However today (1932), it is 56 for a boy and 60 for a girl. So in 20 years life expectancy has increased by not fewer than 15 years. Sickness is as prevalent as ever – Causes of death – Influenza 14,409; Tuberculosis 35,346; Cancer 59,346. In 1900, 142,912 Children died under one year old. In 1930 only 38,908 died under one year of age." In June 1931 the

Independent hoped that Typhoid had been stamped out in Honley though noted in October 29th 1932 that fifty people had contracted typhoid in Denby Vale.)

Mr Dyson conducted the Hartshead Ringers to their best contest result in 1914, when the band won first prize in the Yorkshire Association second section contest. The band never competed in the first section of the contests.

Hartshead's other conductors were: Mr J A Ironside (1903 to 1910) and Mr A Moore (1912). The bands' music repertoire included "Independence", "Sweet and Low", "Blue Bells of Scotland" and "Dreams of Heaven".

Hartshead's last appearance was at the Yorkshire Association Championships of 1925, the year of Mr Dyson's severe illness, so perhaps he did not recover. The band did enter for the championships in 1926, but did not compete. After this the band faded into obscurity as I can find no mention of Hartshead after 1926.

The other Quaker band, "Friends Adult School Hand-bell Ringers, Oldham", seems to have had a life of 17/18 years from 1897 to 1914. Unlike Hartshead, Oldham Friends only entered the British Open Contest at Belle Vue and did not take part in the Yorkshire Contest. Their first entry at Belle Vue was in 1904 under conductor Albert Lawton, of Villa Road, Oldham, who became conductor in 1900.

Oldham Friends began life with a set of 54 bells, purchased in order to provide something of interest for the young men attending the Sunday School. In 1900 a set of 88 bells was acquired. After this the band progressed "beyond all expectations" and competed at Belle Vue in 1904 gaining the "approbation of the judges as well as praise from some of their rivals on this their initial attempt". They also competed again at Belle Vue in 1905, but did not win a prize. In 1906 they were prevented from competing, because of "sickness amongst the members and several working out of town".

Oldham Friends' secretaries included Mr A W Gordon and Mr L Brook. The band worked itself up to a good position by 1907 and the band met with success at Blyth Theatre, Northumberland; Alexander Park, Oldham; Technical Institute, Peel Park, Salford; Oddfellows Hall, Ashton, all in Lancashire, and Oddfellows Hall, Bradford, Yorkshire amongst others. In late 1907 they took delivery of 120 new bells from Shaws of Bradford.

The Band's President at the time was Mr H L Hargraves of

Queens Road and it was "through this gentleman's generosity and enthusiasm that the Oldham ringers sprang into existence" wrote "Cottonpolis" in the British Bandsman.

At the ringers' annual tea party in March 1908 they played "Woodstock" a march; "Alice Where Art Thou?" and "Last Rose

of Summer".

In May 1908 the Bandsman reported that the Oldham Ringers were in fine form, practices were well kept up and that the band was "well prepared for contests or engagements", but the band did not compete in a contest again until the British Open of 1912, when the band's 9 members were conducted by Mr J F Slater, Mus. Bac. F.R.C.O. of Hawk House, King Street, Oldham.

Oldham entered for the British Open again in 1913, but did not compete. They returned to compete at Belle Vue in 1914, but after this date the band disappeared from view and we never hear of them again - a victim of World War 1?

Another Lancashire band to be formed against the run of the mill was Tunstead Church Men's Class Hand-bell Ringers. Tunstead is at Stacksteads near Bacup, in the area of Lancashire towns known as Rossendale. The band appeared on the scene at the British Open in 1911 and competed every year until 1914, after which (yes, you have guessed it) they were never heard of again - another casualty of the Great War?

Tunstead was formed by the men's bible class in October 1908.

Fig. 115: Friends School Hand-bell Ringers, Oldham - formed against the tide in 1897, this band were one of only a handful of Lancashire bands in existance after 1900 (photo courtesy Manchester Cultural Studies Committee)

Fig. 116: Tunstead Hand-bell Ringers c.1911

By 1911 the band seems to have become quite proficient with 8 ringers, and were conducted by Mr Howarth Stansfield, of David Street, Stacksteads.

In 1912, the number of ringers increased to ten and by 1913 there were 11 in the band who were: A Nuttall; J E Lord; J Roberts; Sam Pilkington (who was caretaker/verger of the church); J Rostron; P Aspinall; J Thorpe; J Rushton; F Hargreaves; E Hackington; and R Clegg. Their best result was fifth at the British Open in 1913.

In 1958 Mr Ernest Pilkington, Tunstead Church organist and son of the above Sam, formed a band of 9 or 10 choir boys who used the original bells, and this band lasted about four years. Regrettably in the mid 1980s the Church put the bells up for sale and the chance of a revival of hand-bell ringing in this fine part of Lancashire was lost. However, even so, the spark of tradition is strong in this district and only one mile up the road from Tunstead is Bacup, where each Easter Saturday, the Britannia Coconut Dancers perform in the streets - a tradition probably as old as hand-bell ringing itself and who knows, perhaps one day someone in Tunstead may be moved by this same spark of tradition, to acquire a set of bells and return the art to the village once again.

There is a strong tradition of hand-bell ringing in other towns in this part of Lancashire. The lists of entrants in the British Open gives us the names of some of them - Whitworth, near Rochdale (1864 and 1865); Burnley (1869); St Paul's, Ramsbottom (1891). Other nearby towns with a hand-bell ringing tradition are Over Darwen (1862); Clitheroe (1877); and St Luke's, Heywood (1865, 1891, 1893). This whole area of Lancashire teems with traditions and is well worth a visit.

About eight miles down the road from Tunstead is the town of Accrington. The town's hand-bell heritage is not a great one, but like Tunstead, it is commendable because its band operated when it was not very fashionable to do so in 'turn of the century' Lancashire.

The Accrington tradition seems to have been in two parts, the first was active in the 1880s, and the second part twenty years later. However I have found information on hand-bell ringing in Accrington very hard to come by - despite a visit to the town.

As formerly stated a band of ringers from Accrington took part in a contest at Glossop in 1884. The next mention of the name is when a band call Church Accrington Hand-bell Ringers entered the British Open in 1905, their conductor being Robert Parkinson of Edward Street, Church. Church is in fact an area of Accrington.

The members of the 1905 Church Accrington Handbellband were, Robert Parkinson, James Barnes, Peter Ashcroft, Herbert Furness, Joseph Hartley, Tomas Lightbourn, John Chapman and Percy Aspden, but for some unknown reason Church did not compete in the 1905 contest.

Church seemed to make a habit of changing conductors during the band's rather short-lived existence, the second time around. The band did not enter the British open in 1906, but were back in 1907 with Professor W Prince (M.I.N.M.) Incum. London, as their conductor. The Professor brought about no remarkable change in the band's performance in the contest–. They came well down the list, so in 1908 they returned to the contest with yet another conductor, Edmund Lee, after which the band disappeared from the scene altogether.

At this point I think it will be useful if we recall the Lancashire bands who took an active part in the competitive world of hand-bell ringing between 1900 and 1915.

There were, as already mentioned, Bolton Parish Church; Newchurch, near Warrington; Tunstead; Friends School, Oldham, and Higher Walton. There was one other Lancashire band, Pendlebury, about whom we shall hear later on in our story.

Newchurch and Bolton Parish Church first appeared at the Yorkshire Association Championships in 1913, but with only a handful of isolated Lancashire bands in existence, it must have been difficult to keep up enthusiasm.

There was a completely different situation on the other side of the Pennines. In Yorkshire the hand-bell movement made continued progress. For the few Lancashire bands there were, life must have seemed pitiful in comparison.

The Yorkshire charge of progress was of course, led by the Crosland Moor bands, the United and the Public. Between them the two bands won every British Open bar two between 1901 and 1915, which in itself is a fantastic run of wins. Most bands hadn't won the contest once, let alone achieved a hat trick.

The first of Crosland Moor Public's two hat trick championship wins at Belle Vue, came in 1911-12-13 and at the age of only 33, their conductor, Jimmy Ellis, had a champion band of his own.

By now Jimmy Ellis was attaining the stature of "Chosen Leader" of the hand-bell movement. Jimmy's gift for arranging music for hand-bells combined with his leadership qualities and his skill as an actual hand-bell ringer himself, put him at the top end of the evolutionary chain which began with the formation of Crosland Moor United by Thomas Cartwright in 1890.

Cartwright's own hand-bell ringing skills handbellwere rooted in the Holmfirth Temperance Ringers back in the early 1870s, so Jimmy Ellis had a lot of traditional knowledge from which to draw. His early musical training on the piano as a child also held him in good stead - which rendered him capable of understanding and imbibing all of the knowledge of the United's conductor Albert Townend.

Jimmy Ellis also had the advantage of having members in his band who were prepared to do as he himself had done - listen and learn.

While Jimmy Ellis and the Crosland Moor Public Ringers were blazing the trail to Belle Vue, Albert Townend and Crosland Moor United were doing some trail blazing of their own, as previously mentioned - all the way to Australasia on a tour which was to take them nearly two years to undertake and travel no less than 34,510 miles.

The first murmurings of the tour began after the United Band fulfilled an engagement at the London Hippodrome in March 1911. But this was no one off concert–. It was for two appearances daily, afternoon and evening, for a week!

On the first day each of their performances lasted twenty-five minutes, but this was subsequently reduced to fifteen minutes. The Huddersfield Examiner reported "On every appearance the ringers have had a most enthusiastic reception, encores came thick and fast and the audience would not be content with the conductor bowing acknowledgements, as he did three tunes after every performance."

Among tunes played were "Legend of the Bells", "In my Cottage", the first movement from the "William Tell" overture, "Martha" and "Friendship". Albert Townend told the Examiner: "The manager would gladly have kept us another week, but of course we could not stay, having our work here to attend to".

Whilst in London the ringers toured all the sights, including a walk round a place still visited by hand-bell ringers today - the Mears and Stainbank's their Whitechapel bell foundry.

While in London, as previously stated, the Crosland Moor United Hand-bell Ringers became the first hand-bell ringers to make an 80 rpm record. The Huddersfield Examiner reported, "An enterprising gramophone company has taken some records of the ringers performances". One of these records was found in the BBC record archives in the 1970s, the label on the record simply says "The Gramophone Company". The tune on the record sounds like some sort of country dance, the name of which is not known.

I have not been able to find any other records at Crosland Moor despite an appeal in the Huddersfield Examiner and an extensive oral research in the village.

During United's week's engagement at the London Hippodrome, concert agents, who had been pressing the ringers to undertake a tour of Australasia, were at three of the concerts, "and were so delighted with the success of the performances that they renewed their offers", said the Examiner, who asked Albert Townend if the tour was likely to go ahead; "I don't know I'm sure, we are going to give the matter our careful consideration this week and we shall probably give a definite answer in the course of a few days" was the reply.

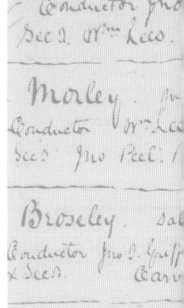

Fig. 117: Crosland Moor United's Signature Tune: "Bellringers' March"

Albert Townend and his band sailed by the Orient Pacific R.M.S. Ormuz, on the 18th August, 1911 to make a tour of Australasia, calling at Gibraltar, Marseilles, Naples, Port Said, Colombo, Freemantle, Adelaide, Melbourne, Hobart and then they landed at Dunedin, New Zealand on October 3rd.Here they opened their tour three days later and "played for six nights before large and appreciative audiences, creating at once a reputation that travelled before them throughout New Zealand and Australia". This information is included within the printed version of "The Bellringer's March", published by J Wood and Sons of Huddersfield in 1912 to commemorate the tour. Albert Townend had "arranged and adapted" the piece especially for the tour and it was adobted by the band as their signature tune. The piece contains a good run of notes for the bass ringers.

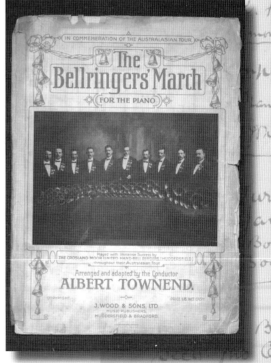

In 1978 I spoke to Harold Godward, conductor of Almondbury Hand-bell Ringers from 1907

right up to the early 1950s. My conversations with Mr Godward were some of the most enjoyable of my research.

Mr Godward had a good knowledge of the "Bellringers' March" and (to my absolute surprise) played the tune on his piano for me. He maintained that the tune was first played by Almondbury, and was given to Crosland Moor United by one of the Almondbury ringers, Jos Dawson. Mr Godward said he thought the tune came from one of the operas and knew it under the name "Les Pantons". Perhaps someone knows more? "We all made polite remarks about Jos Dawson giving it away to Crosland Moor", said Mr Godward with a smile.

I felt a sense of loss on the death of Harold Godward in 1979 aged 88. Not only had I lost a friend, but my own direct link with the halcyon days of pre-Great War hand-bell ringing was irrevocably snapped.

The Crosland Moor United Band, which toured Australasia, consisted of nine ringers and conductor Albert Townend. One of the regular United ringers was unable to make the trip. Albert Townend then asked Albert Jenkinson, a former Almondbury ringer to stand in for the man.

Mr Jenkinson was well experienced in touring with a hand-bell band, as he had been a member of the Almondbury band which toured the USA ten years previously. I think the United ringers took his advice on the rigours of touring as the band had a very strong "U" shaped ringing table specially made from angle iron for the tour. No doubt Mr Jenkinson had recalled the stories of the rough treatment the Almondbury tables and boxes of bells had received on their railway journeys around the USA.

The railways Crosland Moor travelled on were no better. "(Travelling on them was) the most trying experience to which the party had to submit, the trains were slow and the accommodation much below the English standard" said the band's biographer Albert Townend.

During the tour, the band played in eighty cities and large towns and met many people who had come out to settle from Britain, especially from Yorkshire, including the Bishop of Auckland, the Rt Rev'd O T L Crossley, known to the band, as he had once been Vicar of Almondbury.

The band left New Zealand on February 17th, 1912 for Tasmania, playing at Hobart on the 24th and at Launceston and other towns. They again met people from Huddersfield, including a man from Kirkburton who had done very well for himself, owning much land in Devonport.

Albert Townend sent regular reports of the tour, which were published in great detail in the Huddersfield Examiner.

During my research I spoke to Wilfrid Jenkinson, whose father Albert rang in the USA with Almondbury and with Crosland Moor on the Australasian tour. He told me the band was paid £75 a week during the tour. Mr Jenkinson is still proud owner of his father's British Open Championship medals.

From Tasmania the band sailed to the Australian mainland where their first performance was in the Adelaide Town Hall. Every seat was filled and "hundreds were turned away". Other concerts included ones given at Broken Hill and Ballarat. In Australia the band played in thirty-six cities and towns in total.

The tour closed on May 15th when the band sailed home on the R.M.S. Orontes, arriving at Tilbury Docks, Essex on June 23rd, 1912.

In 1961 the Huddersfield Examiner carried a feature on the tour and interviewed Mr Robert Hopson, then aged eighty-three, who was one of the band. He liked Tasmania best of all, liking "everything about the place, the people and the weather". In fact one of the band, Harry North loved the place so much he stayed in Australia, and according to Jim Fisher (a member of the United band in the 1920s) Mr North sent for a set of bells from Mears and Stainbank (Whitechapel).

The United Ringers had been away one day short of forty-five weeks and fourteen of these had been spent sailing. The men arrived back in Huddersfield where they were greeted by their wives and families, and they all travelled the last two miles to Crosland Moor in especially decorated and illuminated trams put on by the local corporation - CIVIC PRIDE, that's what these people had, which seems so distant to us today - Civic Pride is what we all need today, but for some reason it seems sadly lacking - excepting government officials riding around the capital city in Rolls Royces; and in the building of concrete, steel and plastic city and town centres which are a planner's delight, but are not very good for people.

Their travels over, it would seem the Crosland Moor United Band took a long rest, as the year after their return, 1913, seems to have been very quiet for the Band as I can find no mention until the bands entry at the British Open of 1914, the year that Crosland Moor Public were barred from competing due to their championship win in 1913. So, with the 'Public' not being in the contest, the 'United'

223

must have fancied their chances. But a new star was to take over the premier spot in the hallowed hall at Belle Vue in 1914, and this new star was Saddleworth, as they take up their place as one of the great bands of the Twentieth Century. Saddleworth was now the main rival to the Crosland Moor bands.

The Saddleworth Hand-bell Ringers arose from small and humble beginnings, with none of the experienced organisation that started Crosland Moor, although there are parallels.

The Saddleworth band had its origins at St Chad's Parish Church in Uppermill, one of a number of Pennine villages near Oldham, which makes up the area known as Saddleworth, which was in Yorkshire, until the 1974 local government reorganisation. (In 1974 Saddleworth, after much protest, was put into the county of Greater Manchester, but the people of Saddleworth still think of themselves as Yorkshire through and through.)

Exactly when hand-bell ringing began in Saddleworth is at present not known to me, but there was a band connected with St Chad's, Uppermill prior to 1885 when a "new set of 39 additional bells was purchased". The word "additional" indicates that there were hand-bells in use before the new set of 39 bells were purchased, but how many? In 1900 there is evidence of 49 bells, which were known then as the "old 49". This suggests that these bells were in fact the 39 bells bought in 1885, plus 10 others which could have been the pre 1885 bells. These 10 bells may have been used originally by the church's tower bell ringers for change ringing practice.

Unlike Crosland Moor, the Saddleworth Hand-bell Ringers in the first instant were not deliberately set up as a competition/concert band, but as an activity for members of St Chad's Church.

Saddleworth has a long tradition of rushbearings, which were a popular haunt of hand-bell ringers (see earlier chapter on the wakes). Saddleworth's rushbearing festival was held at the end of August and was said to be well established by 1820 and continued until 1912.

The Saddleworth rushbearing festival was started up again in 1975 and is one of Britain's most colourful traditional feasts and is well worth visiting. The rush cart is pulled around the district by scores of morris dancers.

The 1885 Saddleworth Hand-bell Ringers activity continued for some time and then it may have lapsed, because in 1900 a new band was formed under the conductorship of Ben Sykes Taylor. The band's members were Frank Wrigley, William Pownall, Joseph Spencer, James Bax, Leonard Bradshaw, T R Byrom, D Ashley, W

Holden, H lees, E Broadbent, John E Bradbury, H Roberts and C Ratcliffe.

This band continued for only a few short years, after which another band was formed around 1907 and this was the band which was to be the longest and most enduring, and put the Saddleworth Hand-bell Ringers into the hand-bell ringers' hall of fame.

Some of the rules of the 1900 band are worth a mention, such as the following:

Rule 3. That the members arriving at a practice after 8 o'clock be fined one penny.

Rule 5. That any members insisting on being absent for his own pleasure will be subject to being expelled and forfeit all that he has paid (in subscriptions one penny per week).

Rule 8. That every member be fined one penny for bad language.

And these rules were for members of a Church Sunday School! In 1919 a rule said "That there be no smoking, only in specified time

Fig. 118: Saddleworth, taken after their victory at the 1914 British Open. Centre is Mr William Pownall proudly wearing the Diamond Jubilee Medal. The table cover was one of the most beautiful ever made but has now been lost

during practice hours (8 to 9.30 pm).

The Saddleworth Hand-bell Ringers formed around 1907 were different to all the previous formations in that, like Crosland Moor, the band was formed with the idea of entering contests. The band contained some of the members of the 1900 band, one of whom was asked to become conductor - William Pownall, who lived into his nineties. It was with Mr Pownall that the band had some of its greatest successes, including the winning of the Diamond Jubilee British Open at Belle Vue, when the prize, in addition to the Mears Perpetual Trophy, was a special gold medal which had diamonds set in all four corners and in its centre.

This unique and historic medal remained in Mr Pownall's possession until his death when distant relatives came and cleared out his house. The medal's whereabouts is not known. Does anyone have any further information?

The Diamond Jubilee medal was hotly contested by all the other bands, including Crosland Moor United, contesting for the first time since their Australasian tour.

It may come as a surprise to many readers that Albert Townend, United's conductor, helped Saddleworth in rehearsals of the test piece "The Crown Diamonds" by Auber, and as a result perhaps, Crosland Moor United came second. But remember all the bands were members of the Yorkshire Association, and once a band became a member, information was freely given. Albert Townend's association with Saddleworth was to continue for many years.

Albert Townend was a remarkable man. His musical knowledge and expertise was the key to the success of Crosland Moor United and Saddleworth. Always, a good band requires a good leader and conductor, otherwise the whole thing can quickly fall apart.

Albert Townend was a violinist of no mean ability, and taught the instrument privately. He was also a member of Huddersfield's Philharmonic Society. He was a baker/manager for the former bakery of Bellarby's in the town.

While Albert Townend was a conductor paid by Saddleworth to take the last few final rehearsals before a contest, William Pownall was the resident conductor who did all the hard work with the band to get the piece to a sufficiently high standard before Albert Townend was called in for the finishing touches. William Pownall would then conduct the band at the traditional final Saturday morning rehearsal before travelling to the contest, something which most bands seemed to do.

To my regret I never met William Pownall. He died in 1976, aged 96, before my research began. Mr Pownall was fortunately interviewed by the Oldham Chronicle in the 1960s. In the interview Mr Pownall gives a revealing insight into the rise of the Saddleworth Hand-bell Ringers, from their first entry in the British Open when they found themselves outclassed by most of the other bands. The year was 1909 and the Saddleworth ringers used the old 49 bells to play the test piece, an arrangement of Balfe's "Bohemian Girl", using numbers instead of staff notation. Saddleworth came tenth in an entry of 13, but the adjudicator made an encouraging reference to the debut of this young band - and this spurred them on.

The competition taught them two things. Their range of bells was not large enough, and Mr Pownall realised they were not ringing in the same method as the better bands.

He made many inquiries and finally was put in touch with Ben Lodge, the former conductor of the Almondbury United Ringers who had disbanded only eighteen months previously. Mr Lodge lived in Linthwaite, a village about six miles from Saddleworth on the road to Huddersfield.
"I went to see him and he did us proud" Mr Pownall recalled, "He scored me three manuscript copies, treble, tenor and bass, for the following year". So they went to Belle Vue again in 1910 and to their delight moved up several places.

Of using numbers Mr Pownall said "The method was very haphazard, with no rhythm, time or real tune."

Amazingly many bands of today still use numbers instead of staff notation, with some excellent results. Two bands which spring to mind from the later 20th century are Gnosall (although actually they used letters rather than numbers) and Stonnall, two Staffordshire bands who have both made LP records using numbers as music, but if the hand-bell movement wishes to take its place alongside other accepted forms of music making, then clearly acceptance and usage of a standard staff music notation is essential. Whilst numerical and alpha notations are acceptable within the confines of the hand-bell movement, they are not understood by non ringing musicians, who may be called upon to give their professional adjudication on a performance, and if such people are to be encouraged to include hand-bell ringing in the educational system in schools and colleges, the hand-bell movement as a whole, must move towards standard staff notation which on the whole is easier to use than numerical and alpha notations.

(The use of number music is one of the few areas in which Peter [the author] and I [the editor] disagree. Any piece of music, no matter how complicated in timing, rhythm, key or tune, written in the number notation now adopted as standard for number notation by the Handbell Ringers of Great Britain, can be sight read just as easily by those proficient in reading it, as the same music written in staff notation can be sight read by those proficient in reading staff notation, However the standard music notation that has now been adopted by HRGB and other

hand-bell societies around the world is based on piano score staff notation with treble and bass clefs. This was not the standard notation used by most "long set" Belle Vue competition teams. They used individual scores with only the notes of each ringer or pair of ringers marked on them as in orchestral scores, and usually with the tenor and bass parts transposed up into the treble clef.

Before the adoption of the number notation standard by HRGB in 1974 there were (and still are) many number systems in use around the country, from fully notated easily sight readable systems as found at Kings Langley, Herts, and Aldborough, Suffolk, to systems for which one needed to know the tune before it could be played, as found at Prittlewell, Essex. Such latter systems were more of an aide memoir to ringers who were well practised in their pieces, than fully developed sight readable number notation systems in their own right. Unfortunately the systems in use in the north of England at the time tended toward the latter, and were difficult to use for the complicated competition overtures which were required for Belle Vue. Had they been similar to that eventually adopted as the standard for number notation by HRGB, then it is likely that we would now be using it for all hand-bell music worldwide, rather than the present piano style. Ed.)

The Saddleworth ringers must have found the change to staff notation beneficial, because in 1912 the band won the Yorkshire Association Challenge Shield for the winners of the second section contest.

Mr Pownall also told the Oldham Chronicle how he came into hand-bell ringing. "My interest in hand-bell ringing began when I was a schoolboy, but it was not appreciated by the Saddleworth Church Hand-bell Ringers. They used to practise in the bottom room of the Parish School and with other youngsters, I used to watch, listen and interfere!

We kicked up such a row, as boys will, that we always got chased away from the windows we were peeping through. So then we would go back and sneak into the kitchen, turn on the gas and blow down the pipe to put all the lights out. I'm afraid we must have made life very hard for the poor ringers".

While Mr Pownall was busy improving their ringing method, the members of his band were busy raising funds for a new set of bells. They knew the old 49 bells were not sufficient, and launched a public subscription appeal for a new set of 165 bells, similar to the set used by Crosland Moor Public mentioned earlier. These bells cost £96 and the band took delivery of them from the Whitechapel Foundry in 1910, but by January 1914 another appeal was launched to buy an identical set, as the 1910 set was by then wearing out!

The Saddleworth band comprised four treble ringers, three tenor and two bass ringers and was one of many bands that made up the buoyant and successful hand-bell scene between 1903 and 1914, brought about through the hard work and grass roots activity of the Yorkshire Hand-bell Ringers Association. This picture of life is recorded in the pages of the Brighouse Echo, which carried extensive reports of the Yorkshire Association's contest held at the nearby Sunny Vale Pleasure Gardens, Hipperholme, where the Association's contest returned after the 1911 contests at Ecclesfield.

The Echo correspondent wrote of the 1909 contests, "The Northern revival of hand-bell ringing was no flash in the pan, but a revival that possessed every possibility of lasting". In 1913 "There was an excellent entry and a large attendance". In June 1914 the Echo correspondent said, "From all points of view the contests were excellently managed and were the most successful on record".

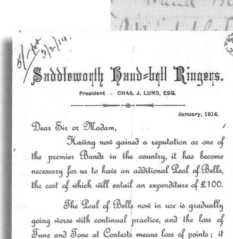

Fig. 119; Saddleworth Hand-bell Ringers' Appeal 1914

The new life in the movement was spotted by the Bell News and Ringers Record, a publication for tower bell ringers which reported in 1911 that "Although this branch of musical art is not as popular as it was 30 years ago, there are indications of an upsurge in the art's popularity".

Although the art was not as popular as it had been in the 1880s, it was technically more advanced in 1912. In fact the movement alerted the attention of the National daily papers during this period, notably the Daily Mail. Under the heading of "Festival of Bells", the Mail said of the 1912 British Open, "In one or two instances the technique of the performers was well nigh flawless. A buzz of animated conversation and cheering greeted the entry of the Crosland Moor Public Band".

In 1913 the Daily Mail again covered the British Open, but with a photograph of Crosland Moor Public as well as an interview with Jimmy Ellis, who told the Mail "In our first victory some of our players were youngsters in short trousers and Eton collars. Even now the oldest player is twenty-seven while the youngest is eighteen. We work hard. Since Easter (it was September) we have rehearsed the piece - nothing else - four nights a week. That's why

229

we win, that and because we endeavour to play with expression. The music of our village is mainly hand-bell ringing".

Jimmy Ellis was a perfectionist, his daughter told me in 1978, "Everything had to be right. If he was playing his piano and there was a rattle or a squeak he would take it apart and would not rest until he found the fault and put it right".

Frank Beaumont, a member of the Public band told me that Crosland Moor used to warm waist shreds in the oven from the local mills and pack it inside and round the bells in their boxes, before setting of to a contest. This brought out the best tone of the bells, although, as he said "some times it would set on fire in the oven, and we had to put it out."

Having attained a knowledge of the hand-bell movement and of the people involved during my researches, I came to know something of the lives and personalities of those I was writing about; so much so that they seemed to enter my subconscious mind.

I well remember a dream in which I visited the Old Hat Hotel in the early years of last century, which was the former headquarters of the Yorkshire Hand-bell Ringers Association (the hotel is still in business today). I could see the delegates of the various bands and I instantly recognised Albert Townend and went over to speak to him. I said "You're Albert Townend aren't you?" "Yes I am" he replied. I asked him if he knew who I was. "You're Peter Fawcett", he said. I told him we were doing our best to get hand-bell ringing going again at Crosland Moor. "Yes, I know", said Albert. I asked him how he thought we were doing with our revival. "I think you're doing alright", was his reply.

I then awoke to find myself back in the 1980s, but the dream was so vivid, I can still smell the smoke in the pub, and to this day I often wonder, was it really a dream?

But at the 1914 Yorkshire Association contests the ringers then were doing some dreaming of their own.

In his remarks after the first section contest the adjudicator Frank Owen, L.R.C.M. from Manchester said that in the playing of the test piece, "Bohemian Girl", the movements in which the bands had been hopelessly at sea were, "A Heart Bowed Down" and "I Dreamt I Dwelt in Marble Halls", but instead of dwelling in marble halls they had appeared to be dwelling in motor cars, which brought laughter from the crowd.

The vitality of the era is best exemplified in the Yorkshire Association's 1912 contests at Sunny Vale when there was a large attendance to see 21 bands compete in three sections. A programme of the 1912 contest was found by the writer in the Mirfield Hand-bell Ringers library of music during research for this book and is an excellent record of the day's action.

There were however three bands absent from the contest, but for the right reasons. Crosland Moor United were on their return from Australasia, Lepton United were in Wales and Horbury were on tour in Canada - a thriving scene, of which the officials and committee of the Yorkshire Hand-bell Ringers Association must have been justly proud.

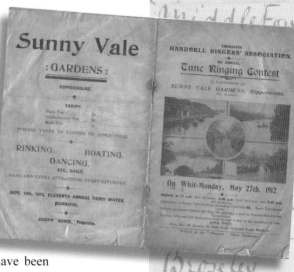

But in their Shangri-La of 1912, little did they realise that forces, both political and social, beyond their control were already at work to shatter their dream. Nor could they guess in their wildest imagination what would soon befall their great efforts.

There were thirteen entries for the Diamond Jubilee of the British Open. Besides the winners, Saddleworth, the entrants were: Crosland Moor United, Pendlebury, Thurlstone Public, Lepton United, Elland C.E.M.S., Birstall St Saviours, Royston United, Gilder Hall, Liversedge Albert, Clifton, Penistone Spring Vale Public and Tunstead (Stacksteads). The last five of these bands did not take part.

The contest was held as usual on Honley Feast Monday, September 21st 1914. Crosland Moor Public, being champion band could not compete. Six days after the British Open, the Crosland Moor Band were guests in a concert at Hanover Church in Halifax.

During the evening the Reverend D.S. Dakin gave a powerful address on "Christianity and War". His theme was "If the Germans came to Halifax". The first World War was just two months old. The Reverend Dakin spelled out the misdeeds the Germans had allegedly already committed and what horrifying things they would do to the town's 'chief' men and to the women if they ever came to Halifax. Could any one of them endure it as a man?

231

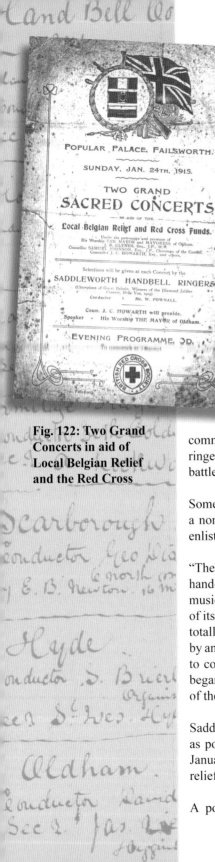

Fig. 122: Two Grand Concerts in aid of Local Belgian Relief and the Red Cross

He would, said the Reverend, be unworthy of the name of a man if he did. War was justified to his mind in the Christian conscience. They had entered into this war as God's ministers of justice and they must make it a victory for civilisation.

The victory would come, but it had very little to do with civilisation. We can only guess what went through the minds of the Crosland Moor Ringers as they listened to the Reverend Dakin's words. Significantly perhaps, Jimmy Ellis kept a report of the concert and Reverend Dakin's address in his scrap book. As the war went into 1915 there were calls in the papers for more men to enlist.

There was great enthusiasm amongst people for the war, and most thought it would last only a few weeks. There were bands who were determined to keep going. Others quietly packed away their bells and music and waited until the fray had ceased before re-forming - some of these never did re-form; amongst them were Gilder Hall, Tintwistle, Tunstead, Royston United, Sowerby Bridge, Oldham Friends and Sowerby.

For Jimmy Ellis and his Yorkshire Association committee, it must have been sickening to see their best young ringers going off to fight a war against other young men on the battlefields of Europe - what talents must have perished.

Some bands of hand-bell ringers such as Skipton Parish Church, a non-competitive band formed in 1890, marched off en bloc to enlist - every member gave his life.

"The British Bandsman", which by 1911, had stopped carrying hand-bell news, debated whether or not bands should stop playing music by German composers, then began the regular publication of its "Roll of Honour" - a list of all bandsmen who enlisted. They totalled up 7,000 names before the feature was gradually replaced by an ever increasing list of obituaries. Eventually, as stories began to come back of men being gassed, shot and wounded, attitudes began to change, and the enthusiastic optimism of the early days of the war was replaced by a more realistic attitude.

Saddleworth was one band which attempted to keep going as long as possible. The band gave concerts in aid of the war effort, In January 1915 the band gave two concerts in aid of local Belgian relief and Red Cross Funds.

A poem, entitled "An Appreciation of Saddleworth Ringers",

232

gives a good indication of the mood of the ringers at that time, both about winning the Belle Vue contest and, about "this bother on the Continent"

AN APPRECATION OF SADDLEWORTH RINGERS

Hast y'erd (you heard) yon music ut floots o'er hill an 'dell?
Ay, mon, it's good old Saddleworth church bell,
It's a nosed (thou knowest = you know) choir, full o' noted singers;
Un all tell thi (thee = you) what, mon,the'n (they are) u set o'good ringers.

Neaw (now), stop a minit, al tell thi (thee) summut (something) tru;
Al tell thi heaw thi (I'll tell you how they) won first prize at Belle Vue.
They set off in t'morning as bold as could be;
Thi one an'aw (then one and all) swore what they'd do or they'd dee (die)
Thi (they) mounted that stage, thi showed such pluck,
Thi carted noan (they cared nothing) for Kaiser or Baron Von Kluck;
They'd gie folks summut to remember an tell,
What music thur wur in a Saddleworth bell;

Thi fixed thur music un scanned the leaves'
Then pu'd (pulled) off thur jackets and rung i shut (in shirt) sleeves
O (all) gazed at one man with eyes so keen,
Displaying as much confidence as ad nar afore seen (as had never before been seen);

Performance wur started wi'Jimmy an Fred.
At very first movement folks jumped up an' said;
"By gum 'this as beawn (is bound) to be a good show.
Who's beawn to beat ure I should like to know.

Just yer (hear) them arpeggios an 'them after heats;
Spencer Parkin an' Rawlings wur treats'
Thi wur fair determined to stop a lot o'swankin;
An' thur wur nob'dy tried harder nur (than) Jimmy Franklin.
A chap stood at th'end at table, so cool an'steady;
Ah believe he goes bit name o'Jack Eddy.
An' what a treat wur Bradbury's chronicle.
It couldn't a bin (have been) put wi a chap wi rheumatic.

Thur wur (There were) Willie Pownall. aye, an'Ross Wood
At ringing treble - what! thur no a (thou knowest are) good?

233

Tha (thou) wants to yer um (hear them) when thur (they are) in thur prime
An al bet tha's never yerd nowt as fine. (and I'll bet thou hast never heard anything as fine)
O (All) said it wur a performance impossible to mend;
They'd had a good tutor in Alf Townend-
A Yorkshire chap wit Yorkshire grit.
A perfect gem at wieldin' a stick.

This victory's won but thurs (there is) another to win-
When we'n (we have) wiped away o (all) this treachery an' sin
We cannot stop a whoam (home) an rest content
While thurs o (there is all) this bother on t'Continent

An' when we'n (we have) fixed t'bar on Germans door
Old England'll be able to look up once moor;
Then when victory's announced we shall all become singers.
An' ah know (and thou knowest) it be proclaimed by t'Saddleworth ringers.

Fig. 123: Saddleworth HBR c.1926 Conductor – William Pownall

Also in 1915 the British Open, traditionally held in September on Honley Feast Monday, was switched to October and held on a Saturday.

There were eight bands who had entered for the contest, Crosland Moor Public, Bradford (Tennyson), Birstall St Saviours, Thurlstone Public, Elland C.E.M.S., Crosland Moor United (who surprisingly were conducted by a Mr M Nettleton of Marsh, Huddersfield),

Penistone Spring Vale Public and Saddleworth with Albert Townend as conductor and William Pownall listed as a ringer. Saddleworth and Penistone however, did not compete. The £15 first prize was won by Crosland Moor Public, the champions of 1913. The same band was the winner of the first section contest at the Yorkshire Association's final contest held in June 1915, before these too were postponed until the end of the war. The public band won by a clear margin of 6 points in front of second placed band Lepton United, having gained 94 marks. The other bands in the first section were Saddleworth and Elland.

In the second section the winners were Bradford Tennyson with 78 points, with Tennyson Place P.M. two points behind. Other bands in the section were Birstall St Saviours, Elland Juniors, Sowerby Bridge, Pendlebury, Bolton Parish Church, Sheffield Hartshead and Liversedge.

So clearly there were bands which attempted to keep together, but between June 1915 and May 1916 Parliament debated the question of conscription, before deciding that every man between the ages of 18 and 40 had to register for service. Millions were called up and the war took its toll. In the battle of the Somme, on the first day (July 1916) 60,000 British soldiers died out of 100,000. By the end of the battle 400,000 were lost in the graveyard of the Somme - a massive waste of life and talent.

The war was a catalyst which changed the whole hand-bell movement and from which it took a very long time to recover, and even then in a very different direction to the course it had been following before the war. Other traditions were likewise affected.

The "War to end all Wars" ended officially in November 1918, but demobilisation took time and it was not until 1921 that the British Open resumed at Belle Vue. The resumption of the Yorkshire Association's Championships took place a year earlier in June 1920. There were five bands in the first section and ten in the second. One year later there were seven entries in the first section and eleven in the second, and in 1922 there was a slight decrease in entries, with five bands in the first section and 14 in the second, but only eleven of these attended.

In section one Elland C.E.M.S. gave a "Masterly rendition of the test piece" which was "Lucrezia Borgia - Operatic Fantasias" (Donizetti arr Seymour Smith) to take first prize and the Yorkshire Challenge Cup. Elland's win was their third successive victory, for which each member and the conductor Fred Squire were awarded a "Special prize" which was probably an Association gold medal. The other bands in the first section were Horbury (conductor A Fothergill), Bradford Tennyson, Pendlebury (J Jones)

and Saddleworth (W Pownall)

In the second section Horbury took first place for their rendition of "La Traviata" (Verdi), the playing of which was limited to 50 bells. Horbury did not in fact enter any competitions between 1911 and 1920, making a comeback at the Yorkshire Championships in 1921 under their conductor Mr A Fothergill, who had trained an almost entirely new band. The other bands in the second section in 1922 were Thornhill (conductor H Ramsden), Thurlstone Public (F Taylor), Ecclesfield (W Whitham), Bradford Tennyson (Kaye Cooke), Woodroyd (T Maude), Armitage Bridge (W Wood), Pendlebury (J Jones), Sheffield Hartshead Friends (W Dyson), Lees St Agnes (W Wood) and Penistone (P Loxley).

16 separate bands entered for the contest, three of which did not compete, leaving 13 bands taking part, - quite a line up for a competition that was only restarted two years previously. The number of bands taking part in these contests was to remain constant for the next six years.

Figure 124:
Fred Squire was one of the leading figures of Hand-Bell ringing in Yorkshire.
He lived at 18 Edward Street, Clifton Common, near Brighouse.
A wood machinist by trade. he was born in 1873 and died in 1947.

The adjudicator at the 1922 Yorkshire Championships was Mr Thos J Hoggett, MUS BAC (DUNE.M) F.R.C.O., of Leeds University who said that in several instances there was a fault to be found in the tuning of the bells. He advised the bell ringers to approach the founders and get the matter attended to. They should not, he said, rest satisfied merely with what was supplied to them.

The 1922 contest at Sunny Vale must have been quite a day for the bands and supporters, as, when not watching or ringing bells, they could have tried their hand at many other activities including "Water cycling".

The Brighouse Echo reported that Miss Zetta Hill, the famous aquatic artist and inventor of the water cycle who attracted crowds at the Crystal Palace at Easter, was at Sunny Vale with her cycle on which she attempted to cross the English Channel. The report added that water cycling as a sport had "caught on" very extensively in the South of England - I wonder if they're still at it?

While such wonders were going on at Sunny Vale, Belle Vue was getting ready for the British Open. The first Open after the Great War had been won by Saddleworth. Elland C.E.M.S. came second, with Crosland Moor Public back in third position. This was one of only two occasions when the Public Band did not take first prize on entering the contest.

The Public Band had lost members during the war. Out of the band's 10 ringers who were with the band in 1915, it is significant that only 2 of these were in the band which became the champion of the British Open by winning in the years 1922-23-24. It was the Public Band's second championship. Even more significant is the fact that, out of the Public's 11 ringers in the 1924 champion band, only 3 of these were members of the band in 1929, but the standard of the band remained high. All of which brings us back to the fact

CROSLAND MOOR PUBLIC HAND RINGERS

that it is often a band which has a good conductor and committee working together which keeps it at the top.

One of the members of the pre-1916 Public Band was Norman Walker who was a member when the Public Band began as Crosland Moor Junior back in 1907. Mr Walker was also a member when the Public Band won its first championship for the years 1911-12-13. Mr Walker returned home from the conflict - but minus an arm. For a ringer who had achieved such brilliance this must have been a devastating blow.

His parents Mr and Mrs Alfred Walker kept the Craven Heifer Inn at Crosland Moor, where the band's successes were celebrated. After the war the Inn was passed on to Norman who was landlord until 1930. Norman's niece, Kathleen Hirst then took over until her retirement in 1988, ending a family connection with the Inn

Fig. 125: Crosland Moor Public Hand-bell Ringers, British Open Champions 1912 with Yorkshire Challenge Cup. Jimmy Ellis by now a Giant on the Hand-bell Scene (photo 1913) Ringers L.to R: E.Lumb, Harold Jepson, Norman Walker, Willy Hanson, Victor Smith, Jimmy Ellis (cond), Lawrence Cartwright, Harry Armitage, Tom Ellis, Harold V. Inman, Lewis Mellor

of 110 years.

While Crosland Moor Public was rebuilding, others had additional problems to contend with. Like most others, Saddleworth disbanded during the war, probably after the introduction of conscription in mid 1916. On their return from the great fight in Europe, the Saddleworth ringers found they had a fight of a different kind on their hands.

The challenge this time came not from the fields of Flanders, but from Saddleworth itself. The new vicar had his eyes on the bells - an old problem! The new vicar was the Reverend John Drury who wrote to William Pownall, the band's conductor, "Regarding the relation of the ringers to the Church". In his letter of April 2nd, 1919, Reverend Drury began by saying "As our men are now being demobilised at a quick rate I imagine you will soon be able to revive the activities of the hand-bell ringers". He went on to say that he had been inspecting the indenture under which the original 39 bells were purchased back in 1885 along with tables, boxes and other properties used in connection with the hand-bells.

Reverend Drury then said he had discovered "From a perusal of the indenture" that the bells and equipment were "handed over to the vicar and church wardens to be used by the hand-bell ringers connected with Saddleworth Church". After quoting other parts of the 1885 indenture, Reverend Drury then came to the crunch point when he quoted the final clause of the indenture, which was "And it is declared that in the event of any hand-bells or appurtenances being hereafter acquired for the purposes of the said ringers, the same shall be held by the vicar and church wardens for the time being of the said church upon the like trusts as those hereinbefore declared".

The 1885 indenture was signed by twelve trustees. The crucial words of the indenture were "For the time being", which is a legal "catch all" term often used in drawing up such documents. "For the time being" can mean for ever.

The vicar then asked William Pownall for more information. How many bells did the band now have? Where they were used in rehearsal, under whose management were they used, and what were the band's rules?

Up to this time everything relating to the operation of the Saddleworth hand-bell ringers had run smoothly to the satisfaction of all parties. Previous vicars had left well alone, in the knowledge that all was well. The only rules the Saddleworth ringers had needed were their own band rules, but realising the new vicar's intentions, a few days after receiving Reverend Drury's letter, Jas

Wood the band's secretary supplied a copy of the band's own idea of a constitution.

The main clauses of the band's own constitution were:

The Society be call "The Saddleworth Hand-bell Ringers"
The President of the Society would be elected by the members.
The bells belonging to the Trustees were to be housed with the conductor and committee of the band. (By this time the band had two sets of 177 bells, purchased by public subscription, as already stated)
Parishioners of Saddleworth and others, not being parishioners, but associated with the Parish Church, would be eligible as members.
The usage of the bells was to be approved by the committee.
The affairs of the Society would be under the management of a committee consisting of the Trustees, two members of the Church Council - to be appointed by the Society and five members of the band, the Secretary, Treasurer and Conductor of the band, elected by the band from their members, seven to form a quorum.

So the message to Reverend Drury was – we, the ringers are in charge, not you.

In reply Reverend Drury sent the band his idea of the constitution. The main clauses were:
The Society would be called the Saddleworth Parish Church Hand-bell Ringers Society.
The vicar of Saddleworth "For the time being" would be president of the Society.
The bells "belonging to the trustees" would be used where they thought fit.
The members of the Society could not use the bells "without the consent of the Trustees".
The "times and occasions" on which the bells could be used had to be approved by the Trustees.
The affairs of the Society would be under the management of a committee consisting of the Trustees - two members of the Church Council, the Secretary, Treasurer and five members elected by the Society, seven to form a quorum.

Reverend Drury said that the President of the Society, must be one of the Trustees and elected by them. The President would "naturally" be the vicar, as being the more "permanent" trustee. He said the band's own constitution was unreasonable.

On April 10th, 1919 there was a meeting between the band's members and the Church Council, but no settlement was reached. Reverend Drury reacted by publishing the 1885 Indenture in the August edition of the Parish Magazine.

By this time the Trustees of the 1885 Indenture had all died. Not to be put off by this, Reverend Drury had a solicitor redraw the 1885 document. This new indenture was identical to the old one apart from containing a list of new trustees - all approved by the Reverend Drury. He then visited the relatives of all the deceased trustees and got them to agree to the new indenture in October 1919. It was all quite legal.

The hand-bell ringers themselves were not short of legal advice. John Bradbury, a member of the band, was a partner in his family firm of solicitors J & J H Bradbury of Ashton- under- Lyne, who wrote to Reverend Drury, saying that the band had been wrongly described as the "St Chad's Hand-bell Ringers" in the parish magazine. The solicitors said the band was to be called the Saddleworth Hand-bell Ringers Society and that in accordance with the Constitution of the Society, the two members of the management committee from the church Council would be approved by the Society and "not by the Church Council". The five members from the band on the committee along with the Secretary, the Treasurer and Conductor would be elected by the band. The solicitor's letter concluded in saying that "In future publications of the Parish Magazine all reference to the Ringers Society and Committee should be in accordance with the particulars before stated".

The dispute between the two sides continued for a couple of years with neither side giving way. In 1923 the Reverend John Drury died. The new incumbent vicar discreetly folded up the indentures, put them back in the Church safe and the matter was forgotten about. Even new members of the band were not told about the dispute.

But in 1970 the 1885/1919 Indenture drawn up by Reverend John Drury was taken out of the safe, dusted down and inspected before it was held up to justify the sale of bells, for a paltry few hundred pounds. There were objections from local people, all to no avail. Albert Braybrook, a member of the Ecclesfield band wrote a letter to "Reverberations", the journal of the Handbell Ringers of Great Britain, saying the sale of the Saddleworth bells was a tragedy. On hearing of the sale, the late Lord Rhodes of Saddleworth, an ardent lover of hand-bell ringing, was said to be incensed by the sale.

The sale of Saddleworth's two sets of bells (177 in each set) may have been legally right - but morally?

The sale could have meant the end of hand-bell ringing in Saddleworth, but their great tradition was not sold with the bells. It stayed within the hearts and minds of local people. Grumbles about the sale lingered on, until in 1983 a set of bells from Girlington, Bradford was purchased by the Saddleworth Festival of Arts

240

(sponsored by Lord Rhodes, a competitive festival held every four years), to reintroduce the art of hand-bell ringing to Saddleworth - thus continuing a tradition of over a hundred years.

A new band was formed and in 1988 the band won first prize in the under 3½ octaves class for hand-bell ringing at the Mrs Sunderland Musical Competition in Huddersfield. Their conductor was Mr Harry Franklin, a ringer with the band in the 1930s. Mr Franklin's father, James, was also a member of the band, joining in 1907 at the age of 14. In the late 1980s Harry returned to live in Saddleworth and became the band's conductor, continuing an association of 77 years.

About three miles down the road from Saddleworth on the edge of Oldham, Lancashire is the village of Lees. Lees has a long tradition of hand-bell ringing. Although the art in the village never reached the heights attained at Saddleworth, Lees did achieve considerable success. Lees, like Saddleworth, had connections with Crosland Moor.

The Lees St Agnes Hand-bell Ringers were originally formed in 1898 with a W. Mills as conductor. The band purchased bells from St Luke's Heywood, which were cast by Shaws of Bradford. The first mention of the art at Heywood, was when a band called Heywood entered the British Open in 1865. The 12 ringers were conducted by David Taylor and the band's address was given as the Kings Arms, Market Place. John Partington, the first Secretary of HRGB and still an active member today can trace his ringing forebears through the Heywood Band. His grandfather used to be a member.

The Lees St Agnes band continued as a non-competition band until 1914. After the war some of the old ringers got together and the band was re-formed in 1920 under the conductorship of James Percy Bardsley and the presidency of William Shaw Bardsley (the conductor's father). The new band rehearsed two nights a week and on Sunday mornings.

Fig. 126: St Luke's, Heywood, Hand-bell Ringers, 1892 John Partington's Grandfather Joseph Partington is on the far right.

In 1921 the band joined the Yorkshire Hand-bell Ringers Association and entered the Association's second section contest,

Fig. 127: Armitage Bridge HBR on winning the Yorkshire Shield 1920 at Sunny Vale. Ringers L. to R. Harold Bates, Harry Gilliott, Fred Hallas, Ben Mitchell, Geo. Froggatt, Willie Wood (Conductor), Arthur France, Ben Shaw, Wilfred Mellor, Harry Smith, Arthur Stocks

but were not in the prizes. The following October they went to Belle Vue and competed in the British Open and again were unplaced.

The band had made good progress, but felt it was not enough to make a name for themselves on the contest platform. So they got Saddleworth's William Pownall to help and purchased a new set of bells cast by Mears and Stainbank. The new bells were tuned to the same pitch as the old Heywood set, making a total of 132 bells.

The casting of new bells in the same pitch as old ones was a common practice, as ringers became used to the sound of their own bells.

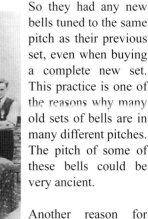

So they had any new bells tuned to the same pitch as their previous set, even when buying a complete new set. This practice is one of the reasons why many old sets of bells are in many different pitches. The pitch of some of these bells could be very ancient.

Another reason for different pitches was because a set of bells was tuned to itself and some hand-bells cast in England still are as regards having similar harmonic characteristics. The retuning to "Standard" pitch, of existing sets, which had been sent in for augmentation and refurbishment, was only introduced in the 1960s, and is now essential if bands are to ring music 'en mass' with other bands..

But back to Lees. With their new bells, the band competed in the 1922 Yorkshire Association Championships. This time they engaged Willie Wood, the conductor of Armitage Bridge Hand-bell Ringers, from near Huddersfield. Mr Wood conducted Armitage Bridge to win the second section at the first contest after the Great War, but he did not bring about a change in fortune for Lees St Agnes, who were again unplaced. "But" said the band's biographer, "they were not disheartened".

The St Agnes ringers received financial support from John and Arnold Dunkerley of Woodhead Mills, who were patrons of the band. The band purchased a new tablecloth made by George Kennins and Son of Little Britain, London. The cloth was embroidered in gold with the name "Lees St Agnes Hand-bell Ringers". This cloth still exists and is one of several fine examples still to be found in the North of England. These cloths are an art form in themselves. Some were worked locally, two examples were made in 1909 and are at Clifton, (Brighouse) and at Crosland Moor. Other fine cloths can be seen at Woodroyd (Honley) and at Hyde in Cheshire.

The St Agnes ringers held an annual concert at the Co-op Hall, Lees. After the disappointing results of 1922, the ringers "still felt that something was lacking", so, for the 1923 season the band decided to take firm and positive action. The test piece for the Yorkshire Association's second section contest was an arrangement of Verdi's opera "Rigoletto".

The big day arrived, the Championships began with the second section contest for which there were nine entries; Thurlstone; Low Moor; Penistone; Spring Vale; Ecclesfield; Bradford; Tennyson Place; Horbury; Elland; Thornhill; Sheffield Hartshead Friends and Lees St Agnes.

The contest began. Then came the call for Lees St Agnes to take the platform. Until this moment it had been a mystery among the other bands as to just who would be conducting the Lees band. The ringers set up their bells on the table and the conductor arrived. There was a surge forward to see who it was. A ringer stood at the back from another band asked "Who is it?" The reply was.....".Jimmy Ellis". Mr Ellis' daughter remembered the ringer's spontaneous reaction to the news, "Oh we'll not win it now, now yond long tall thin sod's come". ('yond' - Yorkshire dialect for 'yonder' or 'that person over there'). 'The ringer's forecast was very accurate - Lees St Agnes won first prize and became the first and only band to take the Yorkshire Challenge Shield out of Yorkshire.

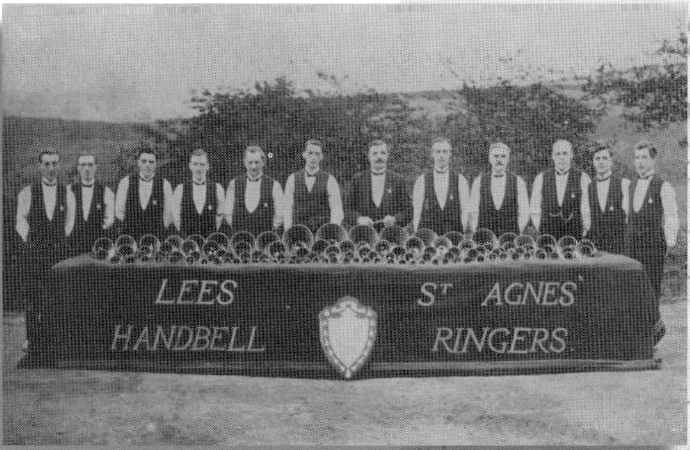

While Jimmy Ellis conducted Lees, Jimmy's own band Crosland Moor Public competed in the first section championship contest, but Victor Smith conducted instead of Jimmy Ellis. Mr Smith was a member of the pre-1916 Public Band. He did not rejoin the band after the war, but did conduct the band on a few occasions in the

Fig. 128: Lees St Agnes HBR showing off the Yorkshire Shield in 1923. The photo shows their resident conductor Mr J.P. Bardsley rather than Jimmy Ellis who conducted them in the competition

243

1920s and 30s.

The absence of Jimmy Ellis as conductor did not seem to help Crosland Moor Public's bid to win the 1923 championship first section, as the band came second to Saddleworth. One year later in the same contest the Public Band with Jimmy Ellis at the helm took the first prize again. Lees St Agnes, conducted by resident conductor James Percy Bardsley, came third in section two.

Jimmy Ellis did conduct Lees on several future occasions at both the British Open and at the Yorkshire Championships. In 1927 Lees again took first prize in the second section, with Mr Bardsley conducting. After coming third at the Yorkshire Championships in 1928 three ringers left the country and the ringers disbanded.

Fig. 129: Lees St Agnes proud after their 1927 winning of the Yorkshire Association shield - Conductor J.P.Bardsley

The Lees St Agnes band had also broadcast from the BBC's 2LO Studio in Marconi House, London in November 1924 only 2 years after the BBC had been incorporated. The studio was very small and hung around with heavy curtains "which were not very clean". There was little room for their large table and less standing room. During the intervals between items they had to stand around in passages. (Saddleworth and Crosland Moor Public had also previously been approached by the BBC, but both bands declined the offer because the fee was not sufficient). Was this the first Radio Broadcast by hand-bell ringers in Britain?

During the winter of 1925-26, the Lees St Agnes ringers were

244

visited by a representative from the Mears and Stainbank of the Whitechapel Bell Foundry and a ringer from the United States, Mr George Ringchrist - he was buying bells for a band in New Orleans from the Foundry. Mr Ringchrist was very impressed with the Lees ringers and asked for permission to use the same pitch as the Lees bells for the bells he was having cast at Whitechapel. This request was granted. Mr Ringchrist suggested that Lees might make a tour of the USA but this was not undertaken.

There was a short revival in 1935 when the bells were lent to Leesfield, and again in 1948 when a band was formed at Leesfield for the Church Centenary. The band was trained by the conductor of the former Lees St Agnes band, and some of the members had been members of the Leesfield band. This band played at the centenary service on June 1st and on June 5th at a concert in the local school.

Hand-bell ringing at Leesfield can be traced back to 1878 when Leesfield first entered the British Open. In 1882 Leesfield won 3rd prize at the contest.

Interest in the art of hand-bell ringing at Lees has resurfaced again. In 1988 Mr Harry Franklin of Saddleworth was asked to assist local people to form a band - so history repeats itself once again.

Another fine Lancashire band which was part of the hand-bell scene of the post-1919 era was Pendlebury. The band was made up of miners, to a man.

The band's best contest performance was in the Yorkshire Championships at Sunny Vale in 1920 when they came 3rd in the first section contest. They were only 5 marks behind the second placed band Crosland Moor Public. The winners were Elland with 110 marks.

The conductor of Pendlebury for their success of 1920 was Harry Nuttall. Mr Nuttall conducted the band for their last contest appearance, which was at the Yorkshire Championships at Sunny Vale in 1927. After this date we hear no more of them.

Harry Nuttall moved to St Anne's on Sea where he took over a hotel. Mr Nuttall became organist at St Anne's Parish Church and also the town's Mayor.

The beginnings of the art at Pendlebury would seem to be sometime shortly before 1905 as in that year the band made its first appearance at the British Open, when their conductor was a Mr M Foy of Park Avenue, Swinton. The members of the 1905 band were: Joseph Dorricott; Thomas Horsefield, James Parks, Samuel Seddon,

George H Parks; James Broadman; Richard Davis; Charles H Broadhurst; William Dorricott and William Wardle, who was later to be killed in a pit accident.

The band competed at Belle Vue from 1905 to 1914, but did not join the

Fig. 1308: Pendlebury Hand-bell Ringers 1905

Fig. 131: Pendlebury Hand-bell Ringers in the 1920s L.to R: Enoch Wynne, Richard Davis, Mr Whitehouse, Arthur Williamson, Joe Dorricott, Harry Nuttall (cond), W. Ryder, Jim Parks, George Parks, ?, ?, ?

Yorkshire Association until 1921. The band had several other conductors, including Mr Arthur Royal (1908 and 1909). With Mr Royal the band won (along with two other bands) a consolation prize of £2 for being just out of the first five at the 1908 British Open. The band's other conductors were Mr P Swindley of Swinton (1911 and 1912) and Mr J Jones (1922).

During my research I made several visits to Pendlebury, a village with its own charm and character on Manchester's North Western reaches. On my first visit, just before Easter 1988, I began my search for information by simply walking into Pendlebury British Legion Club where I showed the barmaid a copy of a programme for a British Open Contest for hand-bell ringers. The programme contained all the names of the old Pendlebury ringers. I asked the barmaid if she knew of anyone who might know anything about the band. "Oh, I'll ask the Secretary. He might know something".

The barmaid took the programme to show the Secretary. A little while later a rather shocked barmaid returned saying, "Hey, this programme's dated 1911! How can we know anything?" Of course I then explained that what I required was to be put in contact with one of the club's more senior members. This was done and one of the club's veterans sent me to St Augustine's Church, where by mere chance, I met Mrs Marion Upton whose father, Richard Davis, had been a member of the band.

Mrs Upton told me the band's first rehearsal room was in St Augustine's Day School. After a while the band moved to a room at Christ Church. While most of the band were church members, the band itself was an independent organisation, founded by public subscription.

The Pendlebury bells were said to be still in Christ Church when it was closed, but during a search in 1988 the bells were found to be missing. Does anyone know of their whereabouts?

Mrs Upton said she thought the band's decline in fortunes came after a series of pit strikes when the men returned to work for less pay.

Another band which was to re-form after the Great War was Ecclesfield. The band competed at the Yorkshire Association Championships at Sunny Vale from 1920 to 1925, always in the second section contest, with the exception of 1921 when they also entered the first section. The band also entered for the 1926 contest, but did not compete. After this the band fell on hard times as all the band's members were out of work. (Ecclesfield also competed at the British Open in 1921 and 1922.)

Ecclesfield's best performance was in 1925 just after they had purchased a set of 170 bells, when they came third in the second section of the Yorkshire Championships, gaining 85 marks, one mark behind the second placed Lees St Agnes and only two marks adrift of the winners, Elland. Ecclesfield's conductor between the wars was Fred Witham who became conductor in 1911.

After the Second World War Mr Granville Mitchell became conductor at Ecclesfield, a post he was to hold until his death in February 1977, after which Mrs Hazel Bradey, the band's present conductor took over. Mr Mitchell is an important figure in the story of the Ecclesfield Hand bell Ringers because when the band was in a weak state after the war it was he (like Reg Proud at Thurlstone) who kept the band going. One of the ways Mr Mitchell accomplished this was to form a band of ringers at Ecclesfield Grammar School where he was a science teacher. (He was to continue with this band until his death). The Grammar

247

Fig. 132: Crosland Moor (Standard Fireworks) Ringers 1950

School band produced some of the recruits who now make up the Ecclesfield (village) Hand-bell Ringers, including Hazel Bradey. Two members of the band joined on the same night in 1919. These same men were to remain members of the band for another 60 years - an all-time record length of service - for which the two men, Ken

Gregory and Albert Braybrook, were made Honorary Presidents of the Yorkshire Hand-bell Ringers Association in 1986.

I spoke to Ken and Albert about their memories of the post Great War era. Albert told me about one exploit which occurred on one of their return trips from Belle Vue after the contest. "Myself and another ringer decided to go down on the train from Belle Vue to the next stop, which was Ashbury Station. We got off and went into the Station's Public Bar, where the rest of the Ecclesfield ringers were, and who should be sat at the first table in the pub, but one of the ringers, Albert Bradshaw and my father. I asked them if they wanted a drink. Albert replied "No, the landlord says we've had too much" I said "Oh, you'd manage one. Well I got them two pints in my hand, I turned round and Albert Bradshaw was so drunk he had fallen off his stool.

Well we got back on the station platform and someone shouted "Aye up, there's a chap on the railway line". Well I pushed my way to the front and it was my father. About a dozen Ecclesfield ringers jumped down from the platform. As drunk as he was and as fast as I pulled him up someone else pulled him down. A railwayman jumped on the line and turned his lamp to red and stopped a train which was coming.

By then the station master and his men were after my father who was himself a railwayman. He would have got the sack if they had caught him. So eventually myself and Herbert Howell got him buried (hidden) and everything was alright. My mother did not speak to him for a fortnight after that"

Albert said the Ecclesfield band had a break from about 1927 to 1930 because all but one of the band's members were out of work. "I was the only one working" Ken Gregory told me. "We got back together late in 1930, and we had to stop again in 1939 for the Second World War and got back rehearsing in 1945 just before the war ended. We used to play for Dutch refugees from the war"

In recent years the Ecclesfield band has been very influential in the redevelopment of the Yorkshire style of ringing. Under their conductor Hazel Bradey, the band has given detailed demonstrations of the almost extinct, but highly developed techniques, which have been handed down through generations of Ecclesfield ringers. Within the band is considerable knowledge on ways and methods of handling a bell to create different effects and sounds, and when to use these to the best advantage.

When I began my research, in the mid 1970s, I spoke to veteran hand-bell ringers who demonstrated to me some of the techniques I had seen used by the older Ecclesfield ringers. These veterans also showed me other techniques which I had not seen anywhere before. It is difficult to give examples in print, but one technique which can be explained was shown to me by a Crosland Moor Public ringer, Cyril Clay on how to play a "trill", as distinct from a "shake" on one bell which is still used by ringers of today. Mr Clay took two treble bells and first held these bells up to shoulder height and rung them with the thumb on the caps. The resulting sound was more even and of better tone with each note more distinct. The volume of sound was also more controllable - a trill should be played slowly at the start and accelerated later, (and not the opposite!) with two bells this can be more easily achieved.

Fig. 133: Opportunity Knocks for the First Time. Crosland Moor (Standard Fireworks) Hand-bell Ringers at Roehampton 1950 with Hughie Green who devised and presented the programme.

These more advanced techniques are at the top end of the evolution of hand-bell ringing. Through workshops held at Weekend Festivals organised by the

Fig. 134: Crosland Moor Scouts HBR Conducted by former Public ringer Kenneth Horsfall 1960s

Handbell Ringers of Great Britain, these techniques, which were in danger of becoming extinct, are now being learned by a new generation of ringers.

Fig. 135: Crosland Moor Public, 1st Prize Winners in the 3½ octaves or under class at the 1985 Mrs Sunderland Musical Competition in Huddersfield, with conductor Richard Sigworth (right) (photo: Fawcett)

Another ringer taught by Granville Mitchell at Ecclesfield Grammar School was Michael King, who himself became a teacher at the nearby Hunshelf Secondary Modern School. At this school Mr King formed a band of ringers in 1966 using the Ecclesfield (village) band's old bells. The school is now comprehensive, but hand-bell ringing continued for 26 years under the conductorship of Mr King. In 1982 the band took the world record for giving the longest recorded hand-bell ringing recital of 52 hours and 9 minutes. This record was extended by the Ecclesfield School Hand-bell Ringers in 1985 to 56 hours and 3 minutes, which still holds today. The band then appeared on the Television show "Record Breakers". In April 1989 they competed on Television's "Opportunity Knocks" and took third place. Viewers voted by telephone.

The first hand bell ringers to make an appearance on Opportunity Knocks was Crosland Moor, who travelled to Roehampton, London in 1950 for the programme, hosted by Hughie Green for Radio

250

Luxembourg. Whether the programme was also on the then fledgling TV is not clear, but the then Secretary of the band Alex Parrett told me he thought it was for TV as well as radio, but the TV programme was only broadcast in London. The pieces they played were the overture to the "Poet & Peasant" opera and "In My

Cottage by a Wood". The latter had obviously been a favourite of hand-bell bands for well over a hundred years as it featured many times in the Belle Vue Lists.

Although the Crosland Moor band disbanded during the 1950s some of the ringers kept the bells ringing for a while. For example Kenneth Horsfell, one of the Public Ringers trained some of the Crosland Moor Scouts to ring during the 1960s, although clearly the troup did not use the full long set of bells, and as explained elsewhere I did my best to form a new band during the 1980s.

Almondbury Hand-bell Ringers also appeared on Opportunity Knocks in 1962. Hughie Green, remembering Crosland Moor, asked the Almondbury ringers how Crosland Moor were getting on, but by then the Moor band, who had been sponsored by Standard Fireworks Limited of Huddersfield, had disbanded and their bells, music and equipment put into store at the Fireworks factory.

Another band which re-formed after the Great War was Armitage Bridge near Huddersfield. The Armitage Bridge ringers achieved immediate success by winning the second section at the Yorkshire Association's first contests after the war in 1920. The band was conducted by William Wood. However, after competing for another two years, the band folded around 1924. One of the band's members, Wilf Mellor, then joined Crosland Moor Public as a bass ringer and enjoyed considerable success.

In 1953 William Wood staged a revival of Armitage Bridge and produced a band with twelve members, some of whom were members of St Paul's Parish Church Youth Group. The band was formed in mid-November and on Christmas Eve played "Christians

Awake". Mr Wood told the Huddersfield Examiner that it was the band's fourth new life. How long this band's fourth new life lasted I do not know.

The other lives of Armitage Bridge began in 1869, when eleven ringers conducted by Henry Pogson competed for the first time in the British Open at Belle Vue. The band also entered in 1870 when the conductor was Alfred Shaw. In 1871 the band won fourth prize out of fourteen entries, the conductor was Seth Coldwell, who also took the band to Belle Vue in 1872 and 1874 when they won the third prize in a line-up of fifteen bands.

From 1869 to 1871 the Secretary of Armitage Bridge was Alexander Lockwood and in 1872 the job of Secretary was taken over by George Boys. This Armitage Bridge band must have disbanded some time shortly after their success of 1874 as the band disappeared from the scene. George Boys then became a conductor of several other bands including Huddersfield Albert and Honley Temperance whom he took to Belle Vue in 1876. One year later Mr Boys (who lived at Park Gate, Berry Brow, near Huddersfield) conducted both Huddersfield Albert and Woodroyd at Belle Vue.

After 1874 there is a gap of 38 years before the name of Armitage Bridge Hand-bell Ringers appears again on a contest list. The year was 1913 when the band entered the Yorkshire Association's second section contest and won the second prize, conducted by a Mr J Dyson. William Wood's father William Henry Wood also conducted the band during this short period. Around 1914 the band went into recess because of the war.

In 1986 a band was reformed at Armitage Bridge. Help was given by ex Almondbury and Clifton ringer Arnold Calvert. The band continued under the conductorship of Pauline Murray.

During my research I couldn't fail to notice one or two other news items, such as the newspaper advertisement in 1926 for Mr John Ward, "Lancashire's famous bloodless surgeon", who was "the only man who has a cure for loose cartilage, water on the knee, heart trouble, spinal trouble, drawn sinews, degenerated muscles, blindness, wasted limbs, paralysis, and underdeveloped brain." It is quite a list and bloodless!

While Mr Ward was curing all, the Huddersfield Examiner reported in 1921 that "Mr Marconi and other experts believe that Mars, or some other planet, was seeking to communicate with the world".

In 1927 there was a total eclipse of the sun, and the year was also to bring another total eclipse, this time of the hand-bell scene at the Yorkshire Championships.

252

WOODROYD HANDBELL RINGERS HONLEY. WINNERS. SUNNY VALE 1921.

No hand-bell ringer's hall of fame would be complete without the band which achieved the almost impossible. The band is Woodroyd.

Woodroyd is a small hamlet of the ancient village of Honley, but a stone's throw from Armitage Bridge. So close were the two villages, that after the Armitage Bridge band folded around 1924, one of the band's members, Harold Quarmby, joined Woodroyd.

The Woodroyd Hand-bell Ringers hold a record which will stand for ever in the annals of the hand-bell movement, when they became the first and only band to gain one hundred marks in a contest - 100 out of 100. This remarkable and historic event happened at the Yorkshire Association's Championships at Sunny Vale on Saturday, May 28th, 1927. Woodroyd were in a line up of seven bands to compete for the first section Yorkshire Challenge Cup, but Crosland Moor Public (who were the holders of the Cup) and Tennyson Place did not compete. This left Thurlstone Public, Elland Church United, Saddleworth, Lees St Agnes and Woodroyd to play the test piece - Schubert's "Rosamunde", op 26 N.I.

The selection opened with bold chords followed by charming very quiet passages, brilliant runs and many tricky parts that required skilful handling. It also included several good bass parts.

At the close of the contest the adjudicator, Mr I Hirst F.W.C.O. of Ilkley, who had not adjudicated such a contest before, said he

Fig. 137: Woodroyd HBR Honley on winning the 2nd Division Shield in 1921

Left to right: N. Illingworth, H. Hirst, C. Welch, J.R. Hallas, G. Maude, H. Hampshire, F. Rathwell, J. Sheard, J. Maude (Conductor), W. Woodhouse, W. H. Maude, B. Webster, L. Webster, W. Denton, J, Welch and F. Hirst.

Fig. 138: Woodroyd (Honley) after achieving the 'impossible' in 1927 (One of their ringers told me that they borrowed the Shield from Lees St. Agnes, who had won the Second Division that year, to make the photo more impressive. Well they had won the First Division with a perfect score so perhaps they can be forgiven!)
Left to right
BACK- W.Denton,
R. Boothroyd,
H. Quarmby,
W.Oldham, J.Booth.
FRONT-
S. Bye, N. Webster,
Charles Older
(Conductor),
H. Beaumount, W. Bray,
H. Hampshire.

had never spent such an enjoyable time. The playing of the bands had been w o n d e r f u l , but he had no difficulty in selecting the first place. The playing of the winning band was truly w o n d e r f u l and he had no hesitation in selecting it for first prize and giving it the maximum number of points. The result was the Yorkshire Challenge Cup and Silver Medal to each performer; 1st Woodroyd 100 marks, conductor Arthur Jenkinson, 2nd Saddleworth 96, (Albert Townend); 3rd Elland C.U. 95 (Fred Squire).

I spoke to Norman Webster who was a member of the Woodroyd band at the time and the band's Secretary for many years, and still retains an interest in the art. Mr Webster told me; "The adjudicator said the reason he had given 100 marks was because the standard of play by the other bands had been so high he felt it necessary to give them high marks, and thus the performance given by Woodroyd had been so excellent, that in order to give Woodroyd even higher points he felt were warranted he had to award 100 marks to the band".

In 1978 I arranged a reunion of the remaining members of the Woodroyd band (virtually the whole 1932 ensemble). They told me the decision to award 100 marks was not correct. Norman Webster said "To get 100 you have to have played no wrong notes. I played a wrong bell." "Yes" said another "so did I. It was simply that Mr Hirst had never heard hand bells before and he was overawed with it all."

Indeed the adjudicator certainly seemed overawed by Woodroyd's performance as his written remarks testify; - "Woodroyd - Andante, good opening, good rhythm, FF's excellent, also PP's. Allegro vivace, fine tempo, wonderful climaxes, wonderful everything. Vivace, marvellous tempo, tone and precision, quite orchestral".

Fig. 139: Echo Handbell Ringers Tour 1987 at St Marys Elland Yorkshire

Orchestral was the watch word as Mr Webster told me, "Our President, Mr Warbrook helped with rehearsal of the test piece and brought a gramophone on which he played a record of the piece played by an orchestra. He would get the contraption wound up and place the needle at the passage of music we were rehearsing and would say, with a broad smile; "That's how I want you to play". Jimmy Ellis was impressed by the performance and told Mr Webster "We shouldn't have played it as good as that at Crosland Moor".

After the proceedings were over, the adjudicator, Mr Hirst, asked the Woodroyd band to play the piece again. He said he could hardly believe what he had heard, as he felt the ringers could not read the music fast enough, as well as picking up the bells of the correct note. The Woodroyd men took the point and turned their music over, placing it face down so they couldn't see it. They then played the whole of the test piece from start to finish without music. This demonstrates an important point. Bands such as Woodroyd, Crosland Moor and Saddleworth rehearsed their music so often that they could play the most difficult piece of music by memory and instinct. The music was used in rehearsals, each part being played over and over again until the ringers knew the music so well that when it came to the final performance they only used the written music as a guide, and to give them confidence. Bands such as Clifton and Ecclesfield still do this today.

In 1987 the Echo Handbell Ringers from Japan toured Britain, when amongst other items, the band performed Passacaglia (G

F Handel); William Tell Overture (G A Rossini) and even played the Flight of the Bumble Bee (N Rimsky Korsakov) and the March from the Nutcracker Suite on BBC television's Terry Wogan Show. Echo always performed their pieces from memory without using any music, just as Woodroyd and other bands had done

Fig. 140: Vivienne Rigby, Ryan Price (Chairman HRGD), Akira Ito (President HRJ) and Peter Fawcett outside Elland Church during Echo's Tour (Phot: Peter Fawcett)

fifty years or more before. Interestingly the style of ringing used by the Echo Ringers was more like the style used by the ringers before the introduction of the 'off table' style and Crosland Moor United's "Chippy Choppy" style of ringing mentioned earlier in our story. The Echo Ringers were formed in 1983 and achieved a very high standard of performance. They had also given concerts in the United States, France and Taiwan. Their conductor during their 1987 tour of Britain was the late Mr Katsumi Kodama.

It is interesting to try and draw comparisons between bands like Echo and Woodroyd, even though the two bands were fifty years apart. The origins of Woodroyd hand-bell ringers go back even further - in fact back to 1877 when the band made its first appearance as Woodroyd Victoria in the British Open. The band was conducted by the already mentioned, George Boys. In 1890 the band was conducted by France Littlewood. In 1891 Richard Heaton conducted the band to third prize in the Open. Mr Heaton was to continue as resident conductor, but in 1903 we find our old friend from Holmfirth, John Moorhouse, conducting the band at the Open. Woodroyd Victoria's last competitive appearance was in the 1905 British Open when Mr Moorhouse was again in charge. Woodroyd Victoria had no duplicate bells, only a small set, perhaps about 50 in all.

Woodroyd Victoria's twelve performers at Belle Vue in 1905 were : E Burhouse, of Back School Street; J Scaife, Shawhead; J E Henderson, Dewent House; G Littlewood; W H Sykes, Thirstin; J T Greenwood, Well Hill; J Dyson, Victoria Place; B J Turner, Fishergreen; B Littlewood; J Chambers, Halling; A Goldthorpe; H F Boothroyd, Brockholes; Conductor - Mr John Moorhouse, South Lane, Holmfirth.

The above band may have continued after 1905 in a small way, but the band entered no contests after this date.

In 1919 the band was re-formed from the young men at the Woodroyd Methodist Sunday School. The second part of the old band's name "Victoria" was dropped and the band was simply called Woodroyd. It is this band that would, eight years later, gain 100 marks in a contest.

This new Woodroyd band was conducted by Tom Maude, a former member of the old Woodroyd Victoria. The new band's members were entirely new to hand-bell ringing. All were young men who were willing to learn. The band consisted of Ronald Boothroyd; Wilfrid Denton; Norman Webster; Raymond Hallas; Lewis Webster; Frank Rathmell; Willie Woodhouse; Horace Hampshire; Laurence Bray; Harry Spooner; Stanley Bye and Wilfrid Oldham.

Norman Webster told me of Tom Maude's conducting method; "Tom couldn't wield the baton and conduct. He would keep time by hitting the table with his stick instead. There was no dust left on the table cover after Tom had finished".

Mr Maude taught his lads how to handle the bells and had his own peculiar statement to get his boys to ring their bells with a wrist action. His maxim was "use your shackles". Mr Webster said "He would say this all the time until we could handle the bells, 'shackling em' we call it".

The band entered the Yorkshire Association's second section contest of 1921. There were eleven bands in the section who all had to play "William Tell" with no more than 50 bells. The time came for Woodroyd to play and the lads used their shackles and took first prize for doing so. In the following two years the band was unplaced, in the second section in 1922 and in the first section in 1923. After this it was felt that action needed to be taken to bring about an improvement in the band's contest performance. The band's committee did in fact take a vote after every performance, as to whether or not a particular performance had been satisfactory. It was stressed that Mr Maude had been very good in teaching the band's members how to handle the bells and conducting in the beginning, but if the band was to reach higher standards of performance, then a conductor with more musical knowledge was required. So in place of Mr Maude, Arthur Jenkinson, a violinist with the Huddersfield Philharmonic Orchestra was engaged. Mr Jenkinson had in fact helped Tom Maude with the final rehearsals before the band's 1921 success.

Mr Jenkinson brought about an immediate improvement as the band took second prize at both Belle Vue and in the first section

257

contest at the Yorkshire Championships of 1924.

The test piece for the first section in 1924 was "Banditenstreiche" (Von Suppe), which was considered horrendously complicated and difficult. The piece was in fact rejected several times by the Yorkshire Association committee, before being selected as a test piece for the 1924 contest. John Terry told me of the reverence in which the piece was held. "It was said that to play Banditenstreiche, every ringer in the band had to use every skill known in hand-bell ringing". John Terry was in fact so fascinated by the piece that he wrote an arrangement of it in 1982 even though he knew there wasn't a band in the country that could play it, his dream music for hand-bells, he called it.

Mr Webster also revered Banditenstreiche. "You had to be a ballet dancer to play it. Some ringers had to step back, others had to move forward". The Woodroyd ringers used their low 32G bell made by Shaws, in the piece. Mr Webster, who rang in the tenors, had to walk round the back of the other ringers to get to the bass to ring the low G bell because the bass ringers were so busy ringing other bells, "There was always a cheer when I did that, at one concert at Hull in the 1930s, the stage was so cramped I couldn't get past the other ringers, I did try, but after a struggle I missed it".

There were those who said the piece was unringable - four bands including Woodroyd proved them wrong. The result was predictable; first, Crosland Moor Public 95 marks, (conductor J H Ellis); second Woodroyd 90 marks, (A Jenkinson); third Elland C.E.M.S. 87 marks, (F Squire). The other unplaced band was Saddleworth.

The test piece for the Yorkshire Association's first section contest in 1925 was M U Balfe's "The Siege of Rochelle". The adjudicator Dr Keighley said that Woodroyd's performance of the piece sounded more like a brass foundry than hand-bell ringing. Mr Webster told me "We didn't damp the bells always at the correct length of note and the ringing table was a bit smaller than the one we were used to, so there was some clashing of bells".

Around 1929 the Woodroyd committee dispensed with the services of Arthur Jenkinson as conductor because, as Mr Webster said "He had got a bit slack and didn't seem to care whether the ringers came to rehearsal or not and there was a clash with one of the bass ringers" and engaged a well known local singer, Leslie Kendall Green. Mr Green made regular appearances in the 1920s at Huddersfield Corporation's Popular Concerts at the Town Hall. Mr Green was also conductor of "Holmfirth Sing" held each year.

258

Under Mr Green, Woodroyd won the Yorkshire Shield in 1930 jointly with Crosland Moor United. Meanwhile Arthur Jenkinson was engaged to conduct Thurlstone, with, as already mentioned considerable success.

Woodroyd along with all the other bands mentioned were all part of the thriving post Great War hand-bell scene which grew up in the 1920s. The era was one in which both the British Open, and the Yorkshire Association Championships re-established themselves. The Yorkshire Association had set about the task of rebuilding the movement with courage and conviction - just as they had done with the Association's formation back in 1903. If they had not done so, the movement today would be much the poorer as the Association left a legacy of high ringing standards which had not been forgotten when the Handbell Ringers of Great Britain was formed in 1967.

The rebuilding of the movement after the Great War was an amazing success. The 1920 Association contests brought just as many entries as they had done on their formation in 1903. Standards, too, had regained most of their pre-war strength, with the crack bands of Crosland Moor, Saddleworth and Elland leading the way, just as they had done before there were any thoughts of war.

But after 1927 the movement went in a decline. This decline continued with a severity never seen before in the annals of the hand-bell movement, culminating in the last Yorkshire Association Championships, which were held in 1932.

This decline was unlike any of those occurring previously. Its causes were far more deep-seated and complex than any of its predecessors. So what were the causes of this new decline? The movement showed no sign of decline during most of the 1920s if competition entries are anything to go by. A total of 15 bands entered the two sections in 1921. This rose to 16 one year later and the number of entries was to remain constant for the next five years up to 1927.

There was a similar pattern at Belle Vue where the British Open resumed in 1921 with a line up of eleven bands, only two less than the number who had entered back in 1914 before war took a hand in matters. Although there was a slightly lower number of entries for the British Open contests post war, than for the Yorkshire Association's own championships - but there was little hint that the movement had been ravaged by the war and the Spanish Influenza.

The Yorkshire Association had set about the task of rebuilding the movement at the turn of the twentieth century with courage and conviction, but now the social and economic face of British Life had suffered the cataclysmic shock of the First World War.

In the nineteenth century, industry had developed around the coal fields, which helped the spread of the hand-bell movement, as already mentioned, but certain areas became heavily dependent on one or more of the interrelated industries. After the war the coal, iron and steel industries were in difficulty. These industries had grown with the growth of the shipbuilding industry and were now in decline.

The decline in the demand for coal, ships, textiles and other staple industrial products led to large scale unemployment in those industries and therefore in the stronghold of the hand-bell movement, which was industrial Yorkshire and Lancashire.

The depression began in the same year in which the Yorkshire Association started its contests again in 1920 at the end of the post war economic boom.

Cuts in government spending in the 1920s and 30s led to the deepening of the depression. This was all too much for the hand-bell movement and the depression began to take its toll. As already mentioned, in 1983, I spoke to former Ecclesfield ringers, Albert Braybrook and Ken Gregory, who told me of the effects that the depression had on their band.

Ken Gregory told me; "We had to give up ringing as all the members of the band except me were out of work. We started rehearsals again in 1931 and continued until 1939 when the Second World War broke out".

As the depression deepened, social conditions in the North of England became almost unbearable. In the 1920s the Brighouse Echo reported that social conditions in the village of Clifton were said to be terrible, and that people in the village were living in houses like pig sties, the people were so poor.

In 1988 I spoke to Ben Cartwright who was a member of the Thurlstone Public Hand-bell Ringers of the 1920s and 30s. Ben told me, "In 1929 the Camel Laird steelworks not far from Thurlstone started to lay men off work. By 1931 it had closed down. Most of the Thurlstone band's members were out of work. I was so poor I was reduced to wearing rags. I was a member of the band which won the Yorkshire Association first section championship three times in succession in 1932, but I didn't have my photo taken with the rest of the band to mark the occasion that year, as I had no decent clothes to wear, only rags. I applied for government assistance, but in those days you were means tested and I was told that I did not qualify for benefit. The means test was a degrading ordeal".

Indeed the means test was hated by the unemployed. The Huddersfield Examiner commented in 1932, "It cost 22 shillings a week to keep a criminal in jail, while many honest people have to live on half that amount". The Examiner described the means test as a "mean test".

The Examiner said that many brass bandsmen were "suffering severe hardship and privation". Indeed they may have been tempted very often to sell their instruments to buy food. My own grandmother, a Barnsley miner's wife, chewed candle fat during this time to stave off the pangs of hunger.

But there were other social factors in the 1920s and 30s which worked against the hand-bell movement and sealed its decline.

The men who returned from the Great War had found a totally different world to the one they left in 1916. Gone were the traditional ways and people's expectations of life.

In September 1932 the new conductor of Huddersfield Glee and Madrigal Society, Mr Roy Henderson, was reported in the Examiner as saying that he was worried about the effects of the wireless, and the effect on people of having too much music. "Music on the wireless. We get too much music. It is chucked about like chaff. Play good music on radio and people don't appreciate it. As we are living in a new age, concert promoters must try harder or, we will end up with all jazz".

Musical taste and expectations had changed with the coming of radio. People became used to hearing music of a high standard - a standard which many concert promoters could not match.

But tastes had also begun to change even before the Great War. In 1911 Irving Berlin composed the tune "Alexander's Ragtime Band" with which ragtime music became a world success.

The changes in musical taste did not go unnoticed. The conductor of the Heckmondwike Concertina band, Mr Fred Tyne, was questioned on the subject in April 1937 by the local newspaper. Mr Tyne's reply was predictable for a man brought up with Victorian music. "Playing? Why some of these youngsters get as far as jazz, then consider they have gone quite far enough!"

This was Mr Tyne's reply to a question as to the outlook of youth on

261

music. He went on to say "Besides, they don't put in the practice we had to put in to become proficient. We were taught in a hard school, but our training was sound. Jazz is alright in its way, but there is something besides".

Mr Tyne's comments on not putting in enough practice and being taught in a hard school are all familiar - exactly the comments I have heard from the older hand-bell ringers - I wonder, does every generation have these opinions?

The cinema also had its effect on the hand-bell movement. In January 1913 the Huddersfield Examiner carried a rather over-the-top article entitled "The evil of the cinema". The correspondent said the moving picture craze was a bad influence upon the workers, "There is hardly a village in the industrial districts of Yorkshire which has not its entertainment. The Picture Palace has taken away from many of our men the desire to use their brains. It is to be hoped that the present craze for the pictures will either die out or be kept within reasonable limits - the youngsters are growing up in the belief that life is simply a matter of living pictures"

The story is a familiar one. The correspondent raises the same fears about the cinema as modern day observers raise about television. The Examiner's correspondent continued "In the Picture Palaces they just sit and gape, and after the show is finished the men go home with their eyes and brains tired. People are not thinking of their work and not talking about work. This matter is a serious one for trade generally".

The writer was, of course, going a mite too far with his prognostications, but his report clearly shows that, even before the war, people were changing the use of their leisure time from actually taking part and doing things actively, to sitting and watching passively - remember before the cinema, radio and gramophone, most people had no choice but to make their own entertainment, but now people could go to a local cinema and see world stars for the first time without travelling to a big city-. Now the stars came to them. Silent screen entertainers such as Charles Chaplin had a massive following. Times had changed-. Gone were the traditional singers and ringers. I wonder what he would think of today's generation who sit for hours in front of television and computer screens

In 1926 correspondence appeared in the Huddersfield Examiner regarding folk songs. It was stated that the only people who would now know any such songs would have to be about 80 or 90 years of age. Folk singing of traditional songs had, in fact declined along with the wakes where chorus songs were sung all day long in public houses.

262

People's tastes in music had changed. Victorian parlour songs were now out of vogue and fireside singsongs became a thing of the past.

The gramophone enormously reduced the sale of sheet music for the home performance. The radio also made concert going a weariness to all except those who lived in places where absolutely first rate concerts were readily available.

All these new leisure activities had an adverse effect on the hand-bell movement and sealed its decline.

But it wasn't just hand-bell ringing which felt the effects of these social changes - other musical organisations were also effected. In June 1932 the Examiner reported that Marsden Choral Society and Staithwaite Glee and Madrigal Society had gone out of existence because of the counter attraction of the pictures, wireless and sports. The report said that Slaithwaite Philharmonic Society was also in difficulty.

So, if such organisations were affected, what chance then for the hand-bell bands? They had to have ALL of their members at a practice or concert in order to give a performance, because they each had their own part each of which was an essential component of the whole piece.

There was another report in the Examiner in June 1932, as to whether Holmfirth Choral Society could continue. At a meeting called to decide if the society should disband, Mr Edred Booth, the society's conductor, complained that sport was ousting music. Mr Booth said there was "too much sport, too many teams, too much hockey and too many girls in shorts!" - now we know where all the hand-bell ringers went!

Having noted the social changes taking place in the early twentieth century that adversely affected all forms of active, participative, local entertainment, we now come to matters that directly influenced the decline of the art of hand-bell ringing.

The single most important event in the annals of the movement took place at Belle Vue, Manchester - the British Open Contest. In 1925 Belle Vue, including the zoo, was taken over by a group of businessmen led by none other than John Henry Iles, who, as stated in an earlier chapter, had rejected requests back in 1908 for a hand-bell contest at Crystal Palace.

The news of the takeover by Iles must have shocked and shaken the leaders of hand-bell ringers. Iles had installed himself as managing director - he now controlled the band contest at both Belle Vue

Fig. 141: John Henry Iles 1948

and Crystal Palace, where in 1922, he had significantly abolished the concertina and reed band contest, after which the day was devoted entirely to Brass Bands, and Iles, once described as "the flamboyant benevolent dictator" now had his clutches on dear old Belle Vue as well.

The takeover was indeed significant for the hand-bell movement and any fears which the hand-bell ringers had were well founded. In 1925 Iles sent a letter to the Yorkshire Hand-bell Ringers Association saying that the hand-bell contest would be scrapped because of lack of interest. This was not accepted by the Association. However, after one more British Open, held in 1926, the Belle Vue hand-bell contests came to an end and Iles had his way. Iles had dealt the hand-bell movement a cruel and crushing blow. If John Jennison was the catalyst for the 1855 revival by organising the first British Open Championship contest at Belle Vue, John Henry Iles was the man who dealt it an almost fatal blow in 1926. With Ile's abolition of the Hand-bell Contest the movement went into a 40 year decline – but it did revive, unlike the concertina bands which suffered a cataclysmic shock from which they never recovered.

John Henry Iles had many irons in the fire and, ironically in the end, it was his downfall. Twelve years after ousting hand-bell bands from Belle Vue he ventured into the film industry which lost him his fortune, and he went bankrupt. Iles died in 1951.

I am quite certain in my own mind that it was Iles who in fact abolished the hand-bell contest so he could devote the day at Belle Vue entirely to brass bands, as he had done at Crystal Palace. This one single act, more than any other, sealed the decline of the art of hand-bell ringing for the next forty years.

"Those born and bred amidst the rugged hills and lovely dales of west Yorkshire and North-east Lancashire were especially charmed with the richness and resonance of the new music.

North Country bell ringers have long maintained their reputation of being good readers of music, the members of the bands usually forming the village and church choirs of the places of worship in their districts. From their childhood these people invariably show a deep love for the music of nature, as well as for that acquired by them as art.

Excellent bands of hand bell ringers had long abounded in these districts".
John Enderby Jackson 1827 - 1903, born in Myntongate, Hull.

Country Hand - Bell Ringers abounded in days of yore throughout Britain. Their repertoire would consist of tunes like, *'Jenny Jones'*, *'The Keelrow'* and other popular tunes of the day.

The Luddite Statue at the top of Knowler Hill, Liversedge in Yorkshire. The design depicts the defiance of the Luddites, but also that they were family men fighting for their livelihoods.
Photo: Peter Fawcett

The British Open Trophy

The British Open Trophy for Hand-Bell Ringing was competed for at Belle Vue, Manchester. When the contest ended it was stated that the trophy should be available if the competition was re-started. This is still the case. (Photo: Peter Fawcett).

The Tintwistle Hand - Bell Ringers around 1905 with Conductor William Gordon

The British Open Silver Medal of Shelley Hand-Bell Ringers Alfred Haigh

Looking resplendent in this 19th century postcard illustration. The Music Hall at Belle Vue where the Hand-Bell Contests took place from 1855 - 1926 shows the vibrance of the era.
Picture from the Fawcett archive.

The face of genius, Ben Cook (1840-1897) who was a giant of the 19th century and a catalyst for change with his introduction of double (duplicate) bells in 1866 and the use of treble (triplicate) bells in 1867.

SHELLEY HANDBELL RINGERS CHAMPION BAND OF ENGLAND 1879

PRESENTED BY THE INHABITANTS OF SHELLEY IN HONOUR OF THEIR BRILLIANT CARREER AS A BAND OF MUSICIANS 1879

The Shelley Band pictured in 1879 were winners of the British Open 7 times. Left to right are: Fred Shaw, Artha Cook, Jesse Cook, Alfred Haigh, Ben Cook (Conductor), Christopher Alderson, Elliot Kilner, William Mosley, William Shaw. Photographs courtesy of Emmanuel Church, Shelley.

William Gordon (1838-1915)

Seen here in his prime around the year 1895.
Gordon is remembered today for his arrangements of popular music for Hand-Bell Bands of any size from two ringers to twelve, much of which has survived to the present day. He never achieved the status of a great conductor unlike some of his contemporaries.

RINGING TECHNIQUES USED TO RING IN ONE CONTINUOUS MOVEMENT AS DONE BY THE YORKSHIRE HAND-BELL RINGERS ASSOCIATION

1. Ringing a Trill
Using two bells of the same size and note, as taught to me in 1984 by Cyril Clay of Crosland Moor Public, Huddersfield.

2. Circulation Ringing
Ringing two bells in a circular movement as as used by Ecclesfield Ringers when playing the overture *'Caliph of Bagdad'* at the HRGB Rally, Brighouse 1981.

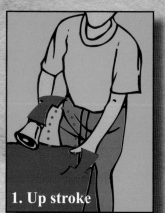

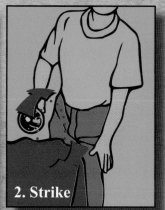

1. Up stroke　　**2. Strike**　　**3. Damp**

3. Staccato Ringing
Staccato ringing in a continuous sideways circular movement, striking on the upstroke and damping the bell on the table in between strokes. As used by Arnold Calvert of Almondbury HBR in the 1930's and with Clifton HBR in the 1970's-80's.

1. Start　　**2. Strike up**　　**3. Backstroke strike**　　**4. Return to table**　　**5. Ready for next bell**

4. Ringing on the upstroke and backstroke
This technique enables the ringer to have his hand immediately ready to pick up the next bell. As used by Arnold Calvert, Almondbury and Clifton.

BIRD'S-EYE VIEW OF THE ZOOLOGICAL GARDENS.

The map legend reads:

D ENTRANCE & HOTEL
ENTRANCE & HOTEL
ANCE & HOTEL ③ STABLES
⑤ LEOPARDS &c ⑥ AVIARY
RS ⑧ & ⑨ VELOCIPEDES & HORSES
E ⑪ SHOOTING JUNGLE ⑫ BOATS & STEAMERS ⑬ REFRESHMENTS
⑮ REFRESHMENTS ⑯ MUSIC HALL ⑰ PARCELS ⑱ HOT WATER ROOM
ATFORM ⑳ REFRESHMENTS ㉑ GREENHOUSES ㉒ FLOWER GARDEN ㉓ BEAR PITS
EWORKS ㉔ STEAMERS ㉕ MAZE ㉖ MONKEY HOUSE ㉗ ELEPHANTS &c ㉗ KANGAROOS
CRANES &c ㉙ MAZE ㉚ SEA LIONS &c ㉛ PENGUINS &c ㉛ EAGLES ㉜ ANTELOPES, ZEBRAS &c
㉝ LLAMAS ㉞ PADDOCK ㉟ PHEASANTS ㊱ EMU HOUSE ㊲ SWANS ㊳ GREENHOUSES
TIC GROUND ㊵ CRICKET & FOOTBALL GROUND ㊶ TENNIS & CROQUET LAWN.

John Jennison with a map of the Belle Vue Zoological Gardens which he founded. Area number 16 is the Music Hall where the Hand-Bell contests were held.
(Images courtesy of Cheetham Library, Manchester.)

ZOOLOGICAL GARDENS
FOUNDED IN 1836
BY JOHN JENNISON
BELLE VUE — MANCHESTER

Ecclesfield at York - 2012. Left to right: Maureen Dewhirst, Molly Barker, Maureen Saxton, Rosemary Foster, Judith Barker, Rosemary Davenport, Hazel Bradey, Lynne Dawson, Steve Woods, James Corbett.

Albert Townend's British Open solid Gold Medals presented after Crosland Moor United's win at Belle Vue in 1901.

Albert Townend
1873 - 1931
One of the greatest Hand
- Bell Conductors of the
20th century. The above
photograph was taken
in 1905 when he was 27
years of age.

"The company at Haigh Hall were ta'en up with our playing, and t'owd Earl danced a Reel in red knee britches to the ringers accompaniment".

Quoted in 1913 by Charles Jowett one of the Wigan ringers reminiscing about an event during the 1860's when they played for Sir James Lindsay, 23rd Earl of Crawford 1783-1869. Haigh Hall Country Park is now owned by Wigan Metro Council and is open to the public.

Jimmy Ellis (1880-1929) of Crosland Moor, Huddersfield seen here in 1912 was a legend in his own lifetime. The most influential Hand-Bell ringer of the 20th century.
Below:
A one-off medal

Despite the fact that I was told the contrary by the organiser of a Scottish Traditional Festival, Scotland's central belt has always had a strong tradition of Hand-Bell Ringing as you can see from the above photograph of Leith Churches Hand-Bell Ringers, 1922. courtesy of 1st Leith Boys' Brigade Ex-Members Association,

Continuing the long Staffordshire Hand-Bell ringing tradition - Stone, formerly known as the Inn Ringers were formed in February 1977 at the Red Lion, Stone, Staffordshire. Back left to right: S. Lindop, R. Smith, M. Woodhouse, P. Mellor, (Musical Director), K. Banks, P. Graetz, S. Martin. Front: S. Johnson, G. Reed, C. Miller, D. Harper, E. Brook, A. Mooney, R. Dawson. Photo taken at Oulton Viallage Hall, May 19th 2012 by the author.

Clifton, Brighouse. Left to right: J. Littlewood, K. Kent, R. Holroyd, C. Sunderland, M. Holroyd, J. Holmes, D. Kent, D. Sunderland. Photo taken at Grassington by the author, May 12th 2012.

Birstall St. Saviours pictured in 1907 at the rear of the Railway Hotel, Smithies. Back left to right: W. Benson, Secretary, N.W. Firth. Front: J.W. Rhodes, R. Clegg, A. Benson, G.H. Rothery, A. Bellis, K. Cooke, (Conductor) J. Colbeck, J. Holliday, T. Hanson, F. Ineson, A. Firth.

The Chimes, Ballymena, Co. Antrim
Scott Dean, John Watson, James Watson and Zoe Dean.

LIST OF PRIZE WINNERS

AT THE

HAND-BELL RINGING CONTESTS

AT BELLE VUE, SINCE 1855.

1855	1856 (Bands Entered)	1857	1858	1859	1860	1861	1862	1863
1 Leigh	Bolton	1 Holmfirth	1 Holmfirth	1 Pendleton	1 Pendleton	1 Wigan	1 Shelley	1 Uttoxeter
2 Oldham Senr.	Holmfirth	2 Leigh	2 Dewsbury	2 Holmfirth	2 Holmfirth	2 Shelley	2 Uttoxeter	2 Meltham
3 Salford	Leigh	3 Barnsley	3 Barnsley	3 Dewsbury	3 Dewsbury	3 Leigh	3 Wigan	3 Wigan
4 Middleton	Macclesfield	4 Pendleton	4 Leigh	4 Wigan	4 Wigan	4 Uttoxeter	4 Dewsbury	4 Oldham
5 Sheffield	Oldham Senr.			Extra Prize—	Extra Prize—	Extra Prize—	Extra Prize—	
6 Hyde	Pendleton			Wigan	Wigan	Wigan	Wigan	
	Prestwich							

1864	1865	1866	1867	1868	1869	1870	1871	1872
1 Wigan	1 Uttoxeter	1 Uttoxeter	1 Uttoxeter	1 Shelley	1 Shelley	1 Shelley	1 Glossop	1 Old Glossop
2 Oldham	2 Dewsbury	2 Dewsbury	2 Shelley Junr.	2 Ratley	2 Scarboro'	2 Hyde	2 Holmfirth	2 Holmfirth
3 Whitworth	3 Wigan	3 Shelley	3 Dewsbury	3 Broseley	3 Leeds United	3 Elland	3 Elland	3 Batley Carr
4 Dewsbury	4 Shelley		4 Meltham	4 Wigan	4 Broseley	4 Leeds	4 Armitage Bdg.	4 Hyde

1873	1874	1875	1876	1877 (Music sent from this date) "Sonata," No. 8. Mozart.	1878 Selections—Mozart's "Don Giovanni," and Haydn's No. 10 "Sonata."	1879 Selections—"Martha," and Haydn's No. 1 "Symphony."	1880 Selections—"Massaniello" and "Il Trovatore."	1881
1 Old Glossop	1 Holmfirth Tem.	1 Holmfirth	1 Shelley	1 Shelley	1 Shelley	1 Old Silkstone	1 Old Glossop Jr.	1 St. Thos. Hyde
2 Holmfirth	2 Howard Bros.	2 Shelley	2 Dalton Victoria	2 Dalton Victoria	2 Dalton Victoria	2 Old Glossop Jr.	2 Barnsley	2 Old Glossop
3 Huddersfield	3 Armitage Bdg.	3 Dalton Victoria	3 Huddersfield	3 Huddersfield	3 Huddersfield	3 Dalton Victoria	3 Hinchcliffe	3 Hinchcliffe
4 Glossop	4 Dinley	4 Huddersfield	4 Holmfirth Tem.	4 Meltham	4 Old Silkstone	4 Elland	4 Dalton Victoria	4 Elland

1882	1883 "La Traviata," and Boccaccio March.	1884 Overt. "Cenerentola," and 'La Verve au Main Polka.	1885 Overtr. "Merry Wives of Windsor," Nicolai, and Enchantment Gavotte, Connoley.	1886 Overt. "Bohemian Girl," and "English Fleet" Polka.	1887 Airs from "Il Trovatore" and Fantasie from "Beatrice di Tenda," Bellini.	1888 Ov. "Crown Diamonds" and "Cuckoo" Polka.	1889 Selection— "L'Etoile du Nord," Meyerbeer.	1890 Overture— "Poet and Peasant," and A Major from "Songs without Words"
"Lucrezia Borgia," and "Rondo" in C. Wolf								
1 Honley Tem.	1 Dewsbury	1 Liversedge	1 Almondbury	1 Almondbury	1 Liversedge	1 Dewsbury	1 Liversedge	1 Dewsbury
2 Birch Vale	2 Hyde	2 Dewsbury	2 Liversedge	2 Liversedge	2 Almondbury	2 Mirfield	2 Mirfield	2 Almondbury
3 Leesfield	3 Elland	3 Almondbury	3 Dewsbury	3 Mirfield	3 Whitefield	3 Almondbury	3 Tintwistle	3 Mirfield
4 Old Glossop Jr.	4 Cheddleton	4 Dalton Victoria	4 Birstall	4 Holmfirth	4 Mirfield	4 Whitefield	4 Dewsbury	4 Birstall
	5 Dalton Victoria	5 Howard Bros.	5 Lepton	5 Birstall	5 Holmfirth	5 Liversedge	5 Birstall St. Sav.	5 Tintwistle

1891 Overture—"Martha," Flotow.	1892 Selection from "Rigoletto a Ernani." Verdi.	1893 Selection— "La Favorita," Donizetti.	1894 Selection— "Robert Le Diable," Meyerbeer.	1895 Selection— "L'Elisire D'Amore," Donizetti.	1896 Selection from Offenbach's Operas, "Orphee aux Enfers," Boyton Smith.	1897 Selection from Sonnambula, No. 1, "Tutte E Sciolto," Wenzel Flachy.	1898 Overture— "Guy Mannering," Bishop.	1899 Selection from Offenbach's Operas, "The Grand Duchess of Gerolstein," Cramer.
1 Liversedge Alb.	1 Liversedge Alb.	1 Almondbury U.	1 Dewsbury	1 Almondbury U.	1 Horbury	1 Almondbury U.	1 Almondbury U.	1 Almondbury U.
2 Almondbury U.	2 Almondbury U.	2 Liversedge Alb.	2 Almondbury U.	2 Dewsbury	2 Almondbury U.	2 Thurlstone	2 Huddersfield	2 Lepton United
3 Woodroyd Vict.	3 Dalton Vict.	3 Birstall	3 Hyde	3 Christ Church, Tintwistle	3 Clifton	3 Almondbury U.	3 Horbury	3 Liversedge Alb.
4 Hyde	4 Crosland Moor	4 Heywood	4 Crosland Moor	4 Thurlstone	4 Dewsbury	4 Clifton	4 Dewsbury	4 Horbury
5 Tintwistle	5 Almondbury U.	5 Crosland Moor	5 Clifton	5 Crosland Moor	5 Thurlstone	5 Horbury	5 Clifton	5 Birstall St. Sav.

1900 Potpourri—"Czaar und Zimmermann," Lortzing.	1901 Selection—"Les Cloches de Corneville," Planquette.	1902 Selection "La Fille du Regiment," Donizetti.	1903 "Genevieve de Brabant," Offenbach.	1904 Selection— "Rigoletto," Verdi.	1905 Selection— "Norma," Bellini.	1906 Selection "Lucludi Lammermoor," Donizetti.	1907 Selection— "William Tell," Rossini.	1908 Selection— "La Traviata," Verdi.
1 Almondbury U.	1 Crosland Moor	1 Crosland Moor U.	1 Crosland Moor U.	1 Huddersfield	1 Crosland Moor U.	1 Crosland Moor	1 Crosland Moor	1 Crosland M. U. Jr.
2 Crosland Moor	2 Clifton	2 Huddersfield	2 Huddersfield	2 Almondbury U.	2 Almondbury	2 Almondbury	2 Birstall St. Sav.	2 Royston United
3 Horbury	3 Liversedge Alb.	3 Clifton	3 Clifton	3 Clifton	3 Clifton	3 Clifton	3 Almondbury U.	3 Dewsbury
4 Clifton	4 Lepton United	4 Liversedge Alb.	4 Almondbury U.	4 Royston United	4 Huddersfield	4 Birstall St. Sav.	4 Dewsbury	4 Lane (Holmfirth)
5 Liversedge Alb.	5 Huddersfield	5 Barnsley	5 Royston United	5 Horbury	5 Lane (Holmfirth)	5 Dewsbury	5 Lane, Holmfirth	5 Barnsley

1909 Selection— "Bohemian Girl," Balfe.	1910 Selection— "Don Giovanni," Mozart.	1911 Selection— "Massaniello," Auber.	1912 Selection— "La Sonnambula," Bellini.	1913 Selection—"The Merry Wives of Windsor," Nicolai.	1914 Selection—"The Crown Diamonds," Auber.	1915 Selection— "Martha," Flotow.	1921 Selections from 1, 3 & 4 "Petite Suite de Concert" S. Coleridge-Taylor.	1922 Overture— "Fique Dame," Franz von Suppe.
1 Crosland M. Pub.	1 Crosland M. Utd.	1 Crosland M. Pub	1 Crosland M. Pub.	1 Crosland M. Pub.	1 Saddleworth	1 Crosland M. Pub.	1 Saddleworth	1 Crosland M. Pub.
2 Birstall St. Sav.	2 Lepton United	2 Lepton United	2 Gilder Hall (Mir.)	2 Gilder Hall	2 Crosland M. Utd.	2 Thurlstone Pub.	2 Elland C.E.M.S.	2 Saddleworth
3 Clifton	3 Clifton	3 Penistone	3 Lepton United	3 Saddleworth	3 Elland C.E.M.S.	3 Bradford Ten'y'n	3 Crosland M. Pub.	3 Elland O.E.M.S.
4 Dewsbury	4 Dewsbury	4 Clifton	4 Thurlstone	4 Clifton	4 Thurlstone Pub.	4 Elland C.E.M.S	4 Bradford Ten'y'n	4 Bradford
5 Crosland M. Utd.	5 Birstall St. Sav.	5 Dewsbury	5 Saddleworth	5 Tunstead	5 Lepton United	5 Crosland M. Utd.	5 Birstall St. Sav.	5 Penistone S. V. P.

1923 Selection— "Norma," Bellini.	1924 Overture— "Raymond," Thomas.	1925. Overture— "Maritana," Wallace.	1926. Overture— "La Couronne D'Or," Alphonse Herman.					
1 Crosland Moor P.	1 Crosland M. Pub.	1 Saddleworth	1 Crosland M. Pub.					
2 Saddleworth	2 Woodroyd	2 Thurlstone Pub.	2 Thurlstone Pub.					
3 Elland C.E.M.S.	3 Saddleworth	3 Lees St. Agnes	3 Lees St. Agnes					
4 Bradford	4 Penistone S. V.	4 Elland Church U.	4 Woodroyd					
5 Horbury	5 Elland C.E.M.S.							

Fig. 142: List of Belle Vue Hand-bell Contests Prize Winners 1855-1926

Chapter 6 –
After the Belle vue Competitions
– 40 year decline and the 3rd revival

The ending of the hand-bell ringing contest at Belle Vue had very little to do with the number of entries. The number of competing bands was slightly down on what it had been before the Great War, but there were still sufficient to make a contest in 1921 when there were 11 entries; in 1923 there were 9; in 1924, 7 entries; 1925, 4 entries, and at the last contest in 1926 there were 9.

There had been periods in the history of the contests at Belle Vue when the entry list had dipped for a while. From 1856 to 1867 there were never more than 9 entries, including 1866, when there were 4 competing bands. So the theory that the contest ended because of lack of entries, does not, I feel hold water in the light of the evidence. However Iles' deception must have been a good one. At a lecture held in Manchester in 2005, organised by the Handbell Ringers of Great Britain to mark the 150th anniversary of the British Open, Iles letter of 1925 stating that there was a lack of support for the contest, was held up as a valid reason for ending the contest. Iles was still deceiving people 80 years later!

Fig. 143: The end of an era. Ballroom Belle Vue burnt down 1958

To complete the Belle Vue story the Zoological Gardens and surrounds became very run down and decrepit during the 1950s, until in 1958 the Ballroom was burned down. Perhaps it was an appropriate yet sad end to what had been the Mecca of more than just hand-bell ringing.

It has been unjustly stated time and time again since the beginning of the revival of the hand-bell movement after the formation of the Handbell Ringers of Great Britain in 1967, that hand-bell ringing declined because of the competitive nature of the movement up to 1932. If this book has one message, it is to show that such theories are not true and has been an unfair judgement on the contest as a medium for the promotion and perpetuation of the art of hand-bell ringing.

It was not taking part in competitions that sealed the decline of the art - but lack of it. The reader may recall (as stated in an earlier chapter) that the decline of the movement gathered pace after 1927 when the entries at the Yorkshire Association contest dropped to just 4. The sharp decline began after the abolition of the British open at Belle Vue. There was, in fact, an afterglow from Belle Vue which spilled over into the 1927 Yorkshire Championships. But gradually it waned in that the movement's national contest and most prestigious event in the calendar of the hand-bell ringers lives, was now missing - an era of 67 glorious years had come to an end.

For some it was all too much, along with all the social changes. So with the glittering prize of the British Open championships now gone, much of the point of continuing to ring was taken away at one single swoop. This was particularly true for bands outside Yorkshire who simply faded away after 1926. Even in the Yorkshire Association championships things were not the same after the afterglow contest of 1927. From 1928 to the final contest in 1932 it was the same four bands who entered each year: Woodroyd; Thurlstone; Saddleworth and Crosland Moor. Appendix 13 sets out the rules for the Association and for what turned out to be the final competition in 1932

Another significant event in the decline of the movement was the death of Jimmy Ellis, the hand-bell ringers' great leader who died of a heart attack in February 1929 at the age of only 49. His death rocked the movement at a time when it needed a good leader. His replacement, Kaye Cooke, did not sufficiently provide the standard of leadership required in such dire times.

The Yorkshire Hand-bell Ringers Association was never formally disbanded, but was simply left in abeyance. Efforts to call a meeting of the Association were made by the Woodroyd Hand-

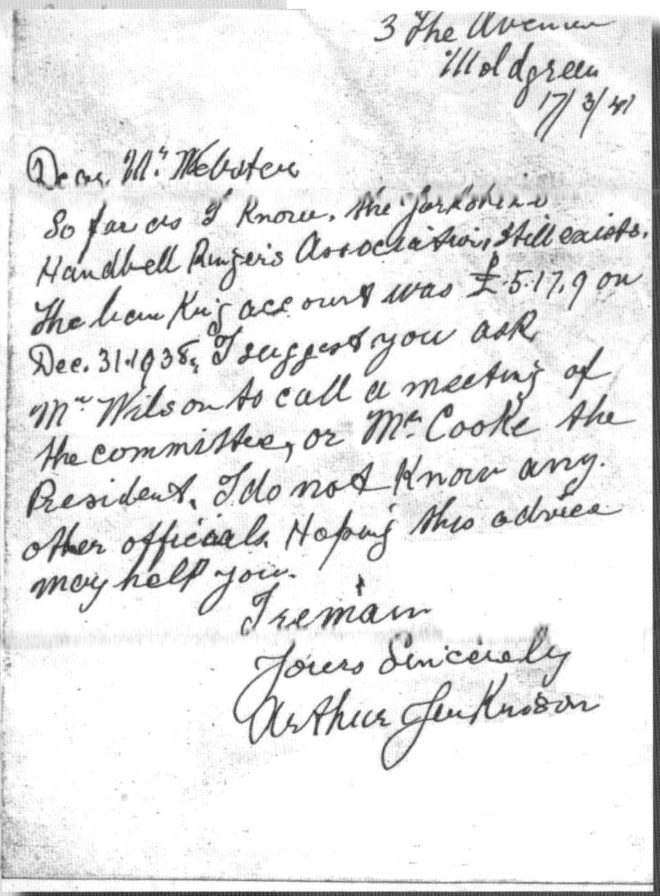

3 The Avenue
Moldgreen
17/3/41

Dear Mr Webster

So far as I know, the Yorkshire Handbell Ringer's Association still exists. The bank's acc ount was £5.17.9 on Dec. 31.1938, I suggest you ask Mr Wilson to call a meeting of the committee, or Mr Cooke the President. I do not know any other officials. Hoping this advice may help you.

Freeman

Yours Sincerely

Arthur Jenkinson

Fig. 144: A. Jenkinson's reply to Woodroyd's request for information on how to call a meeting of the Yorkshire Association

Hyde .
nductor D. Brier
Organis
ed St Ives. Hyd

Oldham .
onductor David
Dec 2. Jas. Le
J. Higgins

bell Ringers who wrote to their former conductor, Arthur Jenkinson, in March 1941. Mr Jenkinson suggested they asked John Thomas Wilson, the Association's Secretary, or Kaye Cooke the President, to call a meeting of the committee. Mr Cooke was in fact never seen again after the final 1932 contest, I wonder what happened to him?

The Secretary of Woodroyd, Norman Webster, then wrote to Mr Wilson asking for a meeting to be called. Mr Wilson's reply was rather weak. He, in fact, asked Norman Webster where the meeting would be held and who would attend, but it was Mr Wilson's job to make arrangements for meetings etc–. He was Secretary of the Association, not Norman Webster.

Eventually, after many months of attempting to get a meeting of the Association called, members of the Woodroyd committee decided that they had done what they could without success. "The matter was not worth bothering about" it said in their minute book. How different things might have been if a meeting had been called. The movement could have been in a better position to promote the art after the end of the Second World War. But it was not to be.

One point Mr Wilson mentioned is important in understanding why meetings and contests of the Association ceased after 1932. Mr Wilson said, in his reply to Mr Webster, that "There was some bitter feeling arising out of the gold medal awards, as the assets of the Association were practically drained to meet the expense and there has been no active interest since". What happened was that Thurlstone Public, in winning the first section contest three times in succession up to 1932 were, according to the rules, now entitled to a gold medal each, but gold was expensive even in 1932. So it would seem that the other delegates of the Association realised that if the gold medals were awarded to the Thurlstone Ringers, then the Association's finances, after paying for the medals, would be down to an unworkable level for the Association to continue its work. The finances of the Association only came to £5.17s.9d. in 1938.

Remember that the number of bands in the Association had gone down to a mere handful after the last British Open in 1926, so the Association had very little cash coming in.

Mr Wilson also said in his letter, "I believe that Thurlstone claim the right to hold both trophies (the Yorkshire Challenge Cup and Shield) until such time as they are beaten in open competition". On my visit to Thurlstone in 1988 I asked one of the ringers, Ben Cartwright, who was a member of the band in the 1920s and 30s, about Mr Wilson's statement in his letter. Mr Cartwright said, "Yes, that is what we agreed to and it still holds good today. The trophies were kept under Laurence Sykes' bed for years".

Fig. 145: A. T. Wilson's reply to Woodroyd's request for a meeting of the Yorkshire Association to be called

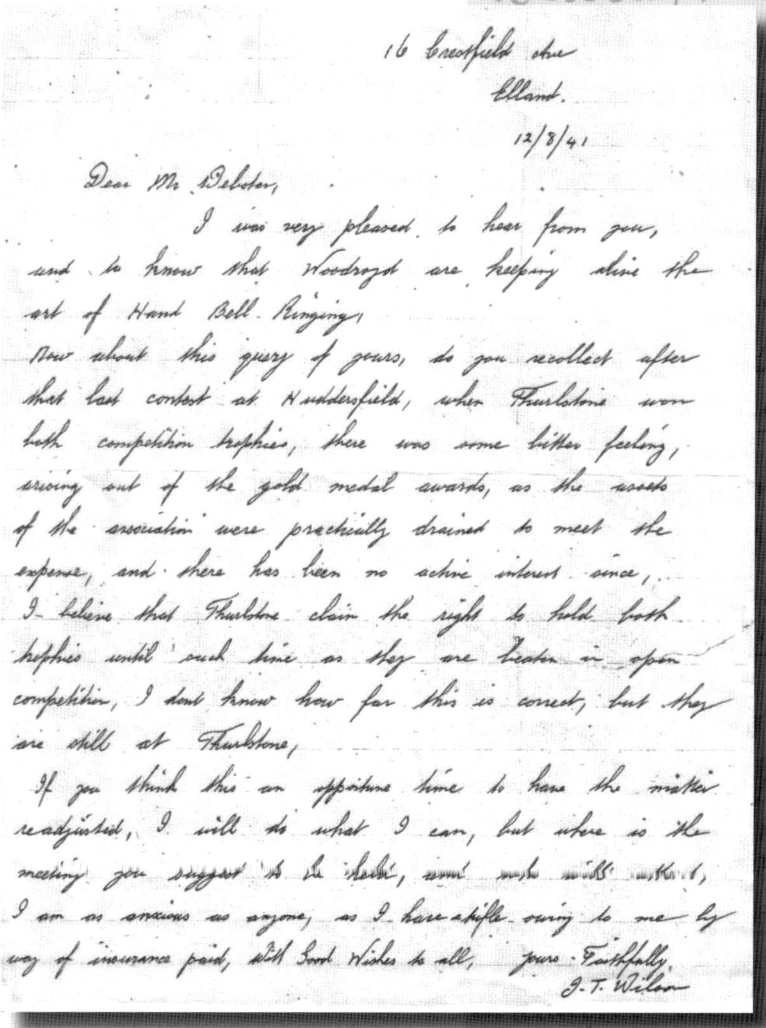

With no contests to enter at all now, many of the ringers in the few bands left functioning, lost interest. One such man was Thurlstone ringer of the 1920s and 30s, Harold Beard. Mr Beard told me, "The contests were the things we looked forward to. We limited our concert appearances so we could go contesting". I asked Mr Beard what he thought of the criticism that had been levelled at contests by modern day ringers. "I cannot understand their views. The contests were our life blood. When they ended, much of the interest we held went with them. The hobby wasn't the same, I myself gave up ringing not long

16 Crosfield Ave
Elland.
12/8/41

Dear Mr Balston,

I was very pleased to hear from you, and to know that Woodroyd are keeping alive the art of Hand Bell Ringing.

Now about this query of yours, do you recollect after that last contest at Huddersfield, when Thurlstone won both competition trophies, there was some bitter feeling, arising out of the gold medal awards, as the assets of the association were practically drained to meet the expense, and there has been no active interest since.

I believe that Thurlstone claim the right to hold both trophies until such time as they are beaten in open competition, I don't know how far this is correct, but they are still at Thurlstone.

If you think this an opportune time to have the matter readjusted, I will do what I can, but where is the meeting you suggest to be held, and make will that, I am as anxious as anyone, as I have a little owing to me by way of insurance paid, with Good Wishes to all, yours Faithfully,

J. T. Wilson

after that last Yorkshire Association contest". Mr Beard then asked me who was saying that competitions were bad for hand-bell ringing. When I told him that Alec Dyson from Thurlstone was one of those, his reply was "Well what did you expect".

Raymond Hollas, a former ringer with Woodroyd, told me the competition was keen, but we were all pals after the contest was over. "The spectators were sometimes keener than the ringers. My grandmother once chased Fred Taylor, the conductor of Thurlstone, round Belle Vue with her umbrella".

Woodroyd's Norman Webster told me, "In 1924 at Belle Vue, when it was announced we had won second prize in the British Open, one of our ringers, Willie Woodhouse, jumped high in the air off the platform in celebration, when he landed, he went straight through the floor! We loved contesting".

Recently I contacted the Brass Band Historian Arthur Taylor. Amongst other things he said "that the one thing that unites hand-bell ringing and brass bands (and concertina bands and drum and fife bands) was that the organisers at Belle Vue saw the commercial value of working class musical competitiveness, and brilliantly organised events - and excursion trains - to make money." Although their motive was commercial, it had the effect with providing hand-bell ringing with a strong focus for nearly 70 years. Its termination by Iles all but removed that focus, and the unfortunate financial result of the 1932 Yorkshire Association's competitions, which effectively prevented any further Y.A. competitions, removed any focus that remained. So it was not competition ringing that killed hand-bell ringing. It was loss of focus. Loss of something to aim for.

(Comment by Editor: It is very good that Peter has so much first hand evidence to show that it was not the hand-bell competitions per se which killed off hand-bell ringing for 35 years, because that was certainly the reason given to me very forceably in the late 1960s. Our hand-bell band 'The Octavius Wigram Hand-bell Band' had thoroughly enjoyed preparing for, playing at, but not winning the hand-bell section in the Richmond Music Festival in Surrey; so at one of the early HRGB Executive Committee meetings, during a discussion on what the Society could do to promote hand-bell ringing, I suggested that we could re-introduce competition ringing as it had been so popular during the 19th and early 20th centuries.

"You're too young to know Philip," said Bill Hartley - surprisingly vehemently, "but it were the competitions that killed hand-bell ringing. Isn't that right Alec?" [to Alec Dyson, Thurlstone's Director who, although not an E.C. member had come with Thurlstone

ringer Tom Briggs who was] *"Aye it was that" said Alec, and Tom agreed. Did Alec smile wryly when he said that? I don't remember. However those comments make so much more sense now I have read about the last Yorkshire Association competitions, the bad feeling left in the minds of the ringers involved, and the fact that the Association had almost been bankrupted by the result. Peter is right. It was not competition ringing per se, which killed hand-bell ringing.*

Interestingly, when Sylvia and I brought our hand-bell Band, The Mount Torrens Ringers over to tour the UK from South Australia in 1986, Thurlstone and Mount Torrens put on a joint concert in Thurlstone village, playing Cubley Brook and Under Freedom's Flag as duets, as well as our various solo pieces. Before the concert Alec proudly showed us the Thurlstone practice room, their bells, music and archives, and the Yorkshire Association Shield and Cup, which the band had won in 1932. It seemed to us that he had a right to be proud of his band, because at that time they were still one of the best in the country. That's why I wanted our young ringers in the Mount Torrens band to see Thurlstone ringing at close quarters, because we were at the two ends of the 'off table' spectrum, we with our 56 bells, and they with their 200 odd bells, and Mount Torrens still had a lot to learn. Ed.)

There was activity amongst several Yorkshire bands after 1932, but this activity was confined locally to each band. These bands stubbornly kept trying to maintain the tradition of hand-bell ringing up to the beginning of the Second World War in 1939. They were Saddleworth, Horbury, Almondbury, Thurlstone Public, Liversedge Albert, Elland, Woodroyd, Ecclesfield, Crosland Moor Public and Penistone Spring Vale, ten bands in all. Which was more than enough to support a meeting of the Yorkshire Association.

As a matter of interest, in 1982 I called a meeting of the Association (which included several members from before 1932) specifically to explore the re-introduction of competition ringing (or at least remove the stigma from it) and to promote Yorkshire style 'long set' ringing which I felt was in danger of being lost. Remember that at that time, and it is still true today, there were at least a dozen 'long sets' of bells in store in the Central Yorkshire area alone just waiting to be re-used. It had gradually dawned on me that the responsibility had fallen on my shoulders to ensure that this heritage was not lost. The meeting was held at the Old Oak Hotel, Liversedge, only a few yards from the site of the New Inn where the Association had been formed 78 years earlier. But sadly I did not get the support which I had hoped for, although some success was achieved when the Association managed to have hand-bell classes included in musical competitions in Huddersfield and Harrogate for several years in the 1980s and 90s, and these attracted several entries from local school hand-bell bands which had not otherwise been involved in outside hand-bell events. Of course by that time the HRGB had been in existence for fifteen years and the recently set up North East Region of HRGB (I was a member of their first Committee in 1977) was actively providing strong support for hand-bell teams in almost the same area as had been covered by the Yorkshire Association, except of course that many HRGB members still believed the myth that it was competitive ringing that "killed hand-bell ringing" which, as we now know, was not true.

Although not currently active the Yorkshire Hand-bell Ringers Association still exists and is therefore the Oldest Handbell Association in the world.

Research has shown, amazingly, that because there were no meetings of the Association, many of these bands thought they were the only ones left and did not know that the others were still in existence too - how important communication is!

It was Mr Tom Ogden, a keen hand-bell ringer with the Moorside Band and a commercial traveller in coffins and accessories around the towns and villages of Lancashire and Yorkshire who, in the main, re-opened

Storthes Hall Mental Hospital,
Kirkburton, nr. Huddersfield.

Woodroyd

Hand-Bell Ringers

Conductor: Mr. C. W. Older

SATURDAY, 11th MARCH, 1939

Commencing at 7.0 p.m.

Soprano Miss Hilda Broadbent	*Contralto* Miss Annie Oates
Baritone Mr. F. Hardcastle	*Humorist* Mr. L. Mackness

Piano Duetists
Madame Taylor and Miss M. Older

Accompanist: Miss Muriel Older

Programme

1. March ... ... " The Golden Crown "
   The RINGERS.

2. Song ... ... " Young Tom O' Devon "
   Mr. HARDCASTLE.

3. Song ... " The Sweetest Song in the World "
   Miss OATES.

4. Humorous ... Lawrence Mackness will entertain

5. ... ... " Star of the Sea "
   The RINGERS.

6. Song ... ... " My Dearest Heart "
   Miss BROADBENT.

7. Pianoforte Duet ...
   Madame TAYLOR & Miss OLDER.

8. Song ... ... Selected
   Miss OATES.

9. Humorous " Selection from his Repertoire "
   Mr. MACKNESS.

10. Song ... ... " Recruits "
    Mr. HARDCASTLE

11. ... ... " Sleigh Bells "
    The RINGERS.

12. Song ... ... " My Hero "
    Miss BROADBENT.

13. Pianoforte Duet ...
    Madame TAYLOR & Miss OLDER.

14. ... ... " Daughter of the Regiment "
    The RINGERS.

15. Song ... ... " Listen ! Mary "
    Miss OATES.

16. Humorous ... More Entertainment
    Mr. MACKNESS.

17. Song ... ... Selected
    Mr. HARDCASTLE.

18. Overture ... " Caliph of Baghdad "
    The RINGERS.

" GOD SAVE THE KING "

Fig. 147: Ashton-under-Lyne, Grammar School Handbell Ringers - Senior Team – 1969 Leader John Partington, first Secretary of HRGB

the lines of communication between the bands. From shortly after the Second World War until 1966 he made it his business to find out where all the existing hand-bell bands were and passed news between them on his regular visits. However he was not the only one who made contact with other bands. For example in 1963 the Ashton-under-Lyne Grammar School Hand-bell Ringers combined a visit to the Loughborough Bellfoundry with a visit to the village of Sileby near Leicester, to visit the town's School Hand-bell Ringers, and in 1964 they visited Ecclesfield to perform with the Grammar School Ringers there. The conductor of the Ashton band was John Partington, whose father Joseph Partington had been a member of Heywood hand-bell ringers in the 1890's. In fact the Ashton-under-Lyne Grammar School Hand-bell Ringers were formed in 1958 using 10 bells belonging to St Luke's Church Heywood. (Lancashire).

Never-the-less it was Tom Ogden's work in building up a network of contacts which was to become the foundation stone on which a new and exciting era would be laid, and the isolation of 36 years from 1932 would be broken in the year England won the Soccer World cup. Tom suggested to Bill Hartley of the Norbury Ringers that it would be a good idea to arrange a get-together of all known hand-bell bands. As a result Bill placed an advertisement in the Ringing World (the towerbell ringers' weekly newspaper) and bands rallied together to perform at Norbury School, Stockport in Cheshire on the 8th October 1966. Interestingly this was exactly one hundred years after Shelley introduced the use of duplicate bells at Belle Vue. Also co-incidentally Stockport was the stomping ground of our old friend William Gordon sixty years before.

At this gathering were bands using the traditional "two in hand" and "four in hand" method, as well as the big bands using bells played from the table in the Yorkshire style. For some, this meeting of ringing styles was a big eye opener. Alec Dyson of Thurlstone, one of the Yorkshire style ringers present that autumn day told me "When we saw them playing with two bells in each hand we were just amazed as we had never seen anyone ring like that. We'd heard about it but never seen it". Indeed, at this gathering the Yorkshire style off table bands met their own ancestry - but they did not know it. Nor did the "two in hand" and "four in hand" bands realise they were demonstrating an earlier form of the art.

The rally was so successful, teams having come from all over England to attend, that another was held in the following year, this time at neighbouring Ashton-under-Lyne, and the ringers there decided to form a national hand-bell ringers' society to promote and revive the art in an organised way – just the same reason for which the Yorkshire Hand-bell Ringers Association had been set up in 1903. Thus, it was at Ashton-under-Lyne on October 7th 1967 that the Handbell Ringers of Great Britain was born, with Dill Hartley as its first Chairman.

But let me jump back to the years of isolation. Two other bands are of interest to this chapter as they both were formed against all odds, one in 1937 and the other in 1938. The first was a West Country 4 in hand group using approximately 2 ½ octaves of bells, called the Martinis, and the second, the Penistone Spring Vale Hand-bell Ringers, a Yorkshire located and Yorkshire off table style, 5 octave long set playing hand-bell band.

I saw the Martinis mentioned in the summer 1993 edition of the Handbell Herald (Journal No.17 of the Handbell Society of Australasia). Brian Martin from Auckland, New Zealand had written to ask if he could put the record straight about the history of his band "The Martinis", a photo of whom had appeared in the previous edition of the Herald. He enclosed an advertising leaflet (below), which showed that Brian started the group (hand-bells accompanied by an accordion) in England in 1937 and they had appeared in many theatres and studios in London and the West Country until 1952. Brian re-formed the group in New Zealand in 1962 where it continued "to thrill audiences with its pleasant, unusual sound" at least until the early 1990s. Brian still has the large silver cup, suitably engraved, which the Martinis won at the Gaumont British Talent Competition in 1938. He also has most of the scripts of their BBC wireless broadcasts as well as the first television appearance they made from the Nuffield Centre in London on 26th February 1952. This is likely to have been one of the first occasions on which hand-bells had appeared on British television.

The Martinis

handbells & accordion ≈ a beautifully
Original ≈ Unique ≈ Entertainment

The group was formed by its present leader in 1937 and appeared in many theatres and studios in London and the west country untill 1952. The group was reformed in NZ in 1962 and has continued to thrill audiences with its pleasant unusual sound.

Some of the more meritorious appearances include :—

winner of Gaumont British talent competition.	1938
BBC radio "Workers Playtime".	1943
BBC radio competition "The Carol Levis Show".	1946
BBC radio "Variety Bandbox".	1947 & 1948
BBC TV "The Nuffield Centre Show". London.	1952

Group reformed in New Zealand 1962.

Finalist "Have a shot" Wellington TV.	1963
"Own Carol Programme". Xmas Day. TV.	1964
"Royal Concert" Queen Mother. (Wanganui)	1966
"Revue 66" National TV.	1966
"On Camera" National TV.	1969
"Afore ye go" National TV. new years eve.	1969
Finalist "The Entertainers" National TV.	1975
"Town Cryer" National TV.	1975

Festival of the Pines. bowl of Brookland. New Plymouth.
1965. 1967. 1977. 1983.
"Stars on Sunday". National TV. 1977. 1978. 1979. 1983

45 years old and as popular as ever ....

"CHRISTMAS DAY INTERLUDE" NATIONAL TELEVISION 1984
GOVERNMENT HOUSE GARDEN PARTY WITH AUCKLAND PHILHARMONIA 1987
AUCKLAND REGIONAL AUTHORITY CHRISTMAS ANNIVERSARY
SPECTACULAR MT SMART STADIUM (25 YEARS) 1988

Fig. 148: The Martinis'
Advertising Leaflet

275

PENISTONE SPRING VALE HANDBELL RINGERS
· FOUNDED APRIL 1938 ·

Fig. 149: A New Band at Penistone, Spring Vale was formed in April 1938, contrary to the general trend. Photo taken outside the Britannia Inn.

Penistone Spring Vale Hand-bell Ringers had its headquarters at Penistone Working Men's Club, but in the 1920s in the band's previous period of active life, their headquarters were at the Britannia Inn on the Sheffield Road at Spring Vale village.

The name of Penistone Hand-bell Ringers first appeared on the entry list of the British Open in 1874 when the conductor was Edwin Biltcliffe, who later conducted Thurlstone. At the 1877 contest, their conductor was a John Biltcliffe. The band entered the contest again one year later, but we don't hear of Penistone again after that until 1911 when they gained third prize at Belle Vue. They were in the contest again in 1914, and after the war in 1922 and 1924. Penistone also entered the Yorkshire Association contest in 1912 and from 1922 to 1927, but after this date the band had a lull in activity until a new band was formed in April 1938 - another example of decline and revival of tradition, what a pity war again intervened. In 1911 the Penistone band comprised F Jessop, F Fearnley, J Peaker, T Chappell, J Fearnley, W Singleton, H Palmer, W Britnell, G Rose and T Singleton, their conductor was Mr I E Falla. The band's conductor in the 1920s had been Mr P Loxley.

There were other bands attempting to keep their tradition alive by training new young ringers. At Almondbury, Harold Godward formed a new band in 1932 with ex-members of the local Boys Brigade. Crosland Moor United trained an entirely new young set of ringers in the mid 1920s, under conductor Albert Townend. On

276

the death of Albert Townend in 1931, Mr Townend's son Hubert Handel Townend took over as conductor for a short while until the United Band folded around 1935.

After the Second World War ended, life returned to something like normal. Various individual members of the pre-war bands still attempted to revive their own hand-bell ringing traditions and keep the art alive. At Almondbury in the 1950s Harold Godward formed a band from local Girl Guides. At Armitage Bridge, Willie Wood also attempted a revival in the 1950s. Austin Rawlins formed a band for a short while at Saddleworth in the mid 1960s. Cyril Clay of Crosland Moor trained a new band in 1945 from workers at the local Standard Fireworks Company where they used to practise. This band enjoyed considerable success, even appearing on television, and continued until 1957. John Thomas Wilson conducted a band at Elland connected with the local Men's Own Brotherhood (MOB!). This lasted until 1939, but in the 1950s Mr Wilson formed another band from local Girl Guides to keep the Elland tradition going. Reg Proud also began a new band at Thurlstone in the early 1960s.

Fig. 150: John Thomas Wilson, (centre) Secretary, Yorkshire Hand-Bell Ringers Association

Chapter 7 - Conclusions

So as can be seen the members of the old bands did try and keep the art of hand-bell ringing alive during the wilderness years of the late 1930s and 40s, 50s and early 1960s. These men just didn't sit back while their tradition rotted away as some modern ringers have thought - they tried their best for the movement in a difficult era when hand-bell ringing was well out of fashion. Their efforts yielded various results, but during those "swing and rock and roll" years it was very hard for an individual who was perhaps getting on in years, to promote an art form which had no backing organisation like the Yorkshire Hand-bell Ringers' Association - an art which many people thought was, to use that awful term, out of date.

Had it not been for the efforts of those few men the hand-bell movement of today would have been very much poorer.

One major legacy the old bands left for the new movement, which began with the formation of the Handbell Ringers of Great Britain in 1967, was the legacy of high standards of ringing–. These high standards of ringing have been passed on to a whole new generation of hand-bell ringers. Although having said that, in my opinion, general ringing standards of today are not as high as they were before World War Two, and, in Great Britain at least, no one band has yet achieved the extremely high standards set by the pre-war crack bands of Crosland Moor, Saddleworth and Elland.

Standards of performance must, I feel, rise, not only to keep public interest but to provide a high enough standard to enable the movement as a whole to survive the next decline when it comes.– History has shown that the tradition of hand-bell ringing is naturally subject to decline and revival. The next decline will come, of that I am sure, and the movement must be prepared for it.

The revival that began in 1967 would not have been as successful as it has been had it not been possible for the new ringers to learn techniques and take some of the standards of the old bands. Old bands such as Ecclesfield have been a big influence on the new bands which have sprung up all over Britain during the last four decades, and the guidance given by pre-war ringers and their influence on the modern movement cannot be understated.

The area where the modern movement has raised standards is in the publication of information on how to form and run a hand-bell band, on how to arrange the music and so on. There is now more information available thanks to the Handbell Ringers of Great Britain, than ever before.

But if after the next decline, future ringers are to be able to pick up the pieces, we must leave them a higher state of the art then at present. It is fair to say though, that standards have risen considerably to heights not thought possible by many back in 1967. It is up to everyone in the movement to raise standards of performance, and the movement must place no restrictions on how this is achieved - all options must be kept open, including contest, if the movement is to prosper and develop.

Tradition means the passing on of information. It does not mean "This is the way it's always been done and this is how it has to be done in the future". Traditions become rich through achieving the best possible results through trial and error. We all learn by making mistakes. We can also learn by the mistakes made by those who came before us.

As we have seen, a tradition is constantly changing to suit the needs of the present - not the past. The past should not rule the future. If the old ringers made one mistake, it was to keep on playing the same old Victorian music. We must not make the same mistake. Every band should include some modern music in its repertoire.

The old ringers developed the tradition and passed it on to us. It is up to every tune ringer to do the same. We are only caretakers of that tradition. The tradition does not belong to us.

Appendix 1
Bibliography, References
and Acknowledgements

A. - Books

Musical Handbells – A comprehensive History of the Bells and their Founders by William Butler (Phillimore & Co. Ltd 2000).

Bells and Man - Percival Price (Oxford University Press)

An Introduction to English Handbell Tune Ringing, by Philip Bedford (Handbell Ringers of Great Britain Chelmsford, Essex, 1974)

The Art of Handbell Ringing, by Nancy Poore Tufts (Herbert Jenkins limited London, 1961).

Discovering Bells and Bellringing, by John Camp (Shire Publications Ltd Aylesbury 1968).

Crosland Moor hand-Bell Ringers-History and wonderful record, by James H Ellis (Huddersfield Examiner 1906)

The Orchestra in England – A Social History by Reginald Nettel (Jonathan Cape Ltd London 1948).

Brass Bands, by Arthur R. Taylor (Granada Publishing Limited 1979).

On brass, by Harry Mortimer (Alphabooks 1981).

Brass Triumphant, by Cyril Bainbridge (Frederick Muller Limited 1980).

History 1750-1986 British Political and social by Peter Lane (Charles Letts & Co Ltd, London 1987).

The Age of Revolution, by E.J.Hobsbawm (Weidenfeld & Nicolson Ltd 1982)

This England 1714-1960, by I. Tenen (Macmillan & Co Ltd 1964)

The Age of Industrial Expansion, by A. J. Holland, (Thomas Nelson & Sons Ltd, London.1968)

The March of History, By Arthur Birnie (McDougall's Educational Coy Ltd 1932)

The Woollen Industry, by Chris Aspin (Shire publications Ltd 1982)

Textile Machines, By Anna P.Benson (Shire Publications Ltd 1983)

Rites and Riots – Folk Customs of Britain and Europe, by Bob Peg (Blandford Press, Pool, Dorset 1981).

See How They Ring! – Travelling Bellringers on the Australasian Popular Stage by Anne Doggett & Gwynn Gillard (BHS Publishing, PO Box 2209, Bakery Hill Post Office, VIC 3354, Australia

B. - Newspapers, magazines, pamphlets.

The British Bandsman, hand-bell ringers news (London 1907-1913)

Reverberations (The Handbell Ringers of Great Britain 1967-)

The Handbell Herald (Handbell Ringers of Australasia 1983 -)

Strike Note (Yorkshire Hand-Bell Ringers Association 1985-86)

Ringing World (Chantry St, Andover, Hampshire. 1911-)

Bell News and *Ringers Record*

List of engagements, prizes won by the Royal All-England hand-Bell Ringers Shelley-1864 to 1873. (John Cowgill, Printer by steam power, Kirkgate, Huddersfield 1874)

Notebook on the Rambling Club of Ringers, by William Laughton 1734 (lodged in the Guildhall Library, London)

A Short History of Horbury Hand-Bell Ringers (1902)

Wheelers Manchester Chronicle (1781-1842)

Manchester Evening Chronicle (1897-1963)

Manchester City News (1825-1926)
Manchester Evening Courier (1856-1926)
Manchester Guardian (1855-1926)
Huddersfield Examiner (1851-)
Huddersfield Chronicle
Huddersfield Echo (1887)
Holme Valley Express (1900-1931)
Halifax Courier
Spen Valley Advertiser
Spenborough Guardian (1867-)
Dewsbury Reporter
Brighouse Echo
Staffordshire Advertiser (1795-1972)

C – Archives

The British Newspaper Library, Colindale, London. NW9 5HE
West Yorkshire Archive Service, Newstead Road, Wakefield.
Manchester Cultural Studies, St Peter's Library, Manchester.
Chetham's Library, Long Millgate, Manchester.
Whitechapel Bell Foundry, London
The G Fieldsend Collection, West Yorkshire Archives.

Acknowledgements

Here I have some difficulty. After the passing of so much time, it is hard to remember everyone who helped me with my work. But if I have missed any one out, then I apologise here. But I certainly enjoyed the company of all whom I met.

Firstly I should thank Dave Russell. It was Dave in 1978, when a student at Bradford University who put me on to the British Bandsman at the British Library . He even gave me references, as he was studying all types of Victorian music making. Dave opened Pandora's box for me. Since then he has become a Doctor, worked at Leeds University, written at least one major work, published a second and updated edition of it, and subsequently retired – all during the time I have been researching and writing this book.

I must thank Nigel Bullen for urging me to write the book in the first place and then producing the first typed paper draft of it.

I must also thank Frank and Margaret Wood for proof reading the first hand written draft of my manuscript, and for encouragement, and inspiration.

I would like to thank Sheila Coles for re-typing the script for me and putting it on to disc.

I must also mention the late Jean Sanderson who undertook the first edit and gave me so much guidance and support.

My thanks to William Butler for his help with the chapter on bell founders and for uncovering the earliest hand-bell music found so far, and to John Partington, (himself a third generation hand-bell ringer and direct link to the Belle Vue Competitions through his grandfather and father) for the early photographs which had been passed down through his family.

And I give my thanks to Philip and Don Bedford for their detailed editing and great effort in bringing the project to a final conclusion, and to Akane Habuki-Bedford for all the food and hospitality she provided during 5 days of intensive editing in Canterbury.

My thanks also to – My wife Áine, Andrew S. Hudson, Alec and Valda Swain, Dr Andy Day, Arthur R. Taylor, Brian and Pam Hopwood, Bruce Baillie for his excellent creative skills in producing the layout design, artwork and illustrations for this book, Bonnie Shaljean, Brendan Farrell, Chris Helme, Colin Armitage, Cheryl Morgan, Cliff Riley, Dick Fawcett (my father), David and Caroline Sunderland, George Francis, Gordon Tyrrall, Hazel Bradey, Ann Gomersall, Ian Hayes, Irene Wood, Keith Gordon, John Atkinson, John Ferguson, Kevin and Lorraine Rowsome, Malcom Wilson, Michael, Joan, Julie and Paul Rhodes, Mrs Wrigley, Michael J Wright, Phillip Lodge, Ronnie Wharton, Roger and Christine Lazenby, Vic Cox, Philip Gregory, Alan Hartley, Lindsay Trevarthen and Ron Massey.

Appendix 2

British Open Championships at Belle Vue, Manchester, 1855-1926

Unfortunately the oft-published list of prizewinners at the Belle Vue Hand-Bell Ringing Contests between 1855 – 1926 is not complete. The reason, as I mention in the book, is because Belle Vue did not print the first list until 1889 by which time they could not remember exactly who had won what and what music had been played by each band taking part. The 1889 sheet listed 1856-57-58-59 only as "Bands Entered" and 1860 reads "No account of Contest", although the following year Shelley's Fred Taylor did help them to fill in many of the gaps from his own memory and records. However the problem was further complicated by the fact that until 1888 the main pieces of the contests were "Own Choice". A further complication was that on this published prize list, the second "Extra Prize" contests, which began in 1859 were not always included on the published lists. Furthermore, the results for 1860 list Holmfirth as taking both 2nd and 4th prizes! – All very confusing.

After looking through miles of pages from scores of daily and weekly newspapers all over the north of England I have managed to fill in the gaps left by Belle Vue with, frustratingly, one exception – the result of the 1856 contest (which I am sure did take place). It was simply that no one could remember the result after 26 years. If any one finds this result please tell me.

Here, with the exception of 1856, is the complete list as reported in Jennison's ledgers and the newspapers of the time:

1855 – Adjudicators – Mr. Elijah Roberts, Eccles; Mr. Seed and Mr. William Waddington, Manchester.

1st Leigh, (Lancashire) - Music Performed –*Waltz, No. 1 (Mozart)*, and *'Lesson 24' (Hook)*, *'Water Piece' (Handel)*, and *'Grand Promenade March' (Holt)*. – 12 Performers. 51 Bells. **2nd Oldham Senior, (Lancashire)** – *'Bell Waltz'* with *Introduction and Coda (H.Johnson)*, and *Grand Introduction and Polonnaise (Henry Johnson:* selection from *' Elfin Waltzes, (Labitzky)*, and *English 'Hornpipe'* – 9 Performers – 43 Bells. **3rd Salford Harmonious Youths – (Lancashire)** – *'Medley Waltz' (Henry Johnson)*, and *'Sturm March Galop. 'Weber's last Waltz*, and *Rondo* from the Overture *'Guillaume Tell' (Rossini)*. – 7 Performers – 53. **4th Middleton, (Lancashire)** – *'Hornpipe waltz' (Mozart)*; *'Cheer, boys, cheer'*, and the *'Huntsman's Chorus*

(Kalkbrenner) – 10 Performers – 42 Bells. **5th Sheffield (Crooks Moor), Yorkshire.** – *'Bell Waltz'(Johnson)*, and *'Bell Polonnaise' with Introduction (Johnson)*, and *'Blue Bells of Scotland'*, with variations *(Johnson)*. – 8 Performers - 50 Bells. **6th Hyde (Cheshire),** *'Charming May Polka,'* and *'Abberiford Polka;* *'Opera Schottiche,'* and *'Anglo-French Alliance Polka*. – 10 Performers – 46 Bells.

* Other bands who took part –
Ripponden, near Halifax, Yorkshire. – *'Auld Lang Syne'*, and *'Keel Row'. ' KattyO'Lynch,'* and *'Elfin Waltz,' first figure (Labitzky)*. – 9 Performers – 44 Bells. **Hurst Brook ,Ashton, (Lancashire)** – *Ap Shenkin,' and 'Hungarian Schottiche,' 'Caller Herrin,'* and *'Albion Polka'*. – 12 Performers – 51 Bells. **Oldham Junior (Lancashire)** – *'Caller Herrin,' and 'Jenny Jones,' 'Copenhagan Waltz,'* and *'Cheer, boys, cheer'* – 9 Performers – 32 Bells. **Holmfirth, (Yorkshire)** – *'Lord Hardwick's March,'* and Song, *'Mariner's Grave,'* with Introduction; *'Rouse brothers rouse,'* (arranged by H, Pogson, and *'Grand March'*. 11 Performers 57 Bells. **Glossop, Derbyshire,** *(eight Brothers)* – *'Deonady's Waltz,'* and *'Bonny Oldham,' 'Jenny Jones'* and *'Keel Row'*. – 8 Performers – 52 Bells. **Stoke-upon-Trent (Staffordshire)** – *'Jenny Lind Polka,'* and Introduction and *Waltz; 'Blue Bells of Scotland,'* and *Introduction and Galop* – 9 Performers – 53 Bells.

1856 - (Bands entered) – **St George's Bolton,** (Edward Lee); **Holmfirth,** (David Hartley); **Leigh, Macclesfield Original (Cheshire)** 7 Performers, 45 bells, (Frederick Swindells) **Oldham Senior,** (Thomas Isherwood); **Pendleton (Lancashire),** 10 Performers, 78 bells; **St Bartholomew's Prestwich, (Lancashire)** 10 Performers, 51 bells.

1857 1st **Holmfirth,** (10), 48 bells, 2nd **Leigh,** (10) 53 bells, 3rd **Barnsley (Yorkshire),** (8), 36 bells, **4th St Thomas's Pendleton,** (10), 78 bells, (Fred Lane).
* Also entered – Hurst Brook, Ashton, (8), 49 bells; **Dewsbury (Yorkshire);** ***Whitefield (Lancashire)** (9) 46 bells, (John Haddock) DNC. – Each band performed 4 pieces, two fixed by the Adjudicators and two of their own selection. Leigh and Holmfirth had to perform a second time to decide who would receive the 1st price of £15.

1858 – 1st **Holmfirth; 2nd Dewsbury,** 52 bells; **3rd Barnsley,** 8 Performers 36 bells; **4th Leigh,** 10 Performers, 53 bells,
* Also entered - St Thomas's Pendleton, Wigan Parish Church.

1859 P– 1st **St Thomas's Pendleton,** (James Green); **2nd Holmfirth,** (Henry Pogson); **3rd Dewsbury; 4th Wigan,** - W. Mason. (Wigan also won the second competition extra prize for performing Julian's 'Martha Quadrills'). For the main contest each band performed Four Pieces of their own selection.
*Also entered – Liverpool (Bell Methodist) – Thomas Gay; **Salford Original** – George Gaskill.

1860 – 1st **Pendleton** - conductor James Green; **2nd Holmfirth** - conductor Henry Pogson; **3rd Dewsbury** - Conductor H. Metcalf; **4th Holmfirth Cond. H. Pogson** Extra 2nd Contest winners Wigan – Conductor William Mason, for performing Overture to 'Lodolaka'.
Also entered – **Shelley, nr Huddersfield (Yorkshire)** – Ben Cooke; Barnsley - Conductor Samuel Wilkinson ; **Heckmondwike, Yorkshire** - Conductor T. Roberts; Wigan, WM Mason

1861 – Adjudicators – Mr John Stewart, Ashton; Mr Wild, Manchester; Mr Belcher, Birmingham, Mr Hanrod, Birmingham, and Mr G. Fish, Band master 2nd Manchester Regiment of Volunteers. – Each band to play two own selection. Second Extra contest £5 - Overture to Home Flowers Waltzes.- Winners Wigan.

1st Wigan £15, (12) K. Benson – Jupiter Quadrilles and The Farmers Rifle Galop. 2nd Shelley – (12) - Ben Cooke – Selections from 'Martha'. 3rd Leigh, (11) -Edward Smith; 4th Uttoxeter (8) - G.Richardson.

* Also entered – York, Campanologian (8) - W. H. Howard; Meltham (8), Yorkshire, - Henry Pogson, Stocksbridge, Yorkshire - Henry Pogson; Heckmondwike, Campanologian - T. Roberts; Pendleton - J. Green.

1862 – Adjudicators – Haydn Wood professor of music, Mr L. Goodwin, pianist, Mr Manton, harpist, Mr. Stewart, Violinist and Mr. Simson, pianist. 9 Bands entered.

1st Shelley - Ben Cooke); 2nd Uttoxeter, (8) - G. Richardson; 3rd Leigh, 4th Dewsbury, 12 Performers, - Thomas Wood.

* Also entered – Stockbridge Deepcar, (12) - Ben Cooke; Over Darwen, Lancashire - Joseph Birch; Hull , St James, (6) - Chas Petty; Newchurch, Lancashire (11) - John Washburton; Meltham, (12) -Geo Kenworthy.

Second contest Extra prize, 'New York Quadrilles'- winners Wigan.

1863 – Adjudicators – Mr Stewart, Ashton-under-Lyne; M. C. A. Phillips, Liverpool; Mr. Jakes, Liverpool, and Mr Goodwin, Manchester.

1st Uttoxeter, (9) - G. F.Gill; 2nd Meltham, (12) - G. Kenworthy; 3rd Wigan - William Mason; 4th Oldham, 12 Performers -David Dyson.

* Also entered – Wigan Swan Meadow Mills, (12) (Edward Benson); Heckmomdwike (12) (Thomas Roberts).

Second contest Extra prize, The last figure in Coot's 'Oure Lancers'- winners Wigan.

1864 – Adjudicators – Mr. Belcher, Birmingham; Mr. Pycroft, Manchester; Mr. Bentley, Manchester; Mr. T. Hanrod, Birmingham.

1st Wigan, (11) - Edward Benson; 2nd Oldham, (11) - David Dyson; 3rd Whitworth (Lancashire), (7) -William Golding; 4th Dewsbury. (12) - Thomas Wood.

Also entered – Wigan Swan Meadow Mills, (11) - Edward Benson. ; Shelley, (12) ; Heckmondwike, (11); Holmfirth, (12) -Henry Pogson ; Meltham, (8); Batley, Prince of Wales,Yorkshire - Richard Garney, (12).

1865 – Adjudicators – Mr. Charles Wilberforce, Liverpool; Mr. John Shinkle, Manchester; Mr. Thistlewood, Manchester; Mr. W. Simson, Manchester; Mr. Manton, Manchester. Each band to play two tunes of their own selection.

1st Uttoxeter, 8 Peformers, Overture to 'Italiana in Algeria' Rossini, and 'The March of the men of Harlech', - G. F. Gill) 2nd Dewsbury (10) - N. Scott. 3rd Wigan, (11) - Edward Benson); 4th Shelley Junior, (10) - Ben Cooke.

*Also entered – Loughborough Campanological, (9) - Henry Bramley; Whitworth, (10) - John Howarth; Heywood (Lancashire) (11) - David Saylor; Oldham, (10) - David Dyson.

1866 – Adjudicators – Mr. Thistlewood, Professional hand bell ringer, Liverpool; Mr. Wild, Professor of music, Birmingham.
1st Royal All England, Uttoxeter, (8) - G. F. Gill; 2nd Dewsbury, (11) - Samuel Scott; 3rd Shelley Junior, (11) - Ben Cooke. * one band did not compete.

1867 – Adjudicators - Mr. Charles Coote, London. Mr. Shickle, Manchester and Mr. N. Weilopolski Phillips, Manchester. 1st Uttoxeter, (8) - G. F.Gill; 2nd Shelley Junior, (11) - Ben Cooke; 3rd Dewsbury, (11) - Natanial Scott; 4th Meltham, G. Kenworthy.
*Also entered - Society of tune ringers Rawmarch, Nr Rotherham,Yorkshire - Samuel Whitworth; Clayton West, nr Huddersfield,Yorkshire, -D. Addy; Wigan Swan Meadow Mills, (10) - Wm. Mason; Batley, (11), - Edward Ward; Ossett, Yorkshire (10) - Joseph Smith.

1868 – 1st Shelley, (11), - Ben Cooke; 2nd Batley, 12 Performers - John Beaumount; 3rd Broseley, Staffordshire 8 - S. Griffiths; 4th Wigan
*Also entered – Clayton West (10) - D. Addy; Wigan Swan Meadow Mills (10) - J. Parkinson; Barnsley (10) - G. Wray; Ossett (9) - Jos Smith; Batley Junior (12) - John Beaumont; Stoke-on-Trent (Staffordshire); Batley; Leeds.

1869 – 1st Shelley, 9 Performers (Ben Cooke); 2nd Scarborough, 11 Performers - Geo Dixon; 3rd Leeds United, (10) - Wm. Birch; 4th Broseley, (8) - S. Griffiths;
*Also entered – Armitage Bridge, 11 performers - Henry Pogson; Batley Junior, (10) - John Beaumont; Glossop Campanological Band, (8 Howard Brothers) - R. Wild; Rotherham, (9) - S. Whitworth; Clayton West Junior, (9) - Henry Dawson; West Bromwich, (9) - Alex Siddous; Holmfirth, (11) - Henry Pogson; Wigan, (10) - Thomas Richardson; Hyde, (11) -S. Brierley; Old Glossop, (8) - Robert Wild; Royal Albert Campanological Band, Birmingham, (8) -Henry Green; Thurlstone, (9) - Joseph Kenworthy; Burnley, (8) - Wm. Harrison; All Saints Society, West Bromwich, - Edmund Cashmore.

1870 – 1st Shelley (9) (Ben Cooke); 2nd Hyde (11) - Sam Brierley; 3rd Elland (11) - J.E. Crowther; 4th Leeds United (8) - W. H. Dixon;
*Also entered - Thurlstone (12) - Joseph Kenworthy; Prestwitch (7) - H. Lyons; Madeley, Staffordshire (7) - E. Morris;
Hollingworth, Nr Hadfield, Cheshire - Sam Higgingbottom; Armitage Bridge (10) -Alfred Shaw; Scarborough (10) - Geo. Dixon; Broseley 8 - S.Griffiths; Dewsbury (12) - Mr Leigh; Swan Meadow Mills (9) - E. Benson; Silkstone, Yorkshire (11) - Joseph Kaye.

1871 – 1st Glossop, 2nd Hyde, 3rd Elland, 4th Armitage Bridge.
* Also entered – Scarborough; Radcliffe Juvinile, Manchester; Hyde; Oldham; Morley nr Leeds; Barrow in Furness, Cumberland; Middleton, Broseley; Almondbury; Madeley Campanologian- Berry Tanter.

1872 – 1st Old Glossop, Selection from Haydn's no 1 Symphony, - Chas Berrisford; 2nd Holmfirth Temperance, 'In Turco in Italia' - J. W. Moorhouse; 3rd Batley Carr Yorkshire, 'Overture Barbar de Sevile' - Mr Lee; 4th Hyde, 'Haydns first grand symphony' (David Cohain);

*Also entered – **Leeds United, 'Hallelujah Chorus"**- Wm. Birch; **Scarborough,** Selection from Flotos opera Martha'- E. Dixon; **Armitage Bridge, 'Overture Barbar de Sivile'** - Geo Boys); **St Paul's Church Shipley, Yorkshire, Jenny Jones from the lays of our Lord'** - A. Whalley; **Almondbury United, Yorkshire, 'Selection from Martha by Furchells'** -A. Hirst; **Middleton Victoria, Lancashire, 'Pla aic Schottiche'** - S. Buckley; **Elland Campanologian, 'Selection from Haydns 1st grand Symphony'** - T. E. Crowther.

1873 – Each band to play a tune of their own selection.
1st Old Glossop, Mendlesons 'Half Hours with the best composers'; 2nd **Holmfirth, Overture to 'Cenerantola' ;** 3rd **Almondbury Nr Huddersfield, 'Overture Caliph of Bagdad'** (Chas Broadbent); **4th Glossop, 'Kyrie and Gloria'** - Chas Howard;
* Also entered – **Hyde – Selection from 'La Traviata'** – Luke Beely; **Meanwood, nr Leeds,Yorkshire, 'Overture to Tancredi'** - G. Hirst; **Barrow-in-Furness, Cumberland, 'Kyrie and Gloria from Mozarts Mass'** - John Marshall; **Workington, Cumberland, 'Selection from Der Freischutz'** - Geo Stuart; **Scarborough, 'Overture to Tancredi'** - Geo Dixon; **Broseley, 'Movement in Hearts of Oak'** - J. S. Griffiths; **Elland, 'Kyrie and Gloria',** - Walter Spencer; **Batley Carr, 'Mozarts 12th Mass',** - Roland Hill; **Brighouse, 'Overture to Tancredi',** - T. F. Crowther; **Thurlstone, 'Overture to Caliph of Bagdad'** - Elias Marsden; **Bingley, Yorkshire, 'Selection from Martha'** - Tom Broadbent; **Disley, Cheshire, 'Warriors Joy'** - John Cooper; **Queensbury, Nr Halifax, Yorkshire, 'Handel, Hallelujah Chorus'** - John Aldroyd; **Loughborough, 'Napoleons Grand March'** - John W. Taylor.

1874 – 14 bands entered 12 competed - **Adjudicators – Mr. C. Warwick Jordan, mus, Bac, Oxon, Lewisham, London. Mr. Saville Swallow, Professor of music, Manchester.** Each band selected their own piece of music.
The following pieces of music were played by the different bands – **"Kyrie and Gloria"** from **Mozart's 12th mass; 'Haydn's Grand Sinfonia, in D'; Selection from Haydn's "No 1 Grand Symphony"; Overture to "Don Giovanni"; Selections from "Der Freischutz"; "Le Cailif de Bagdad"; "Madame Angot"; Martha"; Alelaide" and "Lucrezia Borgia.**
 – 1st **Holmfirth Temperance** (11) – James Charlsworth - **"Beethoven's No 1, Grand Symphony"**(Arrangment Henry Pogson) ; 2nd **Glossop Howard Brothers,** (11) Chas Berisford; **3rd Armitage Bridge** (11) Seth Coldwell; **4th Disley** (10) Joseph Barrow;
* Also entered –**Bingley;** (11) Thomas Broadbent; **Brookfield, Gorton, Manchester** (11) Wm Dunkersley; **Dalton Victoria, Yorkshire** (10) Sam Stead; **Almondbury** (9) Allen Hirst; **Underbank United, Holmfirth** (12) John Moorhouse **"Lucrezia Borgia"**(arranged by Henry Pogson); **Huddersfield** – Allen Hurst; **Meltham** – George Kenworthy; **Shelley**- Ben Cooke; **Stockton, Shropshire** – John Griffiths. The following DNC – Allerdale Model – **Workington, Cumberland** – George Stuart; **Penistone** – Edwin Biltcliffe.

1875 – Bands to play a piece of their own selection. A Special extra prize to the best performance of Quadrilles arranged from Cellier's opera' **The Sultan of Mocha'** by Henry Watson. – 14 Bands entered – **Adjudicators – Mr. E. Rogers, London. Mr. J.W.Young, Professor of music, Manchester. Mr Henry Watson, Manchester.**
1st Holmfirth; 2nd Shelley; 3rd Dalton Victoria; 4th Huddersfield.
*Also entered – **Ainley Bottom (Elland) Yorkshire; Underbank United, Holmfirth; West Bromwich; Newchurch ; Broselely; Bingley; Haworth; Silkstone; Keighley; Brookfield,**

Gorton, Mancheaster; Old Glossop.
A special extra prize of £5 to the best performance of Quadrilles arranged from Cellier's Opera **'The Sultan of Mocha'** by Henry Watson – **1st Holmfirth Temperance; 2nd Dalton Victoria.**

1876 – Adjudicators – Mr F. Dalavanti, of London, and Mr S. Swallow, Manchester.
1st Shelley, £15. (10) **'Beethovan's No 1 Symphony'** (Ben Cooke); **2nd Dalton Victoria,** (Sam Stead); **3rd Huddersfield Albert,** (George Boys); **4th Holmfirth Temperance** (James Charlesworth).
* Also entered – Park Lane Keighley, Yorkshire, (Thomas Broadbent); **Broselely and Stockton United** – John Samuel Griffiths, **Shropshire** (John Samuel Griffiths); **Honley Temperance** – George Boys; **Underbank United, Holmfirth,** (James Moorhouse); **Marple, Cheshire** (Joseph Barrow); **Old Silkstone** (Charles Horsfield); **Bingley Amateurs** (Thomas Broadbent); **St Peter's Collegate Church, Wolverhampton, Staffordshire; Haworth, Yorkshire,** (S. Waite); **Lincoln** – J. T. Parker;
A second contest for an extra prize seven bands performed **'The War March of the Priests'** from **'Athalte'**. **1st £4, Park Lane, Keighley** – Thomas Broadbent; **2nd £3, Holmfirth Temperance** – George Boys; **3rd £2, Shelley** – Ben Cooke; **4th £1, Underbank United, Holmfirth** – James Moorhouse.

1877 – **1st Shelley** (Ben Cooke); **2nd Dalton Victoria** (Sam Stead); **3rd Huddersfield Albert** (George Boys); **4th Meltham** (George Kenworthy).
*Also entered – Low Moor Perseverance, nr Bradford, Yorkshire (Robert Jackson); **Street Side, Ossett, Yorkshire** (Joseph Smith); **Park Lane, Keighley** (James Scott); **Penistone** (John Biltcliffe); **Broseley** (John S. Griffiths); **Woodroyd, Yorkshire** (George Boys).

1878 – Music sent out from this date.
Adjudicators – E. R. Terry, Organist St Peters, London; J. Kenrick Pyne, Organist, Manchester Cathedral; J. L. Goodwin, Organist Church of the Holy Name, Manchester.
'Sonata, No. 5. Mozart'
1st Shelley. 2nd Dalton Victoria. 3rd Huddersficld Albert. 4th Old Silkstone.
* Also entered – Leesfield, (Lees) Lancashire; Park Lane, Keighley; Honley Temperance; Broseley; Kirkheaton, nr Huddersfield; Meltham Temperance; Penistone; Barnsley;
*Holmfirth Band of Hope, DNC.

1879 – 11 bands entered - **Adjudicators – Mr Goodwin. Mr Pine.**
Selections-Mozart's "Don Giovanni," and Haydn's No 20 'Sonata.'
1st Old Silkstone. 2nd Old Glossop Junior, 3rd Dalton Victoria, Kirkheaton, 4th Elland.
Second contest bands who had not won a prize in the Open contest , **1st - £3, New Mills, Derbyshire.**
2nd £2. 10p, Honley Temperance, 3rd £ 1.10p, Park Lane, Keithley, Yorkshire.

1880 – 17 bands entered. Selection – **"Martha" and Hayden's No 1 "Symphony."**
1st Old Glossop junior, 2nd Barnsley, 3rd Hinchcliffe (NB County not listed, it could be any one of ten instances of the name in the north of England), **4th Dalton Victoria. (17 bands entered).**

1881 – Selections – "Masaniello" and "Il Trovatore."
1st St Thomas's, Hyde. 2nd Old Glossop, 3rd Hinchcliffe. 4th Elland.

1882 – Adjudicators – Dr Spark, Organist, Leeds Town Hall. Mr Grosse, of the Richter Concerts, London.
"Lucreza Borgia" and "Rondo" in C. Wolff.
1st Honley Temperance (11), (George Boys); 2nd Birch Vale, Derbyshire (9), (Alfred Bradley);
3rd Leesfield (12), (A. Egerton); 4th Old Glossop Junior (10), (C. Beresford);
*Also entered - Broseley (9); St Thomas's Hyde (11); Shelley (8); Leeds Road, Bradford, Yorkshire (11); Christ Church, Tintwistle (11) ; West Hartlepool, Co Durham (10); Bowden Vale, Cheshire (8).

1883 – (* Five prizes from this date) * 27 bands entered. - Adjudicator – Dr. Haydn Keeton, organist, Peterborough Cathedral. Dr Wm. Spark, organist, Leeds Cathedral.
A portion of "La Traviata." and Boccaccio's Grand March" – (Arranged by Henry Parker)
1st Dewsbury 45 Marks out of possible 50. (Wm. Lee); 2nd St Thomas's Hyde, St Thomas's (Thos. Ashworth); 3rd Elland (J. C. Pennington); 4th St Edward's, Cheddleton, - Used forty-nine bells, viz. G 25 to G 04, Leek, Staffordshire; 5th Tralron Victoria. † (The 2nd & 4th bands played copies specially arranged for them by Mr Wm. Gordon, of Stockport).

1884 - 24 entries, 12 competed. – Adjudicators – Mr C. J. Havart, conductor, Silver Chimes Carilloneours, London. Mr. William Gordon, Professor of Music, Stockport.
Overture to "Cenerentola", Rossini, and 'La Verre en Main'Polka. 'Phillip Fahrbachs'.
1st Liversedge; 2nd Dewsbury; 3rd Almondbury; 4th Dalton Victoria; 5th Howard Bros. Glossop.

1885 – 20 bands entered. Adjudicators – Mr C.J.Havart, conductor of hand bell ringers, London. Mr John. A. Amers, musical director, Newcastle-on-Tyne.
Overture. Merry Wives of Windsor.'Otto Nicolai, and "Enchantment Gavotte. C.M. Connoley.
1st Almondbury; 2nd Liversedge, 3rd Dewsbury, 4th Birstall, 5th Birstall.

1886 – 18 bands entered. Overture. " Bohemian Girl,"and "English Fleet"Polka.
1st Almondbury – Ben Lodge; 2nd Liversedge, 3rd Mirfield, 4th Holmfirth, 5th Birstall.
* Also competed - Gawthorpe Prince Albert's, nr Dewsbury, Yorkshire – Henry B. Pickles.

1887 – 19 bands entered. – Adjudicators – Mr J. Kendrick Payne. Dr. Warwick Jordan. Mr. Fred Vetter.
Selection of six airs from Il Trovatore Verdi and a Fantasia"Come I'Ardova," from Beatrice di Tenda (Bellini).
1st Liversedge Albert (Ben Cooke); 2nd Almondbury (Ben Lodge); 3rd Whitefield, Lancashire (William Gordon); 4th Mirfield (W. Lee); 5th Holmfirth Lane Independent - (John Moorhouse).
* Also – Howden Clough Mills, Birstall; St Helen's Gate, Almondbury.

1888 – 21 bands entered. – Overture **"Crown Diamonds."**and **"Cuckoo" Polka.**
1st Dewsbury, £15 - Arthur Fearnsides; **2nd Mirfield, £10** – J. Pickles; **3rd Almondbury, £7** – Ben Lodge; **4th Whitefield** – Ben Cooke; **£5. 5th Liversedge. £3.**
* Also competed – **Hallamshire; nr Sheffield, Yorkshire; Birstall Congregational, Yorkshire; Batley; The Walford Family.**

1889 – 17 bands entered, 9 competed.- **Adjudicators – Mr. T. E. Embury, senior late bandmaster 52nd Regiment. Mr.R. Johnson, Manchester.**
- Fantasia on Meyerbeer's grand opera, L'Etoile,du Nord."
1st Liversedge Albert (Ben Cooke); **2nd Mirfield** (W.Lee); **3rd Tintwistle** (William Gordon); **4th Dewsbury** (A. Fearnsides); **5th Birstall, St Saviour's** (Ben Cooke).

1890 – 15 bands entered. 12 competed. – **Adjudicators – Mr. J. Kendrick Payne, organist, Manchester Cathedral. Mr. J. O. Shepherd, band conductor at the Courts Theatre, Liverpool.**
Overture – **"Poet and Peasant,"**and A Major from **"Songs without Words."** (Mendelssohn)
1st Dewsbury (Arthur Fernside); **2nd Almondbury United** (Ben Lodge); **3rd Mirfield** (Harry Barlow); **4th Birstall,** St Saviours – Ben Cooke; **5th Tintwistle Christ Church** (William Gordon).
*Also competed - **Barnsley** (Charles Woodhouse); **Hyde**(Joseph Ford); **Liversedge Albert** (Ben Cooke); **Christ Church Hayfield, Derbyshire** (John Brocklehurst); **Woodroyd Victoria** (France Littlewood**); All Souls ? * No Town given,** (Tom Goodhall); **Horbury. * Whetley Mills** – James Augus, DNC

1891 – 23 bands entered. – **Adjudicators – Mr G. Jaeger, professor of music, Paris Conservtorie. Mr F. Vetter, musical director, Manchester.**
Overture – **"Martha."** Flotow.
1st Liversedge Albert, £17, 125 Marks, (Ben Cooke); **2nd Almondbury United, £10,** 117 Marks, (Ben Lodge); **3rd Woodroyd Victoria, £7,** 110 marks (Richard Heaton); **4th Hyde, £5** (A. D. Keate) 90 Marks. **5th Christ Church Tintwistle, £ 2.10s,** 83 Marks (William Gordon).
***Also competed – Birstall; St Lukes, Heywood; Almondbury Junior; Cheddleton, nr Leek,Derbyshire; St Pauls, Ramsbottom, Lancashire; Honley Temperance; Brookfield, (No County given, Nr Cheadle, Manchester ?); Gorton, Manchester; Mirfield; Crosland Moor United** (Thomas Cartwright**); Elland; Keighley Parish Church; Wheatley Mills, Bradford, Yorkshire; Northwich, Cheshire; Hopton Congregational, Yorkshire; Birstall St Saviours; Moorside Nr Oldham, Lancashire; Birstall Congregational.**

1892 – 25 bands entered – **Adjudicators – Carl Kiefurt, Prince of Wales Theatre, London. Mr. J. Kendrick Payne, Manchester Cathedral.**
Selection from "Rigoletto & Ernani"Verdi. (arrangement Royston Smith).
1st Liversedge Albert (Ben Cooke); **2nd Almondbury United; *Joint 3rd Dalton Vitctoria, and Crosland Moor United** (Thomas Cartwright); **5th Almondbury Junior.**

1893 – 25 bands entered – 14 competed.- **Adjudicators – J. O. Shepherd, Royal Court**

Theatre, Liverpool. F. Vetter, musical director, Manchester.
Selection – "La Favorita" Donizetti.
1st Almondbury United; 2nd Liversedge Albert; 3rd Birstall, St Saviours; 4th St Lukes, Heywood; 5th Crosland Moor United (Thomas Cartwright).

1894 – Adjudicators – Mr.J.O.Shepherd, conductor, Royal Court Theatre, Liverpool. Dr Watson, Manchester. 23 bands entered –
Selection "Robert Le Diable." Meyerbeer.
1st Dewsbury – Arthur Fernsides; 2nd Almondbury United; 3rd Hyde; 4th Crosland Moor United (Thomas Cartwright); 5th Clifton, Brighouse.

1895 – 16 bands entered –
Selection – " L' Elisire D' Amore." Donizetti.
1st Almondbury United; 2nd Dewsbury - Arthur Fernsides; 3rd Christ Church, Tintwistle; 4th Thurlstone; 5th Crosland moor United (Thomas Cartwright).

1896 – 23 bands entered – Adjudicators – Carl Kiefurt, London. Mr. J. Kendrick Payne, Organist, Town Hall, Manchester.
Selection from Offenbach's Opera "Orphee aux Enfers," Boyton Smith.
1st Horbury; 2nd Almondbury United; 3rd Clifton; 4th Dewsbury; 5th Thurlstone.

1897 – Selection from Sonnambula, No 1, "Tutto E Sciolto," Wenzel Plachy.
1st Dewsbury; 2nd Thurlstone; 3rd Almondbury United; 4th Clifton; 5th Horbury. * Also – Hyde; Hayfield; Besse-o'-th-Barn; Clifton Juniors; Christ Church, Tintwistle; Birstall St Saviours. The following DNC – Lepton United; St Lukes Heywood; Brighouse; Darton; All Souls, Halifax; Woodroyd Victoria; Heptonstall, nr Halifax, Yorkshire; Crosland Moor United; Liversedge Albert; Mottram, Lancashire.

1898 – 18 bands entered – Adjudicator – Dr Henry Watson, Professor, Royal College of music, Manchester. Mr. F. Vetter, Manchester.
Overture – "Guy Mannering." Bishop.
1st Almondbury United - Ben Lodge; 2nd Huddersfield - J. B. Lodge; 3rd Horbury; 4th Dewsbury; 5th Clifton.
*Also competed – Huddersfield; Lepton United; Thurlstone; Motram, Lancashire; Birstall St Saviours. – The following did not appear (DNC): Sherburn-in-Elmet, nr Leeds, Yorkshire; Crosland Moor United; Heptonstall, Nr Halifax, Yorkshire; Brighouse; Hayfield; Hyde; Tintwistle Christ Church; Clifton Juniors; Darton, Yorkshire.

1899 – 23 bands entered - 11 bands competed – Adjudicators – Mr. J. Ord Hume, composer of music, Royal Scots Greys. Mr. J. Kendrick Payne, Manchester.
Selection from Offenbach's Opera, "The Grand Duchess of Gerolstein."- Arranged by Cramer.
1st Almondbury United, (9) £20 -Ben Lodge; 2nd Lepton United, (11) £12 - S. Shaw; 3rd Liversedge Albert (12) £10 - Kaye Cooke; 4th Horbury (9) £5 -James Woffenden; Birstall St

Saviours (12) £3 - Kaye Cooke.

* Also competed – Dewsbury (10) - A. Fernsides; Crosland Moor United (10) - Albert Townend; Mottram (10) - J. Warhurst; Huddersfield (10) - J. B. Lodge; Royston United Temperance, Yorkshire (12) - S. Butler; Clifton (9) - Albert Sayles.

1900 - 17 bands entered – 9 competed. – **Adjudicators – Dr Henry Watson, Professor of music Royal College of music, Manchester. Mr. F. Vetter, musical director, Manchester.** * – Maximum number of marks = 100.

Potpourri- **"Czar and Zimmermann."** Lortzing.

1st Almondbury United (10) 96 marks - Ben Lodge; **2nd Crosland Moor United** (12) 95 marks - Albert Townend; **3rd Horbury** (9) James Woffenden; **Clifton** (12) Albert Sayles; **Liversedge Albert** (12) - Kaye Cooke.

*Also competed – Birstall St Saviours (12) - Kaye Cooke; Lepton United (12) - S. Shaw; Huddersfield (11) -W. Booth; Mottram (10) - J. Warhurst); Barnsley (12) - R. Stringer. The following DNA – Penistone; Darton; Christ Chuch Tintwistle; Thurlstone; Royston United; Brighouse; Dewsbury.

1901 – 16 bands entered – 14 competed – **Adudicators – Dr Henry Watson, Manchester. Professor George Pritchard, London.**

Selection- **"Les Cloches de Corneville."** Planquett. Arranged by Lieutenant Charles Godfrey, R.A.M., Bandmaster, Royal Hourse Guards, London.

1st Crosland Moor United - Albert Townend; 2nd Clifton; 3rd Liversedge Albert; 4th Lepton United; 5th Huddersfield Albert.

1902 – 22 entries – 11 competed. **Adjudicators – Dr Henry Watson, Manchester. Professor George Watson, London. Maximum marks 100.**

Selection – **"La Fille du Regiment."** Donizetti.

1st Crosland Moor United 98 marks Albert Townend; **2nd Huddersfield; 3rd Clifton; 4th Liversedge Albert; 5th Barnsley. –**

* Also competed – Birstall St saviours; Liversedge Albert; Bingley; Woodroyd; Old Glossop.
* The following DNC – Almondbury; Lepton.

1903 – 15 bands entered – 13 competed. **Adjudicators – Dr Henry Watson, Manchester. Mr, George Pritchard, London.**

Selection – **'Geneviéve de Brabant.'** Offenbach.

1st Crosland Moor United (10) Albert Townend; **2nd Huddersfield** (12) Lewis Booth; **3rd Clifton** (10) Albert Sayles; **4th Almondbury United** (11) Ben Lodge; **5th Royston United** (11) James Watson

* Also competed – **Woodroyd** (13) John Moorhouse; **Lane Congregational Holmfirth** (12) John Moorhouse; **Barnsley** (11) Ezra Stringer; **Liversedge Albert** (12) A. Schofield; **Horbury** (10) James Woffenden; **Bingley** (12) Albert Anderson; **Darfield** (10) Samuel Woodcock; **Chrlst Church Tintwistle** (11) Charles Bray. - ***** The following DNC- **Sheffield Hartshead** (9) J. A. Ironside; **Darton** (12) James Watson.

1904 – 16 bands entered – **Adjudicators – Mr Albert Jowett, mus bac oxon, Leeds. Mr**

George Pritchard, London.
Selection **"Rigoletto"** Donizetti.
1st Huddersfield; 2nd Almondbury United; 3rd Lane Congregational, Holmfirth; 4th Royston United; 5th Horbury.

1905 – 9 bands competed – **Church, Accrington, Lancashire,** DNC. - **Adjudicators – Mr. F. Vetter, Manchester. Mr. George Pritchard, London.**
Selection – **"Norma,"** Bellini.
1st Crosland Moor United (10) 125 marks, Albert Townend; **2nd Almondbury United** (10) 102 marks, Ben Lodge; **3rd Clifton** (10) 86 marks, H. Evans; **4th Huddersfield** (11) 80 marks, Lewis Booth; **5th Lane Congregational Holmfirth** (12) 79 marks, John Moorhouse.
* Also entered – Christ Church, Tintwistle (12) T. Ashworth; **Woodroyd** (12) John Moorhouse; **Birstall St saviours** (12) Kaye Cooke; **Royston United** (11) James Watson; **Pendlebury, Lancashire** (10) M. Foy; **Horbury** (9) W. H. Giggle; **Hayfield, Cheshire** (10) J. Brocklehurst; **Thurlstone** (10) Ben Lodge; **Friends School, Oldham** (12) Albert Lawton.

1906 – 8 bands competed – **adjudicators – Mr. James Watson, London.**
Selection – **"Lucia di Lammermoor'** Donizetti.
1st Crosland Moor United (9) 87 marks, Albert Townend ; **Almondbury United** (9) 81 marks, Ben Lodge; **3rd Clifton** (10) 78 marks, Albert Sayles; **4th Birstall St Saviours** (11) 41 marks, Kaye Cooke; **5th Dewsbury** (10) 37 marks, John Rigg.
* Also competed – Lane Congregational, Holmfirth (10) 35 marks, James Charlesworth; Royston United (10) 34 marks, James Watson. – The following DNC- Friends School, Oldham (11) A Lawton. Christ Church, Tintwistle, - Edward Thornley.

1907 – 14 bands entered – 10 competed – **Adjudicators – Mr Henry Watson, Mus. Doc. (Cantab.). Mr Charles H. Fogg.**
Selection – **"William Tell."** Rossini.
1st Crosland Moor United (9) Albert Townend; **2nd Birstall St Saviours** (10) Kaye Cooke; **3rd Almondbury United** (9) Jos. H. Dawson; **4th Dewsbury** (10) A. Fernsides; **5th Lane Congregational, Holmfirth** (10) –
* Also competed – Clifton (10) A. Sykes; **Lindley,** L. Stansfield; **Liversedge Albert** (10) J. B. Lee; **Almondbury Juniors** (12) Jos. H. Dawson; **Thurlstone** (10) F. Taylor. * The following DNC - **Huddersfield** (10); **Church, Accrington** (8); **Darfield; Barnsley.**

1908 – 13 bands entered – 11 competed – Adjudicators – **Mr George Pritchard, London. Mr. R. Johnson, Manchester.**
Selection **"La Traviata,"** Verdi.
1st Crosland Moor United Juniors - James. H. Ellis; **2nd Royston United** - Jas Watson; **3rd Dewsbury** - Arthur Fernsides; **4th Lane Congregational, Holmfirth** - John Moorhouse; **5th Birstall St Saviours** - Kaye Cooke.
* Also competed – Pendlebury - Arthur Royal; **Church, Accrington** - Edmund Lee; **Almondbury Juniors** – Jos. H. Dawson; **Friend's Hall and Institute, M.A.B.C. Birmingham** – R. C. Bowkett; **Barnsley** – F. Fleetwood; **Clifton** – Albert Sayles. * The following DNC – **Huddersfield; Mirfield.**

1909 – 14 bands entered – one DNC. **Adjudicators - Mr. George Pritchard, London. Mr. Frank Owen, Manchester.**
– Selection **"Bohemian Girl."** Balfe.
1st Crosland Moor Public - James. H. Ellis; **2nd Birstall St Saviours** – Kaye Cooke; **3rd Clifton** – Albert Sayles; **4th Dewsbury** – Arthur Fernsides; **5th Crosland Moor United** – Albert Townend;
* Also entered –; Almondbury – A. J. North; Royston United – Jas. Watson; Barnsley – T. Fleetwood; Thurlstone – Fred Taylor; Clifton Juniors – Fred Squire; Saddleworth – William Pownall; Lepton United - Jos. H. Dawson; Pendlebury – Arthur Royal; Crosland Moor United

1910 – 11 bands competed – **Adjudicators – Dr. Henry Watson, Manchester. Mr Frank Owen, L.L.C.M. Manchester.**
Selection – **"Don Giovanni."** Mozart.
1st Crosland Moor United – Albert Townend; **2nd Lepton** – Jos H. Dawson; **3rd Clifton** ; **4th Dewsbury; 5th Birstall St Saviours.**
* Also competed – Liversedge Juniors; Royston United; Saddleworth; Thurlstone; (10th) Crosland Moor Public; Annesley and Newstead Byron, Nottinghamshire.

1911 – 11 bands competed – **Adjudicators – Mr Charles. H. Fogg. J. W. Beswick.**
Selection – "Masaniello."Auber.
1st Crosland Moor Public - James. H. Ellis; **2nd Lepton United** – Jos. W. Dawson; **3rd Penistone** – E. Falls; **4th Clifton** – H. Evans; **5th Dewsbury** – Arthur Fernsides.
*Also competed – Birstall St Saviours – Kaye Cooke; **Saddleworth – William Pownall; Clifton Juniors – Fred Squires; Ecclesfield, Yorkshire – Fred. P. Whitham; Tunstead (Stackseads) Lancashire – Howarth Stansfield; Royston United – J. Shaw. * The following DNC – Pendlebury – P. Swindley; Thurlstone – Fred Taylor; Liversedge Albert – Kaye Cooke.**

1912 - 13 entered - **Adjudicators – Mr. Charles.H. Fogg. Mr. J. W. Beswick.**
Selection – **"La Sonnambula."** Bellini.
1st Crosland Moor Public – James. H. Ellis; **2nd Gilder Hall (Mirfield) Yorkshire** – Gill Brearley; **3rd Lepton United** – Jos. H. Dawson; **4th Thurlstone** – Fred Taylor; **5th Saddleworth** – William Pownall.
* Also entered – Dewsbury – Arthur Fernsides; Royston United – J. Shaw; Pendlebury – P. Swindley; Tundtead (Stacksteads) – H. Stansfield; Clifton – H. Evans; Penistone – J. E. Fella; Friends School, Oldham – J. F. Slater, Mus Bac., F.R.C.O.; Liversedge Albert – Kaye Cooke.

1913 10 entered 8 competed – **Adjudicators – Mr. C. H. Fogg, Manchester. Mr. F. Coope, Organist, Leeds.**
Selection – **"The Merry Wives Of Windsor."** Nicolai.
1st Crosland Moor Public – James. H. Ellis; **2nd Gilder Hall, Mirfeld** – Gill Brearley; **3rd Clifton** – Albert Sayles; **4th Tunstead (Stacksteads)** – H. B. Stansfield.

293

Also competed – **Royston United** – J. Shaw; **Saddleworth** – William Pownall; **Lepton United** – Jos. H. Dawson; **Thurlstone** – Fred Taylor. – The following DNC – **Friends School, Oldham** – J. F. Slater.

1914 – Diamond Jubilee – 13 entered
Selection – **"The Crown Diamonds."**Auber.
1st Saddleworth; 2nd Crosland Moor United; 3rd Elland C.E.M.S; 4th Thurlstone Public; 5th Lepton United. –
* **Also entered – Pendlebury; Penistone Spring Vale Public; Liversedge Albert; Tunsteads (Stacksteads); Clifton; Birstall St Saviours; Royston United.**

1915 – 8 entered – 6 competed – **Adjudicators – Mr Frank Owen, L.L.C.M. Manchester. Mr. Harry Barlow, Manchester.**
Selection - **"Martha."** Flotow.
1st Crosland Moor Public – James. H. Ellis; **2nd Thurlstone Public** – Fred Taylor; **3rd Bradford Tennyson Place, Yorkshire** – Kaye Cooke; **4th Elland C.E.M.S** – Fred Squire; **5th Crosland Moor United** – M. Nettleton.
* **Also competed – Birstall St Saviours – Kaye Cooke; Penistone Spring Vale Public DNC.**

1916 to 1920 – No Contest due to intervention of World War 1. and the effects of the
Spanish Flu.

1921 Date of contests now changed from September to 3rd week in October.
– 11 bands entered – 9 competed – **Adjudicators – Mr. Harry Barlow, Covent Garden and Halle Orchestras. Dr A.W.Wilson, M.A. Mus, Manchester.**
Selection from 1, 3 & 4 **'Petite Suite de Concert'** S. Coleridge – Taylor.
1st Saddleworth (11) Albert Townend; **2nd Elland C.E.M.S.** (11) Fred Squire; **3rd Crosland Moor Public** (10) James. H. Ellis; **4th Bradford Tennyson Place** (10); **5th Birstall St Saviours** (10) Kaye Cooke.

1922 – 10 bands competed - **Adjudicator – Mr. Harry Barlow.**
Selection from **"Pique Dame"**, France von Suppé.
1st Crosland Moor Public – Victor Smith; **2nd Saddleworth; 3rd Elland C.E.M.S.; 4th Bradford Tennyson Place; 5th Penistone Spring Vale Public.**

1923 – 9 bands competed – Adjudicators – **Mr. Harry Barlow. Mr. Isaac Wharton.**
Selection – **"Norma."** Bellini.
1st Crosland Moor Public – James. H. Ellis; **2nd Saddleworth – 3rd Elland C.E.M.S.** – Fred Squire; **4th Bradford Tennyson Place** – Kaye Cooke; **5th Horbury** A. A. Fothergill.

1924 – 7 bands competed – **Adjudicator – Harry Barlow, Prestwitch. Manchester.**
Overture – **"Raymond."** Thomas.
1st Crosland Moor Public – Jams. H. Ellis; **2nd Woodroyd** – Albert Jenkinson; **3rd Saddleworth** – Albert Townend; **4th Penistone Spring Vale Public** – P. Loxley; **5th Elland C.E.M.S.** – Fred Squire.

1925 – Adjudicator – Mr. Harry Barlow, Prestwitch.
Overture – "Maritana." Wallace.
1st Saddleworth – Albert Townend; 2nd Thurlstone Public; 3rd Lees St Agnes, Lancashire; 4th Elland Church United.

1926 - 9 bands entered – **Adjudicator – Mr Harry Barlow.**
Overture " La Couronne D'Or."Alphonse Herman.
1st Crosland Moor Public 94 marks –Allen Kaye. **2nd Thurlstone Public; 3rd Lees St Agnes; 4th Woodroyd.**

The end of sixty seven years of the BRITISH OPEN HAND-BELL CONTESTS held at Belle Vue, Manchester.

Appendix 3

The Yorkshire Hand-Bell Ringers Association Contests 1904-1932
The results below are a composite of reports gathered from many publications and archives, which I have put together as a complete a record as I can; but is not definitive:

1904 - The Armoury Hall, Queensgate, Huddersfield.
(Contests were usually held around Whitsuntide). Maximum marks to be gained 160.
First Division Contest (unlimited number of bells) Test piece – L'Italian in Algeria. – Rossini.

Results	Band	Score	No. Performers	Conductor
1st	Huddersfield	156	12	Lewis Booth.
2nd	Almondbury	149	10	Ben Lodge.
3rd	Horbury	145	10	J. Woffenden.
	Barnsley		9	E. Stringer.
	Liversedge Albert		11	Kaye Cooke
	Birstall St Saviours		11	Kaye Cooke
	Thurlstone		10	E. Biltcliffe.
	Clifton		10	Albert Sayles
Royston United - did not compete.				(DNC)

Second Division Contest (Limited to bands who had not won a prize at Belle Vue) Test piece – **Reminiscences of Merrie England**, (encompassing familiar old English songs). Maximum marks to be gained 90.

Results	Band	Score	No. Performers	Conductor
1st	Woodroyd	75	11	J. Moorhouse.
2nd	Barnsley	74	10	E Stringer.
3rd	Birstall	73	10	Kaye Cooke.
	Heptonstall		12	W. Sunderland.
	Lightcliffe		9	A Warler.
	Brighouse Park Church		12	P Marshall.
	Holmfirth Lane Congregational		12	John Moorhouse.
	Sheffield Hartshead		10	J.A. Ironside.
	Low Moor		10	K. Cooke.
	Darfield and Sheffield Hartshead Friends -			DNC.

1905 - Public Hall Barnsley.

First Division Test piece – **Il Tancredi** – Rossini.

Results	Band	Score	No. Performers	Conductor
1st	Almondbury Utd	74	9	Ben Lodge.
2nd	Woodroyd	72	12	J. Moorhouse.
3rd	Horbury	71	9	W. H. Giggle. F.G.C.M.
	Crosland Moor Utd	70	10	Albert Townend.
	Holmfirth	62	12	J. Moorhouse.
	Huddersfield	69	11	L. Booth.
	Royston United	54	9	Jas Watson.
	Liversedge Albert	56	11	A. Fernside.
	Thurlstone	66	10	E. Biltcliffe.
	Clifton -		DNA.	

Second Division Test Piece – **Tannhauser** – Wagner.

Results	Band		No. Performers	Conductor
1st	Holmfirth		12	J. Moorhouse.
2nd	Lindley		9	L. Stansfield.
3rd	Thurlstone		10	E. Biltcliffe.
	Lightcliffe (St Matthews)		10	A. Wooler.
	Heptonstall		10	W. Sunderland.
	Dewsbury		9	J. Rigg.
	Birstall St Saviours		11	K. Cooke.
	Low Moor		10	K. Cooke.
	Darfield, and Sheffield Hartshead - DNC .			

1906 - Dewsbury Town Hall.

First Division Test Piece – **Fra Diavolo** – Auber.

Results	Band	Score	No. Performers	Conductor
1st	Crosland Moor United	160	9	A. Townend.
2rd	Horbury	145	10	W.H.Giggle.
3rd	Almondbury United	141	9	B. Lodge.
	Holmfirth		10	J. Charlesworth.
	Huddersfield		9	Wm. Booth.
	Woodroyd, and Clifton –		DNA.	

Second Division Test piece – **Fantasia, Relief of Ladysmith** - Kara Reed.

Results	Band		No. Performers	Conductor
1st	Birstall St Saviours		9	K. Cooke.
2nd	Dewsbury		10	J. Rigg.
3rd	Thurlstone		10	B. Lodge.
	Lindley		8	E. Stansfield.
	Barnsley		10	T. Fleetwood.
	Sheffield Hartshead		11	J. A. Ironside.
	Royston		10	J. Watson.
	Liversedge Albert		10	J. B. Lee.
	Darfield; Heptonstall ; Higher Walton ; Lightcliffe, and Low Moor – DNC.			

1907 - Public Hall Barnsley.

First Division Test piece – **Il Trovatore** – Verdi .

Results	Band	Score	No. Performers	Conductor
1st	Almondbury			B. Lodge.
2nd a tie	Birstall St Saviours			K. Cooke

2nd	Huddersfield		W. Booth.
3rd	Horbury		W.H.Giggle.
	Clifton		Albert Sayles.

Second Division – **Le Diademe** – Herman.

Results	Band	Score	No. Performers	Conductor
1st	Lindley			L. Stansfield.
2nd	Thurlstone			B. Lodge.
3rd a tie	Dewsbury			A. Fernsides
3rd	Barnsley			T. Fleetwood.
	Sheffield Hartshead			J. A. Ironsides.
	Royston			J. T. Morris.
	St Aidan's Ossett			W. H.Giggle.
	Clifton Juniors			Fred Squire.
	Liversedge			J. B. Lee.

1908 - Public Victoria Hall Batley.

First Division Test piece – **Patience** – Sullivan. Maximum marks 100.

Results	Band	Score	No. Performers	Conductor
1st	Birstall St Saviours	86		K. Cooke.
2nd	Horbury	85		W.H. Giggle.
3rd	Holmfirth	80		J. Moorhouse.

Second Division Test Piece – **Fantasia** from the works of Mendelssohn.

1st	Crosland Moor United Junior	95		James.H. Ellis.
2nd	Almondbury Utd.	89		Jos H. Dawson.
3rd	Dewsbury	83		A. Fernsides.
	Higher Walton	72		H. Brearley.
	Holmfirth	74		J. Moorhouse.
	Liversedge	70		J.B. Lee.
	Mirfield	63		J. Taylor.
	Royston	DNC		J.Waterhouse.
	Sheffield Hartshead	DNC		J.A.Ironside.
	St Aiden's South Ossett	75		W.H.Giggle.
	Thurlstone	DNC		F.Taylor.

1909 - Sunny Vale pleasure Gardens Hipperholme, Brighouse.

First Division Test Piece – **Sonata in G, No. 2, Op, 49** – Beethoven. Maximun marks 60.

Results	Band	Score	No. Performers	Conductor
1st	Crosland Moor United	58		A. Townend.
2nd	Birstall St Saviours	56		K. Cooke.
3rd	Clifton	47		A. Sayles.

Second Division Test Piece – **Der Freischultz** – Weber.

1st	Dewsbury	56		A. Fernsides.
2nd	Ecclesfield	55		E. Biltcliffe.
3rd	Clifton Juniors	47		F. Squire.
	Mirfield			J. Taylor.
	Higher Walton			W. North.
	Thurlstone Juniors			T. Taylor.
	Holmfirth			J. Moorhouse.
	Royston United			J. Watson.

1910 - Sunny Vale Pleasure Gardens.
First Division Test Piece – **Mikado** – Sullivan. Maximum marks 100.

Results	Band	Score	No. Performers	Conductor
1st	Crosland Moor Public	93		J. H. Ellis.
2nd	Crosland Moor United	90		A. Townend.
3rd	Birstall St Saviours	77		K. Cooke.
	Clifton	DNC		H. Evans
	Dewsbury	DNC		A. Fernsides
	Horbury	DNC		H. Evans.

Second Division Test Piece – **Maritana** – Wallace.

1st	Lepton United	94		J. H. Dawson.
2nd	Ecclesfield	89		E. Biltcliffe
3rd	Liversedge Albert	84		Kaye Cooke
Thurlstone		83		F. Taylor
Clifton Juniors		82		F. Squire.
Mirfield		75		J. Taylor.
Sheffield Hartshead		61		J. A. Ironside.
Ossett St. Aidan's		DNC		W H Giggle
Royston United		DNC		J. Watson.

1911 – West End Chapel Schoolroom, Ecclesfield.
First Division Test Piece – **Don Giovanni** – Mozart. Maximum marks 140.

Results	Band	Score	No. Performers	Conductor
1st	Dewsbury	125		
2nd	Crosland Moor Public	121		
3rd	Lepton	114		
	Thurlstone	96		
	Liversedge Albert	101		

Second Division Test Piece – **Fantasia, Les Cloches de Bridal** – Arranged by K. Cooke.

1st	Liversedge Albert	110		
2nd	Ecclesfield	107		
3rd	Clifton Juniors	77		
Royston United		DNC		
Sheffield Hartshead		DNC		
Thurlstone.		DNC		

Third Division (49 bells or under, no duplicate bells allowed) Test Piece – **Martha** – Flotow.

1st	Gilder Hall Mirfield	105		
2nd	Bradford Tennyson Place	107		
3rd	Cleckheaton Adult school	95		
	Armitage Bridge DNC			
	Elland Church of England Men's Society DNC			
	One other band entered (unknown) DNC			

1912 – Sunny Vale Pleasure Gardens.
First Division Test Piece - **Le Cloches de Cornville** – Planquette. Maximum marks 100.

Results	Band	Score	No. Performers	Conductor
1st	Crosland Moor Public	98		J. H. Ellis.

298

Results	Band	Score	No. Performers	Conductor
2nd	Clifton	97		H. Evans.
3rd	Liversedge	92		
	Dewsbury	DNC.		

Second Division Test Piece – **Poet and Peasant** – Von Suppé.

Results	Band	Score	No. Performers	Conductor
1st	Saddleworth	91		W. Pownall.
2nd	Elland	86		C. H. Waddington
3rd	Thurlstone	84		F. Taylor.
	Penistone	DNC		
	Sowerby Bridge	DNC		
	Ecclesfield	DNC		
	Sowerby	DNC.		

Third Division Test Piece – **Scottish Airs,** Arranged by Charles H. Cawley.

Results	Band	Score	No. Performers	Conductor
1st	Gilder Hall Mirfield	86		G. Brearley.
2nd	Elland	81		C. H Waddington.
3rd	Newchurch nr Warrington	79		J. Orpme.

1913 – Sunny Vale Pleasure Gardens.

First Division Test Piece – Martha – Flotow.

Results	Band	Score	No. Performers	Conductor
1st	Lepton United	114		J. H. Dawson.
2nd	Crosland Moor Public	110		J. H. Ellis.
3rd	Gilder Hall	109		Gill Brearley.
	Saddleworth	109		
	Elland	101		
	Liversedge Albert	97		
	Clifton.			

Second Division (Limited to 49 bells or under) - **Fantasia, Bohemian Girl** – Balfe. Arrangement C. H. Cawley.

Results	Band	Score	No. Performers	Conductor
1st	Elland	109		F. Squire.
2nd	Armitage Bridge	86		J. Dyson.
3rd	Birstall St Saviours	80		K. Cooke.

Sheffield Hartshead; Sowerby Bridge; Gilder Hall Mirfield; Bradford Tennyson; Newchurch, and Bolton Parish Church also entered.

1914 – Sunny Vale Pleasure Gardens.

First Division Test Piece – Bohemian girl – M. U. Balfe – (Arrangement, Seymour Smith.)

Results	Band	Score	No. Performers	Conductor
1st	Lepton United	106		J. H. Dawson.
2nd	Saddleworth	102		William Pownall
3rd	Crosland Moor Public	101		J. H. Ellis

Clifton; Elland; Liversedge Albert, and Gilder Hall Mirfield also entered.

Second Division (Limited to 49 bells or under) - **Fantasia,** Mendelssohn. (Arrangement, Gordon Meydeh.)

Results	Band	Score	No. Performers	Conductor
1st	Sheffield Hartshead Friends	104		W. Dyson.
2nd	Bradford Tennyson	102		K. Cooke.
3rd	Gilder Hall Mirfield	100		G. Brearley.

Armitage Bridge; Birstall St Saviours; Almondbury United; Bolton Parish church; Ecclesfield, and Sowerby Bridge also entered.

1915 – Sunny Vale Pleasure Gardens.

First Division Test Piece – Poet and Peasant – Von Suppé – (Arrangement, Chas Sheard.)

Results	Band	Score	No. Performers	Conductor
1st	Crosland Moor Public	94		J. H. Ellis.
2nd	Lepton United	88		J. Dawson.
3rd	Saddleworth	87		A. Townend.
	Elland C. E. M. S.	84		F. Squire.

Second Division Test Piece – Zampa – L. J. Herold. Selection by Oscar Verne.

1st	Bradford Tennyson	78
2nd	Tennyson Place PM, Bfd.	76
3rd	Birstall St Saviours	75

Elland Juniors; Sowerby Bridge; Pendlebury; Bolton Parish Church; Sheffield Hartshead and Liversedge Woodfield also entered. Almondbury United – DNC.

1916 – 1919 – No Contest due to World War 1.

1920 – Sunny Vale Pleasure Gardens.

First Division Test Piece – Il Trovatore – Verdi   5 Bands entered.

Results	Band	Score	No. Performers	Conductor
1st	Elland	110		
2nd	Crosland Moor Public	103		
3rd	Pendlebury	98		
	Thurlstone	73		
	Liversedge Albert	66		

Second Division – (Limited to 37 bells or under) Test Piece – **Caliph of Bagdad** – Boieldieu. – 10 Bands entered.

1st	Armitage Bridge
2nd	Bradford Tennyson
3rd	Birstall St Saviours

1921 - Sunny Vale Pleasure Gardens.

First Division Test Piece – Maritana – Wallace.

Results	Band	Score	No. Performers	Conductor
1st	Elland	98		F. Squire.
2nd	Crosland Moor Public	96		J. H. Ellis.
3rd	Saddleworth	84		A. Townend.
	Pendlebury, and Ecclesfield also entered.			

Second Division Test Piece – William Tell – Rossini. 10 Bands entered

1st	Woodroyd	82		Tom Maude.
2nd	Birstall St Saviours	81		K. Cooke.
3rd	Horbury	80		A. Fothergill.

Armitage Bridge; Sheffield Hartshead; Thurlstone; Bradford Tennyson Place; Pendlebury; Lees St Agnes; Ecclesfield, and Bolton Parish Church also entered.

1922 – Sunny Vale Pleasure Gardens.

First Division Test Piece – Lucrezia Borgia – Donizetti. (Seymour Smith).

Results	Band	Score	No. Performers	Conductor
1st	Elland			F. Squire.
2nd	Saddleworth			W. Pownall.
Results	Band	Score	No. Performers	Conductor 3rd

| | Horbury | | | A. Fothergill. |
| Bradford Tennyson (K. Cooke) and Pendlebury (J. Jones) also entered. |

Second Division (Limited to 50 bells or less) Test Piece – **La Traviata** – Verdi. 14 bands entered, 11 attended.

1st	Horbury			A. Fothergill.
2nd	Penistone Public			P. Loxley.
3rd	Thurlstone			F. Taylor.

Ecclesfield (F. Witham); Thornhill (H. Ramsden);
Bradford Tennyson (K. Cooke);
Woodroyd (T. Maude);
Armitage Bridge St Pauls (W. Wood);
Pendelbury (J. Jones);
Sheffield Hartshead Friends (W. Dyson),
and Lees St Agnes (W. Wood) also entered.

1923 – Sunny Vale Pleasure Gardens.

First Division Test Piece – **Tancredi** – Rossini. 7 Bands entered

Results	Band	Score	No. Performers	Conductor
1st	Saddleworth	91		W. Pownall.
2nd	Crosland Moor Public	83		Victor Smith.
3rd	Thurlstone	71		F. Taylor.
Second Division – **Rigoletto** – Verdi.				
1st	Lees St Agnes	80		J. H. Ellis.
2nd	Thurlstone	69		F. Taylor.
3rd	Bradford	60		K. Cooke.

1924 – Sunny Vale Pleasure Gardens.

First Division (6 entries – 4 competed. Test Piece – **Banditenstreiche** – Von Suppé.

Results	Band	Score	No. Performers	Conductor
1st	Crosland Moor Public	95		J. H. Ellis.
2nd	Woodroyd	90		Albert Jenkinson.
3rd	Elland	87		F. Squire.
Second Division Test Piece – **Oberon** – Weber.- (Arranged by Oscar Vern).				
1st	Thurlstone	93		F. Taylor.
2nd	Bradford Tennyson	91		K. Cooke.
3rd	Lees St Agnes	90		J. T. Bardsley.

Thornhill; Penistone Spring Vale Public; Ecclesfield; Low Moor also entered. Armitage Bridge, and Sheffield Hartshead, DNC.

1925 – Sunny Vale pleasure Gardens.

First Division Test Piece – The Siege Of Rochelle – M. U. Balfe.

Results	Band	Score	No. Performers	Conductor
1st	Saddleworth	94		A. Townend.
2nd	Thurlstone	90		F. Taylor.
3rd	Woodroyd	88		A. Jenkinson.
Second Division – (Limited to 48 bells or less) Test Piece – **Martha** – Floto – Arranged by Oscar Varne.				
1st	Saddleworth	87		A. Townend.
Results	**Band**	**Score**	**No. Performers**	**Conductor**

2nd	Lees St Agnes	86		J. H. Ellis.
3rd	Ecclesfield	85		F. Whitham.

Bradford Tennyson; Low Moor; Thurlstone; Penistone Spring Vale; Sheffield Hartshead Friends; Thornhill also entered. Pendlebury DNC.

1926 – Sunny Vale Pleasure Gardens.
First Division Test Piece – **La Dame Blanche** – Boieldieu.

Results	Band	Score	No. Performers	Conductor
1st	Crosland Moor Public	94		Alan Kaye.
2nd	Saddleworth	90		R. Wood.
3rd	Elland	88		F. Squire.

Low Moor; Tennyson Place and Thurlstone also entered. Penistone Spring Vale; Ecclesfield; Sheffield Hartshead, and Thornhill - DNC.

Second Division – (Limited to 46 bells or less) Test Piece – La Serenata - Tosti. – (Arranged by P. Herman).

1st	Bradford Tennyson Place	86		C. Cawley.
2nd	Lees St Agnes	84		J. P. Bardsley.
3rd	Low Moor	82		K. Cooke.

Penistone Spring Vale ; Ecclesfield; Sheffield Hartshead, and Thornhill – DNC.

1927 – Sunny Vale Pleasure Gardens.
First Division Test Piece – Rosamunde – Schubert, op 26, N, 1. Maximum marks 100.

Results	Band	Score	No. Performers	Conductor
1st	Woodroyd	100		A. Jenkinson.
2nd	Saddleworth	96		A. Townend.
3rd	Elland	95		F. Squire.

Crosland Moor Public, and Bradford Tennyson – DNC.

Second Division (Limited to 66 bells or less). Test Piece – Lurline- Wallace – (Arranged by Oscar Verni).

1st	Lees St Agnes	87		F. Bardsley.
2nd	Thurlstone	78		F. Taylor.
3rd	Bradford Tennyson	76		C.H. Cawley.

Low Moor also competed. Penistone Spring Vale; Pendlebury and Thornhill – DNC.

1928 – Sunny Vale Pleasure Gardens. (Contests held 22nd September)
First Division Test Piece – **The Daughter of the Regiment** – Donizetti.

Results	Band	Score	No. Performers	Conductor
1st	Crosland Moor Public			J. H. Ellis.
2nd	Woodroyd			
3rd	Thurlstone			

Second Division Test Piece – **Poet and Peasant** – Von Suppé.

1st	Crosland Moor Public			J. H. Ellis.
2nd	Woodroyd			
3rd	Lees St Agnes			

4 Bands DNC.

1929 – Hope Bank Pleasure Grounds, Honley, near Huddersfield. (September)
Maximum number of marks 100.
First Division Test Piece – **Bohemian Girl** – M. U. Balfe.

Results	Band	Score	No. Performers	Conductor
1st	Crosland Moor Public	95		
2nd	Thurlstone	90		
3rd	Woodroyd	77		

Second Division Test Piece – Bands Own Selection.

1st	Crosland Moor Public	96		
2nd	Thurlstone	94		
3rd	Woodroyd	81		

1930 – Hope Bank Pleasure Grounds. (September) Maximum number of marks 100.
First Division Test Piece – **Les Diamanta de la Couronne** – Auber.

Results	Band	Score	No. Performers	Conductor
1st	Thurlstone	89		
2nd	Woodroyd	86		
3rd	Crosland Moor United	80		

Second Division Test Piece – **Reminiscences of Donizetti** – Arrangement (R. Graham Harvey) – 5 Bands entered but Saddleworth, and Penistone Spring Vale DNC.

1st tie	Woodroyd	79		
1st tie	Crosland Moor United	79		
3rd	Thurlstone	78		

1931 – Hope Bank Pleasure Grounds. (September)
First Division Test Piece – Light Cavalry – Von Suppé.

1st	Thurlstone
2nd	Crosland Moor United
3rd A tie	Woodroyd
3rd	Saddleworth

Second Division Test piece – ?

1st	Saddleworth
2nd	Woodroyd
3rd	Thurlstone

1932 – Victoria Co-operative Hall, New Street, Huddersfield.
First Division Test Piece - ?

Results	Band	Score	No. Performers	Conductor
1st	Thurlstone			
2nd	?			
3rd	?			

Second Division – Test Piece - ?

1st	Thurlstone
2nd	?
3rd	?

Yorkshire Hand-Bell Ringers Association Contests Adjudicators 1904 1932

1904 – Mr A. Jowett, Mus. Bac., Oxon, Leeds
1905 – Mr A. Jowett.
1906 – Mr J.O. Shepherd.
1907 – Mr Lewis Booth, Bradford.

1908 – Thos. Hoggett, Mus. Bac., F.R.C.O. Mus. Bac., F.R.C.O. L.R.A.M.
1909 – Dr A. Eaglefield Hall.
1910 – Mr. A. Jowett, Mus. Bac., Oxon, Leeds.
1911 – Mr. John Rigg.
1912 – Mr. Albert Jowett.
1913 – Mr. Frank Owen, L.L.C.M., Manchester.
1914 – Mr. Frank Owen
1915 – Mr. Thos. J. Hoggett.
1916 to 1919 – No Contests due to World war 1.
1920 – Mr. Frank Owen.
1921 – Mr. Thos.J.Hoggett, Leeds University.
1922 – Mr. Thos.J.Hoggett.
1923 – Mr. A. Jowett.
1924 – Mr. Harry Barlow, Prestwich, Manchester.
1925 – Harry Barlow.
1926 – Dr. Keighley, Ashton-under-Lyne.
1927 – Mr. I. Hirst, F.R.C.O. Ilkley.
1928 – Mr. T.J. Hoggett.
1929 – Mr. Arthur Pearson, Mus. Bac., Oxon, F.R.C.O., Huddersfield.
1930 – Mr. J. Fletcher Sykes, Huddersfield.
1931 – Mr. Frank Owen.
1932 - ? – No record of contest found.

Appendix 4

Pub Bands of Hand-bell Ringers

Taken from addresses in the John Jennison Contests Ledgers 1856 – 1876. (Reproduced with kind permission of Chetham's Library, Manchester.)

This list of names is the first tangible evidence of those hand-bell bands which operated from public houses in olden times. I am sure further research will unearth more of them, but at least now legend has been replaced by fact.

1856 – St Thoma's, Pendleton. Lancashire. – The May Pole Inn, Pendleton. (No longer exists).

1857 - Hurst Brook. nr Stalybridge, Manchester, Lancashire. – The Ring O' Bells, 1 Hillgate Street, Hurst Brook. (No longer exists).

1859 – Oldham Original, The Coach and Horses, 459, Huddersfield road, Oldham, OL4 2HT. (*Still in operation and considered one of the best public houses in Oldham).

1861 - Heckmondwike. The Queens Hotel, Dewsbury Road, Heckmondwike, Yorkshire. (Still in operation).

1862 – 1864 – Dewsbury. The Three Measures Arms, Long Causeway? Dewsbury. (No longer exists).

1863 – Heckmondwike Campanalogian. The Lower George Inn, Dewsbury Road, Heckmondwike. (Demolished in 2009).

1864 – 1867 - Batley. - The George Inn, Wellington Street, Batley. (Now an Asian Restaurant)

1865 – Heywood. - The Kings Arms, Market Street, Heywood, Lancashire. (No longer in existence)

1867 – Rawmarsh. - The Road House Inn, Rotherham, Yorkshire. (No longer in existence)

1869 – Royal Albert Campanalogian Birmingham. The Coach and Horses, Irving Street, Birmingham.

Appendix 5

Examples of John Jennison's Handwritten Record of Entries in the Bell Vue Hand-bell Competitions

Appendix 6

Shelley Hand-bell Ringers
A. List of Engagements and prizes

HISTORICAL NOTES

We can only pay our debt to the past by putting the future in debt to ourselves — John Buchan, Lord Tweedsmuir.

"Hand bells are used by steeple ringers. They need them to learn.

In this country there are any number of small peals to be found wherever there is steeple bells.

Handbells are used also to play tunes and from 1860 to until after the First World War it became popular in Yorkshire especially in the Huddersfield district.

A peal of bells is about 5.50 octaves.

Contests started at Belle Vue, Manchester. Shelley HBR won first prize about 1861 conducted by Ben Cook. The following year nothing as some of the men were worse for drink. That was the last of that band.

A new one was started and won 4th prize at Belle Vue then 3rd the following year, 2nd and 1st prize the next three years.

They were barred from competing for three years and Glossop in Derbyshire won 1st prize those three years.

They then challenged Shelley for £50 that they could beat them. Shelley accepted the challenge and the contest took place at Belle Vue on December 26th 1874. There were three judges. Each band chose a judge and J. Jennison engaged the third. Shelley won the challenge and afterwards won the first prize three years again in 1876, '77 & '78.

They were barred two years at Belle Vue but the band never won another prize as some of the members removed from the district.

Shelley were the first band to use duplicate bells. 61 bells (5 octaves) were considered a good set of bells but after duplicates were brought in peals of 170 were made and a larger table had to be used."

The above notes are a transcript from the original handwritten notes made by my grandfather, Kaye Cooke, which I found whilst sorting out some papers of my mother's (Kaye Cooke's daughter).

Note the change of spelling in the name Cook — between my great-grandfather, Ben Cook, and his son (my grandfather), Kaye Cooke.

I have medals in my possession presented for winning various competitions — the spelling of the surname is used in both its forms. The earliest medal is dated 1868.

J. K. TAYLOR
Bury

SHELLEY HAND-BELL RINGERS.

THIS Band was formed August 24th, 1864, and was dissolved April 18th, 1883, after a very successful career.

The Band appeared at 11 Contests at Belle Vue, Manchester, was twice medalled off, and was debarred from contesting for three years first time, and for one year second time. Two first prizes were won with 8 men, conductor ringing.

The Band appeared at 22 Contests and gained 15½ first prizes, and had one special contest with the Glossop Band at Belle Vue, Manchester, Dec. 28th, 1874, for a prize of £50, and the Championship of England; Shelley won this prize. This Contest arose from Belle Vue circulars debarring Shelley Band from competing during the years 1871-2-3, when Glossop Band took the first prizes these 3 years and claimed the championship. This Shelley Band could not allow, as the three contests were not open ones.

Shelley played the three following pieces:

"Symphony No. 1, in Solomon's Sett"	...	Haydn
"Symphony No. 11, Letter A...	...	Haydn
"Overture to 'Zanetta'" (which is a Masterpiece) ...		Auber

Glossop Band played

"Symphony No. 1, in Solomon's Sett"	...	Haydn
"Half-hours with the best Composers"	...	Mendelssohn
"'Gloria,' (chorus) from Mozart's 12th Mass"	...	Mozart

Shelley first introduced Double Bells in 1866, and Treble Bells in 1867. They also first introduced high-class music at the Belle Vue Contests, Manchester, in 1869, when they played Haydn's "Surprise Symphony,"

which was a great achievement at these Contests. 18 Bands competed at this Contest, which was never exceeded before or after up to the year 1911. At this contest the Glossop Band had no music, and played the "Merry Bells" Polka eight times over from memory.

In 1870 the Shelley Band played No. 1 Symphony, Solomon Sett, Haydn, and in 1877 for an Extra Prize they played the Overture to the "Marriage of Figaro,"—Mozart. The latter selection was only sent out 14 days before the Contest. Shelley took both First Prizes this year.

The Band appeared at over 400 Concerts. The greatest reception was at Mr. DE JONG'S Concert, Jan. 10th 1874, in the Free Trade Hall, Manchester, which was crowded. The Band played the Overture to "Caliph of Bagdad,"—Boildeau, with his Orchestral Band of 75 players. This has not been attempted with any Ringers since.

The original Ringers were:—

FRED SHAW, ARTHA COOK, JESSE COOK, ALFRED HAIGH, ELLIOT KILNER, CHRISTOPHER ALDERSON, WILLIAM SHAW, and BEN COOK, Conductor.

There were five others joined the Band and did good service, viz., CHARLES BERRY, GEORGE HAIGH, ANDREW BARDEN, GEORGE HENRY TAYLOR, and HENRY ROBERTS, but we have had no other photo taken.

The Mechanics' Institute Soiree, Shelley, Dec. 27th, 1880, was the last time the old Band played together, and the last pieces were Handel's "Hallelujah Chorus," and "God save the Queen."

N.B.—Almondbury competed 15 times before being debarred once. Crosland Moor ,, 15 times before being debarred once.

The above particulars were taken from the minutes of the Band book.

{ FRED SHAW,
September, 1911. { ARTHA COOK.

D. Fred Shaw – Obituary

Fred Shaw

One of the old Shelley Hand-bell Ringers

It is with deep regret that we have to announce the death, which occurred at his home, 46, Victoria Terrace, Blackburn, near Sheffield, on Thursday, of Mr. Fred Shaw, manager of the Rainforth Colliery Co., Ltd., Grange Lane, Rotherham.

Recently we published an article dealing with the career of the deceased, who was one of the old Shelley Hand-bell Ringers. After leaving Shelley Mr. Shaw went to reside at Kirkburton, where he will always be remembered for the interest he took in the inauguration of the musical festival there.
For a period of twenty-eight years he did much to improve the musical tone of the district, and at the last meeting was again elected president.
Becoming interested in the Rainforth Colliery about twelve months ago he left this district to

take up duties there, and whilst engaged in the mine a few weeks ago met with an accident. His back was broken, and with the complications which ensued there was practically no hope of his recovery from the first.

Huddersfield Examiner Dec 20th 1913.

E. Ben Cooke's Grave

Fig. 151: Ben Cooke's Grave

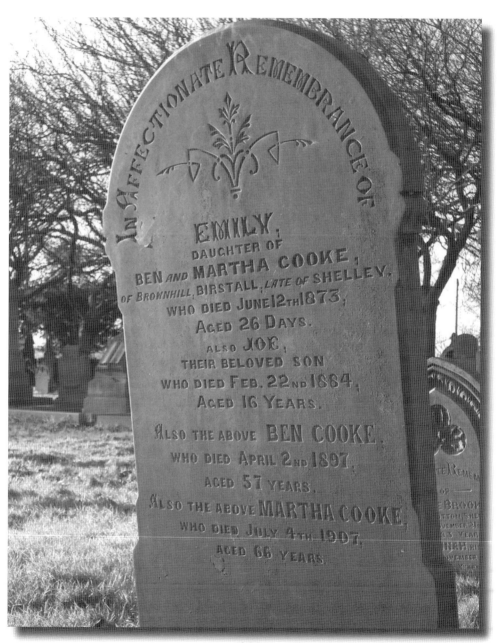

Appendix 7

Almondbury Hand-bell Ringers – Miscellaneous Documents

Almondbury Contract to Tour the USA

MEMORANDUM of AGREEMENT made and entered into the tenth day of May, One Thousand nine hundred and one by and between George H. Hathaway & Co. of Boston, Massachusetts, U.S.A., doing business under the style and title of Redpath Lyceum Bureau, party of the first part and hereinafter for the purposes of brevity called the Bureau, and the following Members of the Almondbury Troupe of Hand Bell Ringers of Almondbury Huddersfield, England.

G. H. Godward	H. Harrison
J. B. Dawson	J. Stansfield
A. Jenkinson	B. Lodge, (Conductor)

the parties of the second part, and hereinafter called for purposes of brevity "The Troupe."

WITNESSETH that for and inconsideration of the sum of One Dollar ($1.00) in hand paid by each of the parties to the other, the receipts whereof are hereby acknowledged and in further consideration of the mutual and reciprocal Covenants and Agreements hereinafter set forth the parties covenant promise and agree together as follows:--

1. The Troupe agree to place at the disposal of the Bureau their exclusive professional Services as Hand Bell Ringers for a series of Concerts in the United States of America and in the Dominion of Canada for a period of twelve weeks, beginning on or about October 14th, 1901-- and the troupe further agree that the Bureau shall have the exclusive right privilege and option of extending the season and securing the Services of the Troupe for a further period after the expiration of the twelve weeks above named on the same terms and conditions as herein set forth, provided, however, that the Bureau shall give Notice of their intention to exercise the said option privilege within six weeks of the Troupe's ... the Bureau ... the said option privilege to be exercised in writing and delivered to Mr. Ben Lodge, or the Leader of the Troupe within the time named:-- The Troupe further covenant and agree that the Bureau shall have the exclusive right privilege or option of renewing this Contract for another season, viz:- "That commencing October 1902, should they wish to do so, on terms mutually arranged but not to exceed the sums specified and set forth in this Agreement. The Bureau to give notice of their intention to exercise such option privilege on or before the 1st of March 1902 in the manner above provided but it shall be entirely optional with the Troupe whether or not they accept the extension of the Engagement for Winter of 1902-3 if offered by the Bureau."

2. The Troupe hereby covenant and agree that they will give Six (6) Evening Concerts and Two (2) Matinees each week (if desired) and will render at all such Concerts and Matinees a programme such as shall be approved by the Bureau and will at all times modify or alter their programme if desired by the Bureau or their representative. Such concerts and Matinees shall be given at such times and places and under such conditions as the Bureau may arrange. The Troupe undertake to appear in good Evening Dress Costumes, and at all times to dress respectably and conduct themselves with propriety both on and off the Platform as befits the nature of the proposed Entertainments should they be given (as is often the case) under the auspices of Churches and other Religious bodies and organizations.

3. The Troupe covenant and agree that under no conditions nor for any reason or on any pretext whatever shall said troupe or any member thereof appear in any Concert or Entertainment for the purpose of taking part therein at any

time during the period of this Contract or any extensions thereof, and it is covenanted that the Bureau may by appropriate legal proceedings restrain the troupe or any member thereof from violating this Covenant, the purpose thereof being to give the Redpath Lyceum Bureau the sole and exclusive right to the professional Services of such troupe and each member thereof during the period of this Contract and its extensions, if any.

Nothing in this clause contained shall however prevent the Bureau from waiving under Special circumstances their sole and exclusive right to the exclusive Services of such troupe or any member thereof to appear professionally at any Concert or Entertainment as may be mutually decided or agreed upon by the Bureau or their authorized Agent.

4. For such Services to be rendered and performed according to the true intent and meaning of this Contract the Bureau hereby agree to pay the Troupe the sum of Thirtysix pounds (£36) per week for each and every week during the continuance of this contract or any extensions thereof-- Salary to commence from the date of the first concert. The Bureau, however, shall have the option of arranging for a rehearsal week immediately after the arrival of the Troupe and whilst they are recovering from the Sea Voyage, such Rehearsal week to commence on or about October 7th and for such Rehearsal week (if arranged) they shall pay the Troupe half-salaries.

The Bureau shall also have the option of suspending the Concerts during the week in which Christmas occurs, should it be found impracticable to arrange for Concerts to be given during that week, and if such week's suspension becomes necessary, the Bureau shall not be liable for Salaries during such time, but shall nevertheless provide Board and Lodging for the Troupe in the same way and manner as if they were at work. The Bureau also agree to pay the usual travelling and Lodging, three meals per day, Baggage transportation to and from Hotels to Railway Depots, also Car or Bus transportation from Depot to Hotel and Hotel to Depot whenever in the opinion of the Bureau or their authorized Agent the same shall be expedient or desirable, and the Bureau agree that lodging for the Troupe shall be provided only at Standard Commercial Hotels, and that the Concerts shall be given in first-class Halls, and the Bureau further agree to provide for 3rd Class Railway transportation from Huddersfield to the place of Embarkation (probably Liverpool) and for second-class Cabin accommodation across the Atlantic but the Bureau reserve to themselves the right to furnish such transportation either in the form of tickets or money.

And it is further agreed that at the termination of this contract or of any extension thereof the Bureau shall pay or provide second Cabin transportation for said troupe from New York City or Boston to Liverpool or other port and third-class tickets from the port of arrival to Huddersfield for such members of the Troupe as return, but should the troupe or any member thereof desire to remain in the United States after the termination of this Contract or any extension thereof, the Bureau shall not be bound to provide such member or members of the troupe with their return fares.

5. It is agreed that the said Troupe may substitute another person for any of the parties hereto if by reason of illness or other cause, any individual member is incapacitated from carrying out the terms of this Agreement, but such substitute shall be competent to fill the vacancy.

Should the Troupe by reason of illness or other cause be incapacitated from giving their performance the Bureau shall

not be bound to pay Salaries until such time as the Concerts can be renewed with the same degree of Artistic excellence as before such illness or incapacity. This Clause shall not be operative on account of any temporary or trivial indisposition of any member of the Troupe.

Signed (George H. Hathaway Co.
        (for Redpath Lyceum Bureau
        (
        (
        (

Witnessed by
Ira G. Law.

LIVERPOOL HOMES FOR AGED MARINERS.

OPENED BY H.R.H. THE DUKE OF EDINBURGH
16TH DECEMBER, 1882.

THE CENTRAL BUILDING, erected at the sole cost of the late Mr. W. CLIFF, is provided for the entire maintenance of Aged Mariners (Shipmasters, Officers, and Seamen). There are now sixty-two inmates in the "Cliff Home."

THE COTTAGE HOMES, in the same grounds, viz.—the "SLACK Cottages," the "DIXON Cottages," the "KELLOCK Cottage," the "SANDER Cottage," the "REYNER Cottages," the "FORWOOD Cottages," the "'AURANIA' and 'ETRURIA' Cottages," the "BACON Cottages," the "PICKUP Cottages," the "ASHTON Cottages," the "BROCKLEHURST Cottages," the "MCINNES Cottages," and the "POTTER Cottages"—are for Aged Mariners who have Wives or other suitable Relatives to live with them, or as may be determined by the Council. Here they have a comfortable house, firing, gas, water, and taxes free, and, in many cases, a small pension, with liberty to engage in ship-keeping or other suitable employment.

THE PARK will admit of additional Cottages being erected and endowed.

OUT-PENSIONS, for Aged Mariners who have friends they prefer to reside amongst, but who cannot maintain them altogether ; and CASUAL RELIEF TO THE WIDOWS OF MARINERS are also included in the objects of the Institution as the funds are provided.

DONORS of £5,000 may name a Ward, and Donors of £1,000 may name a Cabin in the Main Building.

THE further munificence of the late Mr. W. CLIFF, in erecting a Hospital, has placed additional accommodation for inmates at the disposal of the Council as the funds permit.

President—Capt. J. PRICE, R.N.R.   Vice-President—Capt. M. H. FOSTER, A.I.N.A.

Treasurer—J. H. STOCK, Esq., M.P.   Secretary—C. P. GRYLLS, Esq.

Offices—67 & 68, TOWER BUILDINGS, WATER STREET, LIVERPOOL,

Where Subscriptions and Donations may be paid and all information obtained.

AN ENDOWMENT FUND OF AT LEAST FIFTY THOUSAND POUNDS IS AN URGENT NECESSITY.

Programme of Entertainment

In aid of the
LIVERPOOL HOMES FOR AGED MARINERS

Held at Sea on Board

S.S. "NEW ENGLAND"

TUESDAY EVENING, MAY 13th, 1902, at 8 p.m.,

in the

FIRST CLASS DINING SALOON.

President - - - - - Capt. JOHN JAMES.
Chairman - - - - - Mr G. B. CHANDLER.

PART I.

1. Pianoforte Solo ... ... Miss Gertrude Bailey
2. Song ... ..."To the Night" ... ... Miss M. Sparks
3. Selection ... ... Almondbury Hand-Bell Ringers
4. Recitation ... ..."The little small Red Hen" ... Miss M. Fuller
5. Violin Solo... ... Mr B. R Jones accompanied by Miss Spinks
6. Song ... ... Mrs. Kline
7. Recitation ... "The Petrified Fern" ...Miss H. Schurmeier
8. Selection ... ... Almondbury Hand-Bell Ringers

——:o:——

Chairman's Remarks.

Collection on behalf of the Charities.

——:o:——

PART II.

9. Pianoforte Solo ... ... Miss Owen
10. Selection ... ..." Reminiscences" ... Mr C. W. Little
11. Song & Violin Obligato... "La Serenata" ... ... Miss Spinks
12. Selection ... ... Almondbury Hand-Bell Ringers
13. Recitation ... "The Yarn of the Mary Bell" Mr. C. Russell James
14. Song ... ... Mr. Kline
15. Selection ... ... Almondbury Hand-Bell Ringers

"My Country 'tis of thee" and "God Save the King"

Almondbury Hand Bell Ringers.

DIRECT FROM LONDON.

ASSISTED BY

Eva Bartlett Macey, Entertainer,

AND

Walter David, Impersonator.

PROGRAMME.

---

1. MARCH, . "Champion," *Lodge*
   ALMONDBURY HAND BELL RINGERS.
   MR. B. LODGE, MR. G. H. GODWARD, MR. H. HARRISON,
   MR. J. B. DAWSON, MR. J. STANSFIELD,
   MR. A. JENKINSON.

2. MONOLOGUE, . . . *Selected*
   EVA BARTLETT MACEY.

3. WALTZ, "Chimes,"
   BELL RINGERS.

4. BANJO SOLO, . Air Varie, . *Arr. by Macey*
   MISS MACEY.

5. SONG, . . "Kentucky Babe,"
   BELL RINGERS.

6. "A Musical Family," . . *Arr. by Macey*
   MISS MACEY.

7. RECITAL { *a.* "A Character Sketch,"
   { *b.* "The Sweet Girl Graduate,'
   WALTER DAVID.

8. GALOP, . "De Concert,"
   BELL RINGERS.

9. Mr. David and Miss Macey in "Come Here."
   (An Incident.)

10. SELECTION.
    BELL RINGERS.

Exclusive Management Redpath Lyceum Bureau, Boston—Chicago.

313

THE GREATEST OF ALL SUCCESSES

THE FAMOUS
Almondbury Hand-Bell Ringers

(CHAMPIONS OF ENGLAND)

Mr. B. LODGE, Conductor	Mr. G. H. GODWARD	Mr. H. HARRISON
Mr. J. H. DAWSON	Mr. J. STANSFIELD	Mr. A. JENKINSON

———— ASSISTING ARTISTS ————

Miss EVA BARTLETT MACY, Entertainer   Mr. WALTER DAVID, Humorist

Read the following letters and press notices. In fifty concerts since opening of tour the Company has not received one unfavorable criticism.

LETTERS

FREDERICKSBURG, VA., Nov. 20, 1901.
Redpath Lyceum Bureau,

My dear Sirs : The Bell Ringers gave a most delightful entertainment in our city. The audience was large and highly cultivated. All were enthusiastic in praise. They want the Bell Ringers again. I enclose press notices.

Yours respectfully,
KATE T. DILL,
President of Lyceum Association.

NEW BEDFORD, MASS., Nov. 6, 1901.
Redpath Lyceum Bureau,

Gentlemen : I enclose press notices, as desired, and would say the entertainment was accepted as interesting and satisfactory. I have failed to hear any adverse criticisms and am quite sure all were well pleased. The clippings from our papers will perhaps be of value to you.

Yours very truly,
WILLIAM H. WOOD,
Chairman Lecture Committee.

LYNDONVILLE, VT., Nov. 11, 1901.
Redpath Lyceum Bureau,

Gentlemen : The Almondbury Bell Ringers gave excellent satisfaction to our people. They are all right. Miss Macy and Mr. David are equal to anything in their line that we have ever had here,—many say superior.

Yours truly,
E. M. CAMPBELL.

BALTIMORE, MD., Nov. 12.
Redpath Lyceum Bureau,

The Almondbury Hand-bell Ringers fully sustained their reputation at the concert recently given by them in our hall. We have enjoyed the Royal Hand-bell Ringers several times and these men compare very favorably. They give a strong and exceedingly pleasing entertainment.

W. H. MORRISS,
General Secretary Y. M. C. A.

ATTLEBORO, MASS.
Our people were highly pleased with the Almondbury Hand-bell Ringers and the concert was perfectly satisfactory. Miss Macy is a good card.

A. C. EAGLESON.

P. S. Our hall was packed.

CHARLOTTE, N. C., Nov. 18, 1901.
Redpath Lyceum Bureau,

Gentlemen : Your inquiry as to the Bell Ringers received. I enclose you a clipping from the *News,* also one from the *Observer,* both of Nov. 8, 1901.

The Bell Ringers were most favorably received and greatly appreciated, and their performance was most agreeable to an enormous audience, the largest we have ever had on such an occasion.

Very respectfully,
GEO. B. HANNA,
President Y. M. C. A.

ONEONTA, N. Y., Nov. 6, 1901.
Redpath Lyceum Bureau,

Gentlemen : I am very much pleased to advise you that the concert given by the Almondbury Hand-bell Ringers was very satisfactory. The company is a strong one in every particular, and it is hard to mention the feature which is entitled to the first place. The work of the Bell Ringers gave very great pleasure to our people.

An Oneonta audience is said to be cold and unresponsive ; but if this is a fact it was not in evidence at the entertainment, as the applause was hearty from the very beginning.

An exceptional thing for an Oneonta audience occurred when, after the closing number, the people still wished to hear more from the company and tried to secure an encore.

The work of Miss Macy came up fully to what we had heard of her work. This can also be said of Mr. David.

The company we are glad to recommend to all.

Yours truly,
O. B. ROWE.

MORRISVILLE, VT., Nov. 1, 1901.
Redpath Lyceum Bureau,

Gentlemen : We mail you under separate cover two local papers that speak of your entertainment here Oct. 24. In behalf of the committee of the Business Men's Course I wish to state that the Bell Ringers and their assistants gave perfect satisfaction. Many of our people pronounced it the best thing they ever attended in our hall in any course, and we have heard of no one that was not satisfied, which is remarkable.

Yours truly,
A. L. CHENEY.

314

WINSTON-SALEM, N. C., Nov. 14, 1901.
Redpath Lyceum Bureau,

Gentlemen : Your Bureau is to be congratulated upon bringing the Almondbury Hand-bell Ringers to America for a tour. Assisted by Mr. Walter David, impersonator, and Miss Eva Macy, entertainer, this company gave, on the 6th inst., one of the best and most enjoyable entertainments ever given in our hall. They were heard by a large and cultured audience, all of whom speak in the highest terms of the organization.

Very truly yours,
A. W. HICKS,
General Secretary Y. M. C. A.

HAGERSTOWN, MD., Nov. 23, 1901.

The Almondbury Bell Ringer Company entertainment, the first number on our course, came off in fine style ; the Bell Ringers are all right and gave great satisfaction. Miss Macy and Mr. David are the talk of the town ; as entertainers they are hard to beat. The enclosed newspaper clipping will show how the press regards the company.

HENRY HOLZAPFEL, JR.

WORCESTER, MASS., Nov. 5, 1901.
Redpath Lyceum Bureau,

I was pleased with their manipulation of the bells, which, to my mind, was very good, and their rendering of "Kentucky Babe" was very pleasing. I think, without exception they were called for the second selection.

Very truly yours,
C. C. Miles,
General Secretary Y. M. C. A.

PETERSBURG, VA., Nov. 13, 1901.
Redpath Lyceum Bureau,

Gentlemen : The Almondbury Hand-bell Ringers gave us entire satisfaction and were well supported by Miss Macy and Mr. David. Respectfully yours,
J. H. SHERRILL,
General Secretary Y. M. C. A.

ANNVILLE, PA., Nov. 22, 1901.
Redpath Lyceum Bureau,

Sirs : The Almondbury Hand-bell Ringers gave us one of the finest entertainments that was ever heard in this place. The large audience was delighted with their performances. The Almondbury Bell Ringers are pronounced by those to whom bell ringers are not a new thing as being the best they have ever heard.

Yours very truly,
J. WALTER ESBENSHADE,
Chairman Lecture Committee,
Y. W. and Y. M. C. A. of
Lebanon Valley College.

PHILADELPHIA, Nov. 23, 1901.
Redpath Lyceum Bureau,

The Almondbury Hand-bell Ringers Company were a great success. We had a crowded house and the audience was enthusiastic from start to finish, — every number encored. Miss Macy is exceedingly clever in her work, and Mr. David was a genuine surprise to me. He is artistic through and through and has few equals in his line. The whole combination is an unusually strong one. Yours very truly,
CHAS. H. WEVILL.
Central Branch Y. M. C. A.

PRESS NOTICES

Attleboro, Mass. — The first of the series of concerts given under the Y. M. C. A. auspices took place Saturday evening in their hall. The room was filled to its extreme limit and some late arrivals were turned away. The attendance assured the association of all the expenses of the entire course, so they are sure of financial success from now forward. The entertainment was one which received the favorable comment of every one who was there.

The Hand-bell Ringers are something far out of the ordinary entertainers with that specialty, and the reader, humorist, and outside instrumentalist were equally good. The tone of the whole performance was elevated, and while the features were diverting they were of the most commendable sort clear through. — *Daily Sun.*

Fredericksburg, Va. — Should the balance of the entertainments to be given under the auspices of the Lyceum Association in this city prove themselves one half as entertaining as the opening one last evening then the ladies of the association need not lose a moment's sleep over the future of the Lyceum in Fredericksburg. The Opera House last evening, when the Almondbury Bell Ringers began their performance, contained one of the most cultured and appreciative audiences ever in attendance on a similar occasion in this city. Every seat in the house was filled, and from the initial march, rendered beautifully by the Bell Ringers themselves, to the closing selection, the audience was "all attention." The rendition of "Auld Lang Syne," at the close of the entertainment, by the Bell Ringers, was a most fitting farewell, and, from a musical standpoint, was perfect. Every selection played during the evening by

these men, who handle their bells as easily and gracefully as the finished artist handles the violin, was enthusiastically received by the audience. The entertainment would, however, be far from complete without the presence of Miss Eva Bartlett Macy and Mr. Walter David, these two furnishing the fun of the evening. Miss Macy's inimitable banjo playing charmed those present and character sketches by herself and Mr. David kept every one in a roar of laughter. The latter's sermon on Mother Hubbard, her cupboard and dog was a gem of humor, Mr. David's impersonation of the preacher being simply fine. The entire entertainment was a brilliant success.

Charlotte, N. C. — Association Hall was packed last night for the concert of the Almondbury Hand-bell Ringers Company and everybody enjoyed the entertainment. The Bell Ringers were certainly artists in their line and there was a mellowness about the music which made it very enjoyable.

The program was varied by the work of the assisting artists, Miss Macy and Mr. David.

Miss Macy is an elocutionist of rare talent and was repeatedly encored. Her performance on the banjo was very fine.

Mr. David's facial expression is remarkable. He kept his audience in great good humor and his fun will long be remembered. — *News.*

Hagerstown, Md. — The first number of the Star Course was presented last evening at the Academy of Music to a delighted audience. The attraction was the Almondbury Bell Ringers, of England, assisted by Miss Macy, reader, and Mr. Walter David, humorist and impersonator. The performers were in splendid form; the hall was comfortable and beautifully decorated. To all present it was a source of wonder and pleasure that such sweet music could be obtained from bells. Classic and popular selections were alike rendered in the most artistic manner. Miss Macy is undeniably one of the best readers that ever appeared before a Hagerstown audience. Her selections were varied and afforded an excellent opportunity of displaying her abilities as an elocutionist, which, coupled with her splendid stage appearance, made her at once a favorite. Mr. Walter David's mannerisms, sparkling wit and comic acting class him as a natural humorist. Taken as a whole, it was an evening of refined pleasure. — *Morning Herald.*

Hagerstown, Md. — Everybody fortunate enough to be there last night pronounced the Almondbury Bell Ringers, the first of the Star Course series of entertainments provided by Henry Holzapfel, Jr., the star of all the other stars that have previously existed. The bell-ringing, of itself superior and masterly, was only a part of the pleasure. Miss Macy as a reader was regarded the peer of any that has ever appeared here in this rôle. Walter David, humorist and impersonator, leavened the loaf with his drolleries, wit, and naturalness. He has the keen perception of a close observer, and the happy faculty of mimicry that makes the original seem like the counterfeit. The audience showed their pleasure and appreciation of each number, and encores were as frequent as the parts of the set program. — *Globe.*

Morrisville, Vt. — The entertainment by the Almondbury Bell Ringers and their able assistants, Walter David and Miss Eva Bartlett Macy, was a decided success, and a fitting opening of an unusually well-selected course. Each number given by the Almondburys was enthusiastically received, and it was the general opinion that they were fully up to the expectation of all. Especially fine was their rendering of the closing number, "Nearer, My God, to Thee."

Miss Macy, elocutionist and musician, has a charming presence, and gave a variety of entertainments that could not fail to please all. Each number given by her was heartily received, and it would be difficult to choose any one for special mention. She is an artist of rare ability, and should she again visit Morrisville is assured of a hearty welcome.

Mr David as a humorist is one of the best ever heard here. His appearance before the audience was a signal for laughter and applause. The selections given showed him to be possessed of ability far above the average.

Finally, the entertainment was a decided success, and reflects credit upon the management in their selection for the initial number. — *News and Citizen.*

Morrisville, Vt. — The first entertainment of the course at the superb Metropolitan Temple of Art last evening promises well for the success of the course. The hall was filled, and such an average attendance will make a big success of the course. The bell-ringing was thoroughly good, the impersonations by Mr. David were excellent, and the acts of Miss Macy were superb. The writer would place the merit of the entertainment in the order named. Seldom if ever has such music been heard here as was made by Miss Macy on the banjo, and it was easily the feature of the evening from an artistic standpoint. — *Messenger.*

Westerly, R. I. — The opening entertainment in the lecture course given by the choir of the Seventh-day Baptist Church was held last evening. The Almondbury Hand-bell Ringers with their fine peal of one hundred and sixty-two bells was the attraction. All the seats in the church had been sold some days previous to the opening night, and a number of chairs were also occupied. The music by the Bell Ringers was excellent, and fully met the expectation of the large audience. Miss Macy, the elocutionist, from the Emerson School of Oratory, of Boston, rendered her selections in a highly pleasing manner, while Mr. David, the impersonator and humorist, proved a fine entertainer. Repeated encores were given, and the artists responded generously.

Frederick, Md. — The concert at the City Opera House last night by the Almondbury Hand-bell Ringers was a unique and delightful entertainment. The audience was large and very appreciative, and the performers were encored time and again.

"Kentucky Babe" was beautifully rendered by the Bell Ringers, and the audience was especially well pleased with the selection. Miss Eva Bartlett Macy is an elocutionist of signal ability, and her selections were greatly enjoyed. Her recital of the bull-fight, the national sport of Spain, was very fine. Mr. Walter David is a thoroughly trained impersonator, and his two selections were pronounced the best ever heard in this city. Mr. David and Miss Macy in "Come Here" highly delighted and greatly amused the audience. The concert was the first of the Y. M. C. A. course, and if the other entertainments are to be judged by the concert last night the course will be a most successful one. — *Daily News.*

Winston-Salem, N. C. — The committee made no mistake in the selection of the Almondbury Hand-bell Ringers to give the opening entertainment in the Y. M. C. A. Star Course.

The auditorium was crowded last evening with a representative and appreciative audience, and the hearty encore that followed each selection was convincing of the audience's appreciation. The Bell Ringers were superb, while Miss Eva Bartlett Macy fully sustained her reputation as an entertainer. Mr. Walter David was captivating in his impersonations. The company left on the six o'clock train this morning for Charlotte, where it will appear to-night. The Bell Ringers made many friends here, who would delight to have them return and give another of their charming entertainments. — *Twin-City Daily Sentinel.*

Lyndonville, Vt. — The first entertainment of the Lecture Course, given at Music Hall, Saturday evening, by the Almondbury Hand-bell Ringers, assisted by Miss Eva Bartlett Macy, entertainer, and Mr. Walter David, humorist, was a great success, being attended by about five hundred people. The concert by the Bell Ringers was all that could be expected, and the recitals by Miss Macy were well rendered, while it has been said that one of the humorous sketches by Mr. David was worth the price of admission to the entire course. — *Journal.*

Charlotte, N. C. — A very large audience attended the performance of the Almondbury Hand-bell Ringers at the Y. M. C. A. auditorium last night. Every available seat was occupied and many considered themselves fortunate in being able to obtain standing-room. The audience did not hesitate to evince its surprise and delight at the wonderful music made by Prof. B. Lodge

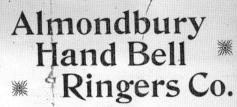

What They Say About The

Almondbury Hand Bell Ringers Co.

Champions of England.

Mr. B. LODGE, Conductor. Mr. G. H. GODWARD, Mr. H. HARRISON, Mr. J. H. DAWSON,
Mr. J. STANSFIELD, Mr. A. JENKINSON.

...ASSISTED BY...

Miss Eva Bartlett Maccy,
Entertainer, Reader, Pianoist, Banjoist.

Mr. Walter David,
Impersonator and Humorist.

Y. M. C. A., FALL RIVER MASS., Oct. 9, 1901.

The Bell Ringers are all right. Miss Macey is entirely satisfactory and David is not outclassed with the others. We were very much pleased with the entire company. Had a good house, and am ahead without further effort. Yours very truly,
W. D. FELLOWS.

LEBANON, N. H., Oct. 17, 1901.

The Bell Ringers are a great success from the word go. We have listened to the Swiss and Spaulding Bell Ringers, but the Almondbury company is the finest thus far. Miss Macey in her easy, graceful stage presence; in her naturalness; in her correct conception and happy rendering of the part she assumes; in the variety of effort to which with marked success she gives herself, make her a prime favorite.

Mr. David is one of the most agreeable managers I have had the pleasure of meeting. His work upon the platform is immensely taking, there is nothing cheap about it, it is first-class. Altogether the entertainment opened up the course finely and all are glad.
Yours cordially,
EDGAR T. FARRILL.

PROVIDENCE, R. I., Oct. 19, 1901.

Redpath Lyceum Bureau, 120 Tremont Street, Boston, Mass.:

DEAR SIRS: It gives me great pleasure to report to you the warm and enthusiastic reception that was given the concert party consisting of the Almondbury Bell Ringers, assisted by Miss Macey and Mr. David, which was held last night in the M. E. Tabernacle, Olneyville Square. We had a very good house, and every number on the program merited and received an encore. The tone and precision with which the ringers rang their selections was marvelous. Then Miss Macey held the audience spell-bound by the eloquent and easy manner in which she performed her musical and literary numbers, while Mr. David caused much amusement by the quaint and able manner in which he performed his share of the program. Altogether it was a splendid performance and everybody was perfectly satisfied.

Please send me open dates for March, 1902, and terms. Wishing the concert party every success, and awaiting your reply, I am,
Yours very truly,
JOE MOSS.

RANDOLPH CENTER, VERMONT, Oct. 23, 1901.

SIRS:—The Bell Ringers gave us a very excellent program, well sustaining their reputation.
Respectfully,
ELLA L. PERRIN.

WESTERLY, R. I., October 25, 1901.

Redpath Lyceum Bureau:

The Almondbury Bell Ringers gave perfect satisfaction. They are all right.
Yours very truly,
JOHN H. TANNER, JR.

BROCKTON, MASS., Oct. 26, 1901.

Redpath Lyceum Bureau, Boston, Mass.:

GENTLEMEN:—We were very much pleased with the Bell Ringers. They gave us an exceptionally fine entertainment and made our opening night a great success. Yours truly,
WILLIAM ELLISON,
Sec. Y. M. C. A. Star Course Com.

WHITE RIVER JUNCTION, Oct. 21, 1901.

The Redpath Lyceum Bureau, 120 Tremont St., Boston, Mass.:

GENTLEMEN:—Replying to yours of 22d inst., beg to say the first number of our course for this season was by the Almondbury Bell Ringers, assisted by Eva Bartlett Macey and Walter David, and was a very pleasing and interesting entertainment. There certainly is a novelty and charm in the music of the bells not found in any other music. The Almondburys played in perfect time, and the fine shading and beautiful technique with which each selection was rendered showed them to be first-class musicians. They captivated the audience at the start, and were repeatedly applauded and encored.

Eva Bartlett Macey, as banjoist and reciter, and Walter David, as impersonator, proved themselves to be artists of a high order, and gave entire satisfaction.

Hoping to have the pleasure of hearing them all again, I remain,
Very truly yours,
G. C. BOGLE,
President Business Mens' Entertainment Association.

BARTON, VERMONT, Oct. 28, 1901.

Redpath Lyceum Bureau, Boston, Mass.:

DEAR SIRS: The Bell Ringers gave us a concert which gave excellent satisfaction to all and was pronounced by many the best concert we have ever had. Their work with the bells was exceptionally fine while the work of Miss Macey and Mr. David made enough variety to make it a complete success. They both did most excellent work.
H. J. STANNARD.

HARDWICK, VT., Oct. 30, 1901.

Redpath Lyceum Bureau, 120 Tremont Street, Boston, Mass.:

GENTLEMEN: Our people are very enthusiastic in praise of the entertainment given last evening by the Almondbury Hand Bell Ringers assisted by Miss Macey and Mr David. Every number upon the program received an encore and Mr. David was obliged to respond a second time to one number. Am very much pleased with the outcome of this our opening number.
Very truly yours,
W. A. DUTTON.

JOHNSON, VT., Oct. 31, 1901.

Redpath Lyceum Bureau:

The Almondbury Hand Bell Ringers, assisted by Miss Eva Bartlett Macey, and Walter David gave splendid satisfaction and was heartily recalled after each selection. Yours,
L. M. JONES.

FALL RIVER, MASS., Oct. 9, 1901.

The Y. M. C. A. entertainment course for the season of 1901-'02, was most auspiciously opened last evening at the Academy. The attendance was very large, in fact the best house for an opening performance that the course has seen in several years, it is believed. And the entertainment furnished was most refined, embracing a programme of musical selections, monologues, character sketches, recitations, etc., that made a decided hit with the audience and encores were demanded after each number and graciously granted If the remaining numbers of the course prove equally attractive then its success is assured for those who attended last evening found in it so much pleasure that they will be anxious to witness the next.

BOSTON HERALD, Oct. 10, 1901.

The first entertainment of the Boston Young Men's Christian Association Star course was given at Association Hall last night. A concert of exceptional merit was given by the Almondbury Bell Ringers of England, introducing their peal of 162 bells. Miss Eva Bartlett Macy, in a clever monologue was well received Walter Davis was more than clever in his impersonations, and his selections, "A Character Sketch" and "The Sweet Girl Graduate," were warmly applauded.

PLYMOUTH, MASS., Oct. 19, 1901.
JUST SUPERB.

The Almondbury Hand Bell Ringers, who are touring this country under the management of the Redpath Lyceum Bureau, visited Plymouth last week Friday. There was a good sized audience in attendance at Davis Opera House, in spite of the short time for advertising the attraction, and every one who went heard what was probably the best hand bell music in the world, as the Almondburys are the champions, and have captured so many first prizes in contests in England, that they have been ruled out as ineligible for this year. Nothing like their work has been heard here, and unless they return, will not be for many a season. Miss Eva Bartlett Macey and Mr Walter David contributed good variety to the programme with recitations, music and sketches, the entire combination being most agreeable, and one the Redpath Lyceum Bureau should feel proud of.
JOHN W. LEE.

RANDOLPH, VT., Oct. 15, 1901.

The first entertainment in the Randolph Center lecture course was given by the Almondbury Hand Bell Ringers' company last Monday evening at Normal hall and was first-class in every respect. The bell ringers handled the bells with accuracy and precision and produced a very pleasing effect. They were assisted by Eva Bartlett Macey, who stands among the first as elocutionist and banjo soloist, and her selections were fine and execution faultless. Mr. Walter David as impersonator is hard to beat. The whole entertainment was of a very high order and was thoroughly appreciated by all present. The encores were frequent and persistent. The evening was dark and rainy, which prevented many from attending that intended to and they were certainly the losers. It is fortunate for any community to have so perfect an entertainment and of such rare merit as this.

JOHNSON, VT., LOCAL, Oct. 31, 1901.

The Bell Ringers gave their entertainment Monday evening to a large audience and it was generally conceded that if it were the only entertainment in the course that one was was well worth the price of the ticket for the whole.

The Almondbury Hand Bell Ringers are under the Exclusive Control of the Redpath Lyceum Bureau, Boston and Chicago.

Appendix 8

Chippy Choppy Whoop Description from the Handbell Society of Australasia's Handbell Herald No. 18

Orchestrating the Whoop

One problem often faced by off-table teams is the whoop created when big bells are replaced on the table during ringing, often spoiling the clarity of a bass run. How do some teams cope better than others? How can the whoop be turned to advantage? What causes the whoop?

The whoop comes from the sudden and complete stopping of a bell's vibrations simultaneously throughout its length – an almost explosive cessation of sound, and is more accentuated with bells below 22C (C4) in size. The problem is greatest where a team's table covering is fairly heavy, e.g. velvet or blanket material, and is negligible where the material is fairly light, e.g. cotton. This is because the bells' vibrations are not cut off suddenly on being put down but ring on slightly through the "give" in the material and the foam rubber. It is worth noting that high-density foam also whoops more than low-density foam.

There are two ways of minimising the problem. The safest way is to use light table coverings especially for bells 22C (C4) and below. The other is to roll the bell from its tip to its handle upon putting it down – provided there is time!

The whoop, being a distinctive off-table phenomenon can be exploited to very good effect, especially in the middle harmony bells of strict tempo pieces like marches. However, the whoop will probably need to be accentuated for such middle harmony bells as it is not as distinct in bells smaller than 22C (C4). To achieve this accentuation, if we are to play a programme of pieces which includes strict tempo, e.g. jazz, William Gordon marches etc., or pieces in which the whoop is deliberately written into the music, my own team, the Mount Torrens Handbell Ringers, place two blankets folded into a strip one foot wide under the light cheesecloth table covering for all the middle harmony bells (approximately 22C-8C [C4-C6]) but not under the bass bells or treble bells (because the bass whoop still needs to be minimised).

If a team wants to exploit the whoop in their playing, firstly the conductor needs to decide which notes need to be whooped and mark them or rehearse the team accordingly. The notes to be whooped will normally be written to be rung on the 2nd and 4th beats of the bar and are therefore pressed into the table padding on the 1st and 3rd beats of the bar to produce a "whoop" on the "on" beat, e.g. from Thurlstone's "Cubley Brook"

Occasionally a better effect is produced if the bells are rung in a slightly syncopated fashion i.e. as a dotted note plus a note of half the value e.g. from "Under Freedom's Flag"

It is for the conductor to decide whether to syncopate the whooping, usually going by the feel of the music – although there are often hints in the music e.g. in "Cubley Brook" the top G of the tune being written on the 2nd and 4th beats ensure a smooth non-syncopated flow. In the 3rd bar of "Under Freedom's Flag" however the embellishment above the tune is actually written syncopatedly so that the middle harmony cries out for the same treatment.

Music which specifically includes the whoop normally has the time value written correctly e.g. from "Waltzing Matilda"

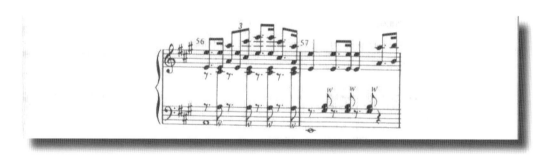

In this case the C#, E and A chords are pressed into the table padding on beats 1, 2, 3 & 4 and rung on the up stroke of each intervening "off" beat (shown as a semiquaver following a dotted quaver rest).

For in-hand and American style ringing, if time, or lack of tables prevent the learning of off-table up stroke ringing, the bells should be rung at an angle of 45 degrees, out and down from the midriff, damping the total side of the bell just below the rib cage on the "on beat". Damping the lip of the bell against the shoulder or collar bone does not produce a satisfactory whoop.

Philip Bedford
1991

319

Appendix 9

Extract made of William Laughton's 1734 Notebook by R.A. Daniell in 1895 and subsequently transcribed by William Butler. (Original lodged in the Guildhall Library, London)

Remarks

On a Rambling Club of Ringers and their performances, giving an account of all their Meetings from first to last, wherein may be seen the famous exploits which have bin done in the Art of Ringing, by that worthy body of Men.

By William Laughton

> *Herein just fifty tales you'll find,*
> *And each set down in prose and Rhyme,*
> *Not one i-m shure was writ in spight,*
> *So Reade and Judge 'em as you like.*
>
> *The Great Butler says:*
>
> *Rhyme the Rudder is of verses,*
> *With which like ships they steer there courses,*
> *And those that write in Rhyme still make,*
> *The one vers for the other's sake.*
> *And one for sense and one for Rhyme,*
> *I think's sufficient at one time.*
>
> *Hud:*
> ### AN APOLOGY
>
> *Now should I write nor sense nor rhyme,*
> *That wou-d be a horrid crime,*
> *But take the gift from whence it came,*
> *Let it be e'er so meanly done.*
> *'Tis the product of a feeble mind,*
> *But something of truth I'm sure you'll find.*
>
> *Lau:*
> ### ON RINGING IN GENERAL
> *28 lines*
>
> *As Ringing is a branch of Musick,*
> *Let none despise those men that use it,*
> *Nor think it mean and scandalous,*
> *Yet at the same time practise wors,*
> *For many men are apt to scoff,*
> *At things which they know nothing of,*
> *And right or wrong be finding fault,*

For want of judgment and of thought.
So censor men leap not at random,
Because they don't rightly understand 'em,
But let such poor unthinking Souls,
Carouse themselves o'erflowing bowls,
Which will shurely pay 'em home at length,
Whilst Ringers enjoy their health and strength.
The greatest blessing that heaven can give,
To be free from illness while we live.
Tho' I cannot say, but now and then,
Ringers tipple as much as other men,
But their exercise throws off those dreggs,
Which would bring others off their leggs,
That use no exercise at all,
But set in a house and drink and call,
As many thousands there are in town,
Which are pleased to run all Ringers down.
But let us pitty 'em with all our souls,
To think they shou-d be sutch stupid owls,
T'condemn sutch a charming exercise,
Which men of sense know how to prize.

To: Mr. George Carbery.
Sr.
You are not insensible (being one of those worthy members yourself) that a Company of us made an agreement to ring at all the peals of 3, 4, 5, and six bells within the City of London and Bills of Mortality, which we should find Ringable, and to Ring at a different place every time of meeting if we should think proper, likewise to Ring a peal, sometimes upon eight Bells, or take a walk into the Country and divert ourselves with a peal, if our fancys should lead that way; for which the snarling criticks were pleased to call us the Rambling Club; the first time of this Honourable Society's meeting was on Thursday the 29th of November 1733, and their last on Satturday the 8th of March 1734 when this worthy body of members broke up after having rung at 35 different peals of Bells, and done severall extraordinary performances in this Art; the merrit of which, caused me to write the following pages, wherein I have endeavoured (as far as my mean capacity is able) to set forth their praise, tho' perhaps far short of what they deserve. But that I'll leave to some more judicious pen: and in the meantime beg your exceptance of this, which if favourably received at your hands, will lay a particular obligation on
      Sr.
        Your most obedient
        Humble Servant to Command,

        William Laughton
Leather Lane, London.
Monday, the 10th of March, 1734

        1.
    Then first - stay let me think,
    Why first of all at Bennett Fink,
    Seven hundred and twenty of plain bob,
    Ay! true my muse a noble job.
            4 lines

2.

St. Olaves Hart Street next comes in,
Two seven hundr-ds we there did ring,
One College Single, the other plain,
Bob if ye please that is the name.

4 lines

3.

To St. Paul at Shadwell next we come,
And there we seven hundred Rung,
Of College Single, I'll tell ye true,
And give every peal and place its due.

4 lines

4.

We met next at St. Botolph's Aldgate,
And there rung two peals as I shall say it,
Grandsire went first, plain bob was next,
Both rung completely I protest.

4 lines.

NOTES

The preceding pages are an accurate transcript of William Laughton's MSS
(Guildhall Library MS. 254), copied originally by R. A. Daniell about 1895, and corrected E.A.
Young. This MSS is in the Central Council Library, M.S. 444.

Daniell made extracts of the remainder of the notebook, and these follow:
"Here follow Indexes to foregoing places and performances, and other tables and
calculations of changes rung, from which I take the following.

Changes on 3 bells	*2,736*
Changes on 5 bells	*2,880*
Changes on 6 bells	*22,320*
Changes on 7 bells	*1,116*
Changes on 8 bells	*24,176*
In all	*53,228 changes*

Methods Rung - Grandsire, Old Doubles, New Doubles, Simonds Doubles, Cambridge Delight
- on 5 Bells

College Single, Plain Bob, Court Bob, Oxford Treble Bob, Morning Exercise,
Cambridge Surprise - on 6 Bells.

Grandsire Triples - 7 Bells

Bob Major and Union Bob - on 8 Bells

"Index to Hang Ups or treats, which you please".

(Here follows a list)

"In all 20 good livings".

Here follow 2 'Songs'. The first presents nothing interesting. The following I extract from the 2nd song.

(The first song is on the Ramblers beginning, the 2nd on the same when ended.)

Likewise we performed Union Bob,
For variety sake it is true,
But no further we troubled our brains,
With any cramp peal that is new.

Then next upon Camberwell eight
Five thousand and forty we rung.
Good ringing most part of it was,
As e'er I desire to hear done.

We struck 'em most charming and true
And sent out their sound for to rove,
For sweetly they sung o'er the fields
Ay, and up to the end of the grove.

....

This is the first Rambling Club
Of Ringers that ever was known
Tho' many there are of good boozers
Through every part of the town.

Nothing is more stupid and dull
Than those that condemn other men
Because they can't think as they do
And do what is done by them.

....

Tune on 10 Bells

35670787	*07677539*
65131356	*96567678*
66566427	*63572461*
78638790	*231235467*

323

Then follows a poetical epistle to "Jerry and Tom" (Jeremiah Gilbert and Tom Greenwood) about commencing a voyage down the Thames to the Isle of Sheppey with a prose account of the voyage of the Isle but containing nothing of ringing interest.

He caught some "Scuttlefish that spews natural inck".

At Erith they dined and had a bowl of punch and then set out on foot for London which (Fleet St.) They reached at 10 the same evening.

They had a very rough passage and he adds:
"'Tis remarkable that four of us had never bin out at sea before, and though the water proved so very ruff yet not one of us was the least sea sick all the voyage."

The epistle explains why Laughton could not keep an appointment with Tom and Jerry and describes what he is going to do on the voyage. In it are the following lines:

> *"If the Sterling Castle we can find,*
> *Captain Geary will use us kind,*
> *We hope to find him in our rounds,*
> *either at the Nore or in the Downs."*

The voyage commenced on Saturday the 31st August, 1734. The party being besides Laughton, Mr. Nathaniel Delander, Mr. John Delander, Mr. Richard Conyers, Mr. Joseph Smith.

NOTE: The above named Geary must be he who took part in the Bob Maximus and afterwards became an Admiral.

Appendix 10

From the Huddersfield Daily Examiner 1904
A report of the
Yorkshire Hand-bell Ringers Association
First Annual Tune-Ringing Contest
(Possibly written by Fred Shaw, formerly of Shelley HBR)

Upon Huddersfield was conferred the honour of being chosen by the Yorkshire Hand-bell Ringers Association as the place for holding their first annual tune-ringing contest, which was brought off to the Armoury on Saturday afternoon and evening. Arrangements were made for two competitions. The first was an open one for the County, and the first prize was the Association's Silver Challenge Cup, a silver medal for each member of the winning band, and a sum of money added, subscribed by tradesmen of Huddersfield. The second and third prizes consisted of silver medals for conductors and members of the respective bands. As a test piece, Rossini's overture, "L'Italian in Algeria" was chosen. The second competition was limited to such bands in the County as had not won a prize at a Manchester Belle Vue contest. The first prize was a silver medal for each member of the band adjudged the best, and the second was a silver medal for the conductor. "Reminiscences of Merrie England", consisting of familiar old English songs, arranged by Wilkins, was the test piece.

The afternoon was set apart for the second competition, which attracted only a few persons beyond the members and more ardent friends of the nine bands who competed in the following order:

No. 1 Heptonstall: twelve performers; conductor, Mr W. Sunderland
No. 2 Barnsley: ten performers; conductor, Mr E. Stringer
No. 3 Lightcliffe: nine performers; conductor, Mr A. Warler
No. 4 Woodroyd, Honley: eleven performers; conductor, Mr John Moorhouse
No. 5 Brighouse, Park Church: twelve performers; conductor Mr P. Marshall
No. 6 Holmfirth, Lane Congregational: twelve performers; conductor, Mr J. Moorhouse
No. 7. Birstall St. Saviours: ten performers; conductor, Mr K. Cooke
No. 8 Sheffield Hartshead: ten performers; conductor, Mr J. A. Ironside
No. 9 Low Moor: ten performers; conductor, Mr K. Cooke

Darfield and Yorkshire (Sheffield) bands also entered for the second competition, but did not put in and appearance. The selection opens with a few bars of diatonic descending octaves leading to a snatch of 'The British Grenadiers' after which follow 'Cherry Ripe', 'Tom Bowling', 'The Girl I Left Behind Me', 'My Pretty Jane', 'Rule Britannia', a snatch of 'Home Sweet Home' and 'Come, Lasses and Lads'. The selection presents practically no difficulties as regards expertness of execution; but its very simplicity was a pitfall to several of the bands, especially in regards to accent and phrasing. Want of definiteness of accent and accenting the wrong notes were common, and often the melody was obscured, partly in consequence of that and partly from accompaniments being too weighty. As a rule the shading was excellent. A few bands, chiefly amongst the early competitors, suffered from having some bells naturally out of tune, and other bands were defective in interpretation and wanting in clearness through being rung with too much force. The worst instances of this fault were in the playing of Low Moor and Sheffield Hartshead. Mr K Cooke's bands suffered from his eccentric and excited conducting, as he adopted the plan of giving two beats when he should have given one, and thereby got unsteady playing and want of smooth and broad phrasing. His rallentandos were also too frequent and prolonged, especially in 'My Pretty Jane'. In the matter of tempo there was great variety, and several lacked buoyancy and smartness in giving the little bit of 'The British Grenadiers' and did not achieve the lilting rhythm of 'Come, Lasses and Lads'. The best conception of the selection was shown by Mr J. Moorhouse and he got much the best interpretation of it out of his Woodroyd band, who were the first to make recognisable the air of the snatch of 'Home Sweet Home' and who gave by far the best accented, phrased, and generally expressive and finished rendering of the piece, marred only by a rather prominent wrong note in the opening of the 'Rule Britannia'. A very similar but less delicate and clear interpretation was given by Lane Congregational ringers, who were not quite accurate in the early part of 'Cherry Ripe', nor perfectly united in 'Come, Lasses and Lads'. Slowness was the chief fault of the Brighouse band; and weak and false accent and want of clearness and balance were the principle defects of Heptonstall and Lightcliffe. Barnsley gave an excellent interpretation of the songs in spite of a little want of clearness in 'Cherry Ripe' and some broken phrasing in 'My Pretty Jane'.

There was a very much larger audience in the evening to hear the first competition, though all the seats were not filled. Out of nine bands entered, only Royston United failed to put in an appearance. The other eight played in the following order:

No. 1 Barnsley: nine performers; conductor; Mr E. Stringer
No. 2 Liversedge Albert: eleven performers; conductor; Mr K. Cooke
No. 3 Birstall St. Saviours: eleven performers; conductor; Mr K. Cooke

No. 4 Thurlstone: ten performers; conductor; Mr E. Biltcliffe
No. 5 Huddersfield: eleven performers; conductor; Mr Lewis Booth
No. 6 Horbury: ten performers; conductor; Mr J. Woffenden
No. 7 Almondbury United: ten performers; conductor; Mr B. Lodge
No. 8 Clifton: ten performers; conductor; Mr A. Sayles

Much more difficult though Rossini's tuneful and expressive overture is than the selection for the second competition, though the same faults were at times shown as the second teams displayed. In spite of once getting rather seriously across in point of time, the Huddersfield ringers gave by far the most musically, clear, and artistic interpretation of the overture. The melody was well brought out, the accent and phrasing were nicely and unitedly marked, and the execution was wonderfully good and expressive. Almondbury United came next in order of merit with a rendering of fuller tone, but not as well balanced, clear, and refined as Huddersfield, nor was the melody as well brought out. A mistake was also made by a player of the treble bells. A very careful and tasteful performance was given by the Horbury ringers, thought the execution and accent were not quite clear or well defined in the early part. Liversedge Albert and Barnsley ringers gave very creditable performances. Thurlstone were unsteady and too forceful and in a less degree these faults appeared in the playing of Clifton and Birstall St. Saviours.

Mr A. Jowett, Mus. Prof. Oxon of Leeds, who was the judge, and had been curtained off in a corner of the platform so that he could not see bands or audience, came forward at close of the contest and announced his awards. He said he would give his decision in the second competition first. In that, there were three or four bands very close together. With reference to playing of some, he wished to point out that force did not always bring music. (Hear, hear). It was possible to throw good bells absolutely out of tune a quarter of a tone by using too much force. In the second competition, which took place in the afternoon, he awarded the first prize to No. 4 (Woodroyd, Honley), with 75 marks out a maximum of 90. The second prize he gave to No. 2 (Barnsley), with 74 marks. No. 7 (Birstall) was third with one mark below – 73. The best band in the first competition that night made a big blunder; but that did not absolutely ruin the band. The total number of points obtainable was 160. The first prize went to No. 5 (Huddersfield) with 156 marks. About that there could be no doubt. They made a serious blunder and might have wrecked themselves in the early part; but they soon recovered themselves and they had the best tone of any band and gave the very best musicianly performance. The second prize, was with 149 marks, went to No. 7 (Almondbury United); and the third prize he awarded to No. 6 (Horbury) with 145 marks.

A great shout was given by the winning bands and their supporters as the numbers were announced. The awards, however, apart from that, must have been satisfactory to all impartial persons who paid attention to the contest from beginning to end.

Appendix 11
Crosland Moor Public – Contracts with Mears & Stainbank to buy Long Sets of Hand-bells

Memorandum of Agreement

made between Crosland Moor Public Hand
Bell Ringers of Huddersfield in the County
of York of the one part, and Mears & Stainbank,
Bell Founders of 32 & 34 Whitechapel Road
London of the other part.

    The said Bell Founders agree to
supply a set of One hundred and sixty
five Hand Bells for a sum of Ninety
four pounds (£94) particulars as follow:-
66 Bells beginning with Tenor 29 C to 005 F
  54   "   as duplicates from 25 G to 201 C.
  42   "   as triplicates from 19 F to 05 F# &
    3 extra bells. 11 G · 4 G & 10 A.
165 bells altogether.

    The said peal to be made of the finest
quality of metal, every bell warranted and
the whole set guaranteed in perfect tune
to the satisfaction of the said Public
Hand Bell Ringers.

    The handles of each bell to be lined
and stitched and the workmanship of
the bell, fittings and handles to be of
the best. The clappers of the bass bells
from 29 C to 30 E inclusive to be split
ball, the others pegged with leathers.
The large springs in these bass bells to be
covered with felts tied tightly round and
above them, the springs to be drilled, and
the felts waxed and stitched on.

If at any time the said peal of bells or any single bell, should prove defective through bad workmanship, the said Bellfounders undertake to replace such bell or bells.

The said Bellfounders undertake to have the whole peal delivered early in July 1909, and the said Company of Hand Bell Ringers, agree to pay the sum of Fifty pounds (£50) within one week of delivery of the bells and the balance, less 5% discount on the total amount, within three months afterwards.

It is also agreed that the Bells be delivered at Huddersfield Station carriage paid, packed in case free of charge and not returnable.

As witness their hands this Seventeenth day of February, 1909.

Mears & Stainbank   SIX PENCE

Witness to the signature
    of Mears & Stainbank.
        G. E. Oliver
            34 Whitechapel Road
                London

Memorandum of Agreement,

made between the Crosland Moor Public Hand Bell Ringers of
Huddersfield in the County of Yorkshire of the one part and
Mears and Stainbank Bell Founders of 32 and 34 Whitechapel
Road London of the other part - - - - - - - - - - - - - - -
The said Bell Founders agree to supply a set of one hundred
and sixtyfive Hand Bells for the sum of Ninetyfour pounds
(£94/-/-) particulars as follows :- - - - - - - - - - - -

66 Bells, tenor 29 C, to 005 F - - - - - - - - - - - - -

54 Bells, as duplicates, from 25 G to 01 C - - - - - - - -

42 Bells, as triplicates, from 19 F to 05 A # - - - - - -

3 extra Bells, viz: 11 G, 4 G, and 10 A - - - - - - - - -

165 Bells altogether. - - - - - - - - - - - - - - - - - -

The said Peal to be made of the finest quality of metal,
every Bell waranted and the whole set guaranteed in perfect
tune to the satisfaction of the said Company of Hand Bell
Ringers. The handle of each Bell to be lined and stitched
and the workmanship of the Bells, Fittings and Handles to be
of the best. The clappers of the bass Bells from 29 C to 20 F
inclusive to be split ball, the others pegged with leathers,
the large springs in these bass Bells to be covered with felt
tied tightly round and above them, the springs to be drilled
and the felts to be waxed and stitched on. If at any time the
said peal of bells or any single bell should prove defective
through bad workmanship, the said Bell Founders undertake to
replace such bell or bells. The said Bell Founders undertake
to have the whole peal delivered by March 14'th, 1915, and
the said Company of Hand Bell Ringers agree to pay the sum of
Seventy Pounds (£70/-/-) within one week of delivery of the
Bells, and the balance, less 5% discount on the total amount

within three months afterwards. It is also agreed that the
Bells be delivered at Huddersfield Station carriage paid,
packed in a case free of charge, and not returnable. - - - -
As witness their hands this Eighteenth day of September,
Nineteen hundred and fourteen - - - - - - - - - - - - - - - -
- -
- -

Mears & Stainbank

Witness to the signature of Mears and Stainbank :-

Leonard. A. Hughes
95 Hainault Road
Leytonstone Essex.

1914 Agreement for the sale of bells to Crossland Moor Public

330

Appendix 12

The 1912 Yorkshire Hand-bell Association Contests Programme

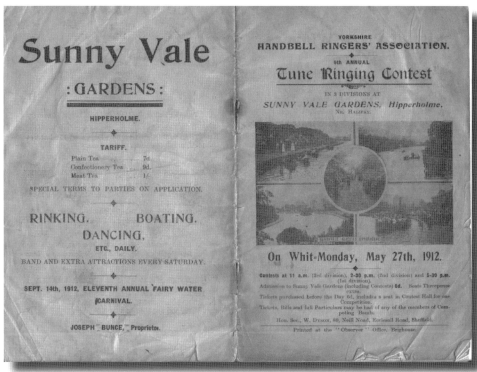

Committee of Association.

Mr. W. H. Giggle	Ossett.
Mr. W. N. Firth	Birstall.
Mr. J. D. Priestley	Crossland Moor Public.
Mr. S. H. Townend	Clifton
Mr. Hellawell	Dewsbury.
Mr. F. Moorhouse	Lepton.
Mr. A. Fothergill	Horbury.
Mr. S. Goodall	Liversedge.
Mr. E. Dalton	Sheffield.
Mr. F. Taylor	Thurlstone.
Mr. A. T. Sorsby	Ecclesfield.
Mr. J. Spencer	Saddleworth
Mr. J. Peaker	Penistone.
Mr. A. Brown	Armitage Bridge.
Mr. W. J. G. Carter	Sowerby.
Mr. C. Heckingbottom	Sowerby Bridge.
Mr. H. Hirst	Gilder Hall, Mirfield.
Mr. A. Plumstead	Chapelthorpe
Mr. V. Broome	Bradford.
Mr. S. Haigh	Elland.
Mr. H. Gould	Newchurch.

FIRST COMPETITION.

First Prize : The Association's Silver Cup, and a Silver Medal for the Conductor and each Member of the Band.
Second Prize : Silver Medal for the Conductor.
Third Prize : Silver Medal for the Conductor.
And proportion of Prize Money.

TEST PIECE.

Grand Selection .. "Les Cloches De Cornville"
CHARLES GODFREY

Judge :—MR. ALBERT JOWETT, Mus. Bac., Oxon., Leeds.

The following Bands have entered :—

1. BIRSTALL S. SAVIOUR'S.

H. Rothery	G. H. Rothery	C. Rhodes
R. Clegg	F. Hudswell	W. Rhodes
J. W. Rhodes	J. Wilson	

Conductor—Mr. K. COOKE.

2. CLIFTON SENIOR.

W. Sykes.	R. Sykes	J. Bottomley
F. Irving	E. Fearnley	A. Schofield
D. Clayton	G. Smith	
N. Smithies	J. Bell	

Conductor—Mr. H. EVANS.

3. CROSSLAND MOOR PUBLIC.

H. Jepson	H. Bradbury	V. Smith
V. Priestley	H. Armitage	L. Mellor
N. Walker	W. Hanson	
T. Ellis	L. Cartwright	

Conductor—Mr. J. H. ELLIS

4. DEWSBURY.

A. Young	A. North	W. Hellawell
A. Heeley	M. Willoughby	J. T. Beaumont
M. Senior	R. Hodgson	

Conductor—Mr. A. FEARNSIDES.

5. LEPTON UNITED.

W. Senior	J. E. Shaw	R. H. Lee
R. H. Brook	W. Ibberson	T. Moorhouse
A. Senior	J. E. Shaw	
E. Kilner	W. Ely	

Conductor—Mr. J. H. DAWSON.

6. LIVERSEDGE.

L. Littlewood	H. Banks	M. Rhodes
P. Whiteoak	F. Barraclough	I. Ross
C. Mortimer	H. Smith	W. Brearley

Conductor—Mr. K. COOKE.

SECOND COMPETITION.

First Prize : The Association's Silver Challenge Shield and
Silver Medal for Conductor and each Member of the
Band.
Second Prize : Silver Medal for the Conductor.
Third Prize :   „   „
Also Prize Money proportionately.

TEST PIECE.
Selection .. Poet and Peasant .. .. Oscar Verne

The following Bands have entered :—

1. ECCLESFIELD.

F. Kaye	A. Kaye	W. Hague
E. Greaves	E. Flather	E. Whitham.
A. T. Sorsby	G. Higgins	C. Flather
A. J. Parramore	T. Hoyland	E. Loxby

Conductor—Mr. F. P. WHITHAM.

2. THURLSTONE.

J. Smith	E. Wood	D. Taylor
F. Peace	R. Norman	T. Sykes
O. Hey	W. Hey	O. Hinchliffe

Conductor—Mr. F. TAYLOR.

11

3. PENISTONE.

F. Jessop	J. Fearnley	G. Rose
F. Fearnley	W. Singleton	T. Singleton
J. Peaker	H. Palmer	
T. Chappell	W. Britnell	

Conductor—Mr. J. E. FALLA.

4. SADDLEWORTH.

R. Wood	F. Howard	H. Spencer
F. Byrom	A. Rawlings	J. B. Wood
J. E. Bradbury	J. Franklin	J. Bradbury

Conductor—Mr. W. POWNALL.

5. SOWERBY BRIDGE.

E. Lawrence	W. Gaukroger	T. Ingham
J. Ackroyd	E. Dobson	H. Wilkinson
C. Heckingbottom	E. Smith	F. Smith

Conductor—Mr. S. HOWARTH.

6. ELLAND.

A. Waddington	H. Bates	R. Siddal
J. T. Wilson	W. Crowther	H. Marsden
W. Bumstead	T. Crowther	R. Eastwood
H. Robinson	T. Robinson	

Conductor—Mr. C. H. WADDINGTON.

7. SOWERBY.

E. Howarth	H. Howarth	R. Riley
G. Normanton	G. Hartley	W. J. G. Carter
H. Hartley	H. Normanton	
H. Riley	W. Smith	

Conductor—Mr. S. H. HOWARTH.

15

4. GILDER HALL (Mirfield).

W. S. Holt	W. Beaumont	H. Hirst
H. Naylor	G. Butterfield	J. Holt
B. Weldrick	H. Singleton	
A. Cartwright	F. Barrowclough	

Conductor—Mr. G. BREARLEY.

5. NEW CHURCH.

W. Green	J. Pye	W. Hampson
F. Reynolds	T. Gould	G. Pye
H. Gould	W. Gould	W. Andrews

Conductor—Mr. J. ORME.

6. SOWERBY.

E. Howarth	H. Howarth	R. Riley
G. Normanton	G. Hartley	W. J. G. Carter
F. Hartley	H. Normanton	
H. Riley	W. Smith	

Conductor—Mr. S. H. HOWARTH.

7. SOWERBY BRIDGE.

E. Lawrence	W. Gaukroger	T. Ingham
J. Ackroyd	E. Dobson	H. Wilkinson
C. Heckingbottom	E. Smith	F. Smith

Conductor—Mr. S. HOWARTH.

8. SHEFFIELD HARTSHEAD.

W. Dyson	H. Kay	T. Furness
E. Dalton	H. Dawson	W. Thompson
J. H. Allen	W. C. Lacy	H. T. Laver
W. Fernley	F. Lacy	

Conductor—Mr. A. MOORE.

4. GILDER HALL (Mirfield).

W. S. Holt	W. Beaumont	H. Hirst
H. Naylor	G. Butterfield	J. Holt
B. Weldrick	H. Singleton	
A. Cartwright	F. Barrowclough	

Conductor—Mr. G. BREARLEY.

5. NEW CHURCH.

W. Green	J. Pye	W. Hampson
F. Reynolds	T. Gould	G. Pye
H. Gould	W. Gould	W. Andrews

Conductor—Mr. J. ORME.

6. SOWERBY.

E. Howarth	H. Howarth	R. Riley
G. Normanton	G. Hartley	W. J. G. Carter
F. Hartley	H. Normanton	
H. Riley	W. Smith	

Conductor—Mr. S. H. HOWARTH.

7. SOWERBY BRIDGE.

E. Lawrence	W. Gaukroger	T. Ingham
J. Ackroyd	E. Dobson	H. Wilkinson
C. Heckingbottom	E. Smith	F. Smith

Conductor—Mr. S. HOWARTH.

8. SHEFFIELD HARTSHEAD.

W. Dyson	H. Kay	T. Furness
E. Dalton	H. Dawson	W. Thompson
J. H. Allen	W. C. Lacy	H. T. Laver
W. Fernley	F. Lacy	

Conductor—Mr. A. MOORE.

ATTRACTIONS PROGRAMME.

❖

SUNNY VALE.   TIME TABLE, WHIT-MONDAY, 1912.

8-30 a.m., Gardens open. 3 Miles of Promenades, amidst the unrivalled scenery of the lovely Shibden Valley.

9-0 a.m., Rinking. Fine open-air covered Rink. Skates 1 hour 4d., Extra time 2d. per hour. Selections by the Military Band Organ.

9-0 a.m., Boating. Two large Lakes, 40 boats. half an hour, 3d. each person. (Minimum per Boat, 6d.)

9-30 a.m., Maze, 1d. Swings, 1d.   Childrens' Swings ½d.

10-30 a.m., Donkeys, 1d.   Ponies, 2d., For a ride of 300 yards.

11-0 a.m., Bands draw for order of playing. Handbell Contest, 3rd Competition commences in the Spacious Dancing Hall, Admission Free. Seats 2d.

12.0 a.m., Dinners and Refreshments. Accommodation to seat 1,000.

2-0 p.m., Motor Launch. Trips round the Large Lake. Adults 2d, Children 1d.

2-30 p.m., Handbell Contest. 2nd Competition. Admission Free. Seats 3d.

3-0 p.m., Dancing. **Heckmondwike English Concertina Band** on the open air Dance Stage.

3-0 p.m., Chute Railway. Lightning Trips, 1d.

4-0 p.m., Teas ready. Catering ad. lib., at very moderate charges (see back page).

6-0 p.m., Rinking, Dancing, Boating, etc.

6-0 p.m., Yorkshire Handbell Championship Competition. Don't miss the Finest Handbell Ringing in the World. Admission Free. Seats 3d.

7-30 p.m., Judge's Awards. Result of Contests.

8-0 p.m., Ballroom. Admission Free.

10-0 p.m., Gardens Close. Thanks to all our Patrons. Good-Night.

Open all day :—Cloak Room, Laughing Mirrors, Automobile Novelties and Devices, Refreshment Booths, Sweet Ice Cream, Toy and Present Stalls, Houp-la, Post Office, Enquiry Office, etc., etc.

JOSEPH BUNCE—Proprietor.

TIME TABLE.

Trams for Halifax, Bradford, etc., from Hipperholme every
15 minutes.

Trams for Brighouse from Hove Edge, every 15 minutes at
10-25, 40 and 55 minutes past the hour.

EXCURSIONISTS RETURN FROM HIPPERHOLME,

For Halifax, 7-27, 7-57, 8-45, 10-12, 11-3.
„ Wyke, Low Moor, and Bradford, 8-15, 8-50, 9-48, 10-23.
„ Leeds, 8-15, 9-19, 9-48.
„ Stanningley, 9-48, Bramley, 9-19.
„ Cleckheaton, Liversedge, and Heckmondwike, 8-15, 9-19,
10-23.
„ Dewsbury, 8-15, 10-23.
„ Elland, Stainland, Huddersfield, etc., 8-48, 10-12.
„ Sowerby Bridge, Hebden Bridge, Todmorden and Lanca-
shire, 7-57, 8-48, 10-12.

EXCURSIONISTS RETURN FROM BRIGHOUSE,

For Huddersfield and Holmfirth, 10-2, 10-40.
„ Mirfield, Wakefield, Dewsbury, 9-30, 9-52.
„ Barnsley and Sheffield, 9-30.

Appendix 13

Rules of the Yorkshire Association its competitions varied 1932

YORKSHIRE HAND-BELL RINGERS' ASSOCIATION. 1932.

GENERAL RULES.

1. - That this Society be called the "Yorkshire Hand-bell Ringers' Association."

2. - That the object of the Association be the advancement and improvement of musical hand-bell ringing, by organizing and holding Contests, Lectures, Meetings, &c., and providing for and facilitating in any way deemed expedient, social intercourse between the members.

3. - That the Association shall consist of any Society of Hand-bell Ringers in Yorkshire or any other County. Each band shall pay an annual Subscription of 15/-. All subscriptions to be paid in advance.

4. - That the government be vested in a President, one Vice-president, Secretary, Treasurer and a Committee consisting of one representative from each band. A quorum of three shall be competent to transact the business providing all have had due notice. The Committee shall have absolute power over the contests, and shall be able to disqualify any unruly member. The Committee shall make all arrangements for the contests, viz:- Selection of Judge, town where Contest is to be held, and all other details connected therewith.

5. - That a General Meeting shall be held every year for the purpose of electing Officers and transacting any other business. Candidates for the position of President, Vice-President, Secretary, Treasurer and Auditors, must be nominated by a proposer and seconder, and due notice given to the Secretary fourteen days before the Annual General Meeting. General and Committee Meetings may be held in any town the Committee may appoint. All Officers shall be elected by ballot, each band having one vote. One Auditor shall retire annually. President and Vice-President to be voted for separately.

6. - That in order to ensure the equality of delegates' expenses, each delegate shall send in annually to the Secretary the railway fares incurred in attending the Committee Meetings. The Secretary shall total up the expenses and divide equally for the whole of the meetings held. The delegates who have not spent the amount arrived at shall pay up to the said amount and those who have spent above the amount shall be re-funded the excess paid, thereby making every delegate on an equality. The Secretary's railway fare shall be allowed and added to the expense account.

7. - That no alteration or addition to these rules shall be made except at the Annual General Meeting. Particulars of any proposed alteration or addition shall be sent to the Secretary no later than 14 days before the General Meeting.

8. - That the private medal die of the Association shall not be lent or used to stamp any medal except for the requisite number of winners who ACTUALLY took part in the Contests.

9. - That the Association general account be made financial each year before any division of profits in the Contests are made. The Association in any case to apportion 12½% of Contest profit before the division of prize money to the winners.

CONTEST RULES.

1. - That Contests be held annually for the Association Cup and Shield, each Band to submit suitable music for the Association Cup. The first to be drawn by the President to be accepted as Test piece, all delegates to submit actual copy. That each Band play an own choice selection for the Association Shield, Winners of Trophies to hold same for not more than one year. That an entrance fee of 10/- be paid by each Band before choice of Test piece, any Band not competing to forfeit such sum, all competing Bands to have such entrance fee returned.
Any band that fails to ring in one contest either through sickness or any other cause loses their deposit.

2. - That in all Association Contests, if only three bands compete two prizes to be allowed; and if four or more compete, three prizes. The prizes in each Competition to be equal in value.

3. - That any band winning either competition three years in succession, shall be granted a special prize in honour of the occasion, the committee to consider the nature of any such prize.

4. - That the railway fares of all members taking actual part in the competitions shall be pooled, and a general average per band taken, each band to pay or receive any amount below or above the average amount, every band to pay equal shares.

5. - That medals or any prize the committee think fit to award prize winners other the trophies shall be purchased from the contest funds.

6. - That the Judge must be in his private apartments before the draw for positions of ringing takes place, at all Contests.
And that no person enters Judges Box until rung for.

7. - That Judges' inclusive fees are not to exceed Three Guineas.

8. - Official Badges will be issued previous to the Annual Contest to admit ringers free to Contest. A deposit of 2/6 to be paid, which will be returned after the Contest on receipt of the full number of badges had, 6d. will be deducted for each badge not returned.

-------- oOo --------

These rules were amended at a meeting held March 19/1932

Appendix 14

Belle Vue Competition Rules 1860 – 1914

ZOOLOGICAL GARDENS, BELLE VUE,
MANCHESTER.

HAND-BELL RINGING
CONTEST,

TO TAKE PLACE

ON MONDAY, SEPTEMBER 24TH, 1860.

THE FIRST TUNE TO BE PLAYED AT THREE O'CLOCK.

PRIZES:—First, **£15**; Second, **£5**; Third, **£2 5s.**; Fourth, **£1 5s.**

THE UNDERMENTIONED BANDS HAVE ENTERED.

PLACE AND NAME OF BAND.	CONDUCTOR OR LEADER'S NAME.
SHELLEY, near Huddersfield ... (12 *Performers*)	BENJAMIN COOK.
WIGAN, Lancashire ...	WM. MASON.
BARNSLEY, Yorkshire ...	ABEL OSBORNE.
PENDLETON, Manchester ... (10 *Performers*)	JAMES GREEN.
HOLMFIRTH, Yorkshire ...	H. POGSON.
HECKMONDWIKE, Yorkshire ...	T. ROBERTS.
DEWSBURY, Yorkshire ...	H. METCALF.

Regulations.

Each Set to ring four tunes or pieces of their own selection. The Judges will observe the nature and difficulty of the pieces performed by each Band, in addition to the correctness of playing.

An Extra Prize of £5 will be given to the parties who play nearest to copy the Overture to "Lodoiska," to be played immediately after the last of their own selection.

No party to compete for the Orginal Prize without also playing for the Extra Prize, nor for the Extra Prize without the Original.

All disputes to be submitted to JOHN JENNISON, Jun., and his decision to be final in all cases before the playing takes place, afterwards the decision of the Judges to be binding. Five Gentlemen of the highest professional standing and respectability will be selected for the office.

ZOOLOGICAL GARDENS, BELLE VUE,
MANCHESTER.

HAND-BELL RINGING
CONTEST,

TO TAKE PLACE

ON MONDAY, SEPTEMBER 22ND, 1862,

THE FIRST TUNE TO BE PLAYED AT TWO O'CLOCK.

First Prize, £15; Second Prize, £5; Third Prize, £3; Fourth Prize, £1 10s.

THE FOLLOWING BANDS HAVE ENTERED:—

No.	Name and Place of Band.	Performrs.	Conductor's Name.
1	WIGAN, Lancashire	12	Edward Benson.
2	OVER DARWEN, Lancashire	11	Joseph Birch, Junr.
3	UTTOXETER, Staffordshire	8	G. F. Gill.
4	ST. JAMES' STREET, HULL, Yorkshire	6	Charles Petty.
5	STOCKS BRIDGE, Deep Car, near Sheffield, Yorkshire	12	B. Cook.
6	SHELLY, Yorkshire	12	Ben Cook.
7	NEWCHURCH, Lancashire	11	John Warburton.
8	MELTHAM, near Huddersfield, Yorkshire	12	George Kenworthy.
9	DEWSBURY, Yorkshire	12	Thomas Wood.

REGULATIONS.

Each Set to ring two tunes or pieces of their own selection, and will be required to produce a Pianoforte or Score Copy of the Pieces they intend to play, which must be given to Mr. Jennison, or some one appointed by him at the drawing; these to be opened simultaneously by the Judges as the Bands go on, but not before. Each Band will therefore please have them wrapped up separately under cover of paper, and on the number being drawn place it on the outside of the wrapper. The Judges will observe the nature and difficulty of the pieces performed by each Band, in addition to the correctness of playing.

AN EXTRA PRIZE OF FIVE POUNDS

will be given to the parties who play nearest to copy the "New York Quadrilles;" to be played immediately after the last of their own selection. It is particularly requested that the Quadrilles be repeated only as marked, and be played but once through, in order to save time, although if repeated an extra time, it shall not be considered to injure the band so repeating them.

No party to compete for the Original Prizes without also playing for the Extra Prize, nor for the Extra Prize without the Original Prizes.

The same conditions as to the conveyance by Rail, to Belle Vue (or Manchester) and Back, as in previous years will be adhered to, and each party will be conveyed Free, where suitable arrangements can be made with the Companies of the lines over which the Bands wish to travel; and if no satisfactory arrangement can be made, the Entrance Money will be returned before the day appointed for the Contest.

ZOOLOGICAL GARDENS, BELLE VUE,

MANCHESTER.

HAND-BELL RINGING CONTEST,

TO TAKE PLACE

ON MONDAY, SEPTEMBER 21st, 1863.

THE FIRST TUNE TO BE PLAYED AT TWO O'CLOCK.

First Prize, £15; Second Prize, £5; Third Prize, £2 10s; Fourth Prize, £1.

THE FOLLOWING BANDS HAVE ENTERED:—

No.	Name and Place of Band.	Performrs.	Conductor's Name.
1	SWAN MEADOW MILLS, Wigan.	12	William Mason.
2	WIGAN.	11	Edward Benson.
3	MELTHAM, near Huddersfield.	12	G. Kenworthy.
4	SHELLY, near Huddersfield.		G. Stephenson.
5	HECKMONDWIKE Campanologian, near Leeds.	12	Thomas Roberts
6	OLDHAM.	11	David Dyson.
7	UTTOXETER.	9	G. F. Gill.

REGULATIONS.

Each Set to ring two tunes or pieces of their own selection. The Judges will observe the nature and difficulty of the pieces performed by each Band, in addition to the correctness of playing. N.B.—Any new system of judging proposed, will be considered, and if thought by the majority of the Bands entered to be superior to the one formerly adopted, will be used on the occasion.

AN EXTRA PRIZE OF FIVE POUNDS

will be given for a piece to be played by each Set, a Pianoforte Copy of which will be sent two months before the Contest to each Band entered for the Original Prizes; to be played immediately after the last of their own selection. The Set who play the nearest to copy to be the winners. No extra entrance money to be paid.

N.B.—No Band to play the same pieces they have played at any previous Contest.

All the Bands to furnish Pianoforte copies of the pieces they intend to play at the time of drawing.

No party to compete for the Original Prizes without also playing for the Extra Prize, nor for the Extra Prize without the Original Prizes.

The same conditions as to the conveyance by Rail, to Belle Vue (or Manchester) and Back, as in previous years will be adhered to, and each party will be conveyed Free, where suitable arrangements can be made with the Companies of the lines over which the Bands wish to travel; and if no satisfactory arrangement can be made, the Entrance Money will be returned.

ZOOLOGICAL GARDENS, BELLE VUE,

MANCHESTER.

MUSICAL CONTESTS

APPOINTED FOR THE YEAR 1865.

FIRST.

BY FIFE AND DRUM BANDS,

ON WHIT-TUESDAY, JUNE 6th, 1865.

TWENTY-FIVE POUNDS will be given, which, with the Entrance Money, 20s. each Band, will be divided into Prizes, the particulars of which will be given after the entries are complete. N.B.—A Side Drum will be given to the best Band as in former years, in addition to the first prize.

REGULATIONS.

No Band to exceed Twenty-five Performers, Conductor included.

Each Band to perform two tunes or pieces, one of their own selection, and one sent to them five weeks before the Contest. No Professional Musician will be allowed to play in any Band.

CONDUCTORS—Any Professional Man may act as Conductor for what Bands he may be engaged (without limit to number), but will *not be allowed to play* in any.

Entries to close on Tuesday, April 25th, 1865.

SECOND,

BY BRASS BANDS,

ON MONDAY, SEPTEMBER 4th, 1865.

FIFTY POUNDS will be given, which, with the Entrance Money, will be divided into four or five Prizes.

REGULATIONS.

Amateur Bands only allowed to play. A Professional Musician may act as Conductor, and may also perform on any instrument; he may also act for as many Bands as he thinks proper, but not to play as a member in one Band, and Conductor in another. The members of each Band must have played together once a week for six weeks before the day of the Contest. A person being a member of another Band, will not be disqualified, but no one to play in more than one Band at the Contest. Entrance Money, 20s. each Band, to be sent on or before *Tuesday, July 25th*, 1865. Two pieces to be performed, one of which will be sent six weeks before the Contest, arranged for the Cornets to be played in B flat; Sopranos in E flat or D flat, at the players' option: and a piece chosen by each Band, which must also be played with Cornets in B flat.

The number of competing Bands not to be less than five, and no Band to exceed 20 in number, Conductor included.

N.B.—No Band to play the same pieces they have played at any previous Contest at Belle Vue.

THIRD,

HAND-BELL RINGING,

ON MONDAY, SEPTEMBER 25th, 1865.

By Sets of not more than twelve performers. First Prize, £15.; Second Prize, £5. Entrance Money, 10s. the Set to form the Third and Fourth prizes.

REGULATIONS.

Each Set to ring two tunes or pieces of their own selection. The Judges will observe the nature and difficulty of the pieces performed by each Band, in addition to the correctness of playing. The two pieces to be plaid in succession.

N.B.—No Band to play the same pieces they have played at any previous Contest at Belle Vue, except they should be required to play off, when they may play one of their old pieces.

All the Bands to furnish Pianoforte copies of the pieces they intend to play at the time of drawing.

Entries to close on *Tuesday, August 15th*, 1865.

Zoological Gardens, Belle Vue, Manchester.

HAND-BELL RINGING CONTEST,

ARRANGED FOR THE YEAR 1914.

OPEN TO GENERAL COMPETITION.

THE 60th (DIAMOND JUBILEE) ANNUAL

TUNE RINGING CONTEST

WILL BE HELD ON

MONDAY, SEPTEMBER 21st, 1914.

£50 will be given in Prizes, particulars of which will be forwarded when the Entries are complete. A Gold Medal, with Diamond inset, commemorative of the Diamond Jubilee of the Contest, will also be awarded to the Band winning the First Prize; and in the event of any Band winning the First Prize for three years in succession, each of the Members will be awarded a Silver Medal, and will not be allowed to compete at the Belle Vue Contest the following year.

N.B.—The CROSLAND MOOR PUBLIC BAND are debarred from competing at this Contest, having won the First Prize three years in succession, viz., 1911, 1912, and 1913.

GENERAL REGULATIONS.

Each Set of Ringers to Ring a Grand Selection from AUBER's OPERA, **"The Crown Diamonds,"** which will be forwarded free of charge on receipt of Entry Fee, 10s.

The decision of the Judges to be binding in all cases after playing takes place.

The Music must not be played in public previous to the Contest.

Post-Office Orders must be made payable to John Jennison & Co., at the Manchester Head Post Office, and must be forwarded, together with the Form of Entry, addressed to John Jennison & Co., Zoological Gardens, Belle Vue, Manchester.

Entries close on Thursday, August 6th, 1914.

Note: The competition rules at Belle Vue set the size of each band to no more than twelve performers.

343

About the Editor

Philip Bedford is a regular International Handbell Symposium massed ringing conductor and workshop clinician. He first turned to hand-bell tune ringing during the mid 1960's as an adjunct to tower-bell and hand-bell change ringing, became a founder member of Handbell Ringers of Great Britain in 1968 and a member of HRGB's Executive Committee in 1971. He was the driving force behind the Society's regionalisation in 1975. In 1974 he wrote the first book published by HRGB – 'An Introduction to English Handbell Tune Ringing', and in the same year, with his brother Don, wrote the first book of music published by HRGB – 'Carol Ringing and More'.

In 1975 Philip and his family emigrated to Australia where they again became heavily involved with hand-bells, organising festivals and workshops throughout the country and founding, in 1983, the Handbell Society of Australasia of which he is the immediate Past President. He held the Chair of the International Handbell Committee from 1992 to 1994, and with his late wife Sylvia organised the 6th International Handbell Symposium in Adelaide in 1994. Indeed he has been one of the HSA representatives on the IHC since its inception in 1990 to the present day.

Philip returned to England in 2002 with his wife Akane and their twin boys where they are all still heavily involved in hand-bell tune ringing.

Philip and Don have now published ten books of hand-bell music for small hand-bell sets written in traditional numerical notation, two of which they have since transposed into normal hand-bell notation (staff notation).

Fifteen of Philip's five octave staff notation hand-bell compositions have been published, nine of which have been selected as massed ringing pieces for International Handbell Symposia.

Philip Bedford   Don Bedford

MUSICAL HANDBELLS

A Comprehensive History
of the Bells and their Founders

William Butler

This hard-backed book of 162 pages is the first comprehensive history of musical handbells and their founders. The result of some thirty five years' research by the author, it begins with the evolution of small bells and moves on to the development of pattern-cast bells by John and Oliver Cor at Aldbourne in the late 17th century. After subsequent founders from this same village, the text moves on to deal exhaustively with more than a hundred other founders from all over England. Indeed, the author needed to visit most counties to consult primary sources and to examine historic handbells in churches, museums, and private collections.

This ground-breaking work gives detailed and extensive references that will provide a sound foundation on which subsequent researchers can build. More than 250 figures illustrate every aspect of the text, including founders' marks and photographs and drawings of the fittings they developed.

Appendices cover such diverse topics as the identification of founders, a chronological list of all known handbell and crotal founders, plus the most comprehensive bibliography of handbell books and papers yet published.

Destined to be the definitive work on the subject, this important new book will be warmly welcomed by everyone with an interest in musical handbells.

ISBN 1 86077 118 1
**Available for £20 post free by e-mailing Bill Butler -
email: bill@barfield.org.uk.**

Traditional Number Music
for Small Sets of Handbells
Arranged by Donald A. and Philip Bedford
for sets of handbells in any key

For 1½ octaves

Carol Ringing and More

    14 carols and 24 popular tunes arranged for 1½ diatonic octaves plus, preferably, the handiest accidentals, although most pieces can be played without them.

Hymns and Things

    Similarly 18 hymns, 6 carols and 31 other arrangements.

Ding Dong Bell

    34 nursery rhymes and lullabies long free from copyright, set in order of complexity from the very easy to the slightly more challenging.   Many can be played on a diatonic 12-bell set.

Ring-a-Roses

    Following on from *Ding Dong Bell* the 26 arrangements continue in complexity from the slightly more challenging to the totally mind bending.   Approximately half the pieces can be played on a straight 12.

For 2¼ octaves

Mainly Folk (in two parts)

    50 arrangements ranging from the very easy but effective to super skilful and challenging – and even more effective!   ***Both parts are also available in staff notation, <u>please state which version when ordering.</u>***

Christmas in Hand

    17 carols, plus *Jingle Bells* and *We Wish You a Merry Christmas.*

Hymns in Hand

    17 arrangements of our favourite hymn tunes.

Nice Old Numbers

    23 old classics and song tunes of yesteryear complemented by a couple of new pieces composed by Philip.

Sweet Sixteen

    From the three collections immediately above we have taken all the arrangements needing no more than 16 bells (not always the same 16) and adjusted the harmonies of some of the other pieces down to 16 bells for playing by 4 ringers 4-in-hand, 8 ringers 2-in-hand, or any combination of the two.

U.K. post free from Don Bedford, 10 Spring Gardens, Narberth, Pembrokeshire, SA67 7BT
E-mail: dondingdong@boompa.plus.com

*In **staff notation** for large sets of handbells*

Philip's challenging arrangements for 5-chromatic-octave sets of hand-bells, many selected for International Symposium massed ringing, are available from him at 44 Nunnery Fields, Canterbury, Kent, CT1 3JT, E-mail: akaneandphilip@yahoo.com.au

INDEX

354

LIST OF ILLUSTRATIONS